"*STRUGGLE OF THE MAGICIANS* WILL BE A BOOK OF IMMENSE interest and value to anyone who engages a teacher on the path of self-discovery. It is a compelling account of the teaching Work of G. I. Gurdjieff and his closest and most brilliant students. The subtitle alone, *'Why Uspenskii Left Gurdjieff'* will undoubtedly capture the interest of anyone familiar with Fourth Way Work. The Fourth Way is a methodology of transformation which grew out of Gurdjieff's pioneering study of human beings and their relationship to consciousness. Uspenskii, in particular, shared his teacher's vision with astute comprehension. Why the two parted has long been a topic of puzzlement to students of these two great men.

"Patterson's writing style is crisp and to the point, and the diary type format he has chosen sets the actions and teaching lessons of this often obtuse teacher in a larger historical context. Mr. Gurdjieff's Work was developed during one of the most turbulent times of recent history, that of the Russian revolution of 1917. It is hard to miss the fact that the years most ripe for the Gurdjieff Work were some of the most costly in terms of human suffering. Patterson tells the story in intimate detail of this small group of individuals committed to the development of human consciousness set against a background which includes the growth of Communism in Russia and the rise of Fascism in Germany. Interestingly enough, Gurdjieff's worst fears at this time were not so much of physical danger as of "acting stupidly." He stood to lose much more than his life and the lives of his students. Travelling with him was the embryo of his vision, which was also destined to face many perils. Fear and the disorientation of war alone could have disabled his Work had he allowed it to fall prey to the dictates of personal survival.

"The *Magicians* referred to in the title also include A. R. Orage and J. G. Bennett, men of outstanding intellect and understanding who were also considered teachers in their own right. But the main focus of the book is the relationship between Gurdjieff and P. D. Uspenskii, for whom Mr. Gurdjieff had the greatest hope. With Uspenskii in place, Gurdjieff hoped to 'step down' and thereby pass on his teaching. It is a delicate affair, this matter of student and teacher, one that requires vulnerability and great courage of heart to risk all of what one thinks himself to be. Uspenskii, especially, was a man of extraordinary intellect who grasped Gurdjieff's ideas readily. He also had the ability to communicate clearly, which made him highly sought after as a teacher. Even Mr. Gurdjieff sought him out, but for a very different reason. Gurdjieff recognized a vital need for his vision to be introduced to the population at large, and he desperately needed a translator who could popularize his Work and make it understandable. He saw Uspenskii as that man.

"But, Uspenskii lacked a piece: that crucial element that can only be gotten through close association with, and eventually direct transmission from, a living teacher. It is this point that makes this book so vitally important to anyone engaged in the master/disciple relationship. Both parties need to have that resist-

ing piece flushed out of the student and brought to realization for the Work to come alive, to grow, to outlive the teacher and to be passed on successfully.

"It seemed that each of Gurdjieff's star students represented a weakness of one of the three centers of man as described in his Work. Uspenskii's downfall came from an inability to loosen himself sufficiently from his overwhelmingly masterful intellect and to stay connected with his teacher through the heart long enough to be birthed into his own transformation. Orage, meanwhile, let his emotions take him away from his teacher's mastery, which was his sole source of real help. J. G. Bennett's weakness seemed to lie in his inability to ground his experience, instead of flitting from one idea to the next, once again missing Mr. Gurdjieff's expertise as the master of movement. In each case it was the student who really broke the connection, not the teacher. A sobering thought and not one to be missed.

"If for no other reason, students of any teacher can benefit from the heartfelt example of these profoundly sincere and dedicated individuals in their search for truth within themselves. Their stories stand out clearly as a warning: The Work of transformation of human consciousness cannot be done alone. It cannot be done without the help of one who has gone before and has dedicated his or her life to serving others in their process. One must have a teacher, a master who can see through the vagaries and even the brilliance of mind to the very seat of being; a master who knows exactly what is needed for each student and can deliver the truth with precise timing.

"William Patrick Patterson himself proves to be a master at gleaning aliveness and insight from the personal writing of Mr. Gurdjieff's students and retelling their stories in such a way that their lessons can be readily applied to one's own personal struggle on the path. Patterson has a ruthless dedication to revealing the truth. For example, by studying carefully the nuance of a single word, he reveals an important aspect of attitude in Uspenskii towards his teacher's dealings with him. The struggle he describes is an internal one, intimate and deeply personal to the author himself. As he states in the introduction, the movement to write this book sprang from his own persistent need to know what happened in Gurdjieff's close company.

"The book is a labor of love which communicates so much more than the superficial facts. It conveys a penetrating respect for the profundity of Mr. Gurdjieff's contribution to the human search for self-understanding and a sense of camaraderie with those who are struggling with the effort to become conscious. *Struggle Of The Magicians* is truly a work of compassion.

"Some of the most piercing insights, however, come from the minute and seemingly unimportant details of this incredible story. Though the focus is on the men in the Gurdjieff group, each struggling to be somebody, like his teacher, ultimately it is the women who shine as embodiments of Mr. Gurdjieff's Work by their action and devout participation. Ironically, in the end it is a woman, Madame de Salzmann, who is entrusted with the primary responsibility of carrying on Gurdjieff's Work."

—*Mudra*

"*STRUGGLE OF THE MAGICIANS* IS AN EXTREMELY IMPORTANT AND valuable addition to Fourth Way literature. Written in diary style entries chronologically set against the back drop of world history, this book makes tremendous inroads toward penetrating the tangled web of information that surrounds and confounds the esoteric movement brought to the West by G. I. Gurdjieff and popularized by his student, P. D. Ouspensky. It also precisely and accurately conveys many of the key ideas Gurdjieff was trying to communicate, thus making *Struggle of the Magicians* a must to see and read for anyone working in this way.

"One major theme of this book is the examination of the teacher-student relationship between Gurdjieff and three of his top students: P. D. Uspenskii, A. R. Orage, and John G. Bennett. More space is devoted to Uspenskii and Gurdjieff's history together and to analyzing their individual characters. Patterson comes up with some interesting insights into what may have motivated the actions of these two enigmatic men, actions that have significantly affected the transmission of the Fourth Way line of Work.

"*Struggle of the Magicians* covers a fantastic amount of ground in telling the story of Gurdjieff's mission to the West and what it engendered. From its humble beginnings in Moscow and St. Petersburg until Gurdjieff's death, the whole movement is covered with clarity and attention to detail. It also affords a look at the early life of P. D. Uspenskii, something relatively uncommon in this literature.

"The book seemed to me to be written very impartially. I noticed no particular bias; it's a simple journalistic accounting of Gurdjieff's, Uspenskii's, and their followers' work in the outer world with a modicum of analysis and speculative explanations. On the whole I found Patterson's explanations to be quite plausible with a high degree of probability. Patterson clearly has an understanding of the Fourth Way material as a user and is able to communicate well. *Struggle of the Magicians* was compelling reading for me.

"I highly recommend this book. In my opinion it is the best book of its kind. Anyone can read *Struggle of the Magicians* and benefit—whether new or old to Fourth Way material."

—*Inner Journeys*

"WHILE LENIN WAS SHACKLING RUSSIA TO COMMUNISM, THAT East-West crossroads was also a world capital of metaphysical movements. In 1915, Madame Blavatsky's Theosophy was flourishing when G. I. Gurdjieff, a Caucasian Greek of great charisma and esoteric acumen, would meet P. D. Ouspensky in a Moscow café, and one of the enduring, pre-New Age systems for personal transformation would be born.

"Patterson's incredibly detailed chronicle of these founding luminaries of the "Fourth Way" is an engrossing, illuminating study of the "struggles"—with themselves and each other—that these two Magi endured while pursuing both common and divergent missions to "wake up humanity" from a deep sleep of self-ignorant automatism.

"Drawing on over 70 published volumes and anecdotal sources, Patterson admirably fleshes out the powerful, enigmatic Gurdjieff and his sometime protege/ 'interpreter' of his teachings and methods, the intellectually prodigious Ouspensky. Patriarch "G." with his proclivities for food and drink and seemingly unbridled shifts between ruthless sarcasm and affectionate humor, is both detested and adored by those who meet him. He's the epitome of the so-called "crazy wisdom" master employing shock-value education, but who also may just be a wily peddler of magic carpets. By contrast, Ouspensky, the apostle who goes his own way in short order, is a study in dignified appropriateness. Respected at a distance for his conceptual prowess, he finds his mentor's erratic behavior intolerable, even insane.

"While *Struggle of the Magicians* is a rewarding, painstaking inquiry into the teacher/student relationship (and also the branchings that such movements typically manifest), the objectivity factor is sporadic. Patterson, as an ardent practitioner of the Fourth Way (see his well-received *Eating The "I"*), clearly favors Gurdjieff's superiority. Though never having met the man, the author canonizes him as a virtual prophet capable of "pure impersonal love," and regularly rationalizes the money-seeking "sheep shearing" of students, the almost manic-depressive episodes, and many other indulgings in less-than-angelic behavior. Ouspensky is drawn as a brilliant but largely failed aspirant who couldn't handle the unconventional proddings to transcend a pristine theory.

"A book of immense interest to Fourth Way aficionados, *Struggle of the Magicians* is a flawed but fascinating record of two highly influential metaphysicians of the 20th century."

—*West Coast Review of Books*

WHY USPENSKII LEFT GURDJIEFF

STRUGGLE OF THE MAGICIANS

EXPLORING THE TEACHER-STUDENT RELATIONSHIP

WILLIAM PATRICK PATTERSON

Edited by Barbara Allen Patterson

Arete Communications, Publishers
Fairfax, California

Design by WordPlay Consulting, Berkeley, CA

Library of Congress Catalog Number is 95-077240
Patterson, William Patrick
Struggle of the Magicians: Why Uspenskii Left Gurdjieff
Bibliography: Includes references, notes, and index
1. Spiritual Teacher-Student Relationship
2. Gurdjieff, His Life and His Mission
3. Uspenskii, Orage, Bennett, Toomer, and Peters
4. Esoteric Psychology and Self-Transformation

Second printing 1998
First printing 1996

ISBN: 1-879514-02-8

Printed on Acid-Free Paper. ∞
The paper used in this publication meets the
minimum requirements of the American National
Standard for Information Sciences—Permanence
of Paper for Printed Library Materials, ANSI Z39.48-1984.

Arete Communications, Box 58, 773 Center Boulevard
Fairfax, California 94978-0058

email: Telos9@aol.com
Web Site: http://members.aol.com/Telos9

The Magus is the highest that man
can approach to God.

— *G. I. Gurdjieff*

Toast to Gurdjieff

God give you the strength
and the manhood
to endure your lofty solitude.

— *Rachmilevitch*

Gurdjieff is a kind of walking God
—a planetary or even solar God.

— *A. R. Orage*

For my mother,
Mabel Scott Patterson,
whose sustaining love
and sacrifice
gave courage
in the face of myself.

CONTENTS

PART III

ACKNOWLEDGMENTS

I wish to extend my sincere appreciation to Henry and Mary Ellen Korman for their generosity of spirit and service in the preparation of the manuscript, seeing it through its many revisions; to Teresa Sanchez-Adams for the high quality of her performance and perseverance in helping with the editing, proofreading, inputting, reference checking, and her creation of the index; to Mary Louise Davis for her critical eye and challenging critique; to Richard Angert for his many labors with the original cover design; and to Gregory Kester for his reference checking. Also, a thank you to Philip Goldsmith and Donna Boss for their support and encouragement. I thank most of all my wife Barbara, who has given so selflessly of her love and time, as well as her professional editing and proofreading skills, in the creation of this book that first saw "the light of day" in the very year we celebrated our silver anniversary.

PREFACE

FROM THE FIRST TIME I READ PYOTR DEMIANOVICH USPENSKII'S *FRAGMENTS OF AN UNKNOWN TEACHING*, OR AS IT WAS RETITLED AFTER HIS death, *In Search of the Miraculous*, I wondered why he had left Gurdjieff. What could it be that would cause a seeker as gifted and hungry for the miraculous as Uspenskii to turn away from the one man who was leading him to it?

The teaching which Gurdjieff brought, and which Uspenskii so faithfully records in *Search*, was for me miraculous in itself. In all my life I had never come across ideas of such scale and dimension and such practicality. I found myself reading the book murmuring "yes-yes-yes." And so coming to that last scene at the Prieuré where Gurdjieff is leaving for his first voyage to America and Uspenskii is telling himself, "My work in the future would proceed quite independently"—was a shock that left a strange disjointed feeling.

Something had gone wrong, but what? Uspenskii's reasons seemed to hide more than they revealed. But it was all quite beyond me. The question of what caused the rupture was quickly submerged in the richness and originality of the teaching. Soon thereafter I entered the Work. Years went by without the question resurfacing. Yet it must have stayed with me, for now and then I would find myself wondering—*Yes, why did Uspenskii leave Gurdjieff?*

As I worked with the teaching, and over the years learned of its historical permutations, the question opened again, demanding an answer. Just as we need to know the story of our lives to make sense of where we have been, are, and are likely going, so too does the 'story' of the teaching. Otherwise, force deflects, ideas disconnect, interpretations personalize. To move into the future, we first need to align the past. The octave of the Work is coming to a crossroads in its evolution. To continue to ascend, it seems to me, a clarity about the past is demanded.

I would like to say everything was this clear for me when I decided to write this book and that I began with the definite intention of answering the question. But the reality was just the reverse. I had assumed, without actually pondering the matter, that the question could not be answered. Or, at least, not by me. And so while the question 'pinched' sometimes, I was not active towards it. This changed when I read Reyner's biography of Uspenskii, *The Unsung Genius,* and upon finishing it, found I had a *new feeling* about the man and his life. In that moment, there came an awareness of an unusual sense of space, one of deep silence and an abiding wholeness—one in which I felt a living presence other than my own. I felt I should write about Uspenskii and how he came to leave Gurdjieff. Though this was felt with a consummate clarity, even so, it largely left me. A few weeks later, in rereading the part in *Search* where Gurdjieff and Uspenskii are together in Essentuki, I found a shift to a new level of understanding. Connections came not made before. For example, I saw how Uspenskii's reaction to Gurdjieff's use of the word *seclusion* in 1915 directly connects to Uspenskii's distrust of where he believes Gurdjieff is leading him three years later. I remembered, too, some original documents I had read some years earlier. Now I saw the possibility of coming to a real answer based on research of the actual written material.

Early on, I decided I wanted Gurdjieff, Uspenskii, and everyone involved from that period to speak for themselves. I would base my research on the written record alone. The reference then, for writer and readers alike, would be one and the same. Interpretations might differ, but the material would be sourced in a common record open to and verifiable by everyone. The words of Gurdjieff, Uspenskii, as well as those of A. R. Orage, J. G. Bennett, Thomas and Olga de Hartmann, C. S. Nott, Jean Toomer, Rodney Collin, Margaret Anderson, Fritz Peters, Solita Solano, and others represent their perspective, their feelings. If our reading is sensitive enough, then the words can be used to step through the words.

Of course, words don't exist alone. When and where they were uttered is important and gives their meaning particular shading. Accordingly, the written record has been set in a time line of dates and places, thus creating a kind of fourth dimension. Included in the time line are historical events, such as the Russian Revolution and the rise of Fascism, for these represent the historical background and atmosphere in which the teaching was presented and practiced. As such, they often had a direct influence on Gurdjieff's and Uspenskii's actions. For example, had Lenin-Trotsky *not* succeeded in seizing power, Gurdjieff's Institute would have been established in Russia and Uspenskii's rupture with Gurdjieff would have played out quite differently. As Uspenskii once wrote, "All things were connected with one another, and not accidentally, but by incomprehensible chains of causes and effects. All things were dependent on one another, and all things lived in one another."

In my first book, *Eating The "I,"* the major theme was relationship as it concerned my family, my wife, and my spiritual teacher, John Pentland. Because of its narrative style and the personal nature of the material, the book's presentation necessarily appeared as subjective (the book's architecture and the recognition behind the written thought is quite otherwise). While the theme of *Struggle of the Magicians* is the same, here the relationship is not personal (for me) and it is between extraordinary and, I believe, archetypal figures. As the text makes clear, there was a struggle going on between Uspenskii and Gurdjieff, as there is, and must be, between any spiritual teacher and student. But their struggle was titanic and far reaching in that both men were magicians,[1] and Gurdjieff, of course, a great deal more.

The relationship between a teacher and student does not easily lend itself to rational understanding, so deep are its modalities, so multiordinal its meanings. What is attempted here is to carry out a rational inquiry in the spiritual sense of such inquiries—rationally ordering events, presenting insights and interpretations of these events, and taking the inquiry right up to the point where value and meaning depend on additional suprarational factors. Guiding our inquiry by the time line of the Gurdjieff-Uspenskii relationship, allowing the available material to build up sequentially, hopefully allowing it to be pondered in a wider

1. The word *magician* is used in the sense given both in Skeat's *The Concise Etymological Dictionary of the English Language* (G. P. Putnam, 1980) as: "Magi, priest of the Persians, enchanter, properly a wise man who interpreted dreams"; and also in Brewer's *Dictionary of Phrase and Fable,* edited by Ivor H. Evans (Harper & Row, 1981): "Among the ancient Medes and Persians, the Magi were members of a priestly caste credited with great occult powers. Ammianus Marcellinus says the Persian magi derived their knowledge from the Brahmins of India and Arianus expressly called the Brahmins 'magi.'" Uspenskii gives a functional definition of a magician as someone who "by their knowledge of the properties of the 'astral sphere'" and by "their ability to act mentally upon astral matter and through it upon physical matter." See *New Model of the Universe,* p.110.

context. Perhaps, then, the moment at which intellectual intuition must enter is rightly approached, increasing the opportunity for a result that shifts understanding toward a higher level. Hopefully, too, by attempting to objectify, to the degree possible, the relationship between Gurdjieff and Uspenskii, a means is developed to begin to appreciate the true significance of what took place while the interworkings of the teacher-student relationship are set in high relief. For this reason, no other, are these old dog bones unearthed.

Without question the place of Pyotr Demianovich Uspenskii in the Gurdjieffian pantheon is unique. He is unrivaled as the chief interpreter of what has become known as the Gurdjieff Work, or the Fourth Way. In fact, far more people are familiar with Uspenskii than Gurdjieff. So it was during their lifetimes and so it has largely remained. Without the clarity and accessibility of Uspenskii's books, the Work would have been much smaller numerically. They provide the needed stepping stones. The body of work Uspenskii left is notable in its intuitive feel for, and faithfulness to, a teaching whose complexity and subtlety extends through many dimensions. That Uspenskii had only his memory and notes to work with in assembling the account of the teaching he portrayed in *Search* makes his achievement even more remarkable. Gurdjieff himself acknowledged this. When Madame Uspenskii sent a draft of a chapter of her deceased husband's book and asked if it should be published, Gurdjieff said unequivocally—"Very good is. Good memory. Truth, was so."

In following Gurdjieff's and Uspenskii's lifeline together, the lives of A. R. Orage and J. G. Bennett necessarily came into view. Both were pupils of Gurdjieff and, like Uspenskii, were intellectually of a very high order. Each could have been of inestimable help in 'stepping-down' and establishing the teaching. Both did so to a degree, but, like Uspenskii, they could follow their teacher only so far. In researching the book, I came to see that these two men played significant parts not only in Gurdjieff's struggle with Uspenskii, but also in his struggle to establish the teaching. I considered using the title "Struggle of the Magicians: Why Uspenskii, Orage and Bennett Left Gurdjieff," but this would have been cumbersome. (May I add that this book should not be confused in any way with Gurdjieff's ballet scenario *The Struggle of the Magicians*, which remains an original work in its own right.)

The question will likely arise as to why the spelling of 'Uspenskii' is used rather than the more familiar 'Ouspensky.' I had believed that the new spelling is closer to how the name actually sounds in Russian, but I understand that is not the case. It is true that the new spelling is increasingly used by academics. Yale University's Sterling Library, for example, lists its archival records under this spelling. But the reason I choose to use

Uspenskii rather than *Ouspensky* is because the new spelling will hopefully suggest a reconsideration as to how we see the man and the part he played, and refused to play, in the dissemination of the teaching. And, more significantly for Uspenskii and the teaching, the intention with which he died.

I chose to organize and write the book's narrative in a diary form as it was best suited to my aim of creating as objective a historical account as possible. As such, I have confined my interpretations to footnotes and to three essays at the end of the book. The reader can follow the main text coming to his or her own conclusions as to value and meaning. Thus having formed his or her own material for, as Mr. Gurdjieff says, "confrontive logic," then read the footnotes and essays, ponder and see if a new perception arises. Agree or not, the writer and reader both at the very least share the same reference base, one built on fact, not whim or sentimentality. This is essential for a deeper penetration of what is actually transpiring behind the words, gestures, and events. For it is only by an awareness of both the subtle to physical planes, and their interpenetration and connection, that we can have any real possibility of understanding as mythic a life as that of G. I. Gurdjieff.

No doubt the reader will find the viewpoint from which the footnotes and essays originate to be quite strong. The viewpoint is the result of a long and active work together with the study of the written material in the light of that work. In my opinion Gurdjieff's two principal biographers, not withstanding their prodigious research, fail to see the significance of the man and his mission. In one case, Gurdjieff is subjected to his biographer's own fantastic imagination, "a flight from reason"; in another, the seriousness of Gurdjieff's identity and mission are obscured, perhaps trivialized, by the biographer's heavy stylization of prose. Worse, both biographers often interpret and judge Gurdjieff from an ordinary human standpoint; his supposed 'venality' being a case in point. With these writers, and so many others, one finds so little esoteric understanding of Gurdjieff and his mission and its importance, not just for his students, but for Western civilization. So often Gurdjieff is given many appellations, all of which write him off as a "rascal guru" or worse. Among those in the Work, he is spoken of as "a philosopher and mystic." But with what philosopher or mystic is he to be compared?

The view is considered radical that Gurdjieff is an original, an avatar, and that the Fourth Way is not merely a synthesis but a reformulation of an ancient prehistoric teaching. Intellectualism and psychologism which only systematizes, never goes beyond societal limits, can never see this. And so Gurdjieff is stuffed where he is too big to fit and, so reduced and levelled, he is subjected to the scrutiny of the ordinary. He once said that he came to tell us that when it rains the sidewalks get wet. Well, it has rained and we still we refuse to see it. Perhaps it is a question of taking responsibility, personal and otherwise, for the gift of rain. We want the gold, but refuse responsibility of payment.

In the reconsideration of Uspenskii undertaken here I have necessarily exposed him to a devaluation. Let it be said that Uspenskii's strengths and achievements are on a level such as few seekers ever reach. It would be a real loss, then, should his books, particularly *In Search of the Miraculous, Psychology of Man's Possible Evolution, Tertium Organum,* and *The Fourth Way,* not maintain their rightful place in the canon of Gurdjieffian literature. That acknowledged, let it also be said that Uspenskii's understanding is not, as most certainly Bennett and Nicoll and all their latter day derivatives are not, on a level of understanding with Gurdjieff's. The notion, therefore, that there could be an Uspenskii line of work, much less Bennett and Nicoll lines, shows a weakness of mind; a kind of tribal sentimentality.

Uspenskii's experience with Gurdjieff—as well as that of Orage, Bennett, Nicoll, Toomer, and Peters—is nonetheless important and useful. We can see ourselves, our own dilemmas and confusion, sacrifice and courage, in the example of their lives. Most importantly, we can see how easily the student can project onto the teacher and teaching his or her own questions and assumptions. Such is the functioning, whatever the level of development, of chief feature and buffers. Lastly, let it be said that this is not a brief for a lock-step student loyalty. (Particularly in our contemporary world-time where so many so readily put themselves forward as teachers.) Self-sincerity is the saving grace. However, sincerity, as Gurdjieff says, has to be learned...

As to dates in *Search*, Uspenskii makes no direct mention of whether he uses the Julian or Gregorian calendars in giving dates. He does say, however, that he left St. Petersburg "on the 15th of October, a week before the Bolshevik revolution." This indicates he is following the Julian calendar. Had Uspenskii used the Gregorian calendar, the date of the revolution would be November 7th. This is because in the twentieth century the Gregorian calendar (established in 1592 by Pope Gregory XIII) is thirteen days ahead of the Julian. Therefore, while Uspenskii is in Russia, all dates pertaining to his and Gurdjieff's whereabouts correspond to the Julian calendar. For all dates after February 1918, when the Bolsheviks adopted the Gregorian calendar, the Gregorian is used.

Though the events related here began more than eighty years ago, the material is presented mainly in the present tense. I do so because that is how I think, feel, and intuit it when I really engage the material. Their story is immediate. The revelations, resistances, the heroic perseverance against momentous obstacles of Gurdjieff, and later Uspenskii, are all of this moment—of, and for, this time. So, in my view, it is not with the past we deal but the present. To keep the body of the main text as free as possible from interpretation, I have confined my remarks to the footnotes.

Lastly, I am well aware that the book treads against one of the fundamental commandments of Gurdjieff's much esteemed Mullah Nassr Eddin who advised: "Never poke your stick into a hornet's nest." Accordingly, let me say that this author has also not only taken to heart, but put into practice, the sage and sly advice of that precious jewel, Mr. Gurdjieff's Karapet of Tiflis.

—William Patrick Patterson
San Anselmo, California

INTRODUCTION

OF ALL THE MEETINGS BETWEEN HUMAN BEINGS, THAT BETWEEN TEACHER AND STUDENT IS ARCHETYPAL. ITS FORM IS ANCIENT, ITS manifestation ever new. So it was with Socrates and Plato, with Shams al-Din and Rumi, with Marpa and Milarepa...and so it is in our own time with Gurdjieff and Uspenskii.

It was some eighty years ago in a noisy Moscow café that Gurdjieff and Uspenskii first met. Gurdjieff was no ordinary teacher; Uspenskii, no ordinary student. Gurdjieff had a mission. He had come to the West to introduce and establish a new teaching, one that would keep the world from destroying itself. He was in search of students to help him achieve his aim. When they met, Uspenskii was already something of a magician. He had made extensive studies of the tarot, magic, and the esoteric teachings of the past, and had conducted a number of experiments. An 'old soul,' he had the power to capture and direct the attention of others and had already published *Tertium Organum* before he met Gurdjieff. He was held in high regard in theosophical circles in Moscow and St. Petersburg where his lectures drew thousands. Nevertheless, as he false reality" that separated him from the miraculous. Uspenskii needed help and he was actively in search of it.

Gurdjieff had what Uspenskii wanted—a way out, a way of understanding, a way of using ordinary life with all its shocks, suffering, and negativity to come to real life. And Uspenskii had what Gurdjieff needed—a powerful intellect that could quickly comprehend the teaching and the oral and writing abilities to communicate it; that is, to 'step-down' the teaching and make it accessible to larger numbers of people. As Gurdjieff would later write, "The first great commandment of God to man is hand wash hand." Gurdjieff offered his hand and expected Uspenskii's in return. In that lay the problem. Uspenskii wanted the teaching, but, like all students, he was wary of 'the payment.' There was only so much he was willing to pay. Beyond that he would not go. Three times he would break with Gurdjieff in the eight-odd years they were together.

What happened with Uspenskii happened as well with two others who Gurdjieff hoped would help disseminate the teaching—A. R. Orage and J. G. Bennett. Like Uspenskii, both were men of exceptional gifts with a strong grounding in the esoteric. Each was capable of capturing, holding, and directing the attention of others. And for all their imagination, each had the capacity to bend the will of others to his own. They, too, in their own right, were magicians. Like Uspenskii, they made incredible efforts, sacrificed, and developed. Yet eventually they too came up against that selfsame demand—the complete dedication to teacher and teaching.

The struggle between Gurdjieff and Uspenskii-Orage-Bennett took place on a very high level. For Gurdjieff was struggling with 'giants,' or as he would say, "power-possessing-beings." All developed through their practice of the teaching and association with Gurdjieff. Yet each failed to ultimately take that final step. Their failure is understandable and in no way is it seen here from any notions of superiority. Anyone who has worked on themselves even a little has some sense of what these men ultimately faced. And yet, given the world-scale of Gurdjieff's mission, the fact that they did not meet the moment, fill the interval, is an incompletion with whose consequences we must all live and work.

To what can their lack be attributed? This is an important question that needs exploring. For, at the very least, in their attitudes, confusions, and behavior, we see our own. Any approach to the question of their leaving Gurdjieff must examine how Uspenskii-Orage-Bennett saw their relationship to the teaching, to Gurdjieff. That's one point of the arrow. The other point is how Gurdjieff perceived matters. Is it possible for us to see, even a little, with Gurdjieff's eyes? That is, can we perceive how Gurdjieff saw himself and his mission?

Certainly Gurdjieff was no one's ideal of a Messenger from Above. As he himself writes in the *Second Series*, he was born into a class of people known as *kaphirs*. A kaphir, Gurdjieff says, is "the name given to people (and this included, in general, all Europeans) who live like animals, without principles and without anything holy in them." A member of the Sarmoung Brotherhood tells Bogga-Eddin to tell Gurdjieff that he would be glad to see him, "a man who—though by origin a kaphir—has succeeded, thanks to his impartial attitude towards all people, in acquiring a soul similar to ours."

Undoubtedly, in Gurdjieff we have no ethereal holy man only tenuously on the planet. No, Gurdjieff was here with both feet planted. He enjoyed life and had a strong earthy side. He had his 'wolf' and his 'sheep.' Man, he often pointed out, is a battleground of two warring natures, the spiritual and the earthy. In perhaps no man in history, with the exception of Padme Sambhava who brought Buddhism to Tibet, have these two natures existed in such polarity. Here was a being whose spiritual character was so inspired as to be imprinted with the mission of establishing a new teaching for our time on earth and who, within the same incarnation, had an earthy nature perhaps equally as desirous. As he himself admitted, at a certain period of his life he could be beset with vindictiveness, self-love, vanity, pride, jealousy, and other passions.

What must it have been like to spend a lifetime reconciling these two natures while, at the same time, fulfilling a mission so colossal, so difficult? Not only were his twin-natures at war, Gurdjieff had to contend with and integrate the disparity between his physical and spiritual bodies. His first 'death' came as a boy lying in a large shell crater on an artillery range. With cannons roaring one hundred yards away, shells flying and bursting over his head, Gurdjieff had the "clear realization... of almost certain annihilation." His emotional center awakened, "The intensity of feeling which flooded through me, and the force of logical confrontation of my thought increased to such an extent that, at each moment, I thought and experienced more than during an entire twelvemonth." The instinctive fear that arose in him brought "an unconquerable living terror." His young body trembled so intensely that "it was as if each tissue vibrated independently." But there was also an awareness for the first time of a *"'whole sensation of myself,' which grew stronger and stronger."* [Author's italics]

In his later journeys with the Seekers After Truth,[1] he was shot three times, "each time almost mortally and each time by a stray bullet." The first in Crete in 1896 when he was nineteen years old. The second in Tibet in 1897. The third in Transcaucasia in 1904. In addition, he also contracted many, what he calls, "specific 'delicacies' of local character" such as scurvy, dysentery, influenza, malaria, hydropsy, and bedinka. As a result of these travels, he reports that there was "implanted in my organ-

1. This is the name used in the Institute's prospectus issued in 1922.

ism for the rest of my life some 'chronically manifesting' factors of evil influence upon my health." And so while his Kesdjan body was coated and anointed, his physical body was ravaged by the effects of bullets and disease. Most likely these were a constant source of pain to him which he dulled by ingesting great quantities of caffeine, nicotine, and alcohol.

However this may be, the indisputable fact is Gurdjieff never betrayed or doubted his mission. From the moment he first met Uspenskii in Moscow in 1915 to his death in Paris in 1949—neither in his words or actions is there ever a contradiction. He knew what he came to do and never wavered. Again and again, he tried to establish his Institute of the Harmonious Development of Man. First in Moscow-St. Petersburg, then Tiflis, then Constantinople, then Germany, then London. Finally after ten years of living with constant pressure and uncertainty he was able in 1922 to establish his Institute in France.

Within less than two years time, however, Gurdjieff suffered a serious car crash and concussion. It brought home to him the recognition that his aim could not be realized through the Institute. He had no idea of what way to go, but he knew this way was not working, so he formally disbanded the Institute. Months later the idea arose in him that if he couldn't pass the teaching on to his generation—then he had to go into the future. For this he must create a *legominism.*[2] A man of action, he must do what he most abhorred: *write.* The result is his great gift to all who will pay the attention to read it, *All and Everything.* And so, in a way he never expected, Gurdjieff fulfilled his mission.

Few have wanted to take Gurdjieff and the teaching he brought at the level of seriousness he demands. We keep him, like a crazy old uncle, somewhat embarrassing, perhaps not thoroughly respectable, locked away in the attic. To take him seriously would mean we must take ourselves and our relation to the teaching seriously. Placed at, say, the level of a teacher, guru, or crazy wisdom master, Gurdjieff makes no problem for us. He is simply one among many. And so we, likewise, can remain 'one among many.' But to begin to see as Gurdjieff saw, to look through his eyes, demands a new orientation outside the usual categories of mind. The question of Gurdjieff's identity is central to an understanding of the teaching he brought. No doubt the teaching can be practiced and one can begin to evolve without coming to the question. But the day will come when that question demands its answer. As will be seen in the lives of Uspenskii, Orage, and Bennett, the answer determines one's limit. For example, if the New Testament were seriously read and its teachings attempted to be lived, one would begin moving in a beneficial direction.

2. A means of transmitting information from initiates to conscious beings over time through the Law of Sevenfoldness.

But the time would come when if it was not believed that Jesus Christ was the only son of God, who was sacrificed for our sins and on the third day arose from the dead...one would not be a Christian, and so to continue would be without real result. As the teaching is centered in conscience, understanding, and redemption, not belief or devotion, what might be called 'the time of decision' may be years in the arising, but come it must. It may come by revelation, intuition, or hard work and pondering, but the question must have its answer.

The seemingly radical but straightforward fact is this: Gurdjieff saw himself as a Messenger from Above. As he writes in *All and Everything*,[3] "our Lord Sovereign sent from time to time His Messengers to the planets of this system, to regulate, more or less, the being-existence of the three-brained beings [human beings] arising on them." The purpose of the Messengers was to aid three-brained beings "in destroying in their presences the crystallized consequences" of self-love and vanity. These Messengers, the ones who are known, have all been 'idealized' through the passage of *Heropass,* or time. It is to such figures that all subsequent Messengers must stand in comparison. That all fail such comparison is hardly surprising.

"My Being," he wrote in italics in the *Third Series, "is necessary not only for my personal egoism but also for the common welfare of all humanity."*

It might be asked: if Gurdjieff was such a Messenger, why does he not have millions of followers as do Jesus Christ, Buddha and Mohammed? The message, or teaching, that each brought became, or was turned into, a religion. As the esotericist René Guénon has so astutely pointed out, every religion must of necessity incorporate into itself "a sentimental element"[4] by which it both broadens its appeal and skews the primordial truth. The teaching of the Fourth Way that Gurdjieff brought is in no regard sentimental. A way of understanding, of conscience, it cannot be founded on anything less than Truth. It addresses the nettlesome ques-

3. The *First Series* of Gurdjieff's writings is commonly referred to as *All and Everything,* and is called so here. However, *All and Everything* is actually the over-arching title he gave to a series of three separate books.

4. Guénon distinguishes between "metaphysic...which is essentially knowledge of the Universal, or if preferred, the knowledge of principles belonging to the universal order" and religion. Wrote Guénon: "The metaphysical point of view is purely intellectual, the religious point of view implies as a fundamental characteristic the presence of a *sentimental element* affecting the doctrine itself, which does not allow of its preserving an attitude of entirely disinterested speculation.... It is this characteristic that gives birth to the inevitable diversity of religious dogmas; hence their incompatibility, for whereas intelligence is one, and truth, in whatever measure it is understood, can be understood in one way only, the same does not apply to feeling, so that religion, in seeking to satisfy the demands of feeling, cannot avoid trying to adapt its form as far as possible to its multiple modes, which vary largely according to race and period." [Author's italics] *Introduction to the Study of the Hindu Doctrines* (Luzac & Co. Ltd., 1993) p. 110 and pp. 124–26.

tions of the significance and purpose of man's life on earth and his potentiality for transformation in accord with the laws of World-creation and World-maintenance. As such, while its ideas have been borrowed and trumpeted by many, and almost always without attribution, it has remained of small attraction in terms of numbers. (Though this is likely to quickly change as societal uncertainty progresses and real need correspondingly increases.) But it might be asked: what intrinsic merit is there in mere quantity? If the reality of Messengers be admitted, why must they come only for the greatest numbers of mankind? That great numbers are influenced points not only to a sentimental element but auspiciousness of historical time and event. So if we are to understand Gurdjieff on any level, we have to challenge our notions and open our minds to a possible new category of perception in regard to him.

The incontrovertible fact is that Gurdjieff saw himself as a herald of coming good, a Messenger from Above,[5] come to the world at a time which he sees as "an empty and aborted interval," bringing an ancient and scientific 'chemistry' calibrated to achieving self-transformation in our contemporary technologized world.

And what of the teaching he brought? So many, such as the Sufis, Cabalists, and certain Christians, claim it as their own. But the fact is, according to Gurdjieff, that the Fourth Way predates them all. When Gurdjieff is asked in St. Petersburg about the relation of Christianity to the teaching, he first says he does not know what the questioner knows about the term Christianity and so a reply is difficult. Then he continues: "But for the benefit of those who know already, I will say that, if you like, *this is esoteric Christianity.*" The operative words are "if you like"; in other words, given your frame of reference, what is most analogous is esoteric Christianity. It does not mean that it is so. Later he will make the radical statement that "the Christian church, the Christian form of worship was not invented by the fathers of the church." And then he will follow it up with the even more astonishing statement that the origin of the Fourth Way was "prehistoric Egypt." Therefore, the elements of the teaching found in these other forms have been borrowed from the Fourth Way which predates them all. The teaching has not been cobbled together then from these forms, as detractors insist, but just the reverse. As Gurdjieff said many times, we are educated to look at life "topsy-turvey."

5. J. G. Bennett appears to have recognized Gurdjieff's identity as such for he writes, "Gurdjieff shows that he himself has gone far beyond the religious or theosophical concept of human perfection and he has also gone beyond the limitations of mystical union." (*Gurdjieff: Making a New World*, p. 246.) Bennett also wrote: "I had reached the conclusion that Gurdjieff was more than a Teacher and less than a Prophet. He was a man with a true mission and he devoted his entire life to it." (*Witness*, p. 379). Unfortunately, he only came to view Gurdjieff in this way in 1948, not 1923 when Gurdjieff asked that he stay at the Prieuré and help him to step-down the teaching.

In conclusion, Gurdjieff also stated there were four principal lines: Hebraic, Egyptian, Persian, and Hindu. And the two mixtures of these lines, theosophy and Western occultism, neither of which, being mixtures, can lead he said "to practical realization [but] give only negative results." Then speaking of the Fourth Way, he declared unambiguously: "The teaching whose theory is here being set out is *completely self-supporting and independent of other lines and it has been completely unknown up to the present time.*"[6] [Author's italics]

What we have here is, if true, monumental.

From Gurdjieff's perspective then, it will require a radical revisioning, if we are to begin to approach a recognition of Gurdjieff's life and the teaching he brought.

But why did he bring it and why now?

Gurdjieff was quite clear about what he called "the terror of the situation." He saw that the lack of conscience and growth of self-will, false individualism, and automatism—"Contemporary culture requires automatons," he said—together with the development of the means of planetary destruction would put mankind's very survival in question.

Unequivocally, Gurdjieff declared: *Unless the 'wisdom' of the East and the 'energy' of the West could be harnessed and used harmoniously, the world would be destroyed.*[7]

It was his view that all leaders, messiahs, messengers from the gods have one fundamental and very important purpose: to find some means by which the two sides of man, and therefore East and West, can live together in peace and harmony. Philosophies, religions, and other such movements had all failed to accomplish this aim, and the only possible way to accomplish it was through the individual development of man. Time was short and it was necessary to achieve this harmony as soon as possible to avoid complete disaster.

He predicted, too, that a day would come when the Eastern world would again rise to a position of world importance and become a threat to the momentarily all-powerful, all-influential new culture of the Western world, which was dominated, according to him, by America—a country that was very strong, to be sure, but also very young.[8]

Gurdjieff was saying all this, and more, in the mid–1920s. Strange and radical as it seemed then, it's now part of the contemporary psycho-babble. Skimming off psychological parts of the teaching, spiritual homogenizers

6. For references to quoted material, see Uspenskii's *In Search of the Miraculous* (Harcourt Brace, 1949), esoteric Christianity, p. 102; Christian church and form of worship, p. 302; principal lines, p. 286.

7. Fritz Peters, *Gurdjieff Remembered*, p. 122.

8. Fritz Peters, *Boyhood with Gurdjieff*, pp. 161–62.

make believe they understand the whole of the teaching. Time has passed Gurdjieff and his teaching by, they claim. Yet as all who have really worked on themselves well know, we in fact have yet to catch up with Gurdjieff, have yet to actually work on ourselves in the cosmological way he described.

Gurdjieff, the man, embodied the teaching. They were one and the same. The selflessness and sacrifice, the will and fierce love of the Truth his life so convincingly demonstrates, are a beacon for us all to truly work to be in life. To begin to look through Gurdjieff's eyes, Gurdjieff must be taken seriously. Only by opening to the possibility that he and his mission are what he says they are can we begin to enter into the life of George Ivanovitch Gurdjieff and relive with him his valiant struggle with the magicians of his day.

PART I

A NEW OR FORGOTTEN ROAD

NOVEMBER 13, 1914. MOSCOW. IN THE OFFICES OF A MOSCOW NEWSPAPER, A THIRTY-SEVEN-YEAR-OLD NEARSIGHTED RUSSIAN JOURNALIST edits material for a forthcoming issue. Only weeks before, he had returned from a journey to the East in search of what he calls "the miraculous." This he sees as "a new or forgotten road," one that would allow him to escape the lies and absurdities of ordinary life, so that he might penetrate its "thin film of false reality" to the hidden reality beyond.

Though he had glimpses of this hidden reality, he understood that his knowledge and efforts were not sufficient. "One thing I see clearly," he says, "that alone, by myself, I can do nothing." He needed to find a school and though there were many such "schools" in Russia as well as in the East, these he found either lacking in real knowledge or personally unsuitable. He was looking for a school of a special type, a school of "a more rational kind." But despite his extensive search in the East—this, his second such journey—he had found nothing. He had come home empty-handed.

So, once again, he finds himself back in Moscow. Though deflated, he has not given up his search. In fact, already his thoughts are of returning to India. Suddenly, a notice in the *Golos Moskvi,* a rival newspaper he is half-reading, makes a connection with these thoughts of the East. The notice heralds the opening of a new ballet scenario written by a Hindu. His attention, formerly diffuse and thin, now fully focuses on the notice. On the screen of his mind imprints the words... *The Struggle of the Magicians.*

At once his attention is caught and aroused. The ballet's title calls forth associations of good and evil, images of black and white magicians warring for souls—all of which mirrors the inner picture he has of life. Reading on, he finds the notice promising that the ballet will give a complete picture of Oriental magic, including fakir miracles, sacred dances, and so forth. All interesting, and yet...yet something about the way it uses language puts him off. He finds the notice's "excessively jaunty tone" irritating. He sees now that it gives a kind of two-sided or 'double' impression. It comes to him: *This notice is not what it appears to be.* The facts say one thing, the tone another. It's as if behind these words someone is laughing. But at whom? And why? Despite these misgivings, he decides to include the notice of the ballet in the coming events section of his newspaper. He does so only after inserting a warning alerting readers that "everything in the ballet that cannot be found in real India but which travelers go there to see."

Though this journalist could hardly know it, this seemingly innocuous notice with its annoying double language is, in effect, the calling card of just that teacher and school for which he has so actively searched these many years. Unlike so many seekers, Pyotr Demianovich Uspenskii is destined to find exactly what he has been searching for—what he calls the *"new or forgotten road."*

∾

In a sense all of Uspenskii's life had been a search. He was born in Moscow on March 5, 1878. Both of his parents were part of Russia's intelligentsia, the educated elite. His mother was a painter with an interest in Russian and French literature. His father, a Survey Service officer, was fond of music and painting. A good mathematician, his father had a lifelong interest in the question of time's fourth dimension. Early on, Pyotr showed an exceptional quality of intellect. As an adult he recalled having "quite clear mental pictures of events" before he was two years old. From the age of three he began to read and says he remembered himself "quite clearly."

When less than four years old, Pyotr received a severe shock—his father died. Thereafter Pyotr and his younger sister lived with their maternal grandparents in their house on Pimenovskaia Street. They were not there long before Pyotr, now four years old, received still another shock. His grandfather, a painter of religious subjects, died. The successive deaths of primal male figures in his life must have had a great impact. Many years later, most likely referring to these deaths, Uspenskii said of his childhood: "I was under less imagination and I saw what life was like at a very early stage." No wonder as a child he did not play with toys. From an early age, then, he had the sense that life in itself was meaningless. "It is only when you realize life is taking you nowhere," he said, "that it begins to have meaning."

At only six years of age, Pyotr was already reading on an adult level. He buried himself in books. Two made an enormous impression on him: Lermontov's *A Hero of Our Time*[1] and Turgenev's *A Sportsman's Notebook.* Lermontov's book is especially noteworthy because the ideas it expresses—the plasticity of time and questions of predestination, fate, and recurrence—are those which will occupy Uspenskii throughout his life. That at a mere six years of age such ideas could not only be of interest but be comprehended gives an indication of the rare quality of intellect that was Uspenskii's.

He became interested, too, in poetry and painting, growing especially fond of engravings and prints. Uspenskii mentions, as well, a certain psychic ability that developed. He and his younger sister often sat peering out the window onto the street below predicting to one another what would happen. Later, when his mother took Pyotr to enroll at his first school, she lost her way. Although he had never been in the building before, Pyotr led her to the right passageway. At the end of the passageway, he told her, they would come to two steps and a nearby window. And from the window, he said, they would be able to see the headmaster's garden with lilies growing and, close by, the headmaster's study. All he described proved to be correct.

When he was about eight years of age, natural science and mathematics captured his attention. Within several years he lost interest. "There was a dead wall everywhere," he would say later. "Professors were killing science in the same way as priests were killing religion." At thirteen, dreams attracted him. This led to psychology which, in its esoteric evolutionary sense, became a lifelong interest. Like many gifted children, Pyotr disliked school. "Work at school was dull," Uspenskii once commented on this period in his life. "I was lazy; I hated Greek and school routine in general." He had moments when he sensed the unity of all things and was overcome with its sensation. Instead of studying his physics book, he read a borrowed book on levers. He experienced that "all round me walls are crumbling, and horizons infinitely remote and incredibly beautiful stand revealed. It is as though threads, previously unknown and unsuspected, begin to reach out and bind things together. *For the first time in my life my world emerges from chaos.* Everything

1. See Notes.

becomes connected, forming an orderly and harmonious whole." [Author's italics] He then asked, "Why am I made to learn a thousand useless things and am not told about 'this?'"

Always sensitive to *time,* he no doubt felt school wasted it. An image in his autobiographical novel, *The Strange Life of Ivan Osokin,* is evoked concerning this period where, as punishment for an infraction, the housemaster orders Ivan Osokin to stand under a clock. In a sense, like a card from a tarot pack, this image could represent Uspenskii's lifelong posture toward, and dilemma in, life. It would not be until the end of his life when, finally cornered, unable to go forward or back, that he would come to the final "miracle," that is, galvanize the clarity and will to step through ordinary time.

At sixteen he left school. Nietzsche entered his life, and with Nietzsche, the idea of eternal recurrence. It was a seminal idea for Uspenskii, one that he would develop later in his "period of dimensions" and continue to work with throughout his life. About this time, he became "very anarchistically inclined." A year after leaving school at sixteen, he experienced another shock—his mother died. By seventeen, he had already lost his father, grandfather, and mother.[2] It was then he began to travel.

Uspenskii was born into a time rife with extremism and revolutionary ferment. In 1879, one year after his birth, *Narodnaia Volia,* the People's Will, was formed. A secret organization, it espoused terrorism as the way to bring down the three-hundred-year-old tsarist regime of the Romanovs. Structured hierarchically and operating in a quasi-military manner, its members pledged to totally dedicate themselves to the revolutionary cause, sacrificing property and life. *Narodnaia Volia's* mission was to assassinate government officials. Four days before Uspenskii's third birthday on March 1, 1881, a *Narodnaia Volia* bomb killed Tsar Alexander II. Six years later, Alexander Ulianov was arrested carrying a bomb in an attempt to assassinate Tsar Alexander III. Ulianov and his co-conspirators believed in an eclectic political brew of *Narodnaia Volia,* Marxism, and German Social Democracy. All were executed.

The execution imprinted Ulianov's younger brother, Vladimir Ilich, later known as Lenin, with a lasting hatred. That same year, Lenin enrolled at the university to study law. Within a short time he joined *Narodnaia Volia* and within months was arrested and expelled. Exiled to Siberia and then deported, Lenin was living in Switzerland when on Sunday, January 9, 1905, thousands of workers led by a priest peacefully marched to St. Petersburg's Winter Palace to present Tsar Nicholas II with a petition of economic grievances. Unable to halt the surging work-

2. See Notes.

ers, the soldiers fired point blank into the crowd, killing 100 people and wounding several hundred more.

The immediate threat of what was known as "Bloody Sunday" was quelled. Strikes among workers and university students then broke out throughout the country. Succumbing to the pressure, the Tsar allowed the legalization of political parties and trade unions and set up a nationally elected *Duma*, or parliament. But the Tsar's image of divine rule had been irreparably damaged, and thus began the slow but inexorable erosion of autocratic rule.

Among the workers arrested for revolutionary activity on Bloody Sunday was Uspenskii's beloved sister. She died in prison in 1908. With this loss, all of Uspenskii's immediate family were now dead. Thus, at thirty years of age, Pyotr Demianovich found himself alone in the world. The meaning of life and the mystery of death now became living questions. Soon he was drawn to theosophical literature, which he read voraciously.

Theosophical literature had been banned in Russia, but after Bloody Sunday controls loosened. In 1908 the Russian Theosophical Society was created and registered with authorities. And at some point Uspenskii began to attend its meetings. In his readings he said he came to realize that there is an "unbroken line of thought and knowledge which passes from century to century, from age to age, from country to country, from one race to another; a line deeply hidden beneath layers of religions and philosophies which are, in fact, only distortions and perversions of the ideas belonging to this line." The idea came that there existed schools that had this knowledge. And so he said, "I decide to start on a long journey with the idea of searching for those schools or for the people who may show me the way to them."

In 1908 he and his good friend, Sherbakov, planned his first journey to the East to make contact with "schools of the distant past, with schools of Pythagoras, with schools of Egypt or with the schools of those who had built Nôtre Dame, and so on." Shortly before they were to embark, Sherbakov died. The feeling that death stalked his heels must have been strong in Uspenskii. Others might have postponed the journey, but, with characteristic resolve, he set out alone.

Traveling to Constantinople, Smyrna, Greece, and Egypt, he had many evocative experiences, some transcendent, yet none substantial. He returned to Moscow and in early 1909 left to live in St. Petersburg. Not finding a school, he began experiments in altering consciousness through hashish and nitrous oxide. Drugs, he soon concluded, were a dead end. During this time, too, he began writing *Tertium Organum,* which he self-published in 1912. The book's impressive clarity and sweep of thought attracted an erudite readership, especially among theosophical circles.

Many doors now opened for him. Through one stepped a beautiful young woman who would be of great influence.

1912. St. Petersburg. Soon after the publication of *Tertium Organum* a beautiful young aristocrat, the daughter of the counsel in the Ministry of Justice and an accomplished pianist, one day came upon the book at a local library. Recently divorced, this twenty-seven-year-old woman was herself filled with a thirst to explore life's meaning. Reading the book she felt an immediate rapport with the author. "Here was a book," Anna Ilinishna Butkovsky told herself, "which seemed to set out to answer the questions I kept asking."

Since the age of seventeen, Anna Ilinishna had read theosophical literature. It evoked in her a strong desire to explore the esoteric worlds she read about. When she attended a lecture at Petersburg's Theosophical Society,[3] it was likely that the author of *Tertium Organum* was still on her mind. Following the lecture, there were questions and at one point the lecturer called into the audience—"Pyotr Demianovich Uspenskii, please be so kind as to give us your opinion on this matter."

A squarely built gentleman of medium height with close-cropped hair and an imposing face rose from a chair. His forehead was high and broad and gave an impression of great intellect. Stubbornness, too, was reflected in his face by a nose that jutted forth and was clipped with a pince-nez. The eyes which peered through the thick lenses reflected a keen sensitivity and uncommon visionary quality.

Through his books, articles, and lectures Uspenskii had become the darling of Russia's theosophical movement. Anna Alekseevna Kamenskaia, the energetic forty-five-year-old General Secretary and co-founder in 1908 of the Russian Section of Theosophy and head of its powerful St. Petersburg branch, spoke of him highly, as did the idealist philosopher Nikolai Berdiaev who called Uspenskii "the most independent and talented theosophical writer in Russia."

For Anna Ilinishna, hearing the sound of the name "Uspenskii" must have been a shock that seemed like a call of fate. At the lecture's close, Anna Ilinishna introduced herself to the author. What the thirty-four-year-old Uspenskii saw through his pince-nez no doubt pleased him, for he sought to make an impression on the vibrant young woman. He confided to her that while, yes, he had attended the lecture, he was also withdrawing from the Theosophical Society.

Nodding toward the people in the hall, he told her scornfully —"These ordinary members are sheep. . . ." He then looked toward the lectern and declared—"But I feel there are even bigger sheep in the 'inner circle.'"

3. See Notes.

Proud and self-confident, the young woman stood her ground.

"You sound as though you are sorry there are no wolves," she challenged.

"Exactly!" cried Uspenskii. "At least wolves display strength. Sheep are simply sheep, and it is hopeless for them to pretend to aspire to be the image of God, and to develop the hidden, higher faculties."[4]

By conversation's end, Uspenskii asked Anna Ilinishna to join him for coffee the following morning at Phillipoff's, a café in Petersburg's bohemian section. The café was on the corner of Trotsky Street and Nevsky Prospekt, the city's main boulevard. As it happened, Phillipoff's was close to both their homes. Uspenskii's apartment was at the corner of the Nevsky Prospekt and Liteiny Street, while Anna Ilinishna lived with her father on another corner of the Nevsky at Nikolaevski Street.

Arriving at Phillipoff's the next morning, Anna Ilinishna found Uspenskii awaiting her, three empty coffee cups in front of him. They spoke together of the ideas in *Tertium Organum,* such as the development of super consciousness and his conclusion, for example, that "a prolonged self-consciousness during sensation, feeling or thinking is a very rare phenomenon in man. As a rule what is called self-consciousness is simply thought, and it takes place *post factum.* True self-consciousness exists in man only as a potentiality, and if it manifests itself at all, does so only by moments."

After discussing more of the ideas, Uspenskii told her of his search for a school "of a more rational kind."

She asked if he would write another book.

He had already started a book, he replied. Its working title was *The Wisdom of the Gods.* He was uncertain about finishing it. He estimated it would take him twenty years to complete.

"Even if it would take so long," asked Anna Ilinishna, "why is it not worth writing?"

"Because what I want to say in that book is so difficult and elusive that I do not feel equal to it," declared Uspenskii, and posturing a bit, he added, "and I must always feel equal to anything that I tackle."

Anna Ilinishna made no reply.

An arrogant smile formed on Uspenskii's face and he feigned an admission: "Although the realization hurt my pride very deeply, I knew I lacked something necessary to do it."

The following day the two met again at Phillipoff's. After a few coffees, Uspenskii, obviously smitten by Anna's beauty and independence of mind, came right to the point: "You are attracted by the purpose of our quest—by

4. Implicit in his words was the declaration that he, Uspenskii, of course, was not a sheep. But the words, too, conveyed the intellectual seduction that she was speaking with someone with the ability to develop such faculties.

the road that we want to travel. And a little by me, too, perhaps?...I don't think that among your other friends you have anyone as *interesting* as I am."

Seeing that these words made no impression, he declared outright: "I came across your orbit like a comet."

Finally, he tried another tack with Anna, saying: "Now, suppose you tell me of any curious experiences you have had."

"Have you ever heard of Nicholas Evreinoff, the theatrical producer and writer," asked Anna Ilinishna.

Yes, he told her, he had seen his portrait in the papers. "Romantic face," he said, "like a Florentine poet of the sixteenth century."

Anna Ilinishna admitted she had an affair with Evreinoff.

Unable to control himself, Uspenskii shouted: "How can you do such things!"

Seeing her face, he quickly caught himself and added: "But I am glad—it shows you are not *'a lady.'*"

Anna protested, indignant.

"I don't mean in that sense," said Uspenskii, foot-in-mouth, backtracking quickly. He meant, he said, that she was a human being *before* she was a lady, "because you aren't afraid of things that Society would disapprove of, or what people may think of you."[5]

However arrogant Uspenskii appeared to Anna, she was attracted by what she saw as his "almost boyish enthusiasm and gentle, poetic radiance." The two continued to meet at Phillipoff's every day at noon and, later on, in the evening as well. One day, as the two were walking along Nevsky Prospekt, they came to the Liteiny and were to pass by Uspenskii's apartment. He invited Anna inside. She hesitated.

"I thought it might give you pleasure to see some of my books," he said. "I went to your house to hear you play, now you should come to mine to look at books!"

True, Anna had invited him to her home to hear her play. She had studied piano under the St. Petersburg Conservatoire's two best professors, one of them the celebrated woman pianist Barinova. Anna Ilinishna had a keen feeling for the essence of music and enjoyed sharing it.

5. Like many men, Uspenskii seems a bit awkward with women. But he was quite taken with them, as evidenced in his autobiographical novel *The Strange Life of Ivan Osokin.* As many of the events in the novel parallel Uspenskii's, it is fair to suppose that Osokin's views reflected his own. For example, in the novel Osokin believed that women were for the most part more interesting than men and belonged to a higher caste. It held that an educated woman like Anna, living in more or less civilized society, would have occupied a privileged position because "for thousands of years," said Osokin, "women have taken no active part in wars, and have rarely had anything to do with politics or Government service. In this way they have avoided the most fraudulent and criminal sides of life. This alone makes women more free than men. Of course, there are different kinds of women; and undoubtedly the modern woman does everything she can to lose her caste."

She knew Uspenskii's invitation wasn't at all the same thing. Moreover, it was risky socially, as young unmarried women did not frequent men's apartments. Still, she agreed.

Uspenskii's "apartment," she found, was one very small room. Its furniture consisted of a bed, chair and table, and a large bookshelf crammed with books in Russian, French, and English. On the table was the final draft of a novel, *Kinemadrama* (later to be retitled *The Strange Life Of Ivan Osokin).* There was also the unfinished manuscript of another of his books, *The Devil.*

Their relationship deepening, Uspenskii and Anna sat hour after hour in coffeehouses, like Phillipoff's, or at bohemian clubs like the Stray Dog, situated nearby in a dark cellar. They were often joined by others of the Petersburg intelligentsia. The well-known writer Volinsky was often present, as was Charkovsky, a bridge engineer, who rivaled Uspenskii in his knowledge of mystic literature. The two could talk for hours on the meaning of the various tarot cards or Charkovsky's current passion, a circular device created by Raymond Lully, a thirteenth-century Catalan mystic and teacher, which organized and related forms of knowledge. They all sat drinking cup after cup of à la Varsovienne, a very strong coffee. Or, because of the prohibition, teacups full of bootleg vodka cut with pineapple juice.

As often as not, Uspenskii usually held court, the words pouring forth like an avalanche, as he talked about ancient texts such as the *Vedas* and the *Zend Avesta*, or perhaps compared, say, the different esoteric schools, relating a historical survey before asking a series of rhetorical questions that he would answer himself.

When the small hours of the morning arrived, the group wandered along the canals such as the Moika, where, at number 12, the poet Pushkin once lived. They ambled along the quays and past the smart hotels like the Europe or the recently built Astoria, past the massive granite pillars of St. Isaac's Cathedral with its golden dome, past the Maryinski and Alexandrinski theaters, and along the old streets of St. Petersburg. With the coming of spring, Petersburg's lustrous "white nights" began to appear. It was a time when darkness never fell, and the group ambled amid shimmering images of Petersburg's pale yellow buildings, its palaces and bridges and famous sphinxes, all the while discussing, talking, arguing, the words still pouring from Uspenskii. With the approach of dawn the group, ever-shrinking, went on to have buns and tea, perhaps more coffee, at the Nikolaevski Station on Znamenski Square.

With Anna, Uspenskii felt like he was about eighteen. In her he saw what he admired in himself—"a driving force and a will to seek and find." For Anna, he came to have two faces. One was the outer face characterized by what she called his "arrogance of erudition." Behind this face was another, she said, "more radiant, countenance filled with a youthful happiness which perhaps no one but myself ever witnessed."

Often their conversations focused on Uspenskii's search and travels. He told her about the esoteric Schools of Builders evidenced by the Cathedral of Nôtre Dame; of the pyramids of Egypt where he said he felt everything "as extraordinarily real, as though I was suddenly transferred into another world, which to my own astonishment I seemed to know very well... [where this distant past] ceased to be past, appeared in everything, surrounded me, became the present." He spoke of standing before the glance of the Sphinx, that which saw life in terms of centuries and millenniums, and feeling all at once, in that moment, "that I did not exist, that there was no I." He told her about Ceylon and the Buddha with the sapphire eyes which, like the Sphinx, spoke "of another life, of another consciousness, which is higher than man's consciousness," and about the Taj Mahal, where he said he had "the sensation of being in two worlds at once...and came to feel that here "before me and all around me was the soul of the Empress Mumtaz-i-Mahal," the divine feminine for whom the immense mausoleum had been built. But of all the subjects, it was always to Uspenskii's chief interest, time's fourth dimension, that the discussion returned. For Uspenskii, it was the Idea of ideas; so much so that his friends called him "Uspenskii Fourth Dimension." At the age of twenty he had even published a book, *The Fourth Dimension.*

The fourth dimension for him was not simply an intellectual idea, however. He had had many experiences of it, most notably perhaps in 1908. He was on a ship in the Sea of Marmara on a rainy winter day standing by the railing watching the waves. The sky was grey and the sea the color of lead, touched with a glint of silver. The waves would crest, their white foam running up to the ship from afar, rear up as though hurling their crests on the deck, and then with a roar throw themselves under the ship.

"I was watching the play of waves with the ship," he said, "and feeling the waves drawing me to themselves. It was not the desire to jump down which one feels in the mountains, but something infinitely more subtle. The waves were drawing my soul to themselves. Suddenly I felt it going to them. It was only a moment, maybe less than a moment. But I entered the waves and, with them, with a roar, attacked the ship. And at that moment *I became all.* The waves—they were myself. The violet mountains in the distance—they were myself. The wind—it was myself. The clouds, hurrying from the north, the rain—were myself. The huge ship, rolling indomitably forward—was myself. I felt that huge iron body as *my body,* all its movements, waverings, rollings and shudderings, the fire, the pressure of steam, the engine—all this was *inside* me."

WINTER 1913. ST. PETERSBURG. Within a year or so of his meeting Anna Ilinishna, Uspenskii began thinking of a second journey to the East. Perhaps this time to Australia. Unable to conceive of finding his teacher there, he told Anna he had dropped the idea.

"But why don't you go to India, then?" she prompted, adding, "And when you come back you can tell me all about what you find there."

Perhaps fearing Evreinoff had returned to Anna's thoughts or she had become bored with him, Uspenskii wondered why she seemed to want him to go.

Her final examination at the Conservatoire, Anna explained, was in the spring. "If I spend all my time at Phillipoff's like this," she said, "I shall never get on with my work."

Uspenskii finally came to a decision "to start on a long journey with the idea of searching for those schools or for the people who may show me the way."

Since 1905 Uspenskii had made his living as a translator and journalist and had no trouble convincing three newspapers for which he freelanced to finance his trip in return for articles. In London, drawing on his theosophical contacts, he met A. R. Orage, the much respected editor of the *New Age*, a literary and political weekly magazine. Besides theosophy, the two men may have talked about another mutual interest, Nietzsche and his concept of the superman.

After London, Uspenskii slowly made his way to Ceylon and later to Madras, India, where he spent six weeks at Adyar, the Theosophical Society's headquarters. He traveled about India visiting places such as Benares, Bombay, Agra, and Delhi. He made contact with a number of schools, but they were, he said, "either of a frankly religious nature, or of a half-religious character, but definitely devotional in tone." The sentimental moral philosophy, the shades of asceticism and spiritualism which permeated such schools, had no appeal for him. Others promised a great deal but demanded, from the beginning, a complete surrender. These interested him somewhat. However...

"Speaking sincerely with myself," admitted Uspenskii, "I could not say that I was able to do this [surrender]. The price seemed too high. As I put it to myself: If I paid with my own self for what I might learn, I should have lost the object for the sake of which I wished to know."

NOVEMBER 1914. ST. PETERSBURG. Anna Kamenskaia, editor of the Russian Theosophical Society's journal *Vestnik Teosofii*, or Theosophical Herald, urges readers to regard the war as a cosmic event of great occult importance which would produce a cleansing that would forge a new spiritual union between the religious East and the scientific West which would be mediated by Russian spirituality.

NOVEMBER 1914. MOSCOW. Returning from his long journey, thirty-seven-year-old Pyotr Demianovich Uspenskii once again finds himself in the offices of a Moscow newspaper editing material for a forthcoming issue. A notice in a rival newspaper he is half-reading suddenly connects with his thoughts of the East. His attention, formerly diffuse and thin, now fully focused on the notice, on the screen of his mind are imprinted the words—*The Struggle of the Magicians.*

∾

DECEMBER 1914. ST. PETERSBURG-PETROGRAD.[6] Once again Uspenskii now finds himself back at Phillipoff's talking with Anna.

"Why on earth did I ever go to India?" he asks Anna. "I found nothing there that I have not read before in books, or heard rumored in some way…nothing new, *nothing.*"

Traveling in India a growing conviction arose in him. Perhaps the teacher for whom he is searching will be found not in the East but in Russia, perhaps even St. Petersburg.

"I have a feeling in my bones," he says. "This is not an exotic city but there must be *someone* here of the kind I am seeking."

FEBRUARY AND MARCH 1915. PETROGRAD. Uspenskii prepares his novel *Kinemadrama* for publication and also gives two public lectures—*In Search of the Miraculous* and *The Problems of Death*—at Alexandroski Hall of the town Duma, or Parliament. The lectures arouse considerable interest with each attended by more than a thousand people.

The Theosophical Society's journal *Vestnik Teosofii* reports:

> P. D. Uspenskii's lectures attracted a huge audience, but they evoked perplexity. The lecturer promised in the program to talk about India. In fact he talked only about disillusionment in seeking the miraculous and about his understanding of occultism at variance with its understanding by Theosophists and the Theosophical Society. With indignation he said that the Theosophists selected ethics and philosophy, not occultism, as their field of effort, and that ethics and philosophy are unnecessary to the Society and unrelated to occultism. Mr. Uspenskii also accused the Theosophical Society of arrogance and sectarianism.

APRIL 24, 1915. ARMENIA. The Turks begin the massacre of over one-and-one-half million Armenians.

6. When Germany declared war on Russia in August 1914, the name "St. Petersburg", German in origin, was changed to the Russian "Petrograd"; Uspenskii, Gurdjieff, and others continued to use the older name.

APRIL 1915. MOSCOW. Uspenskii's Petersburg lectures a success, he now brings his lecture series to Moscow. After one lecture, he meets Vladimir Pohl, a composer, and Sergei Dmitrievich Mercourov, a sculptor. Very soon they tell him about a group to which they belong which engages in various occult investigations and experiments. It is led by a Caucasian Greek, they say. It turns out this very same Greek is the "Hindu" who has written *The Struggle of the Magicians.*

Uspenskii shows no interest, believing occult phenomena to be "a mixture of superstition, self-suggestion, and defective thinking." About meeting this Greek who poses as a Hindu, he is, at best, dubious. Only persistent efforts by Mercourov finally cause him to relent.

The meeting is quickly arranged.[7]

The meeting's venue certainly does nothing to allay Uspenskii's doubts. He is directed neither to a meeting place of the intelligentsia nor to a café of the rich and powerful. Instead, he finds himself opening the door to a small and noisy businessmen's café on a busy Moscow side street. Entering the crowded cafe and seeing the man awaiting him, Uspenskii's concern could only have increased.

No two men could be more opposite in appearance. Uspenskii's skin is light, almost albino, in coloring. Of medium height and squarely built, he sees through a thick pince-nez and speaks and acts in the manner of the intelligentsia. Admirers describe him as having the face of an emperor. In look and action "Uspenskii" gives no doubt as to who he is.

The Caucasian Greek awaiting him at the small café table stares at Uspenskii as he approaches. The man's eyes are dark, intense, piercing. Uspenskii has the dual impression of the eyes having a quality of both emptiness and presence. The impression he creates is "strange" in some way Uspenskii cannot define. The man is swarthy, short, and very powerfully built. Beneath the long nose is a heavy black mustache. He appears to be of an oriental type. In his mind's eye, Uspenskii sees the man in a white burnoose or a gilded turban. The words "Indian raja" or "Arab sheik" enter his mind. Yet the man is dressed like a common merchant. He wears a black overcoat with a velvet collar and a black bowler hat.

Greetings are exchanged. *Georgi Ivanovitch Gurdjieff* is the name given. Uspenskii, who speaks in the faultless Russian of the intelligentsia, finds the Russian this Gurdjieff speaks not only incorrect but, given its

7. Having given public lectures on his search and preparing the publication of his autobiographical novel is, in effect, for Uspenskii to complete his past and, in so doing he prepares for his future. It also signals that a new octave began for Uspenskii in 1913 when he made his second journey to the East. Traveling in India and then assimilating his experiences through his lectures have moved him through two more notes of the octave, re and mi. His meeting now with the Caucasian Greek is in reality his meeting with the magician. It is the octave's shock point.

strong Caucasian accent, coarse. Such an accent is hardly associated with philosophical and spiritual discussions.

Still, always a polite and considerate man, Uspenskii draws up a chair. He almost immediately experiences an uneasy feeling. This Gurdjieff fellow seems "disguised" in some way, and poorly at that. Uspenskii finds himself embarrassed. This man is not what he pretends to be, yet Uspenskii has the odd feeling he has to speak and act as though he is not aware of it.

As with the ballet notice in the newspaper, Gurdjieff has created for Uspenskii a kind of 'double-impression,' one that interests but also irritates and alarms him. No doubt Uspenskii tries not to show his true inner state. And so, unwittingly, he receives a second double-impression, consisting of both his outward expression and his inner feeling.

And so from the outset, with only the giving of his name and perhaps a few words, Gurdjieff begins to act on Uspenskii. That is, Uspenskii is put in the position of seeing one thing yet having to appear as if he does not see it. The contradiction divides Uspenskii. It jams his mind, stops his thoughts, takes him out of his "Uspenskii," and throws him into uncertainty. For a man who prides himself on the power of his intellect, his control and command over himself and others, Uspenskii's position is not only unfamiliar but decidedly uncomfortable.

Though Uspenskii could not know it, Gurdjieff has followed his newspaper accounts of his journey and its aims. He had also directed his pupils to read Uspenskii's books.[8] In this way, he had told his pupils, Uspenskii's level of understanding could be determined and thus it could be known what he would be able to discover.

Although he had found nothing, Uspenskii was no ordinary seeker. He knows a secret: that most people live only to die, that ordinary life is a meaningless charade. This, together with his gift of intellect and thirst for the truth, had enabled him to see through and free himself from the hypnotisms of conventional society. He had entered into subtle domains of esoteric knowledge, and he was capable not only of capturing, holding, and directing the attention of others, but of bending the will of others to his own. He has experienced the change in the sensation of "I," of time and the "long body" of man, he has been tested by "voices." He has experienced the terror and joy of life's infinity, its unity. He knows of the need to become self-conscious, to expand the space-sense. It is true that many of these experiences came from his experiments with drugs, but of this he will say, "Narcotics cannot *give* a man anything he has not already got.... All they can do, in certain cases, is to *reveal* that which is already in a man's soul." He has had the personal power and self-confidence to

8. Having arrived in Russia in 1912, the same year Uspenskii published *Tertium Organum*, it seems likely that Gurdjieff would have read the book.

lecture in Russia's most cosmopolitan cities, St. Petersburg and Moscow, and hold the attention of thousands of people. Compared to the average man, Uspenskii is, in his own right, a magician.

This meeting in a noisy Moscow merchant's café then is no ordinary meeting. Rather, it is a meeting between two magicians. And as with all such meetings the issue is: *whose magic is greater?*

Uspenskii is so put off balance by his initial contact with Gurdjieff, he admits he does not remember how their talk began. If Gurdjieff conducts this meeting as he does others, then he will have begun with questions such as: "Why do you come to me?" "What is your secret intolerance?" "Is your life so unbearable?"

If so, Uspenskii's reply would likely be how he later expressed what he felt at this period of his life. "Ordinary life forces one to swallow customary forms of lying and living in lying," he had said. "I am looking for a way to escape, a new or forgotten road. And it cannot in character be devotional. It must be more rational."

What Uspenskii does remember is that Gurdjieff speaks to him of his Work. Uspenskii's interest is psychology and Gurdjieff explains that while the character of his Work is chiefly psychological, *chemistry* plays a large role.[9] What Gurdjieff means by 'chemistry' Uspenskii is not certain so he associates, telling Gurdjieff about a school in India that studied the chemistry of the human body, altering a man's moral or psychological nature by the introduction or removal of substances.

But this 'chemistry' is not Gurdjieff's.

Uspenskii's material on the subject is slight. Instead of exposing his ignorance, he introduces into the discussion the subject of magic and narcotics.

Gurdjieff answers his questions but doesn't let Uspenskii off the hook. He brings him back to the idea of chemistry saying, "To do this [to know possibilities in advance], a great knowledge of the human machine and of this special chemistry is necessary."

Which of the two has the greatest understanding, which is the magician and which the adept, quickly becomes clear.

Despite the heavy, coarse accent, Uspenskii is deeply impressed with Gurdjieff's manner of speaking. In his answers, Gurdjieff is careful, precise, economical. More important: Uspenskii finds some of Gurdjieff's points of view not only new—but unlike any he's ever heard.

At the end of their talk, Gurdjieff invites him to come back to his house to meet some of his pupils. They take a carriage toward the outly-

9. It is interesting that in reporting this first meeting Uspenskii does not speak of Gurdjieff's presence or power, his great being. Neither does he in any of his subsequent writings or reported conversations. Even intellectuals like C. Daly King, no friend of Gurdjieff's, spoke of the rare quality of being he exuded. Could it be that Uspenskii, so armored and intellectual, did not sense it? Compare what Uspenskii reports to that of Jean Toomer; see p. 104.

ing district of Sokolniki. On the way Gurdjieff gives him to understand he lives in an expensive apartment and that among his pupils are a number of well-known professors and artists. When the carriage draws up in front of a municipal school, and Gurdjieff motions him to get out, Uspenskii must have been surprised. Where is the expensive apartment? Gurdjieff leads him up to the top floor of the school. The 'apartment' turns out to be a large empty flat that costs perhaps no more than ten pounds a month. As for his pupils, Uspenskii finds them nice and decent, but they belong to a layer of Moscow society known as the "poor intelligentsia." Uspenskii cannot understand: why is Gurdjieff so obviously creating in him such doubts about who he, Gurdjieff, is?

A student begins to read aloud a story called "Glimpses of Truth." At the outset the story mentions the newspaper notice for the ballet scenario *The Struggle of the Magicians.* For the third time, like a leitmotif of what their relationship will be, the ballet's title is introduced to Uspenskii.

All the while the piece is read, Gurdjieff sits on the sofa, one leg crossed beneath him, smoking, and drinking black coffee from a tumbler. Now and then he looks at Uspenskii. His movements, Uspenskii notices, have a kind of "feline grace and assurance." The impression slowly forms in him of Gurdjieff being someone quite rare. Uspenskii finds the literary quality of "Glimpses of Truth" unexceptional but still it makes an impression on him.

At the evening's end he goes to leave but suddenly the thought flashes into his mind that he must arrange to see Gurdjieff *"at once, without delay."* Otherwise, he might lose all contact with him.

And so the next day and every day thereafter for the entire week, Uspenskii and Gurdjieff meet and talk at the same noisy Moscow café. What Uspenskii finds especially impressive is Gurdjieff's command of psychology, an area Uspenskii takes to be his specialty. "I saw without hesitation," says Uspenskii, "that in the domain which I knew better than any other and in which I was really able to distinguish the old from the new, the known from the unknown, Gurdjieff knew more than all European science taken as a whole."

At one point, Uspenskii introduces the subject of esoteric schools. There are no general schools, only special ones, Gurdjieff tells him. Every teacher has his specialty and all the students must study it. Uspenskii wants to know in what way Gurdjieff studied. He is told of the Seekers After Truth.

Uspenskii asks about their whereabouts.

Some are dead, some are working and "some," declares Gurdjieff, "have gone into seclusion."[10]

10. In the original draft, the words are not ambiguous—"some are cloistered."

Seclusion. The word's inner ring has monastic reverberations. Uspenskii reacts. He experiences "a strange and uncomfortable feeling."[11]

During one of their talks, Gurdjieff tells Uspenskii that he might learn a great deal if he knew how to read. For Uspenskii—journalist, translator, and author— the remark must have been a great shock.

"If you understood everything you have written in your own book, what is it called?"—Gurdjieff makes something altogether impossible out of the words *Tertium Organum*—"I should come and bow down to you and beg you to teach me."[12]

Gurdjieff tells Uspenskii of the necessity to work on oneself in a group. Uspenskii raises the question of secrecy. "I do not know," he says, "whether you exact a promise from your pupils to keep secret what they learn from you, but I could give no such promise...before everything else, I am a writer, and I desire to be absolutely free to decide for myself what I shall write and what I shall not write."[13]

"One must not talk too much," Gurdjieff tells him. "There are things which are said only for disciples."

"I could accept such a condition only temporarily," answers Uspenskii. He goes on to speak of a group engaged in various scientific experiments who "made it a condition that no one would have the right to speak of or describe any experiment unless he was able to carry it out himself. Until he was able to repeat the experiment himself he had to keep silent."

"There could be no better formulation," says Gurdjieff, "and if you will keep such a rule this question will never arise between us."

On another occasion Gurdjieff tells him that the starting point is that "man does not know himself, that he is *not*...that is, he is not what he can and what he should be." Man, he says, is a machine to which everything happens and as it is not possible to stop being a machine it is imperative that he first know his machine. What needs to be studied is the workings of the machine, its mechanics. In this way, one begins to become responsible for one's actions.

11. Gurdjieff sees the automatic effects that the word "seclusion" sets off in Uspenskii. Three years later in Essentuki all that surrounds this word for Uspenskii will unconsciously play itself out.

12. The implication is that Gurdjieff does understand what is in *Tertium Organum.* Yet Uspenskii, not understanding what he has written, is refusing to bow to Gurdjieff and beg to be taught. Uspenskii appears to miss this subtlety entirely. See *Search,* p. 20.

13. It is seen here that Uspenskii thinks of himself as a writer first, a seeker second. He is perceiving the situation then, not in terms of finding the miraculous, but finding it and writing about it. His identification is understandable, of course, but "the writer" in him is also Uspenskii's "teacher," he who wants to teach others. This —Uspenskii's teacher-"I"—will later become an issue.

"A *man* is responsible. A *machine* is not responsible," says Gurdjieff. The chief delusion of man is that he is convinced he can do but, in fact, everything happens to him. "To do," says Gurdjieff, "it is necessary to be." Everything is connected, Gurdjieff tells him. The planets and moon are living beings. The universe is expanding, not contracting, and the moon is a planet in birth. War is the result not of economics, injustice and the like, but of planetary influences. "Everything that happens on a big scale is governed from outside, and governed either by accidental combinations of influences or by general cosmic laws," Gurdjieff continues. What man does have is a certain possibility of deciding the influences under which he will work.

Having spent the entire week with Gurdjieff, Uspenskii must return to Petersburg. He is preparing new editions of *Tertium Organum* and *Symbolism of the Tarot*, and also, as with these previous books, he will self-publish his autobiographical novel, *Kinemadrama*, first written in 1905 at the age of twenty-seven.

Kinemadrama concerns a romantic young maverick, Ivan Osokin, who has little control over his impulses, is willful, resents authority, and resists responsibility. He always sees life as too dull and boring. Through his stubbornness and rebellion, Osokin has thrown away all his chances in life. In desperation he has a magician send him back into his past so he can repair his mistakes. But, being who he is, he can only repeat them. Such knowledge in itself, he learns, can change nothing. To change, one must have the *will* to change.

"You must realize," says the magician, "that you yourself can change nothing and that you must seek help. And it must be a very deep realization, because to realize to-day and forget to-morrow is not sufficient. One must live with this realization."

The magician tells him he must sacrifice something big to gain the power and knowledge to change, and one must go on making sacrifices. "In order to know, one must learn; and in order to learn, one must make sacrifices. Nothing can be acquired without sacrifice."

Osokin maintains he has nothing to sacrifice.

The magician tells him: "You can sacrifice your life...give me your life and I will see what can be made of you...Twenty, even fifteen years will be sufficient. But during these years you must belong to me—I mean, you must do everything I tell you without evasions and excuses."

∾

Gurdjieff had not come to Russia by chance. Some four years earlier, on September 14, 1911, he had taken a special oath binding him for twenty-one years. It bound him "in my conscience to lead in some ways an artificial life, modelled upon a programme which had been previously planned in accordance with certain definite principles." The purpose of the oath was to help him accomplish what he terms a *sacred task*—to build a new world.

The present period of culture Gurdjieff saw, in terms of the perfecting of humanity, had come to an "empty and aborted interval" in which "the people of our civilization cannot transmit by inheritance anything of value to their descendants." A new teaching was needed, especially for the West. The impetus for his mission was his stark recognition that "Unless the 'wisdom' of the East and the 'energy' of the West could be harnessed and used harmoniously, the world would be destroyed." While such prophecy is common enough today—though still not clearly understood—the idea at that time was revolutionary.

Gurdjieff first appeared in Moscow in 1912.[14] He arrived with about one million rubles and two invaluable collections, one of Chinese cloisonné and the other of old and rare carpets. He brought such an enormous sum because he said he felt it "necessary to be independent, at least in the material sense; the more so, since experience had already shown me that wealthy people never become seriously enough interested in these questions to support a work of this kind, and that others, even with great interest and desire, cannot do much in this respect...."

His plan was to establish an Institute to train students to become "helper-instructors" so they could help in disseminating the teaching. While he will experiment, he knows exactly what he wants to create. The basis of the Institute would be to create conditions, he says, in which "a man would be continually reminded of the sense and aim of his existence by an unavoidable friction between his conscience and the automatic manifestations of his nature."

In the winter of 1913 in St. Petersburg, it seems likely that Gurdjieff—disguised as 'Prince Ozay'[15]—meets Paul Dukes, a twenty-four-year-old Englishman and music student. Dukes is a friend of Lev Lvovitch, a professional hypnotist and healer, who apparently learned his craft while on military service in Central Asia. There he had fallen ill with an obscure malady. He spoke of his "having died" and "come back" through the

14. Biographer James Moore, in his *Gurdjieff: An Anatomy of a Myth* (Element Books Ltd., 1991), states that soon after Gurdjieff came to Moscow and visited St. Petersburg he met and married Julia Ostrowska, a twenty-two-year-old Polish countess. However, he cites no reference. The first she appears in the written record is in Thomas and Olga de Hartmann's *Our Life With Mr. Gurdjieff.*

15. From Dukes' description of the Prince's presence, depth of occult knowledge, and behavior, it does appear that 'Prince Ozay' is Gurdjieff in disguise. Biographer James Webb in his *The Harmonious Circle* (G. P. Putnam, 1980) believes so, but lacking evidence keeps the question open. Moore has no doubt that Gurdjieff is Prince Ozay, but cites no sources. See Notes.

efforts of a shaman of a nomadic tribe. Perhaps it was then that he met Gurdjieff. Whatever the case, Lvovitch speaks to Dukes of Prince Ozay as being a man of whom "there are but few in the world."

Dukes is led to a house at the bottom of a small street near Nikolaevski station. Lvovitch leads him through a very plain apartment to a flat beyond that is larger and more sumptuous. It is decorated in an Oriental manner with the windows heavily curtained, carpets adorning walls, and wrought-iron lamps with colored glass hanging from the ceiling. The Prince is playing chess with another man. He is dressed in a patterned silk dressing gown and a turban. A man of medium height and sturdily built, the Prince at once notices the hole in Dukes' sock and jokes, "You believe in ventilation! Good thing—nothing like fresh air!" He holds out two closed fists with pawns in them, asking Dukes to choose which hand holds the white pawn. Dukes' guess is correct but then he notices that both the pawns in the Prince's hands are white. The Prince quickly beats Dukes.

Over the course of this and many other nights, Prince Ozay tells Dukes many interesting occult facts. The Prince says, for example, that the Lord's Prayer was originally designed as a devotional breathing exercise, the entire prayer to be chanted on a single even breath. "You are a musical instrument, as a piano is," says the Prince, "and you need to be kept in tune. That's where fasting and other exercises come in; you can't possibly reflect finer vibrations when your body—or soul if you prefer—is loaded with a lot of food gurgling in the stomach, or while the blood makes a din chasing about the veins and arteries." He tells Dukes, too, that "God is achieved not through activity but through cessation of activity. Cessation to the utmost limit of diet, breath, and sex. These are the three pillars on which prayer is built. Each has to be trained and disciplined by restraint—there is no other way because they are all runaway horses. Only when the ground is cleared can true building commence. Only from that point can you begin to act consciously."

One evening the Prince asks Dukes: "Are you afraid of risks? Understand this clearly. No man can acquire this kind of knowledge without risking death. God, misapplied, is the Devil. There is only one force in creation. Good and evil lie merely in its application."

In the rising turmoil of the times, Dukes loses contact with both Lvovitch and the Prince.

Gurdjieff left St. Petersburg for Moscow where he established a group. Among his students were the sculptor, Sergei Dmitrievich Mercourov,[16] Gurdjieff's cousin; the composer, Vladimir Pohl; the lawyer Alexei

16. James Moore claims to have discovered that the "M" Uspenskii refers to is Sergei Mercourov. However, James Webb had published "M's" identity eleven earlier. See *The Harmonious Circle,* p. 93.

Yakovlevich Rachmilievitch; Alexander Nikanorovich; and Alina Fedorovna, and Alexander Nikorovich Petrov. They met at the apartment of Rachmilievitch. Gurdjieff was likely looking for a special student of the necessary quality to groom as his assistant to step down the teaching.

None of these students, as well as those in another group he formed, he found suitable. It must have been at this time when Uspenskii's newspaper articles of his journey caught Gurdjieff's eye. Recognizing Uspenskii's potential, he began to put pieces in play that would bring about a meeting. He most likely was responsible for planting the idea of return in Uspenskii's mind. For while in India, Uspenskii received a letter from a woman friend, possibly Anna Butkovsky, suggesting to him that he would find the teacher he was looking for in Russia. (Uspenskii later learned that the woman friend also had a friend who was in one of Gurdjieff's groups.) However it came about, there is no doubt Gurdjieff had the notice for *The Struggle of the Magicians* placed in the *Golos Moskvi*, the Voice of Moscow, and later sent Mercourov and Pohl to Uspenskii's Moscow lectures, all with the intent of arranging a meeting.

For Gurdjieff, then, much had been riding on the meeting with Uspenskii, the dimensions of which only Gurdjieff, and not Uspenskii, could have surmised.

Petrograd. Built in 1703 by Peter the Great on a marshland only a few feet above sea level, St. Petersburg lies on the sixtieth parallel at a level with southern Alaska and is noted for extreme changes of weather. The cultural capital of Russia, it is home to composers Stravinsky, Rachmaninov, and Prokofiev; painters Marc Chagall and Vasily Kandinsky; the writer Maxim Gorky and the poet, Alexander Blok; and Diaghilev and his Ballet Russe. Its palaces and grand homes shine with gold and silver. Cabarets, opera, and the ballet thrive, and the literacy rate is growing. The liberal newspaper *Russkoe Selo* has a circulation of 2.5 million copies.

Yet beneath Petersburg's sparkling surface, signs of discord and disintegration are everywhere. With nearly three-quarters of its population born elsewhere, the city is losing its social cohesion. One out of six of the new arrivals is from Poland or from the Baltic states, but there are also Persians, Chinese and Koreans. Few Russians come from nearby provinces, but from the central and northwest, bringing their peasant clothes and habits in tow. Because of the resulting housing shortage, rents have tripled and are among the highest in Europe. On average, more than three people share a room, twice that of Berlin or Paris. Less than half the city's dwellings have running water.

Necklacing the city, the Neva river, once beautiful, is now seriously polluted by human and industrial waste. The Neva, only forty-five miles long, flows from Lake Ladoga, the largest lake in Europe, to the Gulf of

Finland which opens onto the Baltic Sea. On the river's right bank is the working-class Vyborg district, where infant mortality reaches 25 percent. In industry, women's wages are a tenth to a third that of men's; to supplement their incomes, one woman in thirty, it is estimated, is a prostitute. Though Petersburg's population is young, nearly half the deaths are the result of infectious diseases and epidemics, typhoid and intestinal disease being spread through the city's water supply.

Everywhere people dabble in the occult and hold séances. Everywhere the talk is of living a life of *ogarochnyi*, which meant to burn the candle at both ends with no thought for the consequences. *Sanin*, a popular novel which glorifies vulgar self-gratification, sexual excess, and experimentation, has captured the imagination of the young, many of whom live a life of "Saninism." The novelist Leo Tolstoi speaks of Petersburg as "seething and satiated...its people tormented by sleepless nights, stupefied and deadened by wine, wealth, and lovemaking without love. The spirit of destruction pervaded everywhere. Destruction was thought to be in good taste and neurasthenia to be a sign of refinement." At the Stray Dog, a cellar cabaret on Mikhail Louskaia Square perpetually smelling of sweating bodies, stale smoke and urine, the twenty-two-year-old Futurist poet Vladmir Maiakovskii declaimed to the crowd:

> To you who live only from orgy to orgy...
> To you who love only women and food...
> Why should I give my life for your convenience?!
> I'd be better off serving pineapple water
> To whores at the bar!

Everywhere, too, rumors abound of the "holy devil," the man the Tsarina reverently refers to as "Our Friend," the hypnotic monk, Gregory Rasputin, who increasingly meddles in affairs of state with what the Tsarina describes as his "wonderful, God-sent wisdom." She and the Tsar overlook his whoring and drinking, his blackened teeth, his long, matted hair, and his beard which he uses as a napkin when wolfing down food with his fingers. He is thought to be aiding Tsarevich Alexis, the Tsarina's hemophiliac son, and that, to the Tsarina, is all that matters.

Exacerbating these conditions is the war with Germany. The war is costing Russia 40 million rubles a day, a sum financed through borrowing and the printing of rubles, which has caused the money in circulation to triple. In 1914, 2.4 billion rubles were in circulation. Due to its current rapid rise the amount is estimated to reach 8 billion by 1916. The price of meat has almost tripled; flour more than doubled.

Meanwhile, the war is going badly, the atmosphere darkening. Early losses have caused the war to be fought on Russian territory. "Everything was beginning to totter," remembered Uspenskii. "The hidden suicidal activity which has determined so much in Russian life was becoming more and more apparent." Indeed, the city's suicide rate triples, with two-thirds of those taking their life under the age of twenty-eight.

October 1915. Petrograd. *Vestnik Teosofii*, or Theosophical Herald, prints a statement by Annie Besant, president of the International Theosophical Society, saying that Universal Brotherhood, war, God, and the Brotherhood of Adepts are facts and therefore out of this period of carnage and misery that good would come. Mrs. Besant urges followers to accept what happens and adopt a neutral position.

Autumn 1915. Petrograd. Gurdjieff arrives from Moscow for a few day's visit. He telephones Uspenskii who goes to see him at once. Gurdjieff tells him he is thinking of starting group work here. He wants to organize his work in Petersburg on a large scale, give public lectures and demonstrations and attract a wide variety of people of different levels of preparation. Uspenskii, always cherishing what he sees as his independence, has no interest in group work himself. However, he wants to maintain contact with Gurdjieff, and so agrees to help gather candidates.

Following his meeting with Gurdjieff, Uspenskii goes directly to Phillipoff's. He bursts into the café, going directly to Anna Ilinishna's table. For over an hour she has been waiting for him. He does not greet her or even sit down. Instead, he exclaims—"I have found the miracle!"

The man they have been searching for, he tells Anna, the one who can help them find "the mystic threshold," has been found. (He of course had "found" him months earlier but had said nothing.)

"This man's knowledge goes beyond mere theory," declares Uspenskii, nearly breathless. "He can teach, and give the answers to what we and so many others in different lands and times have sought. But he's very sparing—mean, almost—in communication."

This man, he says, has told him two things which he has never found in any book or any esoteric society. One of the ideas he tells her now: "He says that man, because he is passive, does not actually do things personally, but that everything in him is done, mechanically. A man will say, 'I do such-an-such,' but this is not the genuine 'I,' for he might have twenty-two 'I's'.... What I am trying to say is, there is not one 'I' but many...."

With this as an introduction, Uspenskii takes Anna Ilinishna to the second of Phillipoff's two cafés, just across the boulevard, to meet Gurdjieff. Entering the café, Anna Ilinishna sees a man at a table in the far corner; he's wearing an ordinary black coat and a high astrakhan cap. Introduced to Gurdjieff, she at once notices his "fine, virile features and a look that pierces right through you (though not in an unpleasant way)....His manner is very calm and relaxed, and he speaks without any gesticulation. Even to be sitting with him was very agreeable."

She finds Gurdjieff speaks Russian fluently, though in an exact and very picturesque way. He has "the gift," she says, "of assembling words expressively." Like Russian peasants he is spare with words; "often constructing phrases," she says, "as if for that time only." He uses his voice like an instrument, speaking in many tones—one lazy, another subdued, one having a glint of humor, another passionate with a kind of noble wrath. At last she feels she is "in the presence of a Guru."

JANUARY 1916. PETROGRAD. Boris Stümer, a vain man known for his falsity, is appointed premier and foreign minister. He is a protégé of Rasputin, who has pushed the appointment. This move signals the growing power of Rasputin over the Tsarina and, through her, the Tsar. Of Rasputin, a ballerina of the day remembers, he had "eyes of strange lightness, set close, inconceivable in a peasant face, the eyes of a maniac."

FEBRUARY 1916. PETROGRAD. Gurdjieff now begins to make the 350-mile train trip from Moscow to Petersburg on a regular basis, coming every fortnight. He takes an apartment at Nevsky Prospekt and Pushkin Street. The Nevsky is a boulevard eight miles long and some forty yards across. It seems more than coincidental that Gurdjieff's apartment is at one corner of the Nevsky, Uspenskii's apartment at the second, Anna Ilinishna's at the third, and Phillipoff's at the fourth.

Gurdjieff and Uspenskii, and often Anna Ilinishna, meet every day at Phillipoff's at noon. They talk until five or six in the evening, parting to have dinner, then meeting again for more discussions that often go late into the night. In these discussions, Gurdjieff constantly demands brevity, especially of Uspenskii, who tends to talk on and on, displaying his knowledge.

Gurdjieff soon asks Uspenskii to organize groups for him in Petersburg. Uspenskii agrees but makes a condition.

"Listen, Georgi Ivanovitch," he says, "I will organize these groups for you, but only on the condition that I myself do not enter them. I shall remain *aside*."

"Why?" asks Gurdjieff. He looks at him sideways with one of his characteristic glances.

Uspenskii says, "I could not explain [it] to him. Somehow I disliked the thought that it should be said of me that I belonged to any such groups. I had always been by myself, never belonged even to any literary groups."

Gurdjieff says nothing, only shakes his head.

Uspenskii interprets it: "As if he did not understand me, or as if he were pitying me."

Following this discussion, Uspenskii finds Gurdjieff suddenly begins acting indifferently toward him. Worse, Gurdjieff refuses to answer any serious questions. Ordinarily Uspenskii might react, becoming irritable or sulking, as that is his tendency when he doesn't get what he wants. But Gurdjieff's message is clear.

Uspenskii finally agrees to join a group. Gurdjieff relies on him to gather people for groups and tells him, Uspenskii says, that "nobody would be taken [into the group] without my consent, or remain in the Work without my consent." Uspenskii speaks of this as "the St. Petersburg Conditions."[17]

Uspenskii begins inviting a great number of people to meet Gurdjieff. Most, if not all, are part of the intelligentsia, Petersburg's educated elite. Uspenskii is amazed when Gurdjieff asks 1,000 rubles of those interested in working with him. Uspenskii tells him that only people with private means could afford this amount. Gurdjieff gives a detailed answer as to why he asks for such a payment and ends by telling him—"People do not value a thing if they do not pay for it."

Eventually a preparatory group is established. It consists of six people: Dr. Leonid Stjoernval, a fifty-five-year-old medical doctor; Anthony Charkovsky, a fifty-year-old engineer and bridge builder; Andrey Zacharov, a thirty-seven-year-old railway engineer; Nicholas, a sixty-eight-year-old widower and member of the Senate; Anna Ilinishna Butkovsky, thirty-one years old; and of course Pyotr Uspenskii himself, thirty-eight years old. Later, the Petersburg group will grow to as many as thirty.

During these early group meetings, Uspenskii is fond of parading his knowledge, speaks too much, and doesn't keep to the point. Anna Ilinishna begins to see that her friend is "all outward manifestation." She says that when he got going in front of the group, "Gurdjieff [would] look at him with a curious enigmatic smile and sometimes would stop him in full flood," sometimes even rebuking him, because "behind the quasi-scientific phrases there was no real significance or deep meaning."

Two huge trucks, their height extending to the second floor of the surrounding houses, drive along the Liteiny. Uspenskii notices they are loaded down with unpainted wooden crutches. He imagines similar trucks moving in the streets of Vienna, Berlin, London, Paris, Rome, and Constantinople. All these cities he had visited, knew well, and prized for their contrasts. Now they were all separated "by new walls of hatred and crime."

17. Uspenskii's characterization—*the St. Petersburg Conditions*—is interesting. It's contractual sounding, giving a sense of a certain power and position. The word *position* occurs a number of times in *Search* in particular ways as when later Uspenskii writes of the Essentuki period, "...my personal position in G.'s work began to change." Assuming any position in regard to the teacher or teaching is a desire for security, for stabilization. It's delimiting and leveling.

He tells Gurdjieff of his impressions on the Liteiny. Says Gurdjieff, "What do you expect? People are machines....Everything happens."

At a lecture on knowing oneself, or self-study, Gurdjieff introduces the idea that before all else the structure, functions, and laws of one's organism must be studied. The chief method, he says, for such self-study is the practice of self-observation in which one does *not* analyze but impartially registers what is observed at the moment. This observation of oneself must be related to its given function and center, that is, thinking, emotional, moving, and instinctive centers.

At another meeting Gurdjieff asks the group what is the most important thing they have noticed during self-observation. None of the replies satisfy him. Finally he tells them that "not one of you has noticed that *you do not remember yourselves....*You do not feel *yourselves*; you are not conscious of *yourselves.*"

Walking along the Liteiny in the direction of Nevsky Prospekt, Uspenskii attempts to remember himself. He finds he cannot keep his attention on himself. The incessant noises, the continual movement of people and cars along the street, continually distract him. Irritated with himself, he redoubles his effort and turns onto a quieter street. He reaches the following street and coming to the Nadejdinskaya realizes that his attention has wandered only for short moments. Reasoning that self-remembering is easier on less noisy streets, he decides to experiment. On the Nevsky there is a tobacconist's shop that makes his cigarettes. He will go there, all the while remembering himself, and order cigarettes. Two hours later, taking an *izvostchik* to his printers, he finds himself in the Tavricheskaya when he suddenly wakes up! *"And suddenly,"* Uspenskii says, *"I remembered that I had forgotten to remember myself."*

1916. PETROGRAD. Organized in 1908, the Russian Theosophical Society had focused on theosophy's belief that Russia would play a major role in bringing the East and West together. In that light, amid the deprivations of war, Anna Kamenskaia writes in *Vestnik Teosofii:*

> We are undoubtedly moving on to a higher level of world life. Not without purpose have all the veils been torn away, and previous illusions are burning in the fire of difficult, and, at the same time, profoundly meaningful experiences; not without purpose are we passing through so many shocks; not without purpose are all minds and hearts opening to new ideas and inspirations. But what kind of world view will be capable of expressing this higher level of consciousness? Only that world view which can unify all the complex needs of human life and provide the strength to build a life on earth on the basis of brotherhood, love, and mutual assistance. Theosophy provides such a view.

FEBRUARY 1916. PETROGRAD. The group becoming stronger and more serious, Gurdjieff begins to come every two weeks. He spends the whole day in cafés speaking with people who wish to see him. Then, and only at the last minute, he tells Uspenskii to let others know there will be a meeting that evening. Such short notice makes it difficult for many to come. Puzzled, Uspenskii inquires why. People could only value the ideas, he is told, if they have to overcome obstacles.

Among the ideas Gurdjieff introduces at these early meetings are reincarnation, immortality, and the four bodies of man—the physical, astral, mental, and divine. He contrasts the functioning of an automaton with one who has attained his individuality. He speaks of the absence of unity in man, that man thinks he has only one mind when, in fact, he has three minds: the intellectual, emotional and moving-instinctive. "Man has no permanent and unchangeable I," says Gurdjieff. To come to a real permanent I there must be a fusion of substances. For this, fire is required. A fire is built from friction which is the result of an inner struggle between 'yes' and 'no.' Something significant must be sacrificed in the moment, if this struggle is to be evoked. The higher bodies thus formed possess qualities not found in the physical body, such as a certain electrical conductivity. It also may be possible to magnetize them, make them radioactive, and so forth.

Gurdjieff speaks of the three ways to attain immortality: through work on the body, the emotions, or the mind. These ways are ordinarily referred to as the way of the fakir, monk, or yogi. Each demands that a man begin by doing that which is most difficult—dying to the world. There is another traditional way, as well, though not commonly known. It is the Fourth Way that Gurdjieff introduces. The Fourth Way differs from the other ways in many important and substantial respects, not all of which lend themselves to words. The Fourth Way does not separately work, for example, on body, emotions, and mind, but works on them simultaneously. Furthermore, the pupil is not required to give up anything. He must not withdraw from life but, on the contrary, stay in life and learn to use it for his own development. "A man's life and its conditions," says Gurdjieff, "correspond to what he is." The conditions of his life, its uncertainties, shocks, and suffering are used to come to real life. The principal demand of the Fourth Way is for understanding. For, the greater a man's understanding of what he does, the greater the results. It is practical, immediate, and works with and through ordinary life. Therefore, in contrast to the traditional three ways, the work of the Fourth Way can be more effective, more efficient. (Later he will make a further distinction, saying that unlike the three ways, the Fourth Way is not permanent, it appears and disappears and has a definite aim.)

Later in speaking about real knowledge, associated with the transformation of energies in man and the cosmos, Gurdjieff says that humanity comes into periods when the masses of men lose their reason and mindlessly destroy everything built up over time, and that these periods generally correspond to the beginning of the fall of a culture or civilization. Released at such a time is "a very great quantity of the matter of knowledge. This, in its turn, necessitates the work of collecting this matter of knowledge which would otherwise be lost."

The teaching of the Fourth Way is unusual in that it gives nothing ready-made. Though he can be totally lucid and coherent, Gurdjieff often speaks in ways that seem either to obfuscate or confuse. Gurdjieff teaches using declarations without examples, apparent contradictions, hints, and nuances of all kinds, all of which keep the group on edge and create friction. Teaching in this way makes a demand on the group to become active, to inquire, explore, to think and act independently, to take nothing and no one for granted.

In time, Uspenskii comes to understand something about how Gurdjieff expresses himself: "Our ordinary European logical method of thinking makes us inclined to accept everything literally, that is, if we trust the author, we suppose that with every word, he says exactly what he meant. Eastern thought, however, often uses methods of exposition totally different from ours. Eastern authors often do not define their subject as a whole. They are apt to give only one instance of the possible meaning of the given subject or phenomena without saying that it is merely an instance so that readers are left to understand their words as they like or as they can. Gurdjieff very often did the same thing."

What Uspenskii also sees and likes is the fact that Gurdjieff "appreciated and understood all the good things of life possibly better than anyone. But one felt that he was not attached to them and could at any moment give up everything without losing an atom of his energy and calm." Gurdjieff not only has a total indifference to making things easy or agreeable for himself but never shirks any kind of work. Though he sometimes likes to give large dinners, he often eats and drinks very little. He is totally without any kind of affectation and shows no desire to produce an impression on others. He never pretends to any sanctity or occult powers. He enjoys a joke and has a robust sense of humor. Occasionally, he might "act" or "play" with people's impressions regarding himself, but rather than falseness, says Uspenskii, it "produced an impression of strength." But he adds, "Sometimes there was too much of it."

In forming a group, Gurdjieff tells Uspenskii and the others that its members must agree to engage in self-study, exchange observations, and make a common struggle against their false personalities. In doing so, they must attempt to tell the whole truth to the teacher, sincerity in the group being an absolute demand. Further, members must remember why they came to a group. If they begin to express mistrust toward the teacher, lack of respect and so forth, then they can no longer work with the teacher and must leave.

As the meetings continue, Uspenskii becomes irritated. He is not getting the respect he is due. Gurdjieff, he says, "did not see me, would not give himself the trouble to understand me, that he did not wish to see that in reality I had gone much further from the ordinary outlook than he thought, that many of his ideas were much nearer and much more comprehensible to me than he would admit." Worse, Uspenskii finds Gurdjieff insisting that he give up all his knowledge and start from scratch. But many of the ideas that Gurdjieff speaks about, says Uspenskii, he has already come to himself.[18]

SPRING 1916. PETROGRAD. Gurdjieff gives his first lectures on the seven cosmoses. He points out that the Cabala and other systems speak of two cosmoses but these are *"incomplete"* and, as such, they are inexact. Such teachings, he says, are "merely a fragment split off from another, much fuller, ancient esoteric teaching...the *full* teaching on cosmoses speaks not of two, but of seven cosmoses, included one within another."

Listening to Gurdjieff lecture, Uspenskii realizes the seven cosmoses correspond to the period of dimensions and problems of space and time and higher dimensions, ideas which he has been working on for several years and are the basis of the book *Wisdom of the Gods.* Declares Uspenskii: "It is not merely a coincidence of details—it is absolutely identical. I do not know how it has come about; I have never heard of seven cosmoses related to one another in the ratio of zero to infinity. Nevertheless my 'period of dimensions' coincides with this absolutely exactly."

Bewildered, Uspenskii points out to Gurdjieff passages in his own books and manuscripts where the same ideas are discussed. But Gurdjieff displays no interest. Instead, turning up the heat still more, Gurdjieff quotes verbatim to the group whole pages of Uspenskii's books. He does so, of course, without attribution.

At one point Gurdjieff asks him to say what he can from his point of view, "taking everything just as I said it."

Uspenskii begins by examining the idea of the ratio of zero to infinity and proceeds to work through the dimensions in a manner both comprehensive and insightful.

18. That Gurdjieff, in fact, is working with his emotional center, that Gurdjieff, intentionally, is calling up this state in him with all its self-love and false pride so he can observe it—Uspenskii must not see, for he makes no mention of it. As with many students, it is easier for Uspenskii to comprehend the intellectual aspects of the teaching. The practical aspects, especially when applied to ourselves, tend to escape us.

"There is a great deal of material in what you have just said," comments Gurdjieff, "but this material must be elaborated." He tells him to ponder that time is different in different cosmoses and ends by saying: "Time is breath—try to understand this."

Gurdjieff, like a skilled matador, knows exactly where to stick his sword. Gurdjieff, having shown no interest in Uspenskii's ideas—only to then openly plagiarize them—now insists that Uspenskii give up what is for Uspenskii the *idea* of ideas—the fourth dimension. Gurdjieff tells him he must accept a universe of, not four, but only three dimensions.

For Uspenskii this is tantamount to giving up his first born and, predictably, he rebels. First probing here, then there, Gurdjieff has masterfully forced him into an intellectual corner.

When he speaks to Gurdjieff about this, no doubt hoping for some relief or an explanation, he is told instead that he must put all his knowledge in the fire.

All his knowledge!

Gurdjieff insists. What Uspenskii takes to be knowledge, Gurdjieff says is a mixture of both truth and falsehood. How can one who is asleep discern one from the other? Therefore, all had to be burnt. What is genuine, Gurdjieff tells him, would not be burnt.

The force of Gurdjieff's logic drives Uspenskii until his back is to the wall. Gurdjieff is merciless, he gives him no out, no way to save face. Like a chess master, Gurdjieff's every move has applied just the right amount of pressure at precisely the right time and place.[19]

Finally, after a great struggle, Uspenskii stabilizes and agrees to sacrifice his knowledge. But the cost, in personal terms, is not small. "Naturally," explains Uspenskii, "such submission could not be achieved without great struggle with oneself, and the first results of this was that I entirely lost the power to write."[20]

19. Stripped of all defence, Uspenskii intellectually must agree. But, emotionally, he must find himself caught in a maelstrom of suffering, his powerful mind now unhinged and tossed back and forth between its 'yes' and its 'no'!

20. The idea of sacrifice was not foreign to Uspenskii. In fact, in his *Kinemadrama* it is a central idea. Near the end of the book the magician speaks to Osokin about sacrifice: that he cannot change himself without making sacrifices and that he must sacrifice something big, not only once, but to go on making sacrifices until he gets what he wants. Osokin protests that he has nothing to sacrifice. "Everyone has something to sacrifice," says the magician, "except those who cannot be helped." And later: "A man can be given only what he can use; and he can use only that for which he has sacrificed something. This is the law of human nature." In effect, then, *Kinemadrama* is a foreshadowing. What Uspenskii knows in theory, Gurdjieff leads him to explore firsthand in the reality of his own being.

During this period, Uspenskii says fear is his dominant emotion. Having sacrificed what he most cherishes—his knowledge—Uspenskii feels unprotected, vulnerable, reduced to what he knows not. Speaking of the terror of this state, Uspenskii says he has this "fear of losing myself, of disappearing in something unknown."

At the time, Uspenskii wrote a letter to someone abroad. "I am writing this letter to you," he recounts, "but who will write the next letter signing it with my name and what he will say, I do not know."

This is the primary fear, but many other elements are in it as well. There is "the fear of taking a wrong way," he says, "the fear of making an irretrievable mistake, the fear of losing some other possibilities." But as he continues and gains confidence in himself and the teaching, he says, "all this left me."

At one meeting of the group Uspenskii pontificates about impressions. Finally Gurdjieff cuts him off—"Whatever is this rubbish you're talking?"

Turning to the others in the group, Gurdjieff speaks as if Uspenskii isn't present.

"I suppose he wants to show off his knowledge," Gurdjieff muses. "He's exactly like a cow going round and round a new gate without being able to find a way in. God preserve us from such people!"

Gurdjieff suggests that each of the six—in front of the others—tell the story of their lives.

Dr. Stjoernval, a private man always holding himself in tight control, begins to make such a confession. But to all, it is soon clear he is not telling the truth. He speaks of the event abstractly, in an impersonal fashion, as though he had no hand in it. Anna Ilinishna says one could "sense the struggle between his desire to whitewash the action and his knowledge that it was impossible to deceive Gurdjieff."

Finally, Gurdjieff shoots a piercing look at Stjoernval that stops him in mid-word....

"Another time, doctor, you will be sincere, and recall these matters accurately....Think it over," declares Gurdjieff.

Later Gurdjieff gives his students nicknames. Stjoernval's is "Mean," in the sense that the doctor cannot easily part with anything he possesses, be it money, words or memories. Zacharov's is "Baba," which means in Russian "peasant woman." He is so shy and emotionally frozen that he cannot speak of his inner being. Nicholas' is "Jubilant Old Man." Anna's is "Wavering." To Uspenskii, Gurdjieff gives the nickname "Wraps Up The Thought."

At another meeting Gurdjieff introduces the ideas of knowledge and being. Uspenskii says that the group divided into two camps about this. "The first camp," he says, "thought that the whole thing was from the change of being, that with the change of being we would get more from the knowledge we already have. The second camp (to which I believe I alone belonged) said that even in our present state of being we can get much more knowledge than we have, that we are not so saturated with knowledge that we cannot absorb more. Later I understood that both are necessary."

Despite Gurdjieff's great being and knowledge, there are many things which, as Uspenskii puts it, give "rise to perplexity and doubt. The most unexpected was his eternal and continual playing. He was never simple or natural; one always felt in him some secret, hidden intent. Some people were attracted to him by this playing as one would be attracted by anything incomprehensible, strange and dangerous.... In connection with this play we saw perfectly clearly in him two men, and those who the one attracted did not doubt that the other was surely a mask or part adapted for some definite aim."

1916. PIATIGORSK. Either before or, perhaps after, a journey to Alexandropol to see his family—the last time Gurdjieff is to see his father alive—he meets Professor Skridlov, the archaeologist, in Piatigorsk, at the home of the professor's daughter. With Prince Lubovedsky and Gurdjieff, Skridlov is one of the original members of the Seekers After Truth, first formed in 1892, while the three were walking between the Sphinx and the Pyramid of Cheops in Egypt.[21] Skridlov participated in all the group's major expeditions and he and Gurdjieff have grown quite close. The two have corresponded regularly but have not seen one another since their expedition, most likely in 1896, to the monastery of the World Brotherhood in Kafiristan.

Skridlov must now be in his sixties or seventies, for his hair was slightly graying when they first met at the Pyramid of Cheops twenty-four years before. He is entering upon the last stage of life whereas Gurdjieff, at forty-four,[22] has taken a vow and is embarked on a stupendous mission of bringing a new teaching to the West.[23]

Meeting now, in Piatigorsk, some twenty years since their six-month stay at the Monastery of the World Brotherhood, the two men decide to celebrate their meeting by climbing to the summit of Mount Bechow, a nearby mountain. They of course take the most difficult and daring

21. In the expanded edition of *Our Life With Mr. Gurdjieff* Olga de Hartmann records what Gurdjieff told the group in Essentuki in 1917 about the origins of the Seekers After Truth: "Twenty-five years ago in Egypt, near the pyramids, three tourists met...." Gurdjieff speaks of this meeting in *Meetings With Remarkable Men*, chapter eight, "Prince Yuri Lubovedsky." The place of the group's origin is no doubt as symbolic as it is actual.

22. Dates of Gurdjieff's birth have ranged from 1866 to 1877. Based on facts that Gurdjieff himself gives in *Meetings With Remarkable Men*, the most logical date is 1872. Louise Goepfert Marsh, a secretary of Gurdjieff's and his German translator for *All and Everything*, gives 1872 as his birth date in her essay, "Gurdjieff: An Indication of His Life and Work." Both J. G. Bennett and Olga de Hartmann also believe the birth date is 1872. See Notes.

route, ascending the rocks from the southern side of the mountain. Though not high, Mount Bechow affords a spectacular view of the surrounding countryside. Alone on the summit, the two friends look into the broad expanse and take in the vastness of its silence.

"We saw," says Gurdjieff, "spread out before our eyes an extensive panorama of really extraordinary beauty." To the south and far away the two seekers of truth see the majestic snow-capped peak of Elbrus, the long chain of Caucasian mountains rimming both its sides. Below them sit the toylike settlements, towns and villages of nearly the entire region of Mineralni Vodi, while to the north lies the town of Zheleznovodsk.

Taking in the grandeur of the immensity about them, Professor Skridlov's eyes begin to tear. He tells Gurdjieff that after their stay at the monastery he underwent "a revaluation of all values." He had been totally absorbed only in his own pleasures and interests and those of his children. All he did, all he said, had been vanity.

"The meeting with Father Giovanni killed all this," says Professor Skridlov, "and from then on there gradually arose in me that 'something' which has brought the whole of me to the unshakable conviction that, apart from the vanities of life, there exists a 'something else' which must be the aim and ideal of every more or less thinking man, and that it is only this something else which may make a man really happy and give him real values, instead of the illusory 'goods' with which in ordinary life he is always and in everything full."

This meeting will be the last time that the two essence friends will see one another. Gurdjieff must have spoken of his own feelings as well, but these he does not record.

1916. PETROGRAD. In a group meeting Gurdjieff is asked about the teaching's relationship to Christianity. He says, not knowing what the term means for the questioner, a reply is difficult. "But for the benefit of those who know already,"[24] he continues, "I will say that, if you like, *this*

23. For Skridlov, what lies in the future is a summing up and a winding down, an enjoying of his life. For Gurdjieff the future spreads out into the unknown, but he can be sure it will be filled with ordeals and challenges unlike anything he has yet met. This meeting then between these two great essence friends marks a portentous time for both. Some believe that Skridlov is possibly Gurdjieff's alter ego.

24. In other words, for those who already know what Christianity is, he will say it is a particular form, i.e., esoteric, meaning hidden or not revealed. But the key words here are the conditional "if you like..." If you know what Christianity means and therefore know its origins, what is most analogous to your understanding is to say that the Fourth Way is 'esoteric Christianity.' Sufis and others claim the teaching is derivative in that elements of the Fourth Way can be found in these forms. But rather than having been cobbled together from these forms, and therefore a mixture, as detractors insist, *it is just the reverse.* The astounding truth is that the teaching predates them all. See *Telos,* "Gurdjieff in Egypt," Vol. II, Issues 2, 3, and 4.

is esoteric Christianity." Later he will say that "the Christian church, the Christian form of worship was not invented by the fathers of the church." He then makes the astonishing claim that the origin of the Fourth Way was "prehistoric Egypt." In other words, the teaching predates all the known teachings and religions. Still later, he speaks of four principal lines: Hebraic, Egyptian, Persian, and Hindu. And of the two mixtures of these lines, theosophy and Western occultism, he says that neither, as they are mixtures, can lead "to practical realization [but] give only negative results." Then, speaking of the teaching he brings, he declares unambiguously: "The teaching whose theory is here being set out is *completely self-supporting and independent of other lines and it has been completely unknown up to the present time.*" [Author's italics]

1916. FINLAND. During a group meeting at the Finnish country home of one of the doctor's wealthy patients, Madame Maximovitch, the normally reserved psychiatrist Dr. Leonid Stjoernval exclaims: "Yes! I believe that Georgi Ivanovitch is not less than Christ himself!"[25]

For some time before, he has been sitting quietly, calm and cool as usual, when suddenly, as if coming out of a trance, he explodes like a bombshell, making nervous, excitable gestures, and shouting—"Yes!... not less than...!"

Acting at once, Gurdjieff forcefully cuts Stjoernval off.

Asked about the origin of the teaching, Gurdjieff tells the story of the sly man who in an unknown country and an unknown time was walking by a café when he met a devil who was in a very poor way. The sly man invited the devil into the café and ordered coffee for him. Asked why he was in such a poor state, the devil said, "There is no business. I used to buy souls and burn them on charcoal because they had very fat souls that I could take to hell. All my devil friends were pleased. But now all the fires are out in hell because people today have no souls."

The sly man said, "Teach me how to make souls, and I will give you a sign to show which people have souls made by me."

More coffee was ordered, after which the devil said, "Teach people to remember themselves, not to identify and imagine, and after a time they will grow souls."

25. Whereas Uspenskii's first impression of Gurdjieff was that of a person of power or knowledge, a raja or sheik, Dr. Stjoernval's is that of a loving and suffering Christ. Not surprisingly, Dr. Stjoernval alone of the six (despite protestations of his ever-resistant wife, Elizabeta Grigorievna) will stay with Gurdjieff through all the tumult of the ensuing years until his own death twenty-three years later in Reims, France.

Uspenskii, given his feeling toward religion, must have recoiled at Stjoernval's outburst. He wants nothing to do with devotion. He wants to obtain knowledge. Gurdjieff has said that what must come first is self-study.

So the sly man did just that, organizing groups and teaching people to remember themselves. Some students worked very seriously and did, in fact, grow souls.

When they died they came to the Gate of Paradise, where on one side stood St. Peter and the other the devil.

"Can I just ask one question?" the devil would say to each newly arrived soul. "Did you remember yourself?"

"Ahh, yes, certainly," answered the soul.

"Excuse me," the devil would smile and say to St. Peter, "that is mine."

This went on for a long time until word got back to earth of what was happening at the Gate of Paradise.

Angrily, the sly man's students said to him: "Why do you teach us self-remembering since, when we say we have remembered ourselves, the devil takes us?"

"Did I teach you to say you remembered yourselves?" answered the sly man. "I taught you not to talk."

"But it's St. Peter and the devil," protested the students.

"But have you seen these people, the devil and St. Peter, at group meetings? Very well, don't talk. You see, I not only made an arrangement with the devil, I also made a plan to deceive him. But if you talk..."

Gurdjieff's unpredictable actions, some seemingly so irrational, continue to bother Uspenskii. Rather than suffer it, the idea gradually forms in him that there are two sides, or two personalities, to Gurdjieff. One is a serious, or positive, side; the other "plays." People around Gurdjieff are "sorted out" by these two sides. Some see his serious side which displays his knowledge, his disinterestedness, his Work. In them, Gurdjieff's "play" produces a struggle of "yes" and "no." Others, seeing the negative or play side, view the positive side as a pretense for getting influence and power over people. Still others are attracted by the negative side. Uspenskii believes it keeps them close to Gurdjieff because it corresponds to their own desires and predilections.

However Uspenskii sees Gurdjieff, there remains the nagging question—*Who is Gurdjieff?* It is a question with which every member of the group wrestles. They only know about him what he chooses to tell them. And this is very little. He is undoubtedly a man of enormous power and knowledge, in the real sense of those words—of that the group has no doubt. But, all the same, the question remains.

Says Uspenskii: "What he had been born with and what had been given him by schools, if he had passed through a school—we often spoke of this, and some of us came to the conclusion that Gurdjieff was a genius in his own domain, that he had scarcely had to learn, that what he knew could not be learned and that none of us could expect or hope to become like him."

If his history remains unknown to them, then certainly they could judge him by his behavior. But try as they may, they can't see Gurdjieff. The images he presents, his actions from day to day, are unpredictable.

"One could be sure of nothing in regard to him," declares Uspenskii. "He might say something today and tomorrow something altogether different, yet somehow one could not accuse him of contradiction. One had to understand and connect everything together."

JUNE 25, 1916. The Russian army begins a major offensive against the Austro-Hungarian armies. Despite unexpected success, the depressed atmosphere in urban areas increases as shortages of consumer goods, particularly food stuffs, grows and inflation rises.

MID-SUMMER 1916. PETROGRAD. Gurdjieff is spending most of his time in Petersburg. Some thirty pupils form around him. Meetings are held almost every evening. Gurdjieff, at one point, introduces the idea of chief fault, or chief feature. This is the psychological nucleus around which orbits a person's false personality. "Every man's personal work must consist in struggling against this chief fault," says Gurdjieff.

AUGUST 1916. FINLAND. The group meets again at Madame Maximovitch's country home in Finland, about an hour's train ride from Petersburg. Uspenskii is in "a state of unusual tension." In order to give a shock to his organism, he has been doing a number of short, very intensive fasts, breathing in certain ways, and doing mental exercises to concentrate his attention.[26]

These shocks have produced a certain emotional state, a state, Uspenskii believes, which is "indispensable" to arriving at the facts of the hidden reality he wishes to penetrate. Recognizing the change in Uspenskii's vibration and knowing the work he had done on himself (though, of course, he would never acknowledge that to him), Gurdjieff begins to work with Uspenskii on a more subtle level. Earlier, in a meeting where the Last Supper was discussed, Gurdjieff had said that people who have developed a second, or "astral body" can communicate with one another at a distance. In other words, telepathy was possible.

First, he does the unthinkable.

26. From Uspenskii's manner of speaking about this, it seems probable that he did this on his own and not at Gurdjieff's direction. Otherwise, why would he not have mentioned it? Whatever, the exercises have caused him to be no longer so focused in his forehead. His center of gravity is beginning to switch to his instinctive center. Sensation and feeling are beginning to function. He is becoming more sensitized to himself and the world. He is less dense, more open, transparent.

In front of the five other students, Gurdjieff humiliates Uspenskii, repeating now openly what Uspenskii had told him "in absolute confidence" about Dr. Stjoernval.[27] (Given the doctor's vision of Gurdjieff-as-Christ, it's not hard to guess what that might be.) For an intellectual of Uspenskii's stripe, the exposure of an inferior "I" had to cut deep. But Uspenskii, always in control of his feelings, reports this unmasking as merely "unpleasant."

Having created the necessary conditions, Gurdjieff now begins to show postures and physical movements. Uspenskii observes that Gurdjieff's muscles are relaxed and that he moves with "astonishing assurance and precision." A student, more knowledgeable about the body, at a later time gives this impression of Gurdjieff: "I saw this man in motion, a unit in motion. He was completely of one piece. From the crown of his head down the back of the head, down the neck, down the back and down the legs, there was a remarkable line. Shall I call it a gathered line? It suggested co-ordination, integration, knitness, power....I was fascinated by the way the man walked. As his feet touched the floor there seemed to be no weight on them at all—a glide, a stride, a weightless walk."

Following this wordless teaching of movement, control, and relaxation, Gurdjieff returns to the question of why the members of the group could not tell the story of their lives and the thing they had done of which they were most ashamed.

The tension in the room must have risen dramatically.

With Gurdjieff's question, says Uspenskii, "the miracle began."

Gurdjieff communicates with Uspenskii wordlessly. A voice, says Uspenskii, speaks to him inside his chest.[28]

Uspenskii says: "It all started with my beginning to *hear his thoughts* ...suddenly I noticed that among the words he was saying to us all there were 'thoughts' which were intended for me....After a while I heard his voice inside me as if it were in the chest near the heart."

Gurdjieff questions Uspenskii telepathically and Uspenskii replies audibly. Dr. Stjoernval and Zacharov are visibly astonished. The "conversation" between Gurdjieff and Uspenskii continues for a half an hour.

27. Why does Gurdjieff intentionally break the trust that he has so carefully nurtured? He does so because he is preparing to introduce another level of work. A new level of work demands a new level of trust. Gurdjieff's psychological 'betrayal' emotionally divides Uspenskii who is already emotional but suppressing it. Thus Gurdjieff forces a direct confrontation with the 'yes' and 'no' of negative emotions. The strange impression which Gurdjieff made in that Moscow café the year before, all the little buried doubts about Gurdjieff and getting caught in a relationship, must have resurfaced now with a vengeance.

28. It is not the first time. At the end of their first meeting in Gurdjieff's apartment Uspenskii had a "flash of thought" that he must ask to see Gurdjieff again. But, as he assumed that all his thoughts were his own, he was shut off from this recognition.

At one point, Gurdjieff tells Uspenskii there are certain conditions he has to accept or he has to leave the Work. Gurdjieff gives him a month's time to answer. Uspenskii refuses the time, so certain is he of his allegiance and ability to do. But Gurdjieff, seeing the dragons with which his student will have to contend, insists on the time limit.

Later, on the verandah with Uspenskii, Stjoernval, and Zacharov, Gurdjieff again speaks to Uspenskii telepathically.

"Something he said about me affected me very strongly," says Uspenskii, "and I sprang up from my chair and went into the garden." He wanders about in the forest for an hour or two, finally coming to realize that all Gurdjieff had said earlier, including his own position in the Work, is right.

"What I had considered to be firm and reliable in myself in reality did not exist," he says. That is, he sees the "I" that accepted the conditions was not real.

"But I had found something else. *I knew that he would not believe me*[29] *and that he would laugh at me if I showed him this other thing. But for myself it was indubitable and what happened later showed that I was right.*" [Author's italics]

Uspenskii says later, in regard to his experience in Finland: "There is something in phenomena of a higher order which requires a particular emotional state *for their observation and study.*" In the aftermath of the experience, he also realizes that "certain very definite changes began in my views on myself, on those around me, and particularly on 'methods of action.'" These changes beggar description but, he says: "I can only say that they were not in any way connected with what *was said* in Fin-

29. It is at this point that the real break with Gurdjieff begins, for here is unconsciously revealed what is characteristic of Uspenskii's personality, namely, a dividing and a hiding to preserve his "I." Despite the fact that Gurdjieff had stripped Uspenskii of some of his "I's," he thinks himself able to judge his teacher's understanding —"I knew that he would not believe me...." And decides that what he has found is the implacable truth—"for myself it was indubitable...."

Here then Uspenskii unwittingly breaks a primary rule of the Fourth Way, namely, that the student cannot keep anything secret from the teacher, that he must give up his lies, identifications, and imagination. The student must continually keep questioning his motivations, perceptions, conclusions. Sincerity must be learned. As Gurdjieff said to the Petersburg group: "You do not understand what it means to be sincere. You are so used to lying both to yourselves and others that you can find neither words nor thoughts when you wish to speak the truth."

If the student is not forthcoming about all of his life, if he withholds something, then this "something" becomes the seat of his "I"-hood. He will be sincere about this but not about that, he thinks. But who is it that so decides? It is this "I" that has to be seen.

Not being totally sincere with his teacher, the student breaks the trust and bond between himself and the teacher. Communication thus contracts. The student is no longer open. Rapport ends. No rapport, no relationship. Without relationship, the separation of student and teacher only awaits a trigger event.

land but that they had come as a result of the emotions which I had experienced there. The first thing I could record was the weakening in me of that *extreme individualism* which up to that time had been the fundamental feature in my attitude to life. I began to see people more, to feel my community with them more." [Author's italics]

SEPTEMBER 1916. PETROGRAD. Alexander Protopopov is made acting Minister of the Interior. He has no rank or bureaucratic experience but he is an amateur occultist and a friend of Rasputin's, who has urged the appointment on the Tsarina. Protopopov, a small neurotic man with bright, wild eyes that shift all the time, gives the impression of "resembling an excited seal." Rasputin has also successfully requested that the responsibility for the organization of food supplies be transferred to the Ministry of the Interior. So Protopopov controls not only the Okhrana (the Tsarist secret police) but also food distribution. He will later be accused of deliberately creating food shortages in order to provoke riots as an excuse for repression.

It is in September, too, that Gurdjieff arrives from Moscow. He now takes quarters on the Liteiny nearer to Uspenskii. He has a severe chill and meets with people only in small groups. Uspenskii has not seen him since Finland. He is somewhat uncertain about his experience there. He asks if it is true that what Gurdjieff had said in Finland had frightened him. And, if so, why had he been frightened? Gurdjieff replies that if it's true that he was frightened, it only means he is not yet ready. Despite Uspenskii's questions, he will say nothing else.

Interestingly, on this visit Gurdjieff centers his talks around chief feature, or chief fault. He tells his pupils that they must find a way to struggle with it and to eliminate its involuntary manifestation. He points out his pupils' chief features, telling one that *he is never at home;* another that *he did not exist at all;* another had no *shame;* another, *no conscience.* In some people, he says, their chief feature is so well hidden behind their various formal manifestations that its discovery is difficult. In this case, the person himself is the chief feature and in this sense Gurdjieff refers to Uspenskii's as *Pyotr Demianovich.*

In a later meeting Gurdjieff tells people that they cannot go any further until they come to a definite decision about the Work and him, as "a half-serious attitude could give no results whatsoever." Of the thirty or so people who have gathered around him only two leave. "It is difficult to climb the hill but very easy to slide down it," says Gurdjieff.

OCTOBER 1916. MOSCOW. Uspenskii visits Gurdjieff in his apartment on the Bolshaia Dmitrovka. The walls and floors are covered with carpets and silk shawls hang from the ceilings. Gurdjieff's Moscow pupils come and go. In comparison to the usual banal talking and roles people adopt when together, Uspenskii notices they are "not afraid to keep silent," some not uttering a word for hours. The silence is not heavy or psychological but supportive.

At one of the talks Gurdjieff asks Uspenskii what is the most important thing he has learned so far.

"The experiences, of course, which I had in August [the telepathy in Finland]," Uspenskii answers. If he could evoke such experiences at will, he believes he could discover everything else. But he sees that for this he would have to be able to create the necessary emotional state.

Gurdjieff explains that for this sacrifice is necessary. Not only must one sacrifice one's fantasies but also one's suffering. "A man will renounce any pleasures you like," Gurdjieff declares, "but he will not give up his suffering."

NOVEMBER-DECEMBER 1916. MOSCOW. "Gurdjieff all the time suffered from ill-health, and in the winter of 1916 twice began to develop pneumonia," reports Uspenskii. He stopped coming to Petersburg and so some members of the group go to Moscow for meetings. Gurdjieff's teaching, Uspenskii says, "gave us a certain feeling of confidence and security. We often spoke at this time of how we should feel in the midst of all this chaos [the brewing revolution] if we had not got the system." At this period Gurdjieff, no doubt sensing the impending chaos that would soon engulf all of Russia, introduces the subject of Noah's Ark. Uspenskii had long thought this myth to be an allegory for the esoteric work. The teaching was an "ark" by which students could save themselves during the "flood."

"I felt myself growing in the understanding of abstract subjects," says Anna Ilinishna, "and I noticed that this development also occurred in the other members of the group."

She recounts how much earlier, before leaving Petersburg for the Caucasus, they had been what she calls "ordained" by Gurdjieff. They had all been sitting together, deep in thought, when something made them turn towards Gurdjieff. He spoke in a voice they had never before heard, one both solemn and abstract and with an element of love.

"You started the Quest. You are on the road. You must go on."

One of the group said: "I will go on, Georgi Ivanovitch, because you have put us on the right road."

Replied Gurdjieff: "I will try to hammer into your heads as much as I can of that special knowledge you are after, what Uspenskii calls 'seeking the Miracle.' There will be others coming to join our group, and they, too, will gradually progress. The only condition is that they must make the maximum effort to absorb what they hear, either from me or from one of you six."

Gurdjieff's 'play' continues to irritate Uspenskii—as he says, his moods never led to depression but irritation, a characteristic Gurdjieff quickly noted. Unable to understand what Gurdjieff was doing, Uspenskii says he finally spoke to Gurdjieff about his awkward 'play.' Gurdjieff tells him "that 'play' is indispensable—that in receiving 'yes' a man must simultaneously receive 'no,' and that only the struggle of 'yes' and 'no' in him can create understanding." And he adds: "If there is not 'no,' if there is only 'yes,' faith appears. There must not be faith. I do not wish to infatuate people. Infatuation is always one sided. One side is infatuated while another side knows nothing about it. A serious moment arrives and then this comes out. A man proves incapable of effort, of sacrifice, of serious decision. Only if a man has passed through the struggle of 'yes and no' can he be relied upon, and the greater the struggle was the better and the more steadfast and trustworthy will be from the point of view of the work. 'Play' is not necessary in itself. Men demand it. If they are not repelled, 'faith' appears in them at once, and above all things there must not be faith."

At some point during their meetings Gurdjieff speaks of being "born." Gurdjieff says that this new growth of essence, the appearance of I, means awakening to one's nothingness, the absolute recognition of one's mechanicality and helplessness. What prevents such awakening is that man is hypnotized. He then relates an Eastern story about a very rich magician who has a large number of sheep he keeps for their flesh and skins. Not wanting to hire shepherds or build a fence to keep the sheep from being troublesome and wandering off, the magician hypnotizes them, suggesting that they are immortal and that he, the magician, is a good master who loves them all very much. He suggests to them that if anything bad was to happen to them, it would certainly not happen right then and so there is no need to think about it and, finally, he tells them that they are not sheep at all. To some he confides they are really eagles, to others, men; and to a third group...magicians, a code word for teacher.

DECEMBER 16, 1916. PETROGRAD. Thomas de Hartmann, a Guards officer, who lives in Tsarskoye Selo, the residence of the Tsar, meets Gurdjieff. The location is a seedy second floor café on Nevsky Prospekt frequented by prostitutes, pimps, and the like. Had anyone seen de Hartmann there, he says, "I would have had to leave my regiment." The two speak and at one point Gurdjieff looks around the room and says, "There are usually more whores here." Finally, Gurdjieff accepts him and asks for a customary payment of one thousand rubles. He asks him to contact Uspenskii who should inform him of all that had been said up to now. De Hartmann says of Uspenskii: "From the start he made a very strong impression on me. He was simple, courteous, approachable, and intelligent. . . . In an amazingly simple and clear way he knew how to explain the complicated scheme of worlds, planets, cosmoses, and so forth."

DECEMBER 16–17, 1916. PETROGRAD. Prince Felix Isupov, fearing the increasing influence over the Tsarina, murders Rasputin. First he poisons him and when that fails he shoots "the holy devil" three times. Rasputin's body is wrapped in a heavy linen sheet and driven to Petrovsky Island where it is dumped from a bridge through a hole in the ice. Rasputin has prophesied that if he is murdered, it will bring down the whole country. It is in December, too, that Protopopov is now made full Minister of the Interior.

Before the year's end Gurdjieff introduces the subject of religion and prayer, and what might be called religious "techniques." He goes on to say that humanity is at a "standstill" in its development and risks "a straight path to downfall and degeneration."[30] All around, one sees the growth of personality, the artificial, the unreal, and automatism. "Contemporary culture requires automatons," says Gurdjieff. He again speaks of the Fourth Way, saying that it has no definite forms and is never permanent in that it appears and disappears in accordance with its aim. It always has a definite work to accomplish.

JANUARY 1917. PETROGRAD. Heavy snowfalls and temperature at twenty-two degrees below zero. The city receives only thirty thousand pounds of flour a day instead of the normal two hundred thousand. Sugar becomes scarce, forcing working people, who suck their tea through a sugar cube, to drink it straight. A small helping of potatoes which cost 15 kopecks before the war, is now hard to find at 1.2 rubles. The Okhrana, the Tsarist secret police, reports to the Tsar that "With every day the food question becomes more acute. Never before has there been so much swearing, argument, and scandal. That the population has not yet begun food riots does not mean that they will not in the nearest future."

FEBRUARY 9, 1917. PETROGRAD. Thomas de Hartmann brings his wife, Olga Arkadievna, to their first group meeting in Uspenskii's apartment. Both the de Hartmanns are thirty-one years old and accomplished—he as a composer and conductor, she as an opera singer. Here she meets Gurdjieff. She asks if her husband could somehow avoid going to the front. "No," he says, "when you live among wolves, you have to howl like a wolf; but you should not be taken over by the psychosis of war, and inside you should try to be far removed from all this."

30. Later he will write in *Meetings with Remarkable Men*, p. 8: "...the present period of culture...is, in the whole process of the perfecting of humanity, as it were, an empty and abortive interval."

At a later meeting, Gurdjieff introduces the subject of the intelligence or the consciousness of matter. He says that in nature there is nothing dead or inanimate. He relates the degree of denseness of vibration, or speed of vibration, to the degree of intelligence; while the denseness of matter corresponds to less intelligence. Later, he speaks of the Diagram of Everything Living which shows how the kind of creature and every degree of being is determined by what it eats and what eats it.

FEBRUARY 14, 1917. PETROGRAD. Ninety thousand strikers demonstrate on the Nevsky. They carry banners reading—"Down with the war! Down with the government."

FEBRUARY 18, 1917. Petrograd. Because of the severe weather, throughout the country 60,000 railway cars containing food, fodder, and fuel stand frozen on their tracks. Food and fuel grow scarce. Only ten days supply of flour remains in storehouses.

FEBRUARY 20, 1917. PETROGRAD. Rumors spread that the government plans to introduce bread rationing. Grocery shelves are quickly stripped of all available food. Having no fuel, factories begin to lay off workers and close. Worker strikes begin.

FEBRUARY 23, 1917. PETROGRAD. Weather conditions radically change, the winter temperature soaring to forty-six degrees with sunny skies. Masses of people stream outdoors to bask in the sun. With alcohol prohibited, many are drinking *khanzhn*, a homemade brew of fermented bread reinforced with cleaning fluids. Thousands of women from the Vyborg, the working class district across the Neva from the Winter Palace, march in a parade for the International Women's Day carrying signs such as, "If a woman is a slave, there will be no freedom. Long live equal rights for women."

FEBRUARY 25, 1917. PETROGRAD. Thousands attend a meeting at Vicholayevsky Station. People call for an end to food shortages and the war. Cossack troops do not interfere and many even fraternize with the crowd. A mounted policeman is shot by a cossack and the police fire into the crowd. The Okhrana make many arrests.

FEBRUARY 26–27, 1917. PETROGRAD. Some 160,000 soldiers of the Petersburg garrison mutiny. Riots, looting, assaults on officers. Forty people are killed at Znamenski Square.

The smell of impending revolution hanging in the streets, Gurdjieff leaves by train for Moscow. Uspenskii and some of the group accompany him to Nikolaevski Station. After boarding the train, he comes to the window of his compartment. He is no longer the "Gurdjieff" they know. Now he looks to be, reports Uspenskii, "a ruling prince or a statesman of some unknown kingdom."

Amfiteatrov, a well-known journalist, is also on the train and a few days later he reports in an article of the strange Oriental he has met, a man he has taken to be an "oil king." Speaking of the war with Germany, the oil king notes that "everyone wants to be a millionaire."

Amfiteatrov asks, "And you?"

"We always make a profit. It [the war] does not refer to us. War or no war it is all the same to us. We always make a profit."

As Uspenskii notes, Gurdjieff is speaking of esoteric work, not oil or money.

MARCH 2, 1917. PETROGRAD. Tsar Nicholas II abdicates in favor of his brother, Grand Duke Michael, who is persuaded not to accept. The Provisional Government is thus formed with lawyer and firebrand Alexander Kerensky as its head.

MARCH 12, 1917. PETROGRAD. With the fall of the Tsar, all political prisoners are freed. From Siberia, a small man, only five feet four inches tall, with a pockmarked face and withered left arm, the result of childhood blood poisoning, arrives in the city. A Georgian Bolshevik, Dzhugashvili calls himself Stalin, "man of steel." He and another Bolshevik political prisoner take over *Pravda*, a local revolutionary newspaper. Much later the Bolsheviks will choose to be called "Communists."

MARCH 1917. PETROGRAD. Anna Kamenskaia, the leading Russian theosophist, lauds the revolution.

> What a great and all-encompassing mission has been assigned our beloved Society!
>
> A free Russia will now take her honored place among enlightened peoples and soon will probably be called upon to play a great role in world history, having voiced her particularly 'Russian word' on the questions of the reorganization of social, human, and international relations.
>
> Political and social questions will naturally come to the fore and the heated work of building wisely on new lines will attract all hearts, devoted to the Motherland. The Theosophists will of course participate in this work.

MARCH 24, 1917. PETROGRAD. Uspenskii gathers the principal members of the Petersburg group at Dr. Stjoernval's home. He tells them that the short period of relative calm they are now experiencing is an illusion and everything will soon break up and collapse. As they can do nothing to help, and their own group work here would be impossible, Uspenskii declares that in his opinion, "there is no sense whatever in staying in Russia and we must go abroad." His words are taken to be exaggerated and not greeted with much approval. Most, he says, do not realize the true import of what the revolution brought and others, he says, are "in the grip of the customary illusion that everything that happens is for the best."

Soon after this meeting Uspenskii receives a postcard from Gurdjieff written in February just before the revolution, saying he is going to Alexandropol and asking Uspenskii to "continue the work of the groups until his arrival." He promises to return by Easter.

MARCH 27, 1917. SWITZERLAND. Lenin, the exiled Bolshevik leader, has been negotiating with Germany to allow his return to Russia. The Germans believe that Lenin's lust for power is so great that he will topple the Provisional Government, take over, and withdraw Russia from the war. The German Foreign Ministry requests five million marks for "Russian work" and allows Lenin to cross its territory in a sealed train.

SPRING 1917. PETROGRAD. With still no word from Gurdjieff, Uspenskii begins to look through his notes of a year earlier. Again, he is struck by the similarity of Gurdjieff's presentation of the seven cosmoses to his own period of dimensions. He remembers Gurdjieff's words: *Time is breath.* With this idea as key, the whole idea of cosmoses of zero to infinity opens up for him in a new way. He comes to a completely unexpected confirmation of his own ideas through defining the *present* as the direct sensation of the inhalation and exhalation of breath. For a man, a complete breath is three seconds; for the earth, it is eighty years. He creates a table relating the cosmoses to the period of their breath.

APRIL 1917. RUSSIA. Eighty percent of Russians are peasants. Land seizures rise fivefold. Prices increase dramatically. A pair of shoes which cost 5–8 rubles before 1914, now costs 40 rubles. A bag of rye flour which cost 6 rubles now costs 40 rubles. A potato which cost 1 ruble then now costs 7 rubles.

APRIL 3, 1917. FINLAND STATION, PETROGRAD. The short, stocky forty-six-year-old Lenin—bald with a reddish beard, his slanted eyes and high cheekbones giving him a feral look—gets off the train from Switzerland. He mounts an armored car to speak to the people who await him. His manner of speaking is brusque and often punctuated with a high, sarcastic laugh. But he utters the words the people have waited to hear: "Peace, land, and bread." By "peace" Lenin means not only the withdrawal from the war with Germany but also the overthrow of capital. By "land" he means the confiscation of the estates of the wealthy. Later at Kshesinskaia, the Bolshevik headquarters, Lenin speaks again and insists that the transition from "bourgeois-democratic" to "socialist" revolution be accomplished in a matter of months.[31] A member of the audience remembers:

> I cannot forget that speech, like lightning, which shook up and astonished not only me, a heretic accidentally thrown into delirium, but also the true believers. No one had expected anything like it. It seemed as if all the elemental forces had risen from their lairs and the spirit of universal destruction, which knew no obstacles, no doubts, neither human difficulties nor human calculations, circled in Kshesinskaia's hall above the heads of the enchanted disciples.[32]

APRIL 7, 1917. PETROGRAD. Lenin's "April Theses" is published in *Pravda.* Among the provisions it calls for: No backing of the war with Germany; immediate transition to the second phase of the revolution; refusal to support the Provisional Government; transfer of all power to the Soviets; confiscation of all landlord property and nationalization of all land; the creation of a single National Bank under Soviet supervision; and the Soviet control of production and distribution. A German agent in Stockholm cables Berlin: "Lenin's entry into Russia successful. He is working exactly as we wish."

EASTER 1917. PETROGRAD. Uspenskii still has heard no word from Gurdjieff. A week later, however, Uspenskii receives a telegram. Gurdjieff says he will return to Petrograd in May.

APRIL 21, 1917. PETROGRAD AND MOSCOW. The first Bolshevik demonstrations occur in Russia's two major cities.

MAY 1917. PETROGRAD. Uspenskii has been expecting Gurdjieff's arrival with every passing day. But to no avail.

JUNE 3, 1917. PETROGRAD. At the First All Russian Congress of the Soviets, Lenin declares "our party is ready to assume full power at any time." He calls for the arrest of "fifty to one hundred of our richest millionaires."

EARLY JUNE 1917. PETROGRAD. Uspenskii receives a telegram from Gurdjieff in Alexandropol—*If you want to rest come here to me.*

31. Lenin, to put himself in accord with Marxist thought, argues that Russia's economy is capitalist, not agrarian. Marx had said that economies pass through three stages: agrarianism, capitalism, then socialism. Lenin wants Russia to bypass capitalism (just as China's Mao did later in the century).

32. Eight years later, in writing *All and Everything, First Series,* Gurdjieff will speak of a certain Lentrohamsanin as one of the 313 Hasnamussian-Eternal individuals who, among their other endearing traits, have "the irresistible inclination to destroy the existence of other breathing creatures" and "the feeling of self-satisfaction from leading others astray." Some believe Gurdjieff took Lenin as a model for such an individual.

Within two days, Uspenskii leaves Petersburg by train.

The Caucasus lies some thirteen hundred miles south of Petersburg. With the increasing turmoil, instead of the usual three days, it takes five days to reach Tiflis. Uspenskii had hardly slept throughout the journey. He finds the train station at Tiflis jammed with soldiers, many of them drunk. The influence of Bolshevik propaganda had caused many to leave the Caucasian front. Uspenskii slumbers in an armchair. A glass door separates the buffet from the railway platform outside. Suddenly, from the platform, there are several shots.

Soldiers rush into the buffet, shouting, "Comrades, do not worry. We have only shot a thief."

The thief is said to have stolen three rubles from someone's pocket.

An hour or so passes and Uspenskii hears more shots, more cries.

Another thief has been executed.

Towards daybreak, a third shot. Another thief is shot, but he turns out to be a policeman.

Through the glass door, Uspenskii sees three bloodstained bodies lying on the platform.

He observes that the soldiers are friendly toward the citizens. But, ever the realist, Uspenskii knows this is only the beginning.

"Everybody was still getting bread and shoes," he says. "But it is quite clear that as soon as there should be no bread and shoes, those with guns would get bread and shoes from those without guns."

Uspenskii has no illusions about Bolshevism. He sees it as a "catastrophe, a shipwreck" in which a people cannibalize themselves. "Bolshevism is not a political system at all," he says. "It is something very old, that at different times has borne different names." The Russian name *pougachevchina* describes the essence of Bolshevism, he thinks. In the eighteenth century a man named Pougachev, pretending to be the deceased Emperor Peter III, led an insurrection against Catherine II and for a time occupied nearly half of Russia, plundering the estates, hanging the estate owners and priests, and giving the land to the peasantry.

Societal madness mounting in Russia, Uspenskii believes he must convince Gurdjieff to leave. He thinks of England as a destination.

JUNE 1917. ALEXANDROPOL. Finally, the morning of the seventh day Uspenskii reaches Alexandropol. In the Greek quarter he finds Gurdjieff setting up a dynamo for his younger brother, Dimitri Ivanovitch. He meets Gurdjieff's family, the Giorgiades. They are Greek-Armenian from Asia Minor. They speak Armenian, and are people, Uspenskii says, of "a very old and very peculiar culture." Gurdjieff's relationship with his father impresses Uspenskii. They are obviously very close and loving. The father, Giorgios Giorgiades, is a storyteller, an *ashokh.* An early photo of Gurdjieff hanging in the living room shows that Gurdjieff earned his living as a hypnotist at one time. Outside, standing amid a nearby ancient Armenian cemetery, Uspenskii sees in the distance the snowy peaks of Mount Ararat, the location where myth says Noah's Ark anchored during the Flood.

Uspenskii spends two weeks in Alexandropol. But he fails to persuade Gurdjieff to leave Russia. Uspenskii gives no reasons for Gurdjieff's refusal.[33]

JULY 4, 1917. PETROGRAD. The Bolshevik *putsch* is quelled by release of information about Lenin's dealings with the Germans. Lenin goes into hiding and ends up in Finland.

July 1917. Petrograd. At Kerensky's bidding, the Russian Army mounts an offensive against Austro-Hungarian troops at Galacia. Declares Kerensky: "No army can remain in indefinite idleness.... For the sake of her future, Russia had to perform this historic sacrifice." After initial successes, several hundred thousand men are lost. The Army begins to disintegrate.

EARLY JULY 1917. ALEXANDROPOL. In the morning Gurdjieff and Uspenskii leave for Petersburg. During the journey, their train's departure is delayed a long time at one railway station. Taking advantage of the break, Uspenskii speaks to his teacher about the division of oneself into "I" and "Uspenskii"—and *how can one strengthen the feeling of "I" and strengthen the activity of "I"?*

Gurdjieff tells him that he can't do anything about that. "This should come as a result of *all* your efforts," he says. He tells him that by now he should have a different feeling of his "I."

Uspenskii says he did not have this feeling of "I."[34]

At Mozdok, on the third day of their trip from Tiflis, Gurdjieff appears to suddenly change plans. He will remain in the Caucasus, he says, and Uspenskii is to continue alone to Moscow and Petersburg. He is to give a message to Gurdjieff's students: "Tell them I am beginning new work here," says Gurdjieff. "Those who want to work with me can come."

33. Two important practical considerations may weigh in Gurdjieff's decision to remain in Russia. One, though he speaks a number of languages, Gurdjieff speaks no European ones; and, two, if he leaves, the million rubles he brought to Russia in 1912 are virtually worthless as the rubles cannot be converted into gold (because of the governmental decree of July 27, 1914). It is interesting to note that Gurdjieff, having brought such an enormous sum to Russia, clearly meant to be free of all economic considerations in establishing the teaching. But Fate decreed otherwise. Forced to leave Russia, money became an issue he never intended. How he came to use it as a teaching device is most instructive.

34. A student's questions, their subject matter, intent, and the clarity with which they are formulated, are important because they show the level and direction at which the student is searching. They also give a forefeeling of the future. Here, with this question, it is seen that Uspenskii now approaches the feeling of his own "I." He will come to this in Essentuki in 1918.

Not only has Gurdjieff dashed his plans for escaping abroad, he now directs Uspenskii to return alone to the center of madness. He is not afraid of the physical danger but of "acting stupidly." The future of revolutionary Russia is plain to Uspenskii. It's illogical, stupid, not to leave. But Gurdjieff had made this decision for him. This must really grate on him, but of this Uspenskii will only say: "Now all responsibility towards myself seemed to have been taken from me."[35]

JULY 10, 1917. PETROGRAD. Kerensky asks forty-seven-year-old General Lavr Georgevich Kornilov, son of a Siberian Cossack, to assume command of the armed forces.

MID-JULY 1917. ESSENTUKI. Despite the growing hazard of these days, Uspenskii, Anna Ilinishna, and eleven others make their way to the village of Essentuki nestled in a green valley in the foothills of the Caucasus near Mount Elbrus. On the outskirts, Gurdjieff has rented a country villa, the first of many that Gurdjieff will rent while in the Caucasus. Uspenskii and six others live here with Gurdjieff, while the rest will lodge elsewhere. Work at the villa begins early in the morning and continues late into the evening.

One day a surprise showing is made by Evreinoff, Anna Butkovsky's old lover. Meeting the group on the street, he goes up to Gurdjieff, saying: "I am a difficult, pretentious man. I am ambitious. But here, Georgi Ivanovitch, I bow to you..." Evreinoff stays for a time and then leaves.

It is here in this country villa that for the next six weeks Gurdjieff opens all the doors to the teaching, for the first time allowing Uspenskii and the others to see, as Uspenskii says, "the plan of the whole work." Not only does Gurdjieff reveal the links, connections, and directions of the teaching, but even the origins of its ideas. In effect, Gurdjieff entrusts them with the keys to the kingdom.[36]

35. For an intellectual and individual of Uspenskii's caliber, this had to have set up a real struggle between the 'yes' and 'no' in him. Emotion would have been very strong. It would thus serve to do exactly what Uspenskii asked: How to strengthen his feeling of "I." As Uspenskii would answer in a meeting many years afterward: "It is necessary to create a certain particular energy and that can be created only at a moment of very serious emotional stress. All work before that is only a preparation...."

36. Why *now*—the revolution raging, chaos and hazard everywhere, and even the most promising of his students still not mature in a spiritual sense—does Gurdjieff reveal the intellectual core of the teaching? Because in the growing mass psychosis, death at any time is a possibility. Gurdjieff has had enough experience with "stray bullets" in his life to know he might die at any time. If that happened, then one or more of his pupils, if sufficiently prepared, might be able to at least bring the teaching to the West.

For six weeks the work goes on, the group getting only four to five hours sleep a night, doing housework and chores and the rest of the time doing exercises and listening to lectures. Among the ideas Gurdjieff communicates:

> *Schools are imperative. Man can never attain the necessary intensity by himself. Only super-efforts count. Another person's will is necessary. Unison of centers is chief difficulty in working on oneself. Work on the moving center. Tension among group members is indispensable. Sole possibility of other centers working in a new way is to begin with moving center. Relaxing the muscles. Yoga postures.*[37] *Circular sensation. Feeling the pulse throughout the body. Stop exercise. Voluntary silence. Voluntary suffering. Fasting. Breathing.*[38] *Fourth way. Obyvatel. Only one thing is serious—freedom. Nothing worse than to begin to work on oneself and then to leave it and find oneself between two stools.*

For Uspenskii, who from the beginning secretly kept notes of the meetings, these six weeks in Essentuki were a time of unparalleled richness. Gurdjieff provides a detailed map, as well as exercises and postures, the "new or forgotten road to the miraculous" for which he had so long sought. Standing in the yard of the country villa in the silent early morning and looking out at the cloud-covered top of Mount Elbrus, at over 18,000 feet the highest of the Caucasus mountains, Uspenskii must have felt he stood at its top.

And yet he says, "I always have a very strange feeling when I remember this period." [39]

Whatever the case, he does report that all does not go well with the group. Hard feelings developed between certain members. Given the intensive nature of the work and the close quarters, this is not surprising. And, as Gurdjieff has told them, a "certain tension is indispensable" for chipping away attitudes. As a result of this friction, some event, which Uspenskii does

37. Among the postures Uspenskii reports Gurdjieff doing are *Padmasana* (the lotus) and *Supta Virasana.* Both are advanced asanas, or postures, far beyond the intermediate stage. In *Padmasana* Gurdjieff sat with the legs crossed, the right heel being at the root of the left thigh near the navel. The left leg is placed over the right with heel near the navel. The soles of both feet are turned up. In *Supta Virasana* he sat on the floor on his knees. Then he bent backwards reclining the torso on the floor, the arms stretched out behind the head. This posture, Uspenskii says, Gurdjieff "could adopt to perfection." (See *Search,* p. 350.) Given this demonstration, it is more than likely that Gurdjieff had mastered hatha yoga.

38. Gurdjieff's dire warning about breathing in the *Second Series* (p. 187) has led many people in the Work to believe that any kind of breath work should not be done. But he clearly makes a distinction between 'inflation' and breathing assisted by movements. (See *Search,* pp. 387–88.) Both J. G. Bennett and the de Hartmanns report Gurdjieff giving breathing exercises. A careful reading of his *First Series* reveals the importance Gurdjieff gives breathing in the work of self-perfection as it relates to *Djartklom.*

39. In the midst of his elation, the idea now emerges that he must break with Gurdjieff. He gives a number of reasons for this, but the feeling is that there is something more, something he either is not saying or does not himself know.

not specify, has happened. Uspenskii sees it as "accidental," but Gurdjieff uses it to announce he is disbanding the group and ending all work. The announcement's apparent irrationality shocks Uspenskii.

At first he and the others do not think Gurdjieff is serious, they take it that he is only "playing" or "acting" as usual. Suddenly, Uspenskii cannot fathom Gurdjieff's actions. From this moment his confidence in Gurdjieff, he declares, "began to waver." Instead of "eating" the shock, enduring and absorbing the suffering, he calms himself by making a fatal separation. As he did a year earlier in Finland with the telepathic experience, when he decided to hide a part of his experience from his teacher—creating, therefore, a split between what he would and would not tell Gurdjieff—Uspenskii now makes a further separation—he separates the teacher from the teaching.[40] With his mind, Uspenskii separates Gurdjieff, the man, from the ideas.[41]

AUGUST 1917. PETROGRAD. Lenin convinces thirty-eight-year-old Lev Davidovich Trotsky to join the Bolshevik Party. Trotsky, whose revolutionary credentials extend back to 1905's Bloody Sunday, is a brilliant firebrand, gifted orator, and organizer. His real name was Lev Bronstein; he took "Trotsky" from his Siberian jailer (as Vladimir Ulyanov took "Lenin" from his exile near Siberia's River Lena).

EARLY SEPTEMBER 1917. PETROGRAD. Accused by Kerensky of being a traitor, General Lavr Kornilov sends troops to Petersburg to topple the Provisional government. But they desert and the right-wing *putsch* fails. Generals Kornilov, Anton Ivanovitch Denikin, and others are imprisoned in a converted monastery in the ancient town of Bykhov.

SEPTEMBER 1917. FINLAND. From his hideout, Lenin writes a series of letters to the Bolshevik Central Committee declaring the time is ripe for the seizure of power.

OCTOBER 15, 1917. PETROGRAD. Uspenskii has stayed longer than he expected and now leaves for Sochi. Of these last days in his beloved city he says: "Something disgusting and clammy was drawing near. A sickly tension and the expectation of something inevitable could be felt in everything." He saw the Bolsheviks for what they were, "agents of destruction." They destroyed not so much by their actions but "as by

40. It is tantamount to Peter separating Jesus from the Sermon on the Mount and going on to teach his own version of Christianity as the true version.

41. The act is fatal. The teacher is a living embodiment of the teaching and by splitting the teacher from the teaching, the student unconsciously creates an irreconcilable duality, one for which Uspenskii will sadly pay the rest of his life. Even many years later in writing and rewriting *Fragments of a Unknown Teaching*, Uspenskii appears not to see what happened for he writes, "What the matter was and what particularly provoked me is difficult for me to define even now."

their very existence which corrupts and disintegrates everything around them. This special property of theirs explained their approaching victory and all that happened much later."

OCTOBER 24–25, 1917. PETROGRAD. The Bolsheviks seize power. (By the Gregorian calendar, it is November 7th.) Peasants seize land. The economy totters. The Army's generals are imprisoned.

AUTUMN 1917. SOCHI. Following the teaching in Essentuki, Uspenskii had left for Petersburg to collect his belongings. The rising famine and anarchy meant he could only pack essentials. He must leave behind his library, an intellectual's chief food. Returning to Sochi, he finds that Gurdjieff has taken another country house a little over fifteen miles from the town. Ten people live in the villa, its grounds full of roses. On one side it offers a view of the sea, and on the other a chain of mountains. Despite the beauty, Uspenskii finds the atmosphere greatly changed, not at all like Essentuki.

From Dr. Stjoernval he learns that Gurdjieff and Zacharov are not speaking. Worse, Zacharov is preparing to return to Petersburg. The reason is that Gurdjieff had "a very absurd quarrel" with some Lettish neighbors and Zacharov had manifested in some way so that, from then on, Gurdjieff stopped speaking to him. Uspenskii thinks the situation "pure idiocy," and convinces a reluctant Zacharov to mend matters with Gurdjieff. Zacharov finally does so, but Gurdjieff maintains that Zacharov, having decided to return to Petersburg, should go. "I could not understand it. I would not have let a dog go to St. Petersburg at that time," declares an angry Uspenskii.[42]

NOVEMBER 1917. BYKHOV. Facing certain execution at the hands of the Red Guards, the imprisoned generals escape to South Russia. Says General Denikin of what he experienced en route: "I saw clearly unbounded hatred

42. Unwittingly, Uspenskii here, as elsewhere, puts himself on a level with Gurdjieff, taking himself to be awake enough to judge his teacher's actions. Zacharov perhaps did the same. Why Gurdjieff acted as he did will never be known, but, given the mounting chaos with which the group is surrounded, the bond of trust between student and teacher had to be unshakable. Hierarchy and discipline are essential if the group is to safely walk the fault line of the psychic earthquake that the Bolsheviks had prepared. With the Letts, perhaps, Gurdjieff had acted—"With a *svolotch* [lowest of the low] I am a *svolotch*. With a good man, I am a good man," Gurdjieff said during this time—and Zacharov took this "acting" as real. Whatever, the fact is that psychologically Uspenskii had elevated himself to the chair of the teacher. He believed he could judge Gurdjieff. It is true, however, that Gurdjieff has said to them, "By now you ought better to understand in what my aim consists and by now you ought to see whether you are on the same road as I am or not." Uspenskii may here be shoring up his decision to follow a different road by finding fault with Gurdjieff's actions, thus devaluing the road Gurdjieff is taking. It is interesting to note that Gurdjieff uses the word "road" here, which of course corresponds to Uspenskii's seeking what he calls "a new or forgotten road."

everywhere. Only one desire reigned supreme—to seize and destroy. Its aim seemed to be not to better itself, but to drag down to its level anything that in one way or another stood out or seemed different."

NOVEMBER 1917. TUAPSE. Gurdjieff, Uspenskii, and four others live twenty-five miles north of Tuapse in a house on the Black Sea.

DECEMBER 1917. PETROGRAD. Anna Ilinishna Butkovsky marries the forty-eight-year-old Englishman Charles Hewitt; he represents a British timber importer in Russia. She leaves Russia with her husband; in Paris she runs a fashionable dress salon and also deals in antiques.

LATE DECEMBER 1917. Generals Kornilov, Alekseev, and Denikin form the Volunteer Army, or the White Army, to fight the Bolsheviks. Kornilov takes command in South Russia.

JANUARY 1918. ESSENTUKI. After moving to several more villas, Gurdjieff finally returns to Essentuki in January and rents a house. It is unfinished, with all its rooms looking out onto a verandah but having no windows or doors.

FEBRUARY 1918. ESSENTUKI. Over Uspenskii's signature, Gurdjieff has a circular letter sent out to his pupils in Moscow and Petersburg inviting them to come to him. Showing Uspenskii around the house he has rented, Gurdjieff reminds Uspenskii of his concern of several years before, when Gurdjieff asked group members to pay 1,000 rubles. Only "one-and-a-half persons" had paid that amount, Gurdjieff tells him, and, he declares, "I have now already spent more than was collected then."

FEBRUARY 1918. PETROGRAD. Anna Kamenskaia has urged readers of the theosophical journal *Vestnik Teosofii* to give their support. "At this critical moment in Russian life the voice of *Vestnik* should not be silenced, the hearthfire should not go out. The Editorial Board hopes that those who warmed themselves at this hearthfire will not leave it in this difficult moment and will help to carry forward the light of Eternity into the world." In 1916 its subscription price had been seven rubles; now it is twenty-one rubles. Suffering from the paper shortage and rising printing costs, each issue is smaller than the preceding, until the journal ceases publication.

By the year's end, the Bolsheviks order all religious, occult, mystical groups to cease activities. Kamenskaia and her followers go into the countryside to meet, but by spring "the Red Wave had flooded the countryside" and they return to the city.[43]

43. In 1921, at the behest of Mrs. Besant, Kamenskaia would leave Russia for England. In 1922 the Bolsheviks would open their "antireligious front" in which they closed presses, confiscated literature, and published numerous articles castigating occult societies. This would be followed by the exile or arrest of the more prominent members.

MARCH 3, 1918. BREST-LITOVSK. As the Germans had predicted, the Communists sign a treaty with Germany withdrawing Russia from the war.

MARCH 1918. ESSENTUKI. Some forty pupils from Moscow and St. Petersburg arrive in Essentuki, which lies on the northern slopes of the Caucasus Mountains. From the Petersburg group, besides Uspenskii, also present is Uspenskii's wife, Sophia,[44] and her daughter by a previous marriage, Lenochka Savitsky; Dr. Stjoernval, his wife, Elizabeta; Charkovsky; Nicholas, the government official; Madame Bashmakova; the de Hartmanns, Thomas and Olga; and Zacharov, still weak from an illness. From the Moscow group, there is, besides Gurdjieff's wife, the beautiful and finely formed Julia Osipovna Ostrowska, Alexander Nikanotovich Petrov, one of Gurdjieff's chief pupils and highly gifted in mathematics and engineering; Alexei Yakovlevich Rachmilievitch, one of Gurdjieff's earliest pupils; Lina Fedorovna; Zhukov; and N. F. Grigoriev. One who comes on his own initiative is P. V. Shandarovsky, a well-educated lawyer who plays the violin, a Guarneri.

Strict rules are immediately established in the house. People are forbidden to leave the grounds by day and security is posted day and night. In time, Gurdjieff asks the group to give a name for their society. Uspenskii suggests, "The Society for Struggle against Sleep," but Gurdjieff feels it too obvious. Finally, "International Fellowship for Realization through Work" is selected. A sign is made. It features two symbols, the pentagram and the enneagram. Every day, notices appear on the bulletin board. One demands that each member break all ties with everyone. There must be no identification. Another notice says that all possessions are to be given up. Full members are named, the first three being Uspenskii, Petrov, and Dr. Stjoernval; later Thomas de Hartmann. One notice divides the day into hours with each hour devoted to inner exercises. Physical exercises are given that are much more complex and varied than at the first intensive in Essentuki. Movements and dances are given and various ways of breathing studied. Subjects of discussion during lectures are: Attention. Real confession. Chief feature. Conscience. Crystallization of the soul.

During the group's stay in Essentuki public lectures are given, first with Uspenskii reading a lecture and at another lecture Petrov reads from his paper about the Ray of Creation. Several days after the first lecture

44. Whether Sophia Grigorievna—"Madame Uspenskii" as she is always called— was in fact married to Uspenskii is not clear. The likelihood is that she was not. Born in 1874, and four years older than him, she had twice been married; first to a student when she was sixteen, then to a mining engineer with whom she traveled to remote areas of Russia. A son was killed early in his life and her daughter would be old enough to give birth to a grandchild in 1919. How Uspenskii and Sophia Grigorievna got together and how his relationship with Anna Butkovsky ended is not known.

Gurdjieff calls the group together and says they must know how this Work originated. Following many years of separate work in places where initiation centers were still alive, three people—a man of science, a man of religions and their histories, and a 'man of being'—met by prearrangement at the foot of one of the Egyptian pyramids. They agreed to form groups of people in various places having the right conditions. The real purpose could only become clear when full attention was given to the idea of the crystallization of the soul.

Instead of Gurdjieff lecturing to the public, he has the group put up posters around Essentuki announcing a lecture by the notorious "Dr. Black," a fictional charlatan depicted in satirical poems of the time.

"Why always a suggestion of charlatanism for prospective pupils at the very first meeting?" asks Thomas de Hartmann, and then explains: "Teachers usually surround themselves with an atmosphere of great seriousness and importance, to give newcomers a good impression. With Mr. Gurdjieff it was just the opposite: everything that could repel, even frighten, a new man was always produced. A newcomer had the opportunity to meet Mr. Gurdjieff and to talk with him, but at once there was put before him some obstacle to be surmounted. On the other hand, Mr. Gurdjieff never let a newcomer go away empty-handed if he came with real questions and spoke about something that was of genuine importance to him."

But even with the older students Gurdjieff 'acts' or 'plays.' And now, as a means of increasing the pressure on the group, he 'acts' with everyone.[45] Considering himself a very decent man, the deceit and hypocrisy of ordinary life always rankle Uspenskii. So to find that his teacher employs the same as a means of teaching is more than ironic. Theoretically, of course, Uspenskii says he understands. But he doesn't find this 'playing' always practical.

"In practice," he says, "this 'play' drove away many useful people and kept by him others that were not suitable."

It seemed to Uspenskii that Gurdjieff was not always in full control of his manifestations, which was of great concern to him.

"What always amazed myself and others in his 'play'," he says, "was that sometimes it was too obvious not to be seen, as if he were not trying to hide the whole threads at all, or that sometimes he could not stop himself and 'played' by habit automatically, even when and where there was neither use nor meaning in it."[46]

Others, such as Thomas de Hartmann saw it differently: "As the basis of his Work," he explains, "was to create every kind of impression in a pupil for this transformation [to real I], he could accomplish it only through the playing of roles." He gives the example of a pupil needing

45. For Uspenskii, in particular, this must be hard to swallow.

the experience of injustice and so Gurdjieff plays the unjust man. "Then one had to hold back from reacting badly and not be resentful." If he simply suffered in the usual way, it was not intentional suffering and had no value. Gurdjieff became "our tempter," notes Thomas de Hartmann. "As tempter he provoked in us a strong inner experience of feeling and sensation, which in life expresses itself as what some call 'negative emotion,' and then he strove to enable us to transform it by seeing it and reasoning about it."

Uspenskii speaks of the group disdainfully as having become a "colony." Gurdjieff, he believes, is leading the group "in fact towards the way of religion."[47] Though he does not consider this way wrong, *"it is not my way,"* he declares.

And so he moves Madame Uspenskii and her daughter into a separate house. For two years he has not been able to write. Now he returns to working on the book he began seven years before, *Wisdom of the Gods.* While he continues to speak with Gurdjieff, he refuses to go to the "Home."[48]

For Gurdjieff, the pressures he has to live under at this time are extreme. The million rubles he had brought to Russia, the villa and instruments he had purchased for his Institute, the great energy he had invested—all are now gone. Uncertainty and hazard are everywhere and people are acting, he says, like "infuriated beasts, ready to tear one another apart for the slightest booty." Of this period he says: "For me personally, of all that I went through in Russia, this was the period of most intense nervous strain. All the time I not only had to think and worry about obtaining the most immediate necessities of life, which had become almost unprocurable, but I was also constantly concerned about the lives of the hundred or so people who were in my care."

46. Given Uspenskii's comments at the time, he never appears to have seen Gurdjieff's 'acting' in relation to himself. Like every student, he has difficulty in seeing things involving himself from any but a personal perspective. Yet, at the same time, he invariably distances himself, taking the supposedly impartial stance of the observer. His pet corn is his rejection of all which smacks of the irrational, deceit, the religious, or the cult, and Gurdjieff, of course, has acted accordingly.

47. Though the civil war is all around them, Uspenskii doesn't appear to have understood the context in which Gurdjieff put forward the idea of "religion." To stay in Essentuki meant the group would be sitting ducks for the mass psychosis of the time. The group had to be led over the Causasus. This meant Gurdjieff had to take them between two warring armies. A wrong gesture, a false word, and they all could be shot on sight. The situation demanded that the group put their faith in Gurdjieff and do exactly as he said.

48. Since the previous August, Uspenskii has been caught between a 'yes' and a 'no,' caught between breaking with Gurdjieff and staying on. What he terms his "personal position" in the Work has been changing. He is looking for a way out.

APRIL 13, 1918. EKATERINODAR. In an attempt to capture the town, General Kornilov, commander of the Volunteer Army, is killed by a stray shell. Forty-five-year-old General Denikin, former commander of Russia's Western Front assumes command.

MAY 15, 1918. ALEXANDROPOL. Turkish soldiers advance into Armenia. All in Gurdjieff's family flee except his eighty-five-year-old father, Giorgios Giorgiades, who loads his rifle and sits in his doorway awaiting his fate. He is later buried near his home.

MID-SUMMER 1918. RUSSIA. Only a few months after Russia's withdrawal from the European War, a full-scale civil war breaks out.

MID-JULY, 1918. ESSENTUKI. Quite unexpectedly a cart pulls up in front of Gurdjieff's home. Inside are twenty-eight people, all relatives of his. There are his mother; his younger brother Dimitri Ivanovitch, with his wife and a small child; one of his sisters, Sophie Ivanovna, and her fiance; Georgi Leibovich Kapanadze; two more sisters; and a niece and nephew. Gurdjieff rents a house nearby where they can live.

JULY 16–17, 1918. EKATERINBURG. Tsar Nicholas II, family and servants are murdered.

AUGUST 1918. GERMANY. A regimental runner receives the Iron Cross, First Class for bravery. The medal is rarely given to a common soldier. The runner's name is Adolf Hitler.

AUGUST 6, 1918. ESSENTUKI. In the middle of a civil war, with Bolshevik and White Army soldiers on all sides, and everyone in the grip of a mounting mass psychosis with which he is very familiar, Gurdjieff decides he and his followers must do the impossible: *leave Russia.* Because of the danger and the rigors of the journey, Gurdjieff leaves his family behind.

To get out, the Caucasus must be crossed. The main mountain range of the Caucasus is some 750 miles long and over 100 miles wide. The terrain is often rugged, the roads are poor, and, besides the civil war, there are bandits. The journey seems foolhardy enough, but how to persuade the power possessing beings of the time, infected by paranoia and hatred, to allow such a crossing...?

Only a mind like Gurdjieff's could have dreamed up the unlikely idea of organizing a scientific expedition to the region of Mount Induk in the Caucasus to search both for dolmens and gold. To put it into action, first he has Petrov, a master calligrapher, write a letter for Shandarovsky, a personable and persuasive lawyer, to deliver to the Essentuki Soviet's

Council of Deputies. The impressive looking letter requests permission for the expedition. At the same time, as he had done earlier in placing the ballet notice with Uspenskii, Gurdjieff has a story planted about the expedition in the Piatigorsk newspapers. (It is the higher Soviet Council in Piatigorsk that had the authority to assist the expedition materially.) The story is entirely Gurdjieff's composition; he dictates all its questions and answers: *The expedition intends to go to a remote wilderness, inaccessible to military activities of the civil war. Therefore this scientific work and its discoveries cannot be hindered.*

Soon equipment begins to arrive from Piatigorsk. Having requisitioned and received the necessary supplies of coffee, tea, salt, potatoes, flour, tents and carpets, the group sets out on their journey. Besides Gurdjieff, it includes fourteen people: seven men, five women and two children—all of whom Gurdjieff says are "half-consciously or unconsciously devoted to me." They leave Essentuki with horses and two small carts in two baggage cars pulled by a slow-moving freight train.

Among the men are Petrov, Zacharov, Zhukov, Thomas de Hartmann, and Dr. Stjoernval. Among the women are Mesdames Ostrowska, de Hartmann, Stjoernval, and Bashmakova.

Notably absent is Uspenskii and his family, with his convenient excuse that Madame Uspenskii's daughter, Lenochka, is expecting her first child. Whatever his outward face, he has decided to break with Gurdjieff.

Not until the next day does Gurdjieff's group reach Armavir and only the following morning arrives in Maikop, which is surrounded by fighting Cossacks and Red Army troops. They await the outcome on a farm outside of town. The Cossacks take the town and the group moves on by foot, picking their way between the opposing sides, heading into the mountains. No fewer than five times the group has to cross Bolshevik and White Army lines. All about them is what Gurdjieff says is an "epidemic of fanaticism and mutual hatred." The circumstances summoned all of Gurdjieff's capacities. During this period he says, "miracles were being performed for us...I and my companions moved under supernatural protection." After many trials and hardships, the group finally crosses the mountains and in October reaches Sochi on the Black Sea. After a few days Gurdjieff suddenly announces that the expedition is finished and advises everyone to make their own plans for the future. Only the de Hartmanns, Stjoernvals, and Zhukov remain with Gurdjieff.

Of this period Gurdjieff says—"In my opinion, we got out safely because in the common presences of these people—although in the grip of a psychic state in which the last grain of reasonableness vanishes—the instinct inherent in all human beings for distinguishing good from evil in the objective sense was not completely lacking. And therefore, instinctively sensing in my activities the living germ of that sacred impulse which alone is capable of bringing genuine happiness to humanity, they furthered in whatever way they could the process of accomplishment of that which I had undertaken long before the war."

AUGUST 30, 1918. Lenin is shot twice by a female assassin but recovers.

SEPTEMBER 5, 1918. MOSCOW. The Red Terror officially begins. Prisoners and hostages throughout Russia are massacred. *Kulaks,* rich peasants, are hunted down and shot by the *Cheka,* Lenin's secret police.

NOVEMBER 1918. The First World War ends. The Russian civil war continues.

MID-JANUARY 1919. TIFLIS. Gurdjieff, his wife, the Stjoernvals, and the de Hartmanns leave Sochi by ship for Poti and then take a train to Tiflis. Through an old friend and composer, Tcherepnin, de Hartmann learns that a friend from his early days in Munich, the forty-four-year-old artist Alexander de Salzmann, is painting the scenery for the local opera house. De Salzmann invites the de Hartmanns to dinner. They meet de Salzmann's pregnant wife, thirty-year-old Jeanne Matignon. Born in Geneva, Switzerland, she had been one of the three principal dancers with Jacques Dalcroze, founder of Eurhythmics, a leading European school of dance, at the Hellerau near Dresden. There she met Alexander and the two married in 1911. The de Hartmanns tell them about the teaching. Later, they meet Gurdjieff who says of them: "He is a very fine man, and she—is intelligent." So begins Gurdjieff's fruitful relationship with the de Salzmanns.

That autumn, Gurdjieff decides to re-establish his Institute in Tiflis. He asks Dr. Stjoernval, the de Hartmanns, and the de Salzmanns to name it. He rejects every name until the five come up with The Institute for the Harmonious Development of Man. Rehearsals now begin for the staging of *The Struggle of the Magicians* at the State Theater. Stage sets are designed, music written, dances rehearsed, costumes made. One morning Olga enters the performance hall and sees Gurdjieff taking an axe to the decorations. She thinks he has gone mad. But he says, "Why are you so astonished? We have done it, so we don't need it anymore. Now it can go to the dump." Her husband recounts one of the principles of Gurdjieff's teaching: "Make the pupils do something that is terribly difficult and demands all their attention and diligence, and then destroy it, because, for them, only the effort is necessary and not the thing itself."

JANUARY 1919. ESSENTUKI. Cossacks capture the town. At some point Lenochka, Madame Uspenskii's daughter, has given birth to a son, Leonidas, or "Lonya," Savitsky.

APRIL 1, 1919. SOUTH RUSSIA. Denikin's White Army is supplied with arms and advisors by England and France.

SUMMER 1919. ROSTOV-ON-THE-DON. Uspenskii moves his family from Essentuki to Rostov-on-the-Don. The English journalist Carl Bechhofer-Roberts finds Uspenskii in "rooms [that] were icily cold; draughts blew in every direction; and coal was practically unobtainable owing to the breakdown of the transport system." Uspenskii's sole possessions consist of a shabby overcoat and a ragged frock coat, an extra pair of boots, several extra shirts and pairs of socks, a blanket, towel, tin of coffee, razor, and a file and whetstone. Bechhofer-Roberts says, "He assured me that he considered himself exceptionally fortunate to have so much left." Uspenskii has supported himself and his family over the past year by taking jobs as a porter, a schoolmaster, and a librarian.

JUNE 1919. EKATERINODAR. Uspenskii moves his family to Ekaterinodar, the capital of the Kouban region, located on the bank of the Kouban River in the plain of the Northern Caucasus. One of Russia's richest towns and a center for grain and other raw products, this eighteenth century town is considered the cheapest place in Russia to live. But in other ways it is a virtual hell: Ekaterinodar is a foul smelling, filthy town, a soulless place without history, where the streets, littered now with large numbers of rotting animals, all run at right angles.

SUMMER 1919. CAUCASUS. General Denikin's White Army begins its advance towards Moscow.

JULY 25, 1919. EKATERINODAR. Uspenskii manages to send the first in a series of five letters to Alfred Richard Orage, who is the editor of the *New Age* and whom Uspenskii met in London in 1914 when returning to Russia from his second journey to the East. Uspenskii describes ordinary life amid a revolution. "The prices of all products and necessities have risen by twenty, fifty, a hundred, or six hundred times," he says. "Workmen's wages have risen twenty, fifty, or even a hundred times. But the salary of an ordinary brain-worker—a teacher, journalist or doctor—has risen in the best cases by no more than three times and, very often has not risen at all, but has actually decreased. If you earn 2,000 rubles a month," he says, "you are considered to be doing well; but often one meets with earnings of 1,000, 800, or 600 rubles. But the cheapest pair of boots cost 900 rubles, a pound of tea 150 rubles, a bottle of wine 60 rubles, and so on. On the whole, you may reckon a ruble now as worth a pre-war kopeck, i.e., its hundredth part."

Aware now of Uspenskii's plight, Orage contacts his friend Major Frank Pinder, a British intelligence officer responsible for the Baku-

Batum oil pipeline who is also serving in General Denikin's White Army. Pinder contacts Uspenskii and offers him a job on his staff, paying his salary out of his own pocket.

While in Ekaterinodar, Uspenskii receives a letter from Gurdjieff, who says he has reached Tiflis and has opened there the Institute for the Harmonious Development of Man. Gurdjieff encloses a prospectus for the Institute. Uspenskii sees that he is listed as one of the Institute's "specialist teachers." Gurdjieff says he is preparing his ballet, *The Struggle of the Magicians*, but nowhere in the letter does he mention their past difficulties. Uspenskii sees this as "very characteristic."[49] These difficulties he considers "very real." His decision to leave Gurdjieff had cost him dearly, he says, and he could "not give it up so easily, the more so because all his [Gurdjieff's] motives could be seen."[50]

Others around Uspenskii believe that when the revolution is over they will be able to return to "the old life." But Uspenskii has no such illusions. "In the face of the weakness of the intelligentsia," he says, "... it [Bolshevism] began openly to wage war on culture, to destroy all cultural values, and to annihilate the intelligentsia as the representative of culture."

When he had left Petersburg in 1917, he says, "the ground had fallen away behind me." He now recognizes what so many hide from themselves—there is *"no way back."*

"To no place that I had left," he says, "was it possible to return."

All bridges to his past life are literally burnt behind him.

There is no possibility of return to anything. His whole life, as it were, is wiped out, erased.[51]

Years before, he had foreseen all this. As he had said of the Bolsheviks as early as 1905, "Some of them are very nice people, quite sincere and terribly unselfish. But those will perish. Only scoundrels will survive." He had attended some of their meetings. "They just talked and talked: how bad everything was, how miserable everybody was, and how beautiful everything would be if there were no police, no Cossacks and no General Governors....But when it came to having tea, it transpired that

49. Not seeing he is identified with what, for him, happened in Essentuki, Uspenskii believes his interpretation of his impressions is accurate. Any mention of "past difficulties" by Gurdjieff, whatever tack he may take, only legitimizes Uspenskii's identification. By ignoring it, Gurdjieff forces Uspenskii to keep working with it, keep 'eating' it.

50. Uspenskii apparently forgets that Gurdjieff had said a pupil can never see the teacher. Or, and this perhaps approximates Uspenskii's attitude more closely, ***he no longer sees himself as a pupil.*** In any case, Uspenskii does not go to Tiflis.

51. For a man of rare sensitivity and intelligence, this enormous sense of loss and emptiness—the virtual "death" of his past—must have caused a great emotional wound. But Uspenskii, however great his pessimism about ordinary life, is too strong a man to ever totally give up.

the members of the committee had eaten all the cakes and oranges, and drunk all the tea! So there was nothing left for the rest of us."

Whatever their difficulties, Gurdjieff agrees with Uspenskii about the political situation. Gurdjieff believes "Marxism to be satanic."

Asked by a friend what practical results the Work had produced in him, Uspenskii says that because of it he had acquired a "strange confidence."

"This is not self-confidence in the ordinary sense," he says, "quite the contrary, rather is it a confidence in the unimportance and insignificance of *self*, that self which we usually know." This confidence stems from his realizing that "if something terrible happened to me... it would be *not* I who would meet it, not this ordinary I, but another I within me who would be equal to the occasion." He goes on to say that when Gurdjieff asked him two years before if he had felt a new I inside him, he said that he did not. "Now," declares Uspenskii, "I can speak otherwise."

With that, Uspenskii collects a small group around him and begins to teach the teaching that Gurdjieff had brought. In doing so, he makes a discovery: "Gurdjieff astonished us in St. Petersburg by his capacity to see in people their hidden fundamental features. The nexus was that the whole of one's character is already wound round one particular feature or round an axle or a reel. This capacity in him looked almost miraculous. And now I saw the same capacity in myself." [52]

AUGUST 16, 1919. EKATERINODAR. Denikin captures the city. Against his orders, Denikin's men begin to rape and pillage. Jewish pogroms are mounted.

AUGUST 26, 1919. NOVOROSSIYSK. Denikin captures the city.

SEPTEMBER 20, 1919. KURSK. Denikin captures the city. The White Army is now only 330 miles from Moscow.

SEPTEMBER 26, 1919. Denikin's White Army surrounds the forces of Nestor Ivanovich Makhno, a charismatic guerrilla leader. A semiliterate peasant and anarchist, he sides with neither the Whites nor the Bolsheviks. Makhno's guerrillas, flying the black anarchist flag, withstand the onslaught and inflict a defeat on Denikin's Whites.

AUTUMN 1919. NOVOROSSIYSK. A second letter from Gurdjieff reaches Uspenskii who, apparently, makes no reply. Both Petrov and Zacharov show up in Ekaterinodar, both in a "negative frame of mind" about the Work. Uspenskii's advice: "It is imperative to make a distinction between the system and Gurdjieff."

52. In this way, he rationalizes his 'equality' with Gurdjieff.

OCTOBER 14, 1919. Denikin's army takes Orel. Moscow is now only 245 miles away. Tula is next, only 122 miles from Moscow. Meanwhile, in the Ukraine, Makhno's guerrillas attack Denikin from the rear, cutting supply lines and taking cities.

1919. TIFLIS. "A man of striking appearance. Short, dark and swarthy, with penetrating and clever eyes; no one could be in his company for many minutes without being impressed by the force of his personality. One did not need to believe him infallible, but there was no denying his extraordinary all-round intelligence." This is how the journalist Carl Bechhofer-Roberts describes the Gurdjieff he finds in Tiflis. Uspenskii has given him a letter of introduction, and Gurdjieff takes him to a number of obscure Georgian and Persian restaurants and then to a bathhouse.

In the evenings, Bechhofer-Roberts visits the Institute and watches rehearsals for *The Struggle of the Magicians.* Gurdjieff tells him that the dances "were based on movements and gestures which had been handed down by traditions and paintings in Tibetan monasteries, where he had been. The music, also, was of mysterious tradition. He himself could not play a note, and knew nothing of composition; but the academician [Thomas de Hartmann] who interpreted his ideas assured me that he had learned more of the theory of music from Gurdjieff than in any of the schools. The decorations and costumes were also his work; he had even painted and sewn them himself."

For the third time now, Gurdjieff has tried to establish his Institute. But the promised building from the Tiflis government never materialized and the temporary quarters Gurdjieff was given were unsuitable.

"I finally gave up wasting my time and energy," he says, "in the struggle with the conditions round me."

He decides to leave for Constantinople.

OCTOBER 20, 1919. OREL. The Red Army recaptures Orel from Denikin, breaking the White advance on Moscow and sending it into full retreat. Makhno's guerilla forces continue to ravage Denikin's rear forces, depriving it of much needed supplies.

NOVEMBER 1, 1919. Forty-one-year-old Baron Pyotr Nikolaevich Wrangel, a Caucasian general, takes command of Denikin's remnants. Says Denikin of the struggle: "Not only did the experience cripple the body. It deformed the soul as well."

DECEMBER 1919. Denikin escapes to Europe. The Red Army pursues Makhno, destroying his forces.

EARLY JANUARY 1920. NOVOROSSIYSK. Uspenskii and his family make their way to Odessa and from there to Constantinople.

JANUARY 1920. GERMANY. Hitler becomes chief of party propaganda for the German Workers' Party, which in a few months will change its name to National Socialist German Workers' Party. Party members will be known as Nazis.

LATE JANUARY 1920. CONSTANTINOPLE. Uspenskii, his wife Sophia, and her daughter Lenochka with her one-year-old son Lonya arrive. Twelve years earlier Uspenskii had been here. But that city no longer exists.

The Constantinople he finds is not only noisier but "rapidly acquiring a Western drabness and hideousness." Despite the new and teeming crowds which throng its streets—the repatriated Turkish soldiers, the penniless Russian refugees, the assorted flotsam of humanity—the city, a living museum of long gone Byzantium, seems to Uspenskii more empty.

He and his family live in one of the refugee camps on the island of Prinkipo. A half-hour ferry ride from the city of Constantinople, Prinkipo lies about ten miles southeast in the Sea of Marmara. He visits Péra, the Russian and European quarter where he had previously stayed and where many of his friends lived. But none remain.

He earns money by teaching English to Russian exiles and giving mathematics lessons to children. He begins to give lectures in Péra at the White Russian Club, the *Russky Mayak*. As he did in Rostov and Ekaterinodar, he connects the ideas of esotericism with those of psychology and philosophy.

He receives some good news. *Tertium Organum* has been translated into English and published in America by Nicholas Bessaraboff, an emigrant of the Russian Revolution, and Claude Bragdon.

SPRING 1920. CONSTANTINOPLE. Uspenskii, looking for additional places to hold lectures, meets an Englishwoman, forty-seven-year-old Mrs. Winifred Beaumont, who offers the drawing room of her apartment in Péra. There Uspenskii meets Mrs. Beaumont's lover, twenty-three-year-old John Godolphin Bennett, head of a section of British intelligence in Constantinople. Uspenskii must be surprised, as Mrs. Beaumont is only six years younger than Bennett's mother, and Bennett, it turns out, is still married to his wife Evelyn, pregnant in England. Both Mrs. Beaumont and Bennett are personal friends of Prince Sabaheddin, a nephew of the reigning Sultan and son of a famous Turkish reformer. The Prince also begins to attend Uspenskii's meetings held every Wednesday afternoon. The diminutive Prince, slight and delicate, has an open mind and is well-versed in the subject of self-transformation. He has traveled to the capitals of Europe, and owns a house in Switzerland (where he first met Mrs. Beaumont). Among his many friends is Rudolph Steiner, the founder of Anthroposophy. Also attracted to the lectures is Boris Mouravieff, a rather feline-looking Russian aristrocrat, who will later become a friend of a sort of Uspenskii's.[53]

SPRING 1920. TIFLIS. Gurdjieff's Institute gradually dissolves. He decides to liquidate everything, break with everything that tied him to Russia and renounces "once and for all the idea of making Russia the permanent center of the activities of my Institute." Soon the group will leave for Constantinople.

Earlier, Major Frank Pinder had been captured by the Red Army in Rostov and condemned to death. The sentence was never carried out. He now meets Gurdjieff. As does Carl Bechhofer-Roberts. One afternoon, Bechhofer-Roberts finds Gurdjieff, "a curious individual," sitting at a café with Paolo Yashvili, a Georgian poet, and a group of poets, sculptors and émigré politicians. He says:

> He had a circle in Moscow in the old days, and many members of it had followed him to the Caucasus in 1917 and wandered about with him ever since. He was still surrounded by this entourage of philosophers, doctors, poets, and dancers. He was not exploiting them; on the contrary, several of them were living on his diminishing means. And by them all he was esteemed, almost worshipped, as a guide to the eternal mysteries of the universe.

SUMMER 1920. GERMANY. Hitler designs the Nazi flag. In the middle of its red background is a white disk with a black swastika, the *hakenkreuz.* The red, white, and black colors are ancient symbols of the three forces or *gunas.* It's likely he got the idea of using the swastika from *Ostara,* an anti-Semitic magazine which used the swastika symbol. *Ostara* is dedicated to racial purity and published by a defrocked monk.

JULY 7, 1920. CONSTANTINOPLE. Six months after Uspenskii's arrival, Gurdjieff and his party arrive in Constantinople on a ship from Batum. With him are the de Hartmanns, Thomas and Olga; the de Salzmanns, Jeanne and Alexander; Major Frank Pinder, and assorted others. The group takes separate quarters in Péra.

On the first day Gurdjieff makes a poor man's stew from fat-tailed sheep for everyone. On the second day the group learns that Uspenskii and his family are living in Prinkipo. Gurdjieff asks everyone to bring sheep's heads.[54] Thomas de Hartmann says they "could be bought cheaply, already roasted in an oven and broken in pieces, brains and all,

53. This relationship will have disastrous consequences for Uspenskii.

54. Is there a connection between Gurdjieff hearing that Uspenskii is in Constantinople and his cooking sheep's heads for dinner?

ready for eating. Mr. Gurdjieff was very fond of sheep's head." There is also a soup and, of course, *douziko,* a strong anise-flavored Greek vodka.

Gurdjieff rents an apartment on Koumbaradji Street and soon sets up his "office" at the Black Rose, the rather dubious café frequented by a cross-section of White Russians, officers, whores, alcoholics, drug addicts, and assorted denizens of the night.

Uspenskii had broken with Gurdjieff nearly two years before. They had not seen one another since Essentuki. Now the two meet again at the Black Rose.

"In truth," says Uspenskii, "I was expecting Gurdjieff to come to Constantinople."

He is glad to see Gurdjieff and soon decides that "in the interests of the work, all former difficulties could be set aside and that I could work with him as in Petersburg."[55]

Uspenskii turns over to Gurdjieff his thirty or so students, mostly from the Russky Mayak. Among them is Boris Ferapontoff, a devotee of Nietzsche. Absent are Mrs. Beaumont and young Bennett. Their interest is not strong enough to make a commitment. Uspenskii continues to lecture at Mrs. Beaumont's apartment, perhaps in his role, given Gurdjieff's Tiflis prospectus, as a "specialist teacher."

At some point during Uspenskii's early days in Constantinople, he meets Boris Mouravieff. An intellectual with a great love of books, Mouravieff has a keen, if conventionally disposed, mind and morality. He never trusted, much less understood, Gurdjieff. Given Mouravieff's attitude, his influence on Uspenskii had to be negative.

August 1920. Prince Sabaheddin telephones Bennett to ask if he might invite to Uspenskii's afternoon lectures a newly arrived friend. The Prince tells Bennett that though he had met this friend only three or four times, first in 1908 and the last in 1912, he regards him "as one of the very few men who had been able to penetrate into the hidden brotherhoods of Central Asia." The Prince tells Bennett, too, that he would be meeting "the most remarkable man he would ever know." Coming from the Prince, whom Bennett regards highly, this is high praise.

The Prince's friend arrives at about half-past nine in the evening, long after the lecture is over and Uspenskii has departed, but he shows not the least sign of embarrassment. Bennett observes that the man—his name of course was Gurdjieff—greets "the Prince in Turkish with an accent that was a strange mixture of cultured Osmanli and some uncouth Eastern dialect."

Introduced to the Prince's friend,[56] Bennett says:

55. Setting aside and not working through these "difficulties," Uspenskii keeps in place the conditions for a future break.

"I met the strangest eyes I have ever seen. The two eyes were so different that I wondered if the light had played some trick on me."

The difference, Bennett realizes, is not because of any kind of cast or defect in either eye but, rather, in their expression.

Of Gurdjieff's general appearance, Bennett says: "He had long, black mustaches fiercely curled upwards. He wore a kalpack, that is, an astrakhan cap [and a shaved head beneath]." Gurdjieff tells Bennett, perhaps for effect, that he was born in 1866, thus making himself fifty-four years old, practically twice Bennett's age.

As both Bennett and the Prince have a keen interest in hypnotism, the conversation eventually turns there. The Prince asks Bennett to relate the experiments he has been making. Gurdjieff listens attentively.

"I felt," says Bennett, "that he was not so much following my words as participating in the experience. I have never before had the same feeling of being understood better than I understood myself."

As Gurdjieff speaks about levels of experience in relation to hypnotism, it is quickly evident to Bennett that "this man had specialized knowledge of a kind I had not met with before."

At one point, Bennett speaks of his discovery of the fifth dimension—he had had an out-of-body experience during the war—and his belief that it is the region of free will.

"Your guess is right," answers Gurdjieff. "There are higher dimensions or higher worlds where the higher faculties of man have free play."

He explains to Bennett that theoretical understanding is of no use, as one remains where they are. Even the crystallization of a finer body is not enough in that it, too, is under material laws. He tells him that he himself must change, for, "Within this sphere there is no freedom. Neither your knowledge nor all your activity will give you freedom. This is because you have no *varlik*, no real being."

At one point, Gurdjieff tells Bennett: "You have the possibility of changing, but I must warn you that it will not be easy. You are still full of the idea that you can do what you like."

When leaving, Gurdjieff invites Bennett and Mrs. Beaumont to a demonstration of Temple Dances the next Saturday evening. When Bennett and Mrs. Beaumont go to the demonstration they are surprised to see, of all people, Uspenskii. He had given no indication that he knew

56. Is it to be taken as just a coincidence that Gurdjieff shows up at Mrs. Beaumont's apartment? The Prince's fortunes, financial and political, are at a low ebb and Uspenskii has turned over most of his pupils. So why is Gurdjieff there? A possibility may be that he has heard about Bennett, a brilliant, ambitious, and clever young man, who has an interest in the occult—and has come to recruit him. It is interesting, as well, that Gurdjieff speaks to Bennett of his *idée fixe* of the moment, the fifth dimension. In Petersburg he had insisted Uspenskii abandon his notions of the fourth dimension.

Gurdjieff. Though impressed with the dances, Bennett and Mrs. Beaumont do not become members of Gurdjieff's circle.

SEPTEMBER 1920. Gurdjieff opens his Institute once again, this time on the ground floor of a large house near the Galata Tower in Péra at 13 Abdullatif Yemeneci Sokak, three doors from the Grand Rabbinate and within a stone's throw of the *Mevlanahanesi* of the Whirling Dervishes. Here, as he did in Petersburg, Uspenskii devotes himself to helping Gurdjieff organize the Work. The movements and sacred dances are practiced and self-remembering and self-observation are emphasized, as is work with the centers. Students are told by Gurdjieff that "effort influenced by necessity or desire is no effort. To remember oneself is effort because no external shock can force us. Effort is for the sake of consciousness. Struggle with habits gives a taste of effort. Self-remembering helps balance centers, changes chemical processes, and improves nutrition." Students also study the science of numbers, the Cabala, magical arts, and the traditions of Asian schools concerning religious myths.

Both Uspenskii and Gurdjieff work together on Gurdjieff's ballet *The Struggle of the Magicians,* which is becoming a leitmotif of their relationship. When they first met in April 1915, Gurdjieff had spoken to Uspenskii about his ballet. In the intervening years, however, he had said nothing more. Now he tells Uspenskii that the ballet is not a "mystery" but more of a beautiful spectacle with "a certain meaning hidden beneath the outward form." He says, too, that the ballet has "three ideas lying at the basis." Uspenskii comes to understand it is not so much a ballet, but more "a series of dramatic and mimic scenes held together by a common plot." The dances and movements are to convey certain laws of the universe and thus are "sacred dances." Of particular interest to Uspenskii is that Gurdjieff says the *same* performers will act and dance in both the scenes of the White Magician and also the Black Magician; the movements of the first being beautiful and harmonious, and in the second, ugly and disharmonious. Working with Gurdjieff on the ballet, Uspenskii comes to see sides of Gurdjieff previously hidden—the artistic and poetical.

The Struggle of the Magicians takes place in a large commercial town of the East. Gafar, a handsome rich Parsi, young and full of pride, falls in love with Zeinab, a twenty-one-year-old Indo-Persian beauty. Gafar tries to seduce her but fails, so he enlists the help of the Black Magician. Unwilling at first because Zeinab is a student of the White Magician, he finally puts her under a spell. When the White Magician realizes what has happened to Zeinab, he breaks the spell. Gafar, angry, goes to the White Magician who shows him two possible fates. In both he is old but in one he is happy and cheerful and much loved; in the other he is evil and dissatisfied and regarded with aversion and disgust.

Seeing this creates a great inner struggle within Gafar.

The Magician tells him: "As you sow, so shall you reap. The deeds of the present determine the future, all that is good and all that is bad; both are the results of the past. It is the duty of every man in every moment of the present to prepare the future, improving on the past. Such is the law of fate. And 'May the source of all laws be blessed.'"

The Magician then raises his right hand and, looking upwards, his voice a whisper, says as if in prayer: "Lord Creator, and all you His assistants, help us to be able to remember ourselves at all times in order that we may avoid involuntary actions, as only through them can evil manifest itself."

NOVEMBER 12, 1920. Baron Wrangel's army is defeated by the Red Army at Perekop, 600 miles south of Moscow in the Crimea. He and what is left of his army sail for Constantinople. The Russian civil war is effectively over.

SPRING 1921. Gurdjieff invites Uspenskii to give lectures at his Institute once a week. Gurdjieff takes part, adding, when necessary, to Uspenskii's formulations. The relationship between them becomes more intimate. Gurdjieff visits Uspenskii and Madame Uspenskii in Prinkipo regularly for tea. He introduces Uspenskii to the cultural and dervish life of Constantinople. Work on the ballet moves at a furious pace as Gurdjieff rehearses the group in the subtle psychic and physical demands of his ballet. He has his students dance both the aggressive, inharmonious dances of the Black Magician as well as the reconciled and sophisticated harmonies of the White Magician.

Uspenskii notices that now Gurdjieff begins to dress in black and seems to go out of his way to provoke quarrels and misunderstandings.[57] This behavior alarms Uspenskii and, again, Uspenskii begins to see his teacher as he had in Petersburg—the old sore of Gurdjieff's "playing" reopens.[58]

57. He apparently sees no connection between Gurdjieff working on the ballet with his students and, with it as a 'ground,' working on their emotions through a change in his appearance and behavior. He is, in effect, "playing with the devil," which for Uspenskii is a trigger event.

58. "Gurdjieff had this lightly tinted whiteness. He never stopped playing with all the colors of life; that is why fools cry out against him. Uspenskii, who was a philosopher, tried to stay in the whiteness he had discovered; but if you are the disciple responsible for the kitchen, your duty is to prepare the food. If you refuse to do this, you will be sent away by the Master or you will leave of your own accord and your refusal will be a weight that will burden you for years and possibly even crush you." From Lizelle Reymond, *To Live Within* (Doubleday, 1971), p. 213.

Says Uspenskii, "with Mr. Gurdjieff there are only two 'I's; one very good and one very bad. I believe that in the end the good 'I' will conquer. But meanwhile it is very dangerous to be near him."

Many years later in London, Uspenskii will recount this time in Constantinople with much emotion. He will remember how he and Gurdjieff worked together for "entire days and nights." One night in particular Uspenskii can never forget. The two are sitting in a cafe on Koumbaradji Street just below the former Russian consulate. Suddenly Gurdjieff begins to sing in Persian "The Song of the Dervish," afterward translating it into Russian for Uspenskii. After fifteen minutes or so of singing—when Uspenskii finds himself completely buried under forms and symbols—Gurdjieff commands:

"There, now make *one line* out of that."

Gurdjieff continues singing for another fifteen minutes or so before declaring—"That is another line."

So of all the ideas and feelings to which Gurdjieff alludes, Uspenskii is to sum it all up in one line of poetry.[59]

By dawn, with the town just beginning to awaken, Uspenskii realizes that he had only written five verses and had stopped at the last line of the fifth verse. He is so tired that his brain would "not turn any more."

"It was some special knowledge, very sacred," says Uspenskii. "But we were both very tired."

They retire, agreeing to meet again the following night to resume the translation.

All of Uspenskii's doubts about Gurdjieff now vanish. "I felt sure I could work with him again." Uspenskii says, "That was again the real Gurdjieff."

But the next night Gurdjieff refuses to translate.

Instead Gurdjieff tells him dirty jokes.

"Nothing! Nothing but dirty jokes," cries Uspenskii. "Not even good jokes. Stupid dirty jokes!"[60]

For Uspenskii, there is the continuing problem of what he sees as the "two Gurdjieffs." The one who is serious and the other who plays. Says Uspenskii: "The problem of this 'play' or of the two personalities in Gurdjieff... at

59. Gurdjieff is using one of Uspenskii's strengths—the ability to sum up, or wrap up, long elaborations of thought. The nickname he had given Uspenskii is "Wraps Up The Thought."

60. The teacher sees where the student is because he sees objectively. But the student, interpreting everyone and everything subjectively, cannot see the teacher. Throughout their days together Gurdjieff plays Uspenskii like a violin, plucking his strings, playing cacophony or harmony, but Uspenskii, so focused is he, so identified with acquiring knowledge, never appears to see it in any but personal terms.

times became more acute, at times seemed to disappear—we could never give a final answer to it. I am obliged to say that the majority of people who after a long period of work with Gurdjieff left him, went away because they had ceased to believe in the 'play,' and had begun to see 'reality' in many things which he did and which they could not accept as 'reality.'"

The two men continue their struggle on secondary and unusual ground. It is over the allegiance of Uspenskii's wife, Sophia Grigorievna. There may be a curious parallel here to the struggle of the black and white magicians for the soul of the beautiful and virginal Zeinab.[61] But for the worldly-wise Madame Uspenskii the situation is clear: Gurdjieff is the teacher; her husband, the pupil.

Life in Constantinople and also with Gurdjieff is becoming more difficult and uncertain by the day. Uspenskii begins to think of a way out. "In former Russia," he says, "even in its distant outskirts, work had become impossible and we were gradually approaching the period [here] which I had foreseen in Petersburg, that is, of working in Europe."

Uspenskii expects the plague of Bolshevism to spread to Germany and from there to all of Europe. Should England align itself with the United States, it might avoid Bolshevism. Once again, Uspenskii begins thinking of going to England. But the question is how to get there.

MAY 14, 1921. A telegram from London arrives at Uspenskii's apartment in Prinkipo:

> Deeply impressed by your book *Tertium Organum.* Wish to meet you New York or London. Will pay all expenses.
>
> —Lady Rothermere

Inquiring of Bennett as to who this English woman might be, Uspenskii learns that she is the wife of one of London's wealthy newspaper moguls and has great influence with the Prime Minister, Lloyd George. Earlier Uspenskii had given Bennett three copies of the English translation of *Tertium Organum.*

The telegram must have seemed like a very strong omen. Uspenskii had received a 100 pound check for royalties from his publisher, funds he hoped to use to emigrate to England. With his relationship with Gurdjieff ending, his pupils gone, his wife, Sophia Grigorievna, considering Gurdjieff her teacher, there is no reason for Uspenskii to remain in Constantinople. Bennett convinces the British Consulate that Uspenskii

61. According to Moore, *Gurdjieff: Anatomy of a Myth,* pp. 151–52, "there ensued a sharp tussle between Gurdjieff and Uspenskii for the allegiance of Madame Ouspensky." Moore supports his view with a letter which he claims Madame Uspenskii wrote at this time but, in fact, she wrote the letter three years later at the Prieuré in the autumn of 1924. The letter is quoted here, see p. 116. The original reference is Bennett's *Witness,* p. 158.

is a highly desirable visitor and procures visas for him and his family. A new octave from the West beckons.

At the same time Gurdjieff receives an invitation from the dancing master Jacques Dalcroze to come to Germany. (The invitation has been initiated by Alexander de Salzmann who painted sets for Dalcroze at the Hellerau in Germany.)

MAY 1921. Conditions aren't right and Gurdjieff closes his Institute.

Uspenskii tells Gurdjieff of his idea to write a book giving Gurdjieff's Petersburg lectures and talks with commentaries of his own. Gurdjieff agrees and authorizes its publication. Uspenskii then begins to write *Fragments of an Unknown Teaching*. He will finish the book in the spring of 1925.

JULY 26, 1921. MOSCOW. With Russia experiencing famine in which five million starve to death, Lenin becomes ill. Any loud noise shocks him. The bells on his telephone are replaced with electric lights that flash for incoming calls.

AUGUST 13, 1921. CONSTANTINOPLE. Georgi Ivanovitch Gurdjieff embarks for Germany. Among his entourage most notably is Sophia Grigorievna, Uspenskii's wife, and her family. What exactly has happened between her and Uspenskii is not clear; her choice of teacher is beyond doubt.

AUGUST 1921. CONSTANTINOPLE. Pyotr Demianovich Uspenskii, a still solid, strong-jawed man of forty-two, departs for London, alone.

PART II

MAGICIANS AT WAR

AUGUST 22, 1921. BERLIN. ATTRACTED TO GERMANY BECAUSE OF ITS CENTRAL GEOGRAPHICAL LOCATION AND CULTURAL LEVEL, GURDJIEFF AND his students arrive. Forty-nine-years-old, he must have a sense that time is growing short. If he is to accomplish his mission, he must move quickly. Though funds are always in question, Gurdjieff immediately rents a hall for movements in the expensive Schargendorf district. His café of choice becomes the Romanische Café, along the Kurfurstendamn.

The Stjoernvals have gone to Finland to sell property in order to help Gurdjieff with finances. Among those in his company in Berlin are the de Hartmanns, de Salzmanns, Mesdames Uspenskii, Zhukov, and Lavrona, Boris Ferapontoff, and two gifted dancers, Olgivanna Hinzenberg (who will later marry the architect Frank Lloyd Wright) and Elizabeta Galumnian.

SEPTEMBER 1921. LONDON. Arriving from Constantinople, Uspenskii is feted and treated like visiting royalty by Lady Rothermere. She introduces him to the select of London's aristocratic, literary, and esoteric worlds. He also renews his friendship with A. R. Orage, whom he had last seen in 1914, and who, during his last days in Russia, published his

"Letters From Russia" and arranged for financial help. Though Uspenskii's command of English is far from perfect, his unique esoteric knowledge, his seriousness and intelligence make a powerful impression. A series of lectures is arranged at the Quest Society[1] in early November.

Orage, at forty-eight years of age, is five years Uspenskii's senior. Taller and more angular than the square-framed Uspenskii, Orage is a man of infinite charm and grace. He has established himself in British society as an influential editor and literary critic, and is a friend of people like T. S. Elliot, George Bernard Shaw, and H. G. Wells. Like Uspenskii, he possesses a formidable intellect with a gift for quickly assimilating and articulating metaphysical complexities. Like Uspenskii, he developed an early interest in Nietzsche and is deeply versed in theosophy and the occult. Like Uspenskii, Orage is a magician of sorts, able to capture and sway people's attention and galvanize them into action. The Hindu classic *Mahabharata* is his favorite literary work and he is familiar with both hatha yoga and pranayama.

Having so brilliant an intellect, an influential position, and a large following, Orage expected to meet Uspenskii and this new teaching on equal ground. In terms of personal power, Orage is an imposing figure. A close friend speaks of him as "...not impressing by his features so much as by that which was outside and beyond his features. You were conscious of his aura; you felt his presence so much that you forgot details."

But during their first serious discussion, Orage finds himself no match for Uspenskii, who wastes no time in summarily dismissing all of Orage's views and theories as irrelevant. Remembers an intimate friend of Orage who was present at this meeting:

"Orage was shocked and hurt... [for] at every point where their views clashed, Orage had to realize that he was the novice and Uspenskii the master."

Being so easily outgunned by this Russian journalist, whom just seven years before he felt the equal of, if not the better, could not have been a pleasant experience for a dominating intellect like Orage. But Orage is also a man of great integrity with a genuine thirst for real knowledge. He introduces Uspenskii to members of his psychosynthesis group, which aimed to integrate psychoanalysis with religious perspectives. Among the members are doctors Maurice Nicoll and James Young, both associates of C. G. Jung; E. M. Eder, an intimate of Sigmund Freud; J. M. Alcock; Havelock Ellis; and Dimitri Mitrinović, a Serbian mystic and prophet, and attaché of the Serbian Legation in London.

NOVEMBER 1921. LONDON. Lecturing at Lady Rothermere's studio in Circus Road, St. John's Wood, Uspenskii speaks without gestures, and

1. See Notes.

with no attempt to convince. His style is dry, authoritative. Paraphrasing Gurdjieff, he asserts that the morass of complacency into which mankind has strayed is the result of man being a machine. Worse, this machine's blind self-satisfaction, its ceaseless demand for self-gratification, has led modern civilization to the violence and crime that now breeds at every level of society. If man does not awaken to his true potentialities, and so fails to fulfill the purpose of his creation, he will become a thing of no account. Alluding to Christ, Uspenskii asserts that mankind will be the chaff that is cut down and cast into the fire.

Hard words. An even harder vision. Yet with World War I still hanging in the air like sulfur, no cosmetics are necessary. For a time, people can hear. Indicative of the general reaction is that of Dr. Maurice Nicoll, who rushes home and shakes his wife out of bed, telling her, "You must come and hear Uspenskii. He is the only man who has ever answered my questions."

Declares another, "His looks did not impress me. Nevertheless, when he smiled his eyes lit up with a warm twinkle which encouraged confidence and confidences. His nose made one think of a bird's strong beak; indeed, when sitting in reflection or repose he hunched himself together and looked like a dejected bird huddling up in a rainstorm. He was obviously a man of dominant if not domineering type of character, with determination—or obstinacy—written over his every feature."

Because of the interest generated, a house is put at Uspenskii's disposal for further lectures. Soon, an ardent audience of English intellectuals, professional people, and aristocrats attend lectures three or four evenings a week at Earl's Court, 38 Warwick Gardens. About forty or fifty come on a regular basis, many becoming his pupils. The Fourth Way, the Uspenskiian version, has established itself in the West.

Bennett, having recently returned from Turkey, visits Uspenskii at his hotel on Russell Square. Uspenskii tells him of the success he is meeting with. Bennett says he has decided to return to Turkey and would like to hear some of his lectures. Uspenskii tells him: "Come if you like. But you cannot decide. If you get to Turkey, it is not because you decide. You have no power to choose. No one has power to choose." Bennett does return to Turkey but, as he recounts, "The memory of this talk remained with me, and eventually drew me back to London to study and work with him."

"I spent two hours with the man [Uspenskii]," says Rosamund Bland, a young lady interested in the Work, "and he certainly struck me as being a wonderful person. Incidently, he has the sweetest smile in the world but that is his only attraction from an ordinary point of view, counting out the brains, of course."

NOVEMBER 24, 1921. BERLIN. Gurdjieff gives his first lecture. The theme is man's mechanicality as seen through his habitual postures. The de Hartmanns introduce him to influential friends such as Count Valvitz and Princess Gagarin, but nothing comes of it.

Gurdjieff tries to purchase the Hellerau in Dresden, the former center of Dalcroze's Eurhythmics Institute. Complications result. A legal battle ensues. Germany, despite its Teutonic spirit of self-sacrifice and cultivation of virtue—traits that seemed to make it a natural base for Gurdjieff's teaching—has strangely turned a cold shoulder. Could it have been as simple a thing as Gurdjieff's dark complexion? Whatever— Germany was not to be.

DECEMBER 1, 1921. LONDON. "Uspenskii seemed rather depressed when I last saw him," says Rosamund Bland, "and talked of going away, back to Constantinople, because things were not going well here. As far as I can make out he thinks I am the only one who takes things really seriously and who can be of use to the work from his point of view, and it is not worth his while to spend so much energy in order to perhaps get one person into a condition where they can be useful. If he is going to spend so much force, he must have more result than that."

EARLY FEBRUARY 1922. LONDON. Six months after Gurdjieff's arrival in the West, his Institute for the Harmonious Development of Man remains only an idea. Hearing of Uspenskii's success, the fate of these two men ever entwined, Gurdjieff crosses the Channel. They meet and Uspenskii's attitude becomes "much more definite." He sees again, so he believes, "all the former obstacles that had begun to appear in Essentuki." He doesn't believe it's possible to work with Gurdjieff. Yet, still he expects "a great deal more from Gurdjieff's work." And so he doesn't break entirely. In fact, Uspenskii decides to help Gurdjieff establish his Institute in London.

FEBRUARY 13, 1922. LONDON. Gurdjieff's first talk[2] in London is at the Theosophical Hall at Warwick Gardens. Some sixty people attend. Many, including Orage, already think of themselves as Uspenskii's pupils. Gurdjieff and his translators, Major Frank Pinder and Olga de Hartmann, along with Uspenskii, mount the platform. The audience, awed by Gurdjieff's presence, sits in petrified silence. Gurdjieff, as always, comes right to the point:

"When we speak of ourselves ordinarily we speak of 'I.' We say *'I' did this... 'I' think this... 'I' want to do this*—but this is a mistake. There is no such 'I' or rather there are hundreds, thousands of little 'I's in every one

2. The exact number of meetings in London and the dates on which they were held remain uncertain, given the references in the public sources from that period.

of us.... We are governed by external circumstances. All our actions follow the line of least resistance to the pressure of outside circumstances."

Gurdjieff is asked if it is possible to alter one's emotions through acts of judgment.

"One center of our machine cannot change another center," he answers. "For example: in London I am irritable, the weather and the climate dispirit me and make me bad-tempered whereas in India I am good-tempered. Therefore my judgment tells me to go to India and I shall drive out the emotion of irritability. But then, in London, I find I can work; in the tropics not as well. And so, there I should be irritable for another reason. You see, emotions exist independently of the judgment and you cannot alter one by means of another."

"Mr. Gurdjieff, what would it be like to be conscious in essence?"

"Everything more vivid," is Gurdjieff's memorable, rapier-like reply.

After this first talk, there is no question of who is teacher, who the student for one member of the audience. "I *knew* that Gurdjieff was the teacher," declares Orage. "Uspenskii for me represented knowledge—great knowledge; Gurdjieff, understanding—though of course Gurdjieff had all the knowledge, too."

MARCH 5, 1922. LONDON. Gurdjieff returns from Germany to give a second talk and takes questions. Frank Pinder is translating. At its close he chastises his audience:

"All the questions I have heard tonight are higher mathematics. Nobody knows elementary mathematics.[3] And so such questions are useless."

Later, in speaking privately with Uspenskii, he finally delivers an all-out assault.

> He was working on the wrong lines, Gurdjieff told him. He was too intellectual. He lacked an understanding of the real purpose of the Work and of Gurdjieff himself. All his vast knowledge would be useless, he told him, unless he worked on himself in order to understand basic principles. If he truly wished to understand, he must stop teaching and begin again—work again with Gurdjieff.

It is a scorching appraisal. How could Uspenskii not hear it? Not understand his identification? Believe that he was a spiritual equal, or near-equal, to Gurdjieff? Given that Uspenskii is a man of rare intellect, honest and uncompromising in his search for real knowledge, his blindness here and elsewhere shows the strength of buffers.[4] But Uspenskii didn't hear the appraisal—he heard the assault.

3. This is a subtle criticism of Uspenskii who is a mathematician.

4. Psychological 'partitions' created to lessen shocks and contradictions so that "a man can always be in the right." See *Search*, pp. 154–55.

MARCH 15, 1922. LONDON. Failing to awaken his rebellious pupil privately, Gurdjieff plays one of his last cards. He gives still another talk at Warwick Gardens, this time on the theme of "Essence and Personality." Instead of Uspenskii, Gurdjieff has Frank Pinder translate.

"Normal human beings are the exception. Nearly everyone has only the essence of a child. It is not natural that in a grown-up man the essence should be a child. Because of this, he remains timid underneath and full of apprehensions. This is because he knows that he is not what he pretends to be, but he cannot understand why."

Uspenskii suddenly breaks in, saying that Pinder's translation is not accurate. "Pinder is interpreting for me—not you," answers Gurdjieff.

He then directly attacks Uspenskii, repeating in public now what had been said in private: *Uspenskii is neither mandated nor qualified to teach....*[5]

Later, Gurdjieff remarks to Pinder of the meeting: "Now they will *have* to choose a teacher." Presumably, Uspenskii will have to as well: either himself or Gurdjieff. But for all of Gurdjieff's words and the enormity of his presence, they are without effect. Uspenskii continues to believe in his conclusions. Yet, despite the anger and betrayal he must have felt, he still doesn't break completely with Gurdjieff. In fact, he helps to collect money for Gurdjieff's London Institute. But he does say unequivocally—"I had decided for myself that if the Institute opened in London I would go either to Paris or to America."

And so, as it has openly continued since Uspenskii first broke with Gurdjieff in Essentuki, the struggle between the two continues.[6] The Institute finally opens but Gurdjieff, though the Home Secretary agrees he is no Bolshevik, has a visa problem. Lady Rothermere says she will attempt to wield her influence. But to no avail. Gurdjieff's visa denied, the Institute closes.

Uspenskii's old love, Anna Ilinishna Butkovsky-Hewitt, and he meet in London. Anna is disturbed by the change in him. "He had developed a hard outer shell," she says, "and I wondered then why he had crushed the gentle, poetic radiance of his Petersburg days. Possibly he thought of this side of himself as a weakness, yet it was in this happy mood that his inspiration and vision were strongest: the intellect had nothing to do with it."

5. It is a brutal disrobing. Uspenskii, the pupil Gurdjieff had staked his hopes upon to help him establish his teaching, takes himself to be awake. Uspenskii believes he is able to judge his teacher's motives, his character, and yet Uspenskii had still not worked on essence. His development is only partial. To continue to teach would crystallize him at a level that would make further development impossible. So though the verbal assault is brutal, it is necessary.

6. Though never mentioned by either, it seems reasonable to conclude the struggle, given Uspenskii's experience in Finland, occurs on both the physical and "astral" planes.

JULY 14, 1922. PARIS. With Germany inhospitable to Gurdjieff's Institute and the English door shut, France becomes the choice by default. Gurdjieff arrives from Germany accompanied by the de Hartmanns. They are met by the de Salzmanns.

Soon it is learned that a beautifully furnished château is available at Fontainebleau, forty-four miles from Paris. It is the property of the widow of Fernand Labori, the lawyer who successfully defended Captain Dreyfus, who had been accused of spying. Called the Prieuré des Basses Loges, it has an interesting history, having once been a Carmelite Monastery and, earlier, the home of Louis XIV's famous mistress, Madame de Maintenon.

The château sits behind a high stone wall and heavy iron gates, and, it has not been lived in since 1914. A small fountain lies within the gates of the two-story château; to the rear is a terrace with two more fountains and a long avenue of lime, maple, chestnut, and conifer trees. In the gardens there are an enormous glass orangery, a small house in the gardens known as "Le Paradou," and other outbuildings. The château is set in a park of forty-five acres. An additional 200 acres, bounded by a stone wall, adjoin the Forest of Fontainebleau.

After some strong negotiating by Olga de Hartmann—Gurdjieff told her to remember herself at all times and never to forget her intention—the château is leased, fully furnished, for 65,000 francs with an option to buy for 700,000 francs.

AUGUST 30, 1922. LONDON. Orage tells his friend, the New Zealand short story writer Katherine Mansfield, near death from tuberculosis, about Uspenskii. She begins to attend Uspenskii's lectures. Her husband, John Middleton Murray, does as well, but he is not impressed. "I don't *feel* influenced by Uspenskii....I merely feel I've heard ideas like my ideas, but bigger ones, far more definite ones."

SEPTEMBER 30, 1922. PRIEURÉ. One year after his arrival in the West, Gurdjieff's Institute is established. It will be set up on the same basis as before, that is, "I wished to create around myself conditions in which man would be continually reminded of the sense and aim of his existence by an unavoidable friction between his conscience and the automatic manifestations of his nature." Funds for the Institute—"This child I had conceived," says Gurdjieff—are supplied by the English, notably Mary Lilian, Lady Rothermere, and Ralph Philipson, a Northumberland coal mine owner.

A prospectus for the Institute is written and circulated. It begins:

> The Institute for the Harmonious Development of Man by means of the system of Gurdjieff is, as it were, the continuation of the society known as the Seekers After Truth....

The prospectus continues with a short history of the society and then begins its analysis of the conditions and situation which faces modern man, who, it says, has become "an uprooted being, unable to adapt to his life, alien to all its present conditions." It shows where the problems lie and tells how the Institute will help its students to correct them.

MID-OCTOBER 1922. PRIEURÉ. Though the Institute does not officially open until November, Katherine Mansfield arrives. She has become convinced that Gurdjieff could not only help her with her disease but with a spiritual regeneration as well. Though it is obvious she has not long to live, Gurdjieff allows her to stay.

Her letters[7] give a feeling for what is taking place:

> It's a most wonderful old place in an amazingly lovely park. About forty people, chiefly Russians, are here working, at every possible kind of thing—I mean outdoor work, looking after animals, gardening, indoor work, music, dancing—it seems a bit of everything....A dancing hall is being built and the house is still being organized....Mr. Gurdjieff likes me to go into the kitchen in the late afternoon and 'watch.' I have a chair in a corner. It's a large kitchen with six helpers—Madame Ostrovsky [Ostrowska], the head [Gurdjieff's wife], walks about like a queen exactly—she is extremely beautiful. Mr. Gurdjieff strides in, takes up a handful of shredded cabbage and eats it...there are at least twenty pots on the stove—and it's so full of life and humor and ease that one wouldn't be anywhere else....The cows are being bought today—Gurdjieff is going to build a high couch in the stable where I can sit and inhale their breath! I know later on I shall be put in charge of those cows—Everyone calls them already 'Mrs. Murry's cows.'

OCTOBER 25, 1922. PRIEURÉ. Katherine Mansfield writes to her husband:

> I want to learn something that no books can teach me, and I want to try & escape from my terrible illness. That again you can't be expected to understand. You think I am like other people—I mean—*normal.* I'm not. I don't know which is the ill me or the well me. I am simply one pretense after another—only now I recognize it.
> I believe Mr. Gurdjieff is the only person who can help me. It is great happiness to be here. Some people are stranger than ever but the strangers I am at last feeling near and they are my own people at last. So I feel. Such beautiful understanding and sympathy I have never known in the outside world.

NOVEMBER 1922. PRIEURÉ. Students arrive, ringing the bell by the heavy iron gate. Ushered into the courtyard, they pass the small fountain and

7. According to Gurdjieff, only the constant sensing and knowledge of the inevitability of one's own death, as well as the death of everyone around us, can destroy the egoism that has swallowed up our essence. Katherine Mansfield's last letters stand as a testament to the working of this realization. They reflect the work she did on herself and the understanding she came to in so short a time.

enter a beautifully proportioned château with dormer windows set in a gray slate mansard roof. Inside they find oak paneled walls, ornate Empire mirrors, Oriental carpets, panther skins, Levantine pouffes, and other costly treasures. To the left of the entrance is a wide staircase leading to the top two floors, which have been christened by Gurdjieff "The Ritz," and the "Monk's Corridor," and the attic, "Cow's Alley." To the right is a reception room and long hallway, hung with paintings, leading to an elegant formal dining room, a library which has no books, a large salon with fireplace and a Pleyel grand concert piano, and a study and a game room further on.

Among those assembling are Gurdjieff's oldest students: the Stjoernvals, de Hartmanns, de Salzmanns, Uspenskii's wife Sophia, Elizabeta Galumnian, Olgivanna Hinzenberg, and, of course, Madame Ostrowska. Among those from London ringing the Prieuré's bell, marked "Sonnez fort" (ring loudly), are some very strong and successful people, such as A. R. Orage, Rowland Kenney, Dr. James Young, Misses Merston, Gordon, and Crowdy, Dr. Alsop, Champion Jones, and later, at Uspenskii's direction, J. G. Bennett.

The prospective pupils no doubt have come expecting to be initiated into the esoteric world, but says Gurdjieff, "Everything is body." Though none suspect it, none inhabit their bodies. The head and heart's relationship to the body is practically nil. Hard physical work helps to center and reconnect the pupils with their bodies, allowing their bodies to begin to breathe and eat normally. The pupils then learn what it is to actually inhabit a living, breathing body. Such work also allows pupils to struggle with reactions and attitudes of self-pity, sloth, superiority.

The pupils are put to work scrubbing latrines, felling trees, digging ditches, doing farm work, gardening, housework, laundry and the like. Everyone is up around four in the morning. Breakfast consists only of coffee, toast, bread and butter. For lunch there is stew with vegetables and perhaps a pudding. There follows a late afternoon break for tea, bread and butter. In the evening everyone bathes and dresses for dinner, which is often quite lavish. Generally, guests, older students and Gurdjieff eat in the spacious and well-furnished 'English' dining room, said to be where Madame de Maintenon entertained Louis XIV. There is a large table seating about twenty-five people, with two side tables seating twenty each. Gurdjieff sits in the middle of the large table facing the windows. Directly behind him on the mantelpiece rests a photo of his beloved father. In contrast, the 'Russian' dining room where the younger pupils eat is dark and bare except for a large table and benches. In good weather the pupils eat on the terrace.

After dinner Gurdjieff may give a talk, or Thomas de Hartmann might play music, or perhaps there are movements. Generally, it is midnight before people go to bed. Early Saturday evening the men take a communal Turkish bath; the women bathe earlier. After the men's bath there follows a feast and ritual toasts to idiots. Except for such interludes, the physical, emotional, and mental demands are great. This unrelenting pressure creates conditions in which students can see themselves—not as they imagine themselves to be—but as they really are.

Gurdjieff, of course, does his best to add to the pressure. Says one person, "He constantly manipulated people and situations so as to provoke friction, to create negative emotions between people and give them an opportunity of seeing something in themselves."

Gurdjieff's behavior at the Prieuré raises in his students the full spectrum of emotional reactions, everything "from reverent adoration to diabolical spasms of hatred."

NOVEMBER 4, 1922. PRIEURÉ. Dr. Maurice Nicoll gives up his lucrative Harley Street practice and he, along with his wife Catherine, their young baby, and a nurse, come to the Prieuré. Nicoll's first job, and one he will do for three months, is that of kitchen boy. The job is considered the most demanding at the Prieuré in that the work begins at 5 A.M. with lighting the boilers and lasts till 11 P.M. During that time hundreds of greasy plates, cups, glasses, and pots and pans must be washed with no soap and often no hot water. Meanwhile, his wife helps with the cooking and her sister, Champion Jones, cleans bathrooms. When anything went wrong, Gurdjieff would single out Nicoll as the scapegoat, calling "Nicoll!" and making a gesture of despair.

A Turkish bath is constructed in the form of a grotto on a hillside. Later, Gurdjieff demands a theater be built in a fortnight. Noticing how it is being built, Nicoll asks Gurdjieff, "Why don't you build more solidly?"

"This is only temporary," answered Gurdjieff. "In a very short time everything will be different. Everyone will be elsewhere. Nothing can be built permanently at this moment."

Sometimes in the evenings after dinner and movements, Gurdjieff gives a talk. It would often go on until midnight or later. He pours out a torrent of words lasting for several minutes then pauses for Frank Pinder, to translate.[8] Pinder condenses it all into a sentence or two. Gurdjieff looks at him, shrugs his shoulders, and smiles sardonically.

During the day when he is not in Paris, Gurdjieff can often be seen walking around the grounds urging people on—"Must be done in half the time," he implores.

8. Pinder had perfected his Russian while imprisoned by the Bolsheviks and awaiting a death sentence. Upon his release after the war, the British government made Pinder an officer of the Order of the British Empire.

He purposely places people in situations where they will experience a loss of face. Should false personality appear, he ruthlessly attacks it, forcing the students to see and rely upon that which is real in themselves.

"I cannot change your being," says Gurdjieff, "but I can create conditions, thanks to which you can change yourselves."

Uspenskii arrives at the Prieuré. He describes the students as "a very motley company." He feels, however, "the atmosphere on the whole is very right." He speaks with Katherine Mansfield who seems to him "halfway to death." He is struck by her striving "to find the truth whose presence she clearly feels but which she is unable to touch." She tells Uspenskii:

> I know that this is true and that there is no other truth. You know that I have long since looked upon all of us without exception as people who have suffered shipwreck and have been cast upon an uninhabited island, but who do not yet know of it. But these people here know it. The others, there, in life, still think that a steamer will come for them tomorrow and that everything will go on in the old way. These already know that there will be no more of the old way. I am so glad that I can be here.

Says Thomas de Hartmann of life at the Prieuré:

> The life of a person, like a ball, is thrown from one situation to another. Our prayer was the Work, which concentrated together all spiritual and physical forces. The variety and constant change of tasks continually reawakened us. We are given minimal hours of sleep, just enough to give strength for the following day. Instead of abstinence, there is spending of forces to the utmost, attentive work renewing energies as they are spent, in the manner of a rhythmic flywheel. There is no rejection of life within the Prieuré. On the contrary, life is expanded to the utmost intensity and spirituality.

Of all the newcomers to the Prieuré, the one who is to be the most help to Gurdjieff is A. R. Orage. Forty-nine-year-old Alfred Richard Orage has come to the devastating recognition that—"my intellectual life...was leading me nowhere."

For the seven years preceding his meeting Gurdjieff, the most influential figure in Orage's life was Serbian mystic Dimitri Mitrinović, who championed the idea of a panhumanity based on a vision of a united Christian Europe. Had it not been for Mitrinović, Orage believes he could not have come to what he called "the best and hardest decision of my life—to follow Gurdjieff."

Resigning as editor of the *New Age* and asked by his secretary why he was leaving, Orage answered—"I am going to find God." The ever fastidious Orage, now greatly overweight, arrives at the Prieuré and finds himself relegated to a small room, more like a cell. He undergoes a daunting experience of dawn-to-dusk labors, mostly mopping latrines and digging ditches until his hands bleed. Often Orage is awakened during the night and ordered to continue his digging. This he is to do until he receives permission to stop. Then, the trench dug, he is told to fill it in, which he does with no outward complaint.[9]

A Yorkshire country boy, Orage had grown up doing farm chores, but this is no help at the Prieuré. Too many years of soft living had taken its toll. Orage descends into the pit of despair:

"I had had no real exercise for years [and so] I suffered so much physically that I would go back to my room, a sort of cell, and literally cry with fatigue...I asked myself, 'Is this what I have given up my whole life for? At least I had something then. Now what have I?'"

Gurdjieff describes the Institute as "a hatching place for eggs. It supplies the heat. Chickens inside must try to break their shells then help and individual teaching is possible. Until then only collective method."

Fritz Peters, who came to the Prieuré in 1924 at eleven years of age, gives an insight into what was going on. Years afterward, speaking about conscious labor and intentional suffering that newcomers to the Prieuré were confronted with, he says:

> For the average person, it consisted largely in a preliminary period of joining in reasonably hard manual labor in a group....After a while, one became conscious of being thrust into somewhat frustrating circumstances having to do with the work—such as being forced to work with someone whose temperament clashed with yours, being taken off a job as soon as you became too interested in it, etc. Most of the novice students seemed to be put through a period of purposeful frustration. Inevitably, given the reputation of the school and its stated aims, they began to wonder just exactly what was being accomplished by doing physical labour, and nothing else. The frustration would usually increase because no one, including Gurdjieff, would answer their questions—they were simply told that for the time being they were to do as they were told. When they reached some kind of breaking point, they would suddenly be given an exercise—usually being told that they should observe themselves consciously while they worked and learn about themselves. If they stayed long enough they were gradually taken into the inner circle where they attended readings or listened to lectures and participated in the exercises....

Writing many years later, Orage's friend and biographer Philip Mairet says:

> It was precisely the complete submission to a will not his own that was, for Orage, the novelty and the value of the experience. He had known before what it was to be greatly influenced by others, which is

9. This is reminiscent of Milarepa's treatment by his teacher Marpa. See Lobsang P. Lhalungpa's, *The Life of Milarepa* (E. P. Dutton, 1977).

> quite another matter...but this was an explicit surrender to the spiritual authority of another, in order to attain something which, by definition, one could not know at one's 'present state of development.' Such a submission opens up immense possibilities of psychic and spiritual change, either positive or negative or both. The results doubtless depend upon the spirit in which such loyalty is given, much more than the way in which it is accepted. And the spirit in which Orage gave his fealty was sincere and devout.

At one point Orage's resistance to physical work ends—"When I was in the very depths of despair, feeling that I could go on no longer, I vowed to make an extra effort, and just then something changed in me." He finds he is able to work manually and at the same time keep his mind occupied with counting and other exercises. In doing so, his emotional being awakens, and experiences of a serene and ecstatic order open to him.

At this point Gurdjieff comes to him, declaring, "Now, Orage, I think you dig enough. Let us go to café and drink coffee."

For friends who visit him at the Prieuré, they are amazed to see an Orage with better color, one who is thinner, harder, and more virile-looking; one who sometimes even showed an almost childlike spontaneity.[10] In a space of months, the Prieuré has become for Orage "a house of devotion and Gurdjieff his spiritual preceptor."

Orage and Katherine Mansfield have talked nearly everyday. She had tried to write but had torn up her work. One day Orage goes to her room and finds that "her face shone as if she had been on Sinai." Once Orage and she had been lovers, and she speaks to him of the "Katherine Mansfield" he had known. She has been a camera, she says, but a selective one. Her attitude has determined what observations she selects. She has been passive, not creative. The result, she says, "like everything unconscious," has been evil. The "slices of life" she has portrayed in her short stories have been "partial, misleading, and a little malicious." Not one of her stories would she dare show to God.

In the future, she tells Orage, she would widen the lens of her camera and use it for a "conscious purpose"—showing how life appeared to a "creative attitude." To illustrate what she means, she says: "Two people fall in love and marry. One, or perhaps both of them, has had previous affairs, the remains of which still linger like ghosts in the home. Both wish to forget, but the ghosts still walk. How can this situation be presented?"

She says "the late lamented Katherine Mansfield" would of course see it in terms of her "passive, selective and resentful attitude," and the result

10. Because he had the courage to endure physical hardship and psychological despair, Orage had come to the experiencing of ecstasy—that is, his consciousness had been able to stand outside the body, knowing it and how it related to the universe.

would be "one of her famous satiric sketches, reinforcing in her readers the attitude in herself."

But as she is now she would see the situation as "an opportunity for the exercise and employment of all the intelligence, invention, imagination, bravery, endurance, and in fact all the virtues of the most attractive hero and heroine." Such a story, she continues, need not have a happy ending as the problem might be too large, but the sympathy of the reader would be supported "by the continuity and variety of the effort of one or both of the characters, by their indomitable renewal of the struggle, with ever fresh invention." Her aim was to make human virtues, not human failings, interesting.

On a second visit, Uspenskii and Katherine Mansfield sit in one of the salons and she tells him in a feeble voice that she has long looked upon people as those who "have suffered a shipwreck and have been cast upon an uninhabited island, but do not yet know of it. But these people here [at the Prieuré] know it. . . . I am so glad that I can be here."

DECEMBER 24, 1922. PRIEURÉ. Writes Katherine Mansfield:

> We are going to [celebrate Christmas] in tremendous style here. Every sort of lavish generous hospitable thing has been done by Mr. Gurdjieff. He wants a real old fashioned *English* Xmas—an extraordinary idea here!—& we shall sit down to table 60 persons to turkeys, geese, a whole sheep, a pig, puddings, heaven knows what in the way of dessert, & wines by the barrel. There's to be a tree, too & Father Xmas. I am doing all I can for the little children so that they will be roped in for once. I've just sent them over colored paper & asked them to help to make flowers. It's pathetic the interest they are taking. Our pudding was made in a baby's bath, stirred by everybody & Mr. Gurdjieff put in a coin. Who gets the coin gets our darling new born calf for a present. The calf—1 day old—was led into the salon to the beating of tambourines & to a special melody composed for it.

DECEMBER 26, 1922. PRIEURÉ. Katherine Mansfield writes to her husband:

> You see, my love, the question is always *'Who am I?'* and until that is discovered I don't see how one can really direct anything in one's self. *'Is there a Me?'* One must be certain of that before one has a real unshakable leg to stand on. And I don't believe for one moment these questions can be settled by the head alone. It is this life of the *head,* this formative intellectual life at the expense of all the rest of us which has got us into this state. How can it get us out of it? I see no hope of escape except by learning to live in our emotional & instinctive being as well and to balance all three.
>
> You see, Bogey, if I were allowed one single cry to God that cry would be *I want to be REAL.* Until I am that I don't see why I shouldn't be at the mercy of old Eve in her various manifestations forever.

> But this place has taught me so far how unreal I am. It has taken from me one thing after another (the things never were mine) until at this present moment all I know really, really, is that I am not annihilated and that I hope—more than hope—believe. It is hard to explain....
>
> Our cowshed has become enriched with 2 goats and two love birds. The goats are very lovely as they lie in the straw or so delicately dance towards each other butting gently with their heads. When I was there yesterday Mr. Gurdjieff came in and showed Lola and Nina who were milking the cows the way to milk a goat. He sat down on a stool seized the goat & swung its hind legs across his knees. So there the goat was on its two front legs, helpless. This is the way Arabs milk. He looked very like one....

DECEMBER 31, 1922. PRIEURÉ. Katherine Mansfield writes:

> I have been leading a very tame semi-existence here. My heart, under this new treatment, which is one of graduated efforts and exercise, feels decidedly stronger, and my lungs in consequence feel quieter, too. It's a remarkable fact that since arriving here I have not had to spend one entire day in bed—an unprecedented record for me! I feel more and more confident that if I can give this treatment a fair trial—as I intend to do—and stay on for six months at least, I shall be infinitely stronger in every way. More I do not venture to say.

JANUARY 9, 1923. PRIEURÉ. John Middleton Murray comes for the celebration of the Russian New Year on the thirteenth. He finds his wife Katherine pale but more beautiful than anyone he had ever seen. He says she seemed "a being transfigured by love, absolutely secure in love." She shows him around the grounds. In the evening there is dancing. At ten o'clock she says good night and, climbing the staircase to her room, she hemorrhages. Within a half-hour, her eyes "wide with terror," she takes her last earthly breath. Three days later in the Protestant cemetery at Avon, Fontainebleau, in the presence of Gurdjieff, her husband, her lifelong friend Ida Baker, her sisters, and some of her friends from the Prieuré, Katherine Mansfield is buried. On the large grey slab that is her grave stone are carved these words from Shakespeare:

> But I tell you, my lord fool, out of this
> nettle, danger, we pluck this flower, safety.

Katherine Mansfield's death brings a storm of invective onto Gurdjieff, whom many blame for her death. One such is the writer D. H. Lawrence, who says: "I have heard enough about that place at the Fontainebleau where Katherine Mansfield died, to know it is a rotten, false, self-conscious place of people playing a sickly stunt."

1923. MUNICH. Fritz Thyssen, head of a steel trust, meets Hitler. Impressed, he donates $25,000 to the obscure Nazi Party.

German newspapers print anti-Semitic tracts. The polluted atmosphere of extremism that Gurdjieff found in Russia with the rise of Bolshevism now arises in Europe with Fascism.

1923. PRIEURÉ. Uspenskii says he crosses the Channel "fairly often" to visit Gurdjieff. On several occasions, Gurdjieff invites him to live at the Prieuré. Indicative of his inner attitude, Uspenskii interprets the invitation as a "temptation." Though he still has an interest in Gurdjieff's Work, he maintains: "I could find no place for myself in this work nor did I understand its direction."

As he had in Essentuki, he says that he finds at the Prieuré, "many destructive elements in the organization of the affair itself and [I see] that it had to fall to pieces."

Later he will say that "from the very beginning, there came into the life of the Institute many strange currents, incompatible with its ideas, aims and plans and they very soon made further development of these ideas quite impossible. In my opinion the chief cause of this was the unfortunate choice of people who Gurdjieff admitted to the Institute."

MAY 1, 1923. PRIEURÉ. Nicoll's father is seriously ill. He leaves his wife and daughter at the Prieuré and returns to England.

MAY 23, 1923. PRIEURÉ. Gurdjieff lectures on "The Three Powers." Man, he says, has three powers, which are physical, psychic, and moral. The first depends on the structure of the human machine and its tissues. The second on the quality of the thinking faculty and the material it contains. The third power "is very hard to change, for it takes a long time to form. If a person has common sense and sound logic, one or another action may change his opinion and his will. But changing his nature, his moral make-up, needs long pressure."

MAY 24, 1923. PRIEURÉ. Gurdjieff lectures on love saying:

> There are two kinds of love; one, the love of a slave, the other, which must be acquired by work. The first has no value at all, only the second has value, that is, love acquired through work. This is the love about which all religions speak. If you love when 'it' loves, it does not depend on you and so it has no merit. It is what we call slavish love. You love even where you should not love. Circumstances make you love mechanically.
>
> Real love is Christian, religious love—no one is born with that love, one must be specially trained in it. Some are trained from childhood, others in old age....Love may be of different kinds. To understand what kind of love we are speaking of, it is necessary to define it.

> Now we speak about love of 'life.' Everywhere where there is life, beginning with plants (for they too have life) and animals—in a word, wherever life exists—there is love. All life is a representation of God. He who sees the representation will see Him who is represented. Every life has love and is sensitive to love. Even inanimate things such as flowers which have no consciousness, understand whether you love them or not. Even unconscious life reacts in a corresponding manner to each man and reacts to him according to his reactions. Who does not love life does not love God.

JULY 1923. LONDON. Bennett, involved in a whirlwind of international business, speaks to Uspenskii about his feeling that he has lost touch with his spiritual aims. Bennett had been to the Prieuré for a weekend visit in January. Now, despite Uspenskii's ambivalence toward Gurdjieff, he advises Bennett to go for a long visit.[11]

AUGUST 1923. PRIEURÉ. Nicoll returns to the Prieuré. Gurdjieff tells him: "When you return to Institute [you are] two men—one happy to meet friends, old associates, and so forth. The other does not begin to be felt until you arrive. Suddenly you begin to fear. He thinks of all the difficulties to be faced. He thinks seriously."

The tempo and difficulty of the work is speeded up. And, of course, doubts surface. There is much friction. As always, Gurdjieff fuels the doubts. Nicoll wonders "...whether the difficulties Gurdjieff knows he creates are equal in value for work with those he does not know he creates."

Uspenskii receives a telegram from Madame Uspenskii telling him to come to the Prieuré immediately. Though still wavering in regard to his relationship with Gurdjieff, he does go and almost immediately meets with Gurdjieff. After a long and painful silence, Gurdjieff confides to Uspenskii that he is "very dissatisfied with the work and the attitude of several people in the Institute and that the momentum of the Work was such that he could not control it in the same way."

Later, assembling all his students, Gurdjieff divides them into seven groups. In the first group he puts Dr. Stjoernval, Dr. James Young, A. R. Orage, and Frank Pinder; in the last group he puts Madame de Salzmann, Madame Uspenskii, and her daughter Lenochka. Having prepared the conditions for the shock, Gurdjieff now declares that only the first group is to remain—all others must leave the Prieuré.

Letting that announcement set in, Gurdjieff follows it with another emotional bombshell: he is discontinuing all work with Uspenskii.

11. Given what will later happen between Uspenskii and Bennett, is Uspenskii sending him to Gurdjieff for Bennett's own good, or trying to get rid of him?

He adds that though he personally has nothing against some people in the last group, he is obliged to put some people there because of their connection with Uspenskii.

To the very last Gurdjieff tries to jar Uspenskii into seeing the spiritual trap of power and pride that ensnares him.

Before leaving the Prieuré, Uspenskii sees Gurdjieff alone.

Gurdjieff asks: "Did you understand what I said and did you understand what you must do?"[12]

Uspenskii replies: "I understand both."

"In that case," declares Gurdjieff, "we have no need of long talk."

Having previously publicly rebuked and humiliated Uspenskii in front of his students in London, Gurdjieff now has given the same "medicine" in front of the Work's senior students, Uspenskii's friends and wife. The moment had to cut deeply...and all the more so because Uspenskii believes Gurdjieff's actions are the result of a betrayal by some of his former pupils, principally Orage and Mrs. Page, a wealthy Englishwoman.

Apparently, for some time now, Uspenskii's behavior in London has been under strong attack at the Prieuré. Uspenskii is blamed for the closing of Gurdjieff's Institute in London. He did not obtain the necessary visa. But Uspenskii claims—and there is no reason to doubt his veracity—that Lady Rothermere said she would see the Home Secretary about the visa. Later, the visa denied, Orage asks her whether she had done so. Lady Rothermere makes the excuse that she has asked her cousin to do so. The reason she gives is that she was going on a vacation. It is Uspenskii's claim that she asked Orage if he would lie about this and Orage agreed.

Further, newspaper articles have appeared that seem to indicate Uspenskii thinks that the teaching belongs to both Gurdjieff and Uspenskii. The *London Daily News* quotes Uspenskii as saying "Gurdjieff and I have reached our present state of knowledge by long and hard work in many lands." The same interviewer writes: "... in Gurdjieff he [Uspenskii] found a kindred spirit who had gone farther on the same road." Uspenskii maintains he had not seen the articles before their publication and says he is misquoted.

After studying the articles, Orage reports to Gurdjieff that "it is evident to him" that Uspenskii saw the articles before publication.[13] It is also reported by Mrs. Page that during Uspenskii's lectures he had said that "Institute work was not necessary."

12. What Uspenskii must now do is not clear and Uspenskii makes no further comment. Later, Gurdjieff will invite Uspenskii to return to the Prieuré but he refuses.

13. Orage's appraisal may not have been wholly objective. He may have the "disciple's disease," i.e., the desire to be his teacher's favorite with the consequent spiritual poisons, jealousy, and rivalry. Much later, when Uspenskii's *A New Model of the Universe* is published, Orage will dismiss it as "The New Muddle of the Universe."

Uspenskii writes Mrs. Page a letter:

> Dear Mrs. Page,
> I am sending to you a copy of my letter to Orage and ask you very much to help him to find out who was the cause of all these stupid lies which come to me now from all quarters.
>
> Yours sincerely,
> P. D. Uspenskii

At the Prieuré a much irritated Uspenskii confronts Mrs. Page and calls her a "troublemaker."

"Why can't you tell the truth, and say that you lied?" he asks.

"How can I say that?" she answers. "I do not know."

Others, such as Dr. Young, are also spreading stories about Uspenskii. Understandably, Uspenskii is upset. Both Orage and Young belonged to his first group in London, and so Uspenskii realizes: "If they repeat these lies, or say they do not know they are lies, that shows by itself that there is nothing to be expected."[14]

The experience must have been disillusioning, especially since he had done so much for these people, and also had obtained funding for the Prieuré. As J. G. Bennett notes, "Uspenskii was a brilliant and dedicated exponent of Gurdjieff's ideas, and also a man who inspired confidence by his obvious integrity and sincerity. No one else in Gurdjieff's entourage could have gained the confidence of so many wealthy and influential English people." And it was the English, not the French or Germans, who financed the purchase of the Prieuré.

When Gurdjieff moved to the Caucasus, the Moscow and Petersburg groups merged. There were people, says Uspenskii, "[from] Moscow who did not know of "Petersburg conditions," and, more important, he had not approved any of these people. Still, Gurdjieff continued to hold him responsible, blaming him for their various behaviors. The same happened in Constantinople, and again now at the Prieuré.[15] Uspenskii writes that even at the Prieuré Gurdjieff tells him:

"You remember that I said to you several times that many wrong types came to the work. You are not careful enough in the choice of people."[16]

Gurdjieff had found Uspenskii's "corn" early on and continually kept it under heel. To Uspenskii, a consummate intellectual, the highest manifestation of man-number-three possible, it is not just unfair—but irrational! Absurd! Objectively, it is a master stroke. The use of irrational

14. Underlying this social poisoning is the rivalry and jealousy anyone who is close to the teacher is likely to draw from their peers.

15. Hence, perhaps, giving a new perspective to Uspenskii's comment that the Prieuré people were "a very motley company."

blaming is in fact Gurdjieff's Kurdish "red pepper,"[17] one he specially prepared for Uspenskii. Irrationality of any kind always irritated Uspenskii, and to be blamed so was unthinkable. So this is Gurdjieff's "Uspenskii pepper," one that would never fail to jam Uspenskii's "Wraps Up The- Thought" intellect and open him to the vagaries of his emotional center.

For Uspenskii, listening to Gurdjieff lecture on the Table of Hydrogens, The Diagram of Every Living Thing, octaves and triads and inner considering and false personality and the like—this was "food" his intellectual center feasted upon, for that was his center of gravity. But with the emotional center, that part of himself so underfed and misunderstood—he drew a line. That, he put off limits.[18]

Gurdjieff's senior students take a hard view of Uspenskii and his breaking with Gurdjieff. For example, says Frank Pinder, "All that Uspenskii had of value, he got from Gurdjieff, and that only with his mind. He had a perfunctory fling at the movements; and even confessed to being lazy. Gurdjieff's main quarrel with him was that he, Uspenskii, thought he knew better, and was apt to kick over the traces.... Uspenskii apparently thought that he understood Gurdjieff and his inner teachings—which he did not, and Gurdjieff had to make him choose whether to stay with him and submit to discipline, or break away.... Uspenskii knew the *theory,* better than anyone possibly—he had the knowledge, but he did not *understand.*"[19]

For his part, Uspenskii does not hold Pinder and Orage in high regard. He believes the Prieuré is bound to fail because the "principle of

16. What Uspenskii makes of this is not known but since Essentuki, so he says, he "ceased to understand." He never states directly what that was. Presumably, it is the direction he believes Gurdjieff is taking the Work. Uspenskii wanted "a school of a more rational kind," and he believes Gurdjieff is moving in the direction of devotion. His impression of Gurdjieff, too, is a factor. In sum, because of Gurdjieff's 'acting' or 'play,' he can hold no single concrete impression of him. He is, then, of many minds, or many "I's," about Gurdjieff. Insisting perhaps on rationality, Uspenskii fails, or refuses, to see Gurdjieff's ambiguity as part of the Fourth Way teaching.

17. In *All and Everything, First Series,* Gurdjieff writes of the uses of "the red pepper pods of the Transcaucasian Kurd," pp. 21–22. Many years later, in speaking of self-remembering, Uspenskii says, "It is necessary to create a certain particular energy or point (using it in the ordinary sense), and that can be created only at a moment of very serious emotional stress. All the work before that is only preparation of the method." *A Further Record,* p. 52.

18. Like many intellectuals, Uspenskii appears to have a wish to control the world, model it, put it in some sort of rational, understandable shape. He also had a wish to teach others. And, of course, he had a wish for the miraculous. Gurdjieff's mission was to bring a new teaching to the world and Uspenskii was his handpicked emissary, the man who would "step- down" the teaching, make it comprehensible, and faithfully spread it. But few men of Uspenskii's caliber want to be second-in-command. He was a wonderful stallion but, if he was to be of any use, he had to be "broken."

seniority" has not been followed. "People who did not belong to groups before," he says, "like Pinder and Orage, they were given certain power over people who were much older in the Work; it did not work—it could not go on."

After his fateful summons to the Prieuré, Uspenskii will see Gurdjieff several more times before taking what is effectively his final departure from the Prieuré and Gurdjieff's Work. Gurdjieff invites him to return for Russian Easter, holding out the carrot that he would tell him how the Work can be continued, but Uspenskii has had enough.

AUGUST 1923. PRIEURÉ. Twenty-seven-year-old John Godolphin Bennett arrives. Highly intelligent, a visionary, a leader with natural gifts for commanding others' attention, and a fledgling magician in his own right, Bennett is a promising candidate to fulfill the role in teaching which Gurdjieff had seen for Uspenskii.

One day Gurdjieff takes Bennett aside and tells him, "Now only your mind is awake: your heart and body are asleep. If you continue like this, soon your mind also will go to sleep, and you will never be able to think any new thoughts. You cannot awaken your own feelings, but you can awaken your body. If you can learn to master your body, you will begin to acquire Being....Remember yourself as two—you and your body. When you are master of your body, your feelings will obey you."

During the coming weeks Bennett makes some breakthroughs. Gurdjieff, dressed in a smart French suit, as is now his custom, invites Bennett to accompany him on a business trip to Melun. Upon their return Gurdjieff cuts off into a forest road. The two end up in a clearing overlooking the Prieuré some hundred feet below. Speaking Turkish—Bennett is the only student versed in that language—Gurdjieff confides that this view of the château is his favorite. He talks of the future, telling Bennett of his plans to buy more land. He will then build an observatory, there being many facts about planetary movements that astronomy has overlooked. The impression he creates is that there is much to do, much to learn, many opportunities.

A few days later, Gurdjieff again approaches Bennett declaring—"You have the possibility of learning to work....You have seen that it is possible to be directly connected with the Great Accumulator of Energy that is the source of all miracles. If you could be permanently connected with this source, you could pass all barriers." He goes on to relate that "Ever

19. Pinder and Orage, and certainly Bennett, even Nott, are not to be taken as unbiased observers. As Uspenskii pointed out in *Tertium Organum*: "The reason why men understand one another so little is that they always live by *different* emotions. And they understand one another only when they happen simultaneously to experience identical emotions." Also, there is the factor of competition and jealousy which breed their own special strains in any organization, especially a spiritual one.

since I was a young boy, I have known of the existence of this power and the barriers that separate man from it, and I searched until I found the way of breaking through them. This is the greatest secret that man can discover about human nature. Many people are convinced that they wish to be free and to know reality, but they do not know the barrier that prevents them from reaching reality. They come to me for help, but they are unwilling or unable to pay the price."

Speaking about being and knowledge (as he had to Uspenskii and others seven years before in Petersburg), Gurdjieff warns Bennett of the danger of losing everything, if he relies on knowledge alone. Thinking of Uspenskii perhaps, he warns Bennett with great seriousness: "With too much knowledge, the inner barrier may become insurmountable."[20]

Gurdjieff declares: "If you devote all your energies to the task, it may take two years before you can work alone."[21]

You can work alone, Gurdjieff tells him.

Gurdjieff tells him exactly what he wants to hear. Whether or not Gurdjieff meant it, Bennett, rarely doubting himself at the right time, never questions.

A skilled agent of British intelligence, Bennett must sense the trap Gurdjieff has laid. He plays a last card. He has no money, Bennett says.

"I am not interested in your money," counters Gurdjieff, "but in your work. There are plenty of people who will give me money, but very few who will work. I will give you the money you need."

Gurdjieff then sweetens the pot. He offers to take Bennett with him on his forthcoming trip to America to act as his interpreter. Bennett is no doubt seeing himself sitting next to Gurdjieff, just as Pinder had in London.

Gurdjieff dangles another lure. He tells Bennett that later on he will be able to give lectures himself.

Then Gurdjieff delivers the masterstroke—"At present you will have to take because you have nothing to give. Later you will be ready to give your last shirt to help the work—as I am ready to give mine."

Gurdjieff's words make a great impact on Bennett, yet not so great that he stays on. Walking past the Prieuré's flowing fountain, Bennett opens the high wrought iron gate to the street. He calms himself with the words, "I will go away and make money, and then I will return." Once closed, it is a gate Bennett will never again open.

20. To a man like Bennett, freedom—his notion of freedom—is everything. When he then asks how long would be needed if he decides to stay, it sounds like he is looking for a way out.

21. The words must have singed Bennett's brain. He had expected twenty years. Mercurial, zesting after adventure, what Bennett most fears is being trapped. Raised in a family with a no-account father, he had been his mother's pride and joy, her "young king."

AUGUST 21, 1923. PRIEURÉ. "For one section of the people here," says Gurdjieff, "their stay has become completely useless. If this section were to be asked why they were here, they would be completely unable to answer or they would answer something quite nonsensical, would produce a whole philosophy....Whoever does not make use of the conditions here for work on himself and does not see them—then this is no place for him. He is wasting his time by remaining here, hindering others and taking someone else's place....He who can be a conscientious egotist here, can be in life not an egotist. To be an egotist here means not to give a hoot for anyone, myself included, to regard everyone and everything as something by which to help oneself. There must be no considering with anything or with anyone....There is only one salvation: to remember day and night that you are here only for yourself and everything and everyone around you must either not hinder you or you must act so that they do not hinder you. You must make use of them as a means for attaining your aims. Yet everything is done here except that. This place has been turned into something worse than in ordinary life. Much worse. All day long people are either occupied with scandal, or they blacken one another, or they think things inwardly, judge and consider with each other, finding some sympathetic, some antipathetic; they strike up friendships, collectively or individually play tricks on each other, concentrate on the bad sides of each other."

OCTOBER 1923. PRIEURÉ. Gurdjieff speaks of Orage going to America to teach the Work. He suggests to Maurice Nicoll that he should accompany Orage. Highly educated, intuitive, and a natural communicator, Dr. Nicoll is another possible candidate to help Gurdjieff establish the teaching. Orage and Nicoll could help balance each other. But Nicoll, for all his intuition, is blind both to the need and the possibility. Always the aristocrat, he graciously bows out. And so Nicoll, wife, baby, and nurse depart for London. This is the last of Gurdjieff they will ever see. From here on they will content themselves with Uspenskii's version of the teaching.

NOVEMBER 1923. LONDON. WARWICK GARDENS. Nicoll and his wife attend Uspenskii's meetings. Nicoll visits Uspenskii's flat. As they greet, Nicoll notes the scratches on Uspenskii's hands. Uspenskii explains they are the work of his eight-year-old cat, Vashka, whom Nicoll describes as "a big, brindled beast with brilliant eyes." Uspenskii is quite fond of Vashka. It will only play with meat, not eat it. So Uspenskii feeds it lobster, asparagus, and olives.

On one of his visits, Nicoll finds Uspenskii working on a chapter, "Christianity and the New Testament," for his book *A New Model of the Universe.* About the room are a number of dictionaries as well as copies of the New Testament in Greek, German, French, Russian, and English. He writes with a pencil, of which he has many, all sharpened to very fine points. When he speaks of a biblical passage to Nicoll, Uspenskii first looks at the translation in each of the versions, then compares it with the Greek.

NOVEMBER 8, 1923. MUNICH. Hitler's beer hall putsch fails. He is imprisoned. Begins to write *Mein Kampf* (My Struggle).

DECEMBER 1923. PRIEURÉ. Gurdjieff has managed to extricate his family from Russia. They now arrive: his mother, suffering from a chronic liver illness; his younger sister Sophie Ivanovna and her husband Georgilibovitch Kapanadze; and his brother Dimitri and his family.

Dimitri had been quite well off before, having been mayor of Alexandropol and owning both a cinema and shoe shop. His daughter Luba remembers of those days that "My father used to help my Uncle George in his traveling, you see. My father worked; he was a family man. My Uncle was all the time going somewhere. He used to come home for one or two weeks and get clothing and money and then he would go. Sometimes it was a couple of years—nobody heard anything, nobody knew if he was alive or dead and suddenly he would appear again."

While Gurdjieff and his brother were close, Luba says, "My father was not interested at all in what was going on [at the Prieuré]. He used to say [to him] 'You're talking rubbish.' My Uncle used to love my father, but they used to fight like dog and cat about everything. My father would never agree with my Uncle and my Uncle would never agree with him. You see, my father was a bon viveur. He used to go out all the time, play cards, drink—enjoy life. They looked very much like each other, but you'd never think it was two brothers. They didn't have at all the same ideas."

DECEMBER 13, 1923. PARIS. First public demonstration of the sacred dances at Paris' Théâtre des Champs Élysées draws mixed reactions; some experience their newness and sacred quality, others believe they have no aesthetic value. Afterward, Gurdjieff sends Dr. Stjoernval and Orage to New York to drum up interest in the teaching and prepare for the arrival of Gurdjieff and his dance troupe.

He has spoken with Orage about what he will find there. Americans, Gurdjieff believes, have more possibilities for good than any other nation, but they are so at the mercy of wrong ideals brought from Europe, and eventually distorted even further—they have come to power and money so easily, that their civilization may decay and rot long before it is ripe.

He has given Orage the tasks of generating interest in the teaching and raising enough money to support the stay in America. The first task Orage, by intellect and training, is well-equipped for, but to the second task he has a strong personal aversion. As a friend says, "...his family had suffered much from poverty when he was a boy and he hated it. Equally he hated having to slave for money and almost as much he disliked asking for money for any purposes—even one not his own."

JANUARY 4, 1924. Before Gurdjieff and his troupe sail to America three hundred thousand francs are "swallowed up" paying for the Paris demonstrations, steamship tickets, the most urgent bills at the Prieuré, making provisions for those who would stay behind, and so forth. And so, three days before he is to depart, Gurdjieff says, "I found myself at the last minute in a super-unique tragi-comic situation"—he had no cash reserve.

Only a few days earlier his mother and several members of his family had arrived from Russia. He says he was in his room "searching in my mind for a way out of the incredible situation that had arisen," when his mother came in and returned an expensive brooch to him that he had given her for safekeeping. Gurdjieff says of this event:

"What occurred was one of those interventions that people who are capable of thinking consciously—in our times and particularly in past epochs—have always considered a sign of the just providence of the Higher Powers. As for me, I would say that it was the law-conformable result of man's unflinching perseverance in bringing all his manifestations into accordance with the principles he has consciously set himself in life for the attainment of a definite aim."

Uspenskii is present at Gurdjieff's departure. It reminds him, he says, of Gurdjieff's leaving Essentuki and "all that was connected with it." Once again, as he had in Essentuki in 1918 and Constantinople in 1921, Uspenskii decides to break with Gurdjieff.

Years later Uspenskii would say as to why he broke with Gurdjieff: "Gurdjieff had gone off the rails—become mad—and I wanted to save the System."

JANUARY 1924. LONDON. "I have asked you to come because I must tell you that I have decided to break off all relations with Mr. Gurdjieff."

So Uspenskii informs his key group at Ralph Philipson's flat in Portland Place, London. "This means that you have to choose," he declares. "Either you can go and work with him, or you can work with me: but if you remain with me, you must give an undertaking [understanding] that you will not communicate in any way with Mr. Gurdjieff."

Philipson, who had made substantial contributions to the purchase of the Prieuré, as well as helping to underwrite Uspenskii's work in London, asks the reason behind this decision.

"Mr. Gurdjieff is a very extraordinary man. His possibilities are much greater than those of people like ourselves. But he also can go in the wrong way. I believe that he is now passing through a crisis, the outcome of which no one can foresee. Most people have many 'I's. If these 'I's are at war with one another it does not produce great harm, because they are all weak. But with Mr. Gurdjieff there are only two 'I's, one very good and one very bad."

"I believe," Uspenskii continues, "that in the end the good 'I' will conquer. But meanwhile it is very dangerous to be near him. We cannot be of any help to him, and in his present condition he cannot be of any help to us. Therefore, I have decided to break off all contact. But this does not mean I am against him, or that I consider what he is doing is bad."[22]

Uspenskii's difficulty, as Frank Pinder sees it, is that: "Uspenskii could never forget Gurdjieff's attacking him in front of his pupils." Pinder feels Uspenskii projected himself "in a role in which he saw himself as a successful religious teacher—though he may not have been conscious of this. . . . Uspenskii, for all his great brain, was, for what was real, unintelligent; and it was inevitable that Uspenskii should cut himself and his pupils off from Gurdjieff. It is strange that there can be talk of 'Uspenskii's Teaching,' and 'Gurdjieff-Uspenskii System': the Teaching is *Gurdjieff's*."

At the close of Uspenskii's remarks at Philipson's flat, Uspenskii is asked: "How will we exist? Will we continue on the same line as we have been going, or by some other new line or connection with Mr. Gurdjieff's work?"

"We are connected with the inner meaning of the work," answers Uspenskii, "but as an organization we are not connected."

Kenneth Walker, a prominent Harley Street surgeon asks, "This work can be done effectively here as in Paris, can't it?"

"Yes, practically," says Uspenskii.

He speaks of the Petersburg conditions and then tells the group: "You must decide, do you want [a] separate organization or [to have] one with [the] Institute because later I will base my ideas on one decision or another."

Says Kenneth Walker, "St. Petersburg conditions worked well in Petersburg so they should work well in London."

"From my point of view," says Uspenskii, "people [at the Institute] were taken without tests, without knowing who they were and many things went wrong."

Later in the meeting Uspenskii says, "My opinion is that we must organize separately."

Someone asks what would happen if the struggle went the wrong way.

22. This is sounding very much like an Uspenskiian version of *The Struggle of the Magicians*. In fact, it is Uspenskii, too, who is passing through a crisis, a crisis of sincerity, though such is his state he does not know it. His possibilities are much greater than other students. His voice is influential and for him to go the wrong way means many people will follow him.

Returning to what he had said earlier, Uspenskii says, "He could go mad. Or else he could attract to himself some disaster in which all those round him would be involved."

Bennett is among those present. He agrees not to communicate with Gurdjieff. As do Nicoll and many others.

The Uspenskiian work begins. The die now cast, there will be not one work, but two.

And so, less than a year and a half after Gurdjieff founded his Institute at the Prieuré to establish the teaching in the West, the octave is deflected, the force of the teaching halved. Uspenskii entrusts the translation of *Fragments* to Baroness O. A. Rausch de Traubenberg who lives in Paris. He asks Boris Mouravieff to supervise it.

Curiously, though this break seems permanent, Uspenskii will be seen with Gurdjieff now and then through the years until their final meeting seven years hence on the terrace of the Café Henri IV at Fontainebleau-Avon.

Hearing of his former student's decision to break with him and teach his own line of the Work, Gurdjieff's thoughts might have returned to a time seven years earlier in St. Petersburg when he had spoken with Uspenskii and Anna Butkovsky.

Supposedly exasperated at the lack of seriousness of the young group, Gurdjieff had stormed out of the meeting, slamming the door behind him. Uspenskii had rushed after him and convinced him not to abandon the group.

The next day Gurdjieff had met with the group and explained that man had no genuine I. He was, rather, many "I's." Speaking of the teaching, he said: "One must know how to act swiftly, grasp the object [teaching] and never let go....For will there ever be another opportunity? Probably never! And when it's been lost, a man will try to satisfy himself with some kind of imitation of what he's lost...'Paradise lost!' According to his talent and intellect, sometimes it may work, sometimes not. But then he, too, will start trying to 'preach' about it to others. From preachers like that, Lord deliver us!"

JANUARY 1924. NEW YORK. Orage's first talk is at the Sunwise Turn Bookshop, a center for New York's avant-garde, located at East 31st Street just off Fifth Avenue in Manhattan. In attendance is a cross-section of New York intelligentsia.

Tall and easy of manner, quick and brilliant of mind and speech, Orage begins his presentation thus:

> The Institute for the Harmonious Development of Man...which is based on the system of G. I. Gurdjieff, is really a continuation of the society called the 'Seekers After Truth.'

He goes on to sketch the preparations for the formation of the Institute in Russia through its founding at Fontainebleau-Avon in France. Then he states:

> The life of our time has become so complex that man has deviated from his original type....Our civilization has taken away from the natural and essential qualities of his inherited type, but it has not given him what was needed for the harmonious development of a new type, so that civilization, instead of producing an individually whole man adapted to the nature and surroundings in which he finds himself and which really were responsible for his creation, has produced a being out of his element, incapable of living a full life, and at the same time a stranger to that inner life which should by rights be his...the world perception of man of our time and his way of living are not the conscious expression of himself as a complete whole; but, on the contrary, are the unconscious manifestation of only one of the three parts of him [intellectual, emotional, instinctive-moving].... Each truly conscious perception and expression of man must be the result of simultaneous and co-ordinated working of all three centers, each of which must take its part in the whole task.

Orage's talk makes a strong impression. Many in the audience are New York literati, among whom are Margaret Anderson and Jane Heap, co-editors of the *Little Review*, a lively review of the arts.[23] Says Margaret Anderson after the talk, "[Orage is] the most persuasive man I have ever known."

A fateful meeting occurs the following morning. Orage returns to the Sunwise Turn and spies a young, attractive blonde woman. Remembering that she had attended his talk but listened with a certain levity he inquires, "How did you enjoy the talk?"

Orage, who always liked an intellectual challenge, especially from women, finds the young woman does not disappoint.

"Not at all," immediately answers tall, fair-haired Jesse Dwight. Hardly half Orage's age, she is not in the least overwhelmed by him.

Though having little interest in what he says, she is attracted to Orage and the two soon fall into chatting. He learns that her frankness and independence are bred from a long line of Connecticut clergymen and scholars. And not only is she beautiful and well-connected, but this young lady also happens to be a co-owner, with Marjorie Content, a wealthy photographer, of the Sunwise Turn.[24]

23. The *Little Review*, founded in 1914 by Margaret Anderson, who defined it as "A Magazine of the Arts, Making No Compromise with the Public Taste," published the avant-garde of its day, many of them steered to its pages by poet Ezra Pound, the magazine's "foreign correspondent." Among its writers: James Joyce, Ernest Hemingway, William Butler Yeats, T. S. Eliot, Jean Cocteau, and Gertrude Stein.

Orage's great charm is animated by a blessing which Mairet, his friend and biographer, calls "a feminine element." As he points out:

> The acute sensibility and responsiveness of mind in which lay so much of Orage's personal magnetism was due to a feminine element in his character of which he was well aware, though he could never wholly accept it. He feared it, as men often do, and made matters more difficult by additional efforts to stiffen his character and harden his mental texture, which, as is usually the case with such efforts, especially if undertaken in mature years, were far from achieving their object but brought on tortured and precarious feelings. He became unable to miss a shot at golf without glancing round anxiously in fear that some stranger had noticed the blunder.

Born January 22, 1873, Orage's early life was marked by poverty and promise. Orage's father died when he was only one-and-a-half years old. A schoolteacher, the father had gambled away his small inheritance. And so his unexpected death when he was hardly past forty left his family penniless. Young Orage mastered all his school subjects so easily that the schoolmaster provided special prizes for him. Taller than his peers and blessed with a vivid intelligence, a passion for reading, and the voice of a natural singer, Orage was also the star performer in the school's annual play.

His later life showed a pattern of mixing his working life with his love life. When only twenty-three, in 1896, he married Jean Walker, an ardent theosophist. Her family opposed the marriage as being premature; more likely, class and circumstance was the basis. Orage, for all his gifts, was a poor Yorkshire country boy, and Jean, the daughter of a well-to-do Scottish family. Initially the marriage blossomed. Orage and Jean shared theosophical and aesthetic interests and she helped him with the activities of the Leeds Arts Club, a club he and some friends had formed "to affirm the mutual dependence of art and ideas."

In 1906, the young couple moved to London. Lecturing on theosophy, he met Beatrice Hastings,[25] a vivacious and talented divorcée from South Africa formerly married to a professional boxer. Orage's wife, Jean, was no match for the irrepressible Beatrice, and Orage soon separated from Jean, taking Beatrice as a lover.

24. What a great help she could be to him in the task Gurdjieff gave him—establishing the teaching in America. What man, indeed a stranger in a strange land, facing such a monumental responsibility, would not feel with Orage that this enchanting young woman is heaven-sent? In fact, Jesse Dwight would prove his undoing. In her he is meeting the greatest challenge to his spiritual life that he has yet met, and he does not in the least surmise it.

25. Just as theosophy had brought a significant woman, Anna Butkovsky, into Uspenskii's life, so it brings Beatrice Hastings into Orage's. Both seem to be classic *shakti*, i.e., a woman blessed with high energy, intelligence, daring, cunning, independence, and a warrior spirit.

In 1907 he founded the *New Age*, a political and literary weekly. Beatrice soon came to share not only his bed but his office as well, helping Orage to edit the weekly. Soon, she became one of its principal contributors. Gifted but unstable, she had lively arguments with Orage over the Women's Suffrage movement, only then emerging. Orage, an ardent Nietzschean, strongly opposed it in his editorials, although he condemned the methods of those suppressing it.

During his affair with Beatrice, Orage had a liaison with a new young short story writer from New Zealand, Katherine Mansfield, whose stories he published in the *New Age*.[26] Though Orage preferred Katherine, the more forceful and domineering Beatrice pushed her aside. Beatrice, ever the free spirit, on a holiday with Orage and the painter Modigliani in France, danced nude on the tables of Parisian cafés. Though he enjoyed her fire and independence, Orage was unable to commit to her. In 1914 she left him, the affair finally ending acrimoniously in 1916.[27]

While at the Sunwise Turn, Orage has another fateful meeting with a man who will become a lifelong spiritual friend. Noticing a young Englishman, an employee of the bookshop, who had also attended his talk, Orage asks what impression he got from it.

"None at all. I could not get the hang of it," replies C. S. Nott.

"Never mind," Orage says. "Gurdjieff is arriving in a week's time with forty pupils to give demonstrations of sacred dances and exercises. Why don't you come?"

Says Nott, "It was as if I were meeting someone whom I had known intimately and had liked, and from whom I had been separated for a very long time."

JANUARY 23, 1924. NEW YORK. Gurdjieff's troupe makes its first appearance at Manhattan's Lesley Hall on West 83rd Street. Orage gives the introduction. In the audience is C. S. Nott, whom Orage had invited. Nott hears a low voice calling offstage—"Remember yourself, you idiot!" The voice is Gurdjieff's.

Nott is taken with the sacred dances and the music. The highlight for him is a series of movements called the "Big Seven" or "Big Group." The program said the movements were based on the enneagram and had been

26. Her first story, *The Child-Who-Was-Tired*, is about an overworked peasant mother who, to keep her baby quiet, smothers it. Orage ran it in the *New Age* on February 24, 1910.

27. Orage's inability to make a lasting commitment, along with his mixing of his love and working lives—first with his wife, Jean, then Beatrice and Katherine, emerges as a pattern. The pattern will repeat in America with Jesse Dwight. This time Orage, perhaps believing he is breaking the pattern, commits.

taken from the Aisors, a Christian sect tinged with Sufism, located near Mount Ararat.

A few days later, Orage and Dr. Stjoernval come to the Sunwise Turn. Nott is there. He says:

> At once I sensed that I was a mere youth in the presence of these adult men. Very soon I made another and more striking comparison; Gurdjieff arrived, very impressive in a black coat with an astrakhan collar and wearing an astrakhan cap. With a twinkle in his eyes he began to joke with the others. Then he walked round, and I found him standing beside me. I looked up, and was struck by the expression of his eyes, with the depths of understanding and compassion in them. He radiated tremendous power and "being" such as I had never in all my travels met in any man, and I sensed that, compared with him, both Dr. Stjoernval and Orage were as young men to an elder.

JANUARY 26, 1924. PETROGRAD-LENINGRAD. At the outbreak of the First World War St. Petersburg's name was changed to Petrograd; now it is changed yet again to Leningrad, "the city of Lenin." Uspenskii must not have rested well this night.

FEBRUARY 2, 1924. NEW YORK. The troupe's second performance is given at the Neighborhood Playhouse on MacDougal Street in Greenwich Village. New York responds favorably to Gurdjieff's presentation of sacred dances. A large amount of money is collected. Among those present at the performance is the thirty-year-old writer Jean Toomer, a tall, magnetic figure, whose novel *Cane* had been an instant critical success the year before. Toomer, a lemon-skinned black writer whose ancestry includes Jewish, Indian, German, French, Dutch, and Welsh blood, has had, like Uspenskii, an oceanic experience of being: "All I had formerly thought and felt about a larger being and a higher consciousness," says Toomer, "became for me a living reality of higher experience...[which became unbearable...but it left] an unforgettable taste." Toomer was familiar with German and Swedish gymnastics and had studied the Alexander Technique [a body work] and had a keen sense of the body. When he first saw Gurdjieff he says: "I saw this man in motion, a unit in motion. He was completely of one piece. From the crown of his head down the back of the head, down the neck, down the back and down the legs, there was a remarkable line. Shall I call it a gathered line? It suggested co-ordination, integration, knitness, power....I was fascinated by the way the man walked. As his feet touched the floor there seemed to be no weight on them at all—a glide, a stride, a weightless walk." He describes Gurdjieff's face: "his complexion is swarthy, his dark eyes wide-spread, his nose finely modelled and even delicate compared with the rugged four-square lower face, and he has a tigerish black moustache."

Of Gurdjieff himself, Toomer says: "He seemed to have everything that could be asked of a developed human being, a teacher and a master. Knowledge, integration, many-sidedness, power—in fact, he had a bit too much power for my comfort....I held back, Gurdjieff's power disturbed me. I was not sure of it, and I wanted to be sure before I placed myself wholly in his hands."

In his diary, Toomer comes closer to his impression of Gurdjieff. "Power[28]—something more than strength of body, something in addition and other than strength of mind. Though he contained it, it came out of him, this deep, pervasive, unfathomable power. I soon became sure that I had never seen any other man with power of this kind. But how was he using it? For good? For evil? How would he use it on me should I become one of his pupils? From this time on I had no peace until I had finally settled this question so far as I was concerned."

FEBRUARY 15, 1924. NEW YORK. Gorham Munson, a literary disciple of Waldo Frank, the novelist and social critic, attends a demonstration by Gurdjieff and his troupe. He writes to Frank:

> The sensation in New York for the past month has been the visit of Gurdjieff, Orage, and a troupe of pupils from Fontainebleau. They came unheralded, give out no addresses, assign no purpose for their visit, and put on quite suddenly demonstrations for invited audiences. It is the very devil to find out when and where they are demonstrating, and it is the very devil to get admitted. At last, however Lisa [Munson's wife] and I were placed on their list. I have seen two demonstrations and heard three lectures. The dancing is quite undreamed of. Ritual dances from the East, temple dances of esoteric cults, monastic experiences: I have never seen so much complexity, contradiction, and detailed variety held together in an unaccountable unity. It is a dance of design (of complicated geometry) rather than of motion. Strictly impersonal. Also there are demonstrations of tricks, semi-tricks, possibly thought-transference, and these have been concentration tests. Gurdjieff is the most powerful man I have ever seen: God or Satan himself—almost. Everyone is talking—literati, society, little girls—amazing rumours spread.

Margaret Anderson gives a potent first impression of Gurdjieff.

> I had just time to look carefully at a dark man with an oriental face, whose life seemed to reside in his eyes. He had a presence impossible to describe because I had never encountered another with which to compare it. In other words, as one would immediately recognize Einstein as a "great man" we immediately recognized Gurdjieff as the kind

28. For Toomer, the difficulty is Gurdjieff's power. For Uspenskii, it is Gurdjieff's 'playing' and his use of devotional methods. For Bennett, it is commitment (his own). For Orage, the difficulty will be even closer to the bone.

> of man we had never seen—a seer, a prophet, a messiah?...We looked upon this man standing in the wings as a messenger between two worlds....I think I really thought of Gurdjieff, at first, as a sort of Hermes, teaching his son Tat....What philosophers have taught as 'wisdom,' what scholars have taught in texts and tracts, what mystics have taught through ecstatic revelation, Gurdjieff would teach as a science—an exact science of man and human behavior—a supreme science of God, world, man—based on sources outside the scope, reach, knowledge or conception of modern scientists and psychologists.

FEBRUARY 26, 1924. MUNICH. Correspondents from the world press and leading German newspapers cover Hitler's trial for treason. It lasts twenty-four days. In that short time Hitler's speaking ability and nationalistic spirit transform the defeat of his putsch into a triumph. All the world hears of this man who readily admits his desire to get rid of the Reich government. About his view of himself he minces no words. "The man who is born to be a dictator is not compelled," declares the thirty-four-year-old Hitler, "he wills it. He is not driven forward, but drives himself. There is nothing immodest about this. Is it immodest for a worker to drive himself toward heavy labor? Is it presumptuous of a man with the high forehead of a thinker to ponder through the nights till he gives the world an invention? The man who feels called upon to govern a people has no right to say, 'If you want me or summon me, I will co-operate.' No! It is his duty to step forward."

1924. LONDON. Writers Aldous Huxley and Gerald Heard attend Uspenskii's lectures. The occult writer A. E. Waite also comes. Listening to Uspenskii discourse on the need for man to realize he is a machine, Waite walks out crying—"Mr. Uspenskii, there is no love in your system."

SPRING 1924. NEW YORK. Orage, the consummate lecturer, is attracting larger and larger audiences to his exposition of Gurdjieff's teaching. Besides Margaret Anderson, Jane Heap, and Jean Toomer, he draws into his orbit authors, poets, critics, actors, and budding psychologists. Among them are: Waldo Frank, his wife Margaret Naumberg, Muriel Draper, Rebecca West, Zona Gale, Gorham Munson, Carl Zigrosser, Schuyler Jackson, Edwin Wolfe, John O'Hara Cosgrave, and the philanthropist Mabel Dodge Luhan.

Says thirty-five-year-old Waldo Frank, the literary lion of the time: "Orage blights the claims of humanness. With valedictory sentiment, wipes sentiment off the slate. With logic swift as a machine, he discredits logic. With courteous manner, drops spiritual bombs into the laps of ladies who adore him."

For writer-editor Gorham Munson what stands out is Orage's intelligence. He and his wife are introduced to Orage by Jean Toomer and Margaret Naumberg. Says Munson: "I felt that this man's *note* was intelligence, and I have never met a man who struck it with as much clarity....He gave no sign of middle age. No hint of grey in the dark hair, and only a slight recession of the hairline near the part on the left. No sign of corpulence."

Munson's wife, Elizabeth, a former dancer, later recounted: "I felt his alertness and his relaxation," she later said. "I felt in Orage something always in motion but not hurried, not tense, not forced—an easy swiftness which could change its course deftly and resume the original direction with perfect sureness. Quick intelligence, quick feeling and understanding, and an extraordinary speed of perception—a sort of lightning functioning."

Toomer spent a weekend at Waldo Frank's who had written the foreword to Toomer's first novel, *Cane*. Frank and his wife Margaret Naumberg, both psychologists and well-off financially, had long been at odds. When Toomer visited he and Margaret quickly entered into an affair. She later left Frank to live with Toomer. Gorham Munson, a friend of both men, was caught in the middle. He refused to take sides. Of Toomer, Munson says: "His sex nature was sweet and pure, and I imagine that he was a genuine lover and genuine person in his sex contacts."

Orage's meetings are held first in the apartment of a psychoanalyst, then at 24 East 11th street, Jean Heap's apartment in the Village, and finally in Muriel Draper's more spacious Murray Hill apartment at 24 East 40th Street. Draper is the socialite architectural critic of *The New Yorker* who Gurdjieff delights in calling "Mrs. Trapper," much the same as he refers to the lesbian Jane Heap as "Mees Keep."

Soon, an attractive, young blonde is seen sitting adoringly at the Englishman's feet. The temptation proves too much for Orage. Before long he succumbs to an affair with Jessie Dwight. He must have had his doubts, for Orage has long recognized his weakness for women. In England he had spoken of the need to free himself from the need for female companionship. As he wrote earlier in the *New Age*:

> Long after the liability to complete subjection to female illusion is over, men sometimes continue to experience perturbations of their equilibrium in the presence of women. In few instances are these perturbations violent enough to overthrow the mind entirely, but for the moment they undoubtedly do cause the judgment to reel and stagger and the resulting conversation and actions to become distorted. These residual phenomena, however, are to be distinguished from the similar phenomena of adolescence by the fact that they no longer inspire hope but disgust or, at least, annoyance.[29]

Settling in Manhattan, Orage moves into a tiny apartment in Chelsea. He works steadfastly to build interest in Gurdjieff's teaching and to form groups. Some two hundred people, many drawn from New York's intelligentsia, will show interest in joining Orage's groups. Soon Jesse Dwight leaves Sunwise Turn to become his personal secretary. Far more stable than Beatrice Hastings or Katherine Mansfield, Jesse Dwight is a woman who knows what she wants and will sacrifice to get it; the "sacrifice" in this case being to align herself with Gurdjieff's teaching.[30] For his part, Orage seems to be at right angles to himself. Intellectually, he is opposed to granting women independence, but emotionally strong-willed, independent women are his great attraction.

An interesting portrait of Orage in action is published in a Waldo Frank essay *Mystery in a Sack Suit:*

> ...Here were true intellectuals who despise Greenwich Village. Here were socially elect who looked down on Park Avenue as a gilded slum. Here indeed were men and women dry and fresh, smart and solemn, rich or merely famous—perpendicular extremes of our extremely perpendicular New York. And now if you looked still closer, you saw that they were listening with passionate concern to a man they call Orage and Orage was most intempestuously sitting in an upholstered armchair, smoking a cigarette and cavalierly smiling. He seems a proverbial schoolboy, slightly damaged by the years, yet on the whole intact—as he sits enwreathed in all those seeking brains and eager eyes. He has a hard body in a tight drab suit. He has hair like a cap drawn close upon his skull. The finger tips are yellow with tobacco. The face is gray with thought. And its prominent part is the nose. The nose is the pinnacle of Orage. Intense brow, willful jaw, keen eyes, ironic mouth—they all converge upon this proboscidean symbol of pertinence and search.
>
> ...He talks more of Behaviorism, Astronomy and Mechanics than of what is commonly called religion. And he believes in literally nothing. Nothing that is, I mean. This is what makes him so detached. He knows all the scriptures from the *Mahabharata* to Hart Crane, and he is detached from them all. Even Buddha believed in the world enough to cry against it, to invent harsh disciplines to combat it. Not Orage. He despises the world so well that he is at peace with it wholly....His sensuous hospitality is the sign of his contempt. Even so, his boy face is the counterfeit of candor; and his language, which for fluent clarity has few peers in England, weaves a mist about him. Orage knows not alone the *Pali Canon,* but as well the

29. Like Uspenskii's Osokin, Orage sees his situation clearly enough but has not the requisite self-remembrance and will to change it.

30. It may be that a part of her is interested in the teaching. But, from her original comment to Orage and her battle with Gurdjieff, that part never substantially grew.

> Jesuits and Machiavelli. He barbs you with his words; he swathes and soothes you with his perhaps too unctuous manner—and himself glides by.... The Puritan Socialism of Bernard Shaw—dear Shaw who takes liquor, meat, tobacco, coffee, tea and women so seriously that he does not take 'em at all—was not for Orage. Shaw stayed on in England: Orage—who takes 'em all—has come to our wider land.

Many in New York want to go to the Prieuré, among them the young Englishman, C. S. Nott. But there is a problem. Nott tells Orage that a young American woman he is seeing has "become resentful" of his interest in the Gurdjieff system. She has refused to go to any more meetings and blames Nott for a loss of interest in what they had both worked for—"social reform and the good of others." When he told her of his plans to go to the Prieuré, she declared—"You will have to choose between Gurdjieff and me."

Replies Orage, who soon will be no stranger to the problem:

> You must remember that American women, more than any others, are spoilt. Of course, all women want their own way but one of the tragedies of American life is that women have succeeded in getting it to the extent of dominating men. The passive force has become the active. One of the consequences is the enormous number of divorces here compared with Europe. Gurdjieff blames men for the deterioration in the status of women in America. The strange thing is that Americans regard it as a sign of 'progress'... In a real civilization woman understands her function and has no wish to be other than a woman.

APRIL 1, 1924. GERMANY. Convicted of treason, Hitler enters Landsberg prison to serve a five-year sentence.

APRIL 8, 1924. NEW YORK. The day of the opening of the New York branch of the Institute for the Harmonious Development of Man. After a dinner in honor of Mr. Gurdjieff at a Russian restaurant, he and friends and several pupils of the French branch retire to the apartment of a Mrs. R. for coffee and liqueurs. Gurdjieff is asked about the finances of the Institute and its annual budget. He answers at great length.

Gurdjieff's first visit to New York is a success and Orage, whatever his inner resistance, has no trouble raising the money needed. He tells Nott: "Gurdjieff says that the attitude to finance is all part of the dream state that we live in. If men could wake up it would very soon be changed. Gurdjieff's attitude to money is different from that of anyone I have met.... Gurdjieff may appear to be throwing money about, but he calculates and uses it for certain non-personal ends."

APRIL 23, 1924. PRIEURÉ. Feast Day of St. George the Victor, Warrior of God, Knight of Christ. This day, says Gurdjieff, is to be regarded as the Institute's "Coronation Day."

JUNE 1924. NEW YORK. Gurdjieff returns to France. Of the impact Gurdjieff and Orage make in their initial contact with America, Claude Bragdon, the architect and author who had translated *Tertium Organum,* best sums it up: "It was Orage, the perfect disciple, the Plato to this Socrates [Gurdjieff], who was responsible for most of the success which attended the movement in America. His charming manner and brilliant mind did much to counteract the bewilderment in which Gurdjieff so often left his auditors."

JUNE 1924. PRIEURÉ. Arriving for a stay are Margaret Anderson and her two young nephews, Fritz and Tom Peters, Jane Heap and Georgette Leblanc, an actress and singer, and former mistress of Maurice Maeterlinck, the playwright. At dinner one evening they are surprised to see Uspenskii, since they had heard he had left the Institute.

"Uspenskii," says Margaret Anderson, "sat at Gurdjieff's left and acted like a small boy, laughing more than he meant to, saying what he meant not to, flushing with the Armagnac forced upon him.... Though Uspenskii must have taken part in this ceremony a hundred times, I always felt that he had never discovered its significance; that he knew ideas but didn't know people."

Anderson speaks with Gurdjieff who tells her: "I cannot develop you. I create conditions; you develop yourself."

Anderson, Georgette Leblanc, and Jane Heap become residents of the Prieuré.

Georgette says to Margaret, "We have spent our lives walking about under parasols."

Thinks Margaret, always highly imaginative, "Yes, white parasols, like those used by Catholics in midnight Mass at New Year's."

Georgette's impression of Gurdjieff is that "He resided on the earth as on a planet too limited for his own needs and function. Where did he manifest his real existence?...I was not astonished that he was little known, that he was not surrounded by thousands of followers. Neither money nor influence could open the doors of the Prieuré—Gurdjieff created all possible obstacles to discourage any idler-spirits who might push their way into a world where they did not belong."

The women will live at intervals at the Prieuré for two years. Margaret and Georgette will encounter Gurdjieff more rarely thereafter until 1935.

June 1924. Prieuré. Eleven-year-old Fritz Peters is interviewed by Gurdjieff on the terrace. The boys' mother has been hospitalized for a year, and Anderson and Jane Heap have legally adopted the boys.

Told that Gurdjieff is a prophet or someone very close to the second coming of Christ, the young boy dreads the meeting. He is relieved when he meets Gurdjieff.

"The actual meeting," says Peters, "did not measure up to my fears. 'Messiah' or not, he seemed to me a simple, straightforward man."

Among the questions Gurdjieff asks him is what he wants to know.

"I want to know everything," Peters replies.

"You cannot know everything. Everything about what?"

"Everything about man."

Gurdjieff sighs and tells him, "You can stay. But your answer makes life difficult for me. I am the only one who teaches what you ask. You make more work for me."

Peters was put to work from 6 A.M. to 11 P.M. cleaning out the stable and taking care of the horse and donkey. Not only was he differentiated from others there by his age but also he was, understandably, not searching for anything. He was also there, as he says, "against my will—in the sense that any child is at a boarding school against his will—or at least, hardly by choice."

The children at the Prieuré included Fritz and his brother Tom, Dr. Stjoernval's son, Tolik Mercouroff, Madame de Salzmann's daughter Busic, and later two sons, Michel and Claude, as well as Gurdjieff's niece Luba, her sister Lida and cousin Valya. There were some ten children in all and they were able to attend the readings and lectures, if they wished.

At Orage's urging, Jessie Dwight had come to the Prieuré. Her attitude toward Gurdjieff ranges from detachment to passive-aggressive. She breaks the Prieuré's rules and avoids tasks she either does not like or considers beneath her. Gurdjieff discovers her reading letters from Orage and immediately delivers a shock, ordering that all mail must first be given to him. She resents Gurdjieff's influence over Orage and resists all Gurdjieff's efforts toward her. She apparently never questions herself and has not the least idea of Gurdjieff's mission and what is at stake.

Alexander de Salzmann, exasperated, bursts out—"If you'd only admit you're a squirming idiot,[31] what a marvelous initiate you'd be."

SUMMER 1924. GERMANY. Hitler begins to dictate *Mein Kampf* from his cell at the old fortress of Landsberg, high above the River Lech. Hitler's book gives his rationale for what has gone wrong with European civilization and his plans to change it.

31. A squirming idiot is a person with a particularly unpleasant personality trait.

JULY 8, 1924. CHAILLY. It is a hot day and Gurdjieff and Olga de Hartmann are in Paris. They are expected to return to the Prieuré. He tells her to have a mechanic check his car thoroughly, especially the steering wheel. On this day, too, he signs papers giving her power of attorney should anything happen to him. Though it is customary for the two to return together, he tells her he will drive alone. She is instructed to take a train.

Leaving Paris, Gurdjieff drives his small black Citroën as he always does. On the open road he travels at 115 kilometers an hour [71 m.p.h.]; through towns he cuts the speed to 90 kilometers [56 m.p.h.]. Near the hamlet of Chailly, the Citroën approaches a crossroads where the road from Paris to Fontainebleau meets the N 168 road from Versailles to Choisy-le-Roi. Suddenly, out from a side road appears a car. The Citroën swerves and shoots off the road, veering past a signpost, and heading into a grassy area between some trees and a stone embankment. The Citroën hits the embankment head on, snapping the steering-wheel, and comes to a dead stop against a tree. The immense force of the impact crumples the front axle and fenders, crushes the radiator, throws the engine off its seating, and smashes the windows and doors.

A passing policeman finds Gurdjieff, unconscious and bloody, his head laying on a car cushion. He has a severe concussion. He has either been thrown from the car, somehow crawled out, or the driver of the other car pulled him out and left. He is taken to a hospital. Olga de Hartmann finds him and has him brought to the Prieuré on a stretcher, his head wreathed with bandages. He is still unconscious. He is carried up to his second floor bedroom and put to bed. For five days he lies in his corner room of the Prieuré unconscious. He is being kept alive on oxygen. Doctors come and go at intervals. Tanks of oxygen are delivered and removed. There is a hushed atmosphere everywhere as if everyone is involved in a silent prayer for his recovery. Finally, he awakes only to find himself, as he says, "a bit of live meat in a clean bed." Madame de Hartmann takes over the running of the château while Madame Ostrowska and Dr. Stjoernval nurse Gurdjieff.

Uspenskii believes he had foreseen some accident like this. He says, "Gurdjieff lost contact with the source after Essentuki. His behavior goes contrary to his teaching. He drives a car as if he were riding a horse."

Some days after the car crash Uspenskii and his friend Boris Mouravieff[32] visit the crossroads where Gurdjieff's Citroën had hit the tree. Mouravieff says that Uspenskii was "despondent and crushed." After a prolonged silence, Uspenskii said: "I'm frightened…this is dreadful.…Georgi Ivanovitch's Institute was established to escape from the influence of the law of accident under which men spend their lives. Well, see how he himself has fallen under the influence of this very law.…I still wonder whether it's really a pure accident?—Gurdjieff used always to make light of honesty together with all the rest of human personality. Has he not gone too far?—I tell you, I'm terribly afraid!"

All the talk at the Prieuré is of the motor accident. But for Gurdjieff it is no accident at all. That, he says, is "their usual superficial understanding."

"As I supposed from the first when I recovered my senses," he says, "and as I am now quite convinced—it was the last chord of the manifestation toward me of that 'something' usually accumulating in the common life of people, which...was first noticed by the Great, really Great King of Judea, Solomon, and was called '*Tzvarnoharno.*'"[33]

LATE JULY 1924. PRIEURÉ. Jean Toomer arrives from America. His concern about Gurdjieff having so much power he had come to see was really "a deep-seated unwillingness to put my life under the direction of anyone other than myself, and a stubborn belief that I could make my own way, unaided by such help as I would receive in the course of ordinary life." Now ready to work with Gurdjieff, Toomer finds him incapacitated, with no one allowed to see him except those caring for him. A great gloom hangs over the Prieuré. Toomer finds there is little to no working going on, and what there is is done half-heartedly. In New York he has heard about the benefits of manual work from Orage, and so soon begins working in the vegetable garden and helping to uproot tree stumps, saw logs, and make roads.

In time, Gurdjieff begins to be seen walking slowly along the paths with a cane, his head bandaged, his dark swollen eyes concealed behind dark glasses. He looks a shell of his former vibrant self. With him are Mesdames Ostrowska and de Hartmann. Though it is the height of summer and the weather is quite warm, Gurdjieff is bundled in his thick black coat and astrakhan hat. Students approach him; he does not recognize them, his sight is so impaired. He does not speak. Against doctors' warnings, he has made a tremendous effort to get out of bed. Slowly, only taking a few steps at a time before stopping, he has made his way

32. Mouravieff has a strong animus toward Gurdjieff and does all he can to fan Uspenskii's concerns about his former teacher. His viewpoint and the accuracy of quoted material are to be taken accordingly. Gurdjieff, himself, answers why the accident happened in *The Herald of Coming Good*, in speaking about *Tzvarnoharno.* As to "honesty with all the rest of human personality," if Uspenskii in fact said this, it would mean he has forgotten what Gurdjieff said in St. Petersburg—"You do not understand what it means to be sincere...." *Search*, p. 249.

33. *Tzvarnoharno* or not, the crash shocks Gurdjieff into seeing what perhaps he has known but has refused to allow himself to see: namely that, regardless of his pupils' gifts, it is impossible, given their self-love and vanity, to prepare and train the required "helper-instructors" needed to disseminate the teaching.

down the staircase and out onto the terrace. Always behind him carrying a chair for him to sit upon, is eleven-year-old Fritz Peters, his designated "chair-carrier." After fifteen minutes or so, his wife and Madame de Hartmann take him back to bed. Each day Gurdjieff forces himself to stay outside a little longer. Despite his physical condition, as C. S. Nott observes, "One could still sense and feel the undiminished force of his being."

Recovering, Gurdjieff soon is directing the work from a bench or chair. He seldom speaks and has not smiled since the accident. One day a fallen tree is being hoisted from a watery ditch. Thomas de Hartmann and C. S. Nott are up to their knees in water. The tree falls back into the ditch hitting Nott on a leg he has previously injured. Instantly, Nott cries out, "Damnation!" Everyone stops and stares at him. "It's all right," says Nott, "no harm done, just uncomfortable."

Gurdjieff, watching, starts to smile and everyone starts to laugh. Says Nott, "A new feeling, almost of joy, emanated from everyone," and from that day forward, Gurdjieff begins to talk a little. Toomer, who has taken to the physical work, finds that with Gurdjieff's return "things begin to hum....It is perfectly amazing what his presence does. Extra life, extra zest, extra power, extra will springs up in us. Everybody works hard all day long and sometimes into the night." The hard work, consciously done, redirecting the attention from the mind and giving attention to both the body and the work at hand, begins to have an effect on Toomer and soon puts him "in simply wonderful shape, feeling that I could continue on and on, wanting no other life than this. All other life seemed, by contrast, flat, undynamic, unstretching, ungrowing and, above all, unreal, a mere dream-life of vague surfaces and a stir of words." And Toomer learns the real value of manual work as a means of transformation:

> Manual work is usually done for the sake of outward results, for the products, that is a farmer works to grow crops, a carpenter to build a house. Here at the Prieuré we were to work chiefly for the sake of purification, growth, increased ability and consciousness. Each job, to be sure, was to be done as well as we could do it. Work standards were anything but lax. Each of us was to improve as a workman, acquiring competence and skill. Tools and materials were to be cared for as real craftsmen care for them. But we were not to be attached to the fruits of our labor. The aim was the same as that expressed in the *Bhagavad Gita,* "Be free from attachment to results." People who became overly egotistical about their accomplishments were likely to find their pet projects mysteriously disrupted.

Toomer gets a new sense of manual work as chemistry. He says:

> When you work the way we did, the blood is drawn down from the head into the body. The blood, pumped vigorously through the body by this intellectual and sustained activity, is purified. The purified blood revitalized, well-nigh regenerates the body. Then there is a

> surge upwards into the brain. After several weeks the purified blood courses back into the head, revitalizing and well-nigh regenerating the mind. The total result is a recharged body-mind, a body purified, energized, strengthened, a mind able, lucid, with greatly increased power to grasp and comprehend.

Toomer is reading the aphorisms on the wall of the Study House. When he reads—*You are here having realized that you have only yourself chiefly to contend with. Therefore thank those who give you the opportunity*—he says:

> The saying took instant hold of me, found purchase in my very roots; for it crystallized practice that I had engaged in, none too consistently at all, but very earnestly, off and on, ever since that boyhood illness.[34] The new slant was the unmistakable pointing to oneself, the emphasis put on contending with oneself, not with others. The entirely new angle was the allure of actually thanking those who gave us the opportunity. I could remember, on several occasions in the past, being spontaneously grateful to those who had made me face myself and see things I didn't want to see, so that I had to struggle to overcome them. But thank *everyone* who calls out your faults, your anger, your impatience, your egotism; do this consciously, voluntarily; make determined practice of it—here indeed was an entirely new effort, an effort whose value struck me at once but whose full significance was to become clear only after years of application.

As Gurdjieff's physical strength returns, he takes more and more part in the Institute's activities and begins to answer questions and explain various aspects of the teaching. Says Toomer: "Each day was a full day. Indeed, more effort and more experience are packed into a day at the Institute than in an ordinary month. It gives you a measure of man's reserve power, a standard of human capacity."

AUGUST 26, 1924. PRIEURÉ. Gurdjieff calls everyone into the Prieuré's main salon. Earlier he had dictated to Olga de Hartmann the speech he wished to give. He begins:

"I was very ill. Now, thank God, I feel better and continue to be better...."

Gurdjieff stops.

He hands the dictation to Olga, telling her to read:

"What happened to me, how it happened, I do not know. I remember nothing. I went to the place where it happened and imagined how it happened. There are not many people who could speak with you like

34. At ten years of age Toomer was stricken with severe stomach ailments that greatly altered his life. "I had been strong. Now I was weak. I was compelled to exert efforts to get strong again. Life had taken away from me what it had given, and I was forced over years to obtain it by exertion."

this after such an accident. In principle, I had to die, but accidentally I stayed alive."

Gurdjieff then apologizes if he offended anyone in the weeks after the accident, as his memory was weak. He says only three or four days ago his memory came back to him and "I can live as before, not as an animal." His first thoughts were: "Did die or not? How will everything be now? And what about the Institute? I saw that I was alive...." He has, however decided to close the Institute.

"First of all," he says, "there are very few people who understand. I gave all my life for my Work, but the result from other people in general was not good and that is why I think it is not necessary for those few to sacrifice their lives here." People can leave immediately or stay on as guests for two weeks. He will sell the Prieuré but, he says, "All the same, I cannot throw away all my Work....In two weeks I will begin a new work. The names of those who may stay will be posted. Others will have to leave."

Gurdjieff gives some organizational instructions and then returns to his main point:

"Again, I repeat that the Institute is closed. I died. The reason is that I was disenchanted with people after all that I have done for them and I have seen how 'well' they have paid me for it. Now, inside of me everything is empty."

Besides his "disenchantment" with his students, Gurdjieff says, "the second reason is that I wish to live for myself. I have to rest and use all the time for myself. I don't wish to continue as before, and my new principle is—everything for myself."

Everything for myself. These last words have a quality of uncharacteristic self-pity but they are also historically relevant.

Many years before, on September 11, 1911, Gurdjieff had taken a special oath binding himself for twenty-one years, he writes, "in his conscience to lead in some ways an artificial life, modeled upon a program which had been previously planned in accordance with certain definite principles."

So, nearly thirteen years later, Gurdjieff appears to end his oath. He no doubt took his mission to be a failure. To establish the teaching in the West, he needed to put someone in his place. He needed to find and prepare a student with a Western mentality who could step-down the teaching. Otherwise, it would never take root. He had failed with Uspenskii, with Bennett and, perhaps, at this juncture, he saw no great promise in Orage.[35]

Gurdjieff's sudden closure of the Institute is a thunderbolt whose reverberations are felt for many days. Wrote Toomer of this time sometime later:

> Most of us were shot straight into the air, and stayed there, suspended, an uncomfortable length of time. Day after day you would see people, sometimes in twos and threes, sometimes alone, in conference with

> Gurdjieff, talking over their future course of life, where they would go, what they would do. I had such a conference. Gurdjieff said I might stay on, if I wished. I thought it over. Not much work would go on. But had I come here only to go away in a few months? Where would I go? What would I do? Finally, after quite a struggle, something clicked in me and I decided to return to New York.

AUGUST 1924. LONDON. Says Uspenskii: "Gurdjieff's work at the Prieuré," he says, "failed simply because the principle of seniority was not followed....People who did not belong to groups before, like Pinder and Orage, they were given certain power over people who were much older in the Work; it did not work—it could not go on."

AUTUMN 1924. PRIEURÉ. The car crash and Gurdjieff's later actions fuel the swirl of question and rumor around him as to who he is. For Madame Uspenskii it is not an issue: "I do not pretend to understand Georgi Ivanovitch," she declares. "For me he is X. All that I know is that he is my teacher and it is not right for me to judge him, nor is it necessary for me to understand him. No one knows who is the real Georgi Ivanovitch, for he hides himself from all of us. It is useless for us to try to know him, and I refuse to enter into any discussions about him."

AUTUMN 1924. NEW YORK. Through the door of the Sunwise Turn[36] steps C. Daly King. A Yale graduate living on private income, he has a keen interest in Egyptology and psychology. The bookshop is where twenty-nine-year-old King buys all his books. The previous January he and his wife had attended two performances of Gurdjieff's troupe and

35. Despite his understanding and being, he had been unable to make any of his students sufficiently aware of their identification with the properties of what he calls *Kundabuffer*, the blind egoism that puts man-in-quotation marks at the center of the universe. The car crash has opened him to what he probably had known but would not admit for some time. Namely: none of his would-be students at the Prieuré could break through this identification either. In the summer of 1963, Bennett lectures, "He certainly was under some special kind of obligation, that in the particular work he had to do, he should not assume a position of being a great teacher, with a large number of pupils depending upon him. It was often very obvious that with the greatest of ease, if he had chosen to do so, he could have exercised the power he had to attract people. He could have had thousands of people round him...." Ten years later, Bennett, able to see the large picture, would add, "They (his old and intimate pupils) saw him as their teacher, concerned with the spiritual progress of his pupils, whereas, he was concerned with the impact which his work and ideas could have on the world over a long period of years. This is why he so frequently refers to the realization of his aims after his death."

36. The Sunwise Turn plays a prominent place in Orage's life. Not only is the bookstore the venue of his first American talk, but it is here that he meets Jesse Dwight, C. S. Nott, and now C. Daly King, all of whom become significant figures in his life. Gurdjieff even mentions the bookstore and Jesse Dwight in his *Third Series*.

found the dances "totally unusual and impressive to a degree." In the ensuing months Jesse Dwight had often invited him to attend a meeting of Orage's but he had always declined, picturing it as a group of "fanatics meeting privately to discuss strange notions."

Finally, bowing to Jesse Dwight's persistence and logic—*she* was not a fanatic, was she?—King reluctantly attends a meeting. Intellectual to a high degree, King expects "a proselytizing harangue." He goes armed with an incredulous attitude, ready to object to every point. But he finds that the tall slender Englishman in the inconspicuous dark business suit presents the teaching with "complete and utter *rationality*." Moreover, Orage makes clear that no starry-eyed believers or woolly thinkers are countenanced.

"My incredulity was not admitted," says King. "Instead, it was demanded that I adopt skepticism toward what I heard, that is, that I should neither believe nor disbelieve."

Upon his return to New York Jean Toomer, without authorization and unable to resist his desire to be a teacher, however premature, sets up his own Gurdjieff study group, imitating Gurdjieff, affecting his mannerisms, even using Russian words. Says his friend Gorham Munson: "Jean had a lot of nerve to do that; he was really not qualified to do it." The group only lasts five or six meetings. He then returns to Orage's group.

Orage is quick to recognize the young man's possibilities and begins to work closely with Toomer. At one point after a question about will, Orage tells Toomer: "Work hard while you feel like it, and then, when you no longer want to, work twice as hard. It is the work done after wish ceases that really counts. When desire ends, then and then only can will come into play. When you automate activity slows down and would stop, then is your chance for voluntary, nonhabitual action."

DECEMBER 16, 1924. PRIEURÉ. *It happened in the 223rd year after the creation of the world through space flew the ship Karnak....*

Some four months after ending his formal teaching at the Prieuré, Gurdjieff begins to dictate to Olga de Hartmann. And with this Gurdjieff begins to bring into the world his magnum opus, *All and Everything: Beelzebub's Tales to His Grandson.*

It is well known that Gurdjieff took a dim view of contemporary writing, science fiction in particular. But it was the only means open to him to complete his mission. He says:

"Since I had not, when in full strength and health, succeeded in introducing in practice into the life of people the beneficial truths elucidated for them by me, then I must at least, at any cost, succeed in doing this in theory, before my death."

To Orage has fallen the task to raise money in America to free Gurdjieff to write *All and Everything.* Though not a welcome order, he does this admirably.

During 1924, Uspenskii finishes the introduction to *Fragments of an Unknown Teaching.*[37] In a passage concerning evil, later deleted, he writes that he asked Gurdjieff if there can be conscious evil. Gurdjieff says there certainly can be, though it is possible only in a very elaborate way, and in very rare cases.

"Anything that produces big phenomena can have mind and intelligence behind it," he says.

He pauses, then asks Uspenskii—"Why are you upset?"

"It means changing all I had thought before."

"It becomes even more interesting," says Gurdjieff. "It is one thing to have against you only mechanical forces and quite another to have intelligence; it is one thing to struggle with intelligence, and another to struggle with mechanical forces."

Gurdjieff, though pale, looking dreadful and walking with difficulty, wills himself to keep writing *All and Everything,* either dictating to Madame de Hartmann or scribbling in notebooks in Armenian.

Meanwhile, Orage is becoming ever more enamored of his young secretary. Says a close friend: "He wasted his substance in talk and falling in love." Gurdjieff sees her as a squirming idiot "spoiled out of all proportion to her position."

DECEMBER 20, 1924. GERMANY. Hitler is released from Landsberg prison.

1925. NEW YORK. Toomer has written to Orage that he "would like to learn from you, to work with you, more than formerly....Substances in me are turning to Gurdjieff, and, more immediately to you." Orage gives him permission to form a group in Harlem. This comes to nothing and Toomer leaves for Chicago.

1925. PRIEURÉ. Gurdjieff often sits on a bench in the garden while writing his book. Frequently his wife and aged mother come and sit on either side of him. "One of them always adored by me was my old mother and the other, my uniquely and sincerely beloved wife." His mother has a chronic liver condition and his wife has cancer. Like his mother, his once tall and beautiful wife is now stooped and walks with

37. In the original draft, he writes of his personal association with Gurdjieff in one section and of the teaching in a second. Only at a later time does he interweave the two sections into one, this blending giving a much more profound result.

the aid of a stick. Accompanying his mother on her walks to his bench are four animals. A cat walks in front of her, two peacocks at her side, and behind a dog. It is obvious from the conditions of these two women—"uniquely nearest to my inner life," says Gurdjieff— that both will soon die. To his mother's death he is reconciled, as this is "the normal destiny of every person of esteemed age." But the prospect of his wife's early death calls up a strong feeling of "'implacable revolt' against the injustice of casual, self-willed destiny." Seeing them, he feels every kind of association of suffering and so as not to "experience this unpleasant process, [I] immediately buried myself in the question of writing."

MARCH 1925. NEW YORK. Orage receives some chapters of *All and Everything.* Orage sends it back.

"It is completely unintelligible. I've no idea what it is about," he says.

Not long after, a revised version arrives. "This is entirely different," says Orage. "Now I begin to smell something very interesting."

Later Orage says of the book: "It is really an objective work of art, of literature of the highest kind; it is in the category of scripture....It is consciously designed to have a definite effect on everyone who feels drawn to reading it. Anyone who tried to rewrite it would distort it."

C. Daly King has continued to attend meetings. Orage sees his promise and the two men often have lunch together. Says King of his mentor: "I have never encountered any other mind of the shining clarity which Orage's achieved nor have I met any other teacher who so completely understood that no human being can ever be taught anything, that the true teacher's task is to assist another to learn."

MARCH 20, 1925. NEW YORK. At a meeting whose theme is chief feature, Toomer decides that his was the desire for power. "Orage thought that this came pretty close to the mark," Toomer writes. And Orage added, "We say that the chief feature must die. Meanwhile, observe it in all acts."

Toomer describes himself in the third person as having "a long slim body with long tapering fingers. He had the sensitivity of an artist, the lips of a sensualist, the eyes of a fanatic."

MAY 1925. PRIEURÉ. Gurdjieff has nearly fully recovered from the car crash, though his eyes continue to trouble him. Because of his inactivity, he has begun to put on weight. But, says C. S. Nott, "He is also radiating more 'light.'" Life at the Institute has returned to its usual course with movements in the Study House, meals in the 'English' dining room, and Turkish baths on Saturdays. Gurdjieff again is giving tasks in the forest and gardens but, reports Nott, he does "not take much active part himself." Another small black Citroën has been purchased and Gurdjieff has resumed his trips to Paris.

Wherever he goes, Gurdjieff carries with him a supply of cheap exercise books and pencils. No matter where he is he writes. Often, it is an effort and he must, through a variety of means, compel his organism to allow him to write. Once he asks C. S. Nott to meet him at the Café de la Paix at eleven o'clock in the morning. They drink a glass of Armagnac together. For the next two hours Gurdjieff writes, not saying a word, stopping only to order coffee or drinks.

"All the time I am sitting there," says Nott, "it is as if I am being charged with electricity, magnetized with energy from Gurdjieff; as if a force is passing between us. Although I have felt listless and tired when I arrived, and had sat for two hours apparently doing nothing, I am now charged to the brim with bubbling energy, like a battery."

At one o'clock Gurdjieff finally finishes and closes the exercise book.

"You see," he tells Nott, "what a lot I have done. Very good work this morning. Now take this back to the Prieuré and ask Madame de Hartmann to have it typed."

June 1925. Prieuré. Gurdjieff's mother dies. Madame Ostrowska's cancer grows worse. As the summer goes on she takes to her room permanently.

Summer 1925. Prieuré. Fritz Peters and his brother had left in October. They now return. He finds Gurdjieff, sitting on the terrace at one of the marble-topped tables shaded by a striped umbrella, writing *All and Everything.* Gurdjieff makes Peters his "caretaker." He is to clean his room, bring him food, and so forth.

Gurdjieff speaks to "Freets" (Fritz Peters) about the work he is doing with his wife. It is extremely difficult he says "because I try to do thing with her which almost not possible. If she alone, already she be long time dead. I keep alive, make stay alive, with my strength; very difficult things. But also very important—this most important moment in life for her. She live many lives, is very old soul; she now have possibility ascend to other world. But sickness come and make more difficult, make impossible for her do this thing alone. If can keep alive few months more will not have to come back and live this life again."[38]

38. Gurdjieff's statement "live this life again" directly refers to Uspenskii's idea of eternal recurrence. As Gurdjieff told Uspenskii in St. Petersburg, "This idea of repetition is not the full and absolute truth but it is the nearest possible approximation of the truth. . . . But what you say is very close to it. And if you understand why I do not speak of this, you will be still nearer to it. What is the use of a man knowing about recurrence if he is not conscious of it and does not change?" *Search,* p. 250.

JULY 1925. PRIEURÉ. Orage, with Jesse Dwight, returns. It is Orage's delicate job to edit *All and Everything* in a way that makes it clear and yet remains faithful to Gurdjieff's intention.

Besides writing the book in Armenian, Gurdjieff dictated it in Russian and a pidgin French, as he says that no single language could give him sufficient freedom of expression for his complicated ideas and theories. The Armenian was translated into Russian by Madame Galumnian, an Armenian pupil, and then translated from Russian into literal English by Thomas de Hartmann. It was for Orage to shape the words into appropriate English form, making literal what was to be taken literally, symbolic what is to be taken symbolically. To be rightly assimilated, Gurdjieff's ideas had to enter the psyche in a form that forced the reader to have to work to extract substance.

By now Orage, in the full bloom of 'falling in love,' falls more and more under the influence of Jesse Dwight. Like Uspenskii and Bennett before him, he is blind to his identification and its significance. Gurdjieff, ever watchful over his "super idiot," notes Orage's growing infatuation with his tall blond secretary. Gurdjieff tries to make him see what is happening, what she represents.

One wet morning Orage and Nott are sitting in the dark, empty Russian dining room. The two men are having tea. Gurdjieff appears wearing a light grey suit and carrying a walking stick and, as Nott observes, "looking very handsome." He stops by their table, lights a cigarette and begins to talk about his accident. Nott does not understand the meaning behind his words but intuits that Gurdjieff is "speaking in parables [on more than one level], conveying something to Orage."

Gurdjieff tells them that it was his habit when driving from Paris to the Prieuré to put his hand out of the window to pick an apple off a row of trees that grew near the spot where his car crashed. He did so on this occasion and the wheel of his car must have bumped into something. He remembered nothing. He must have unconsciously taken a cushion from the Citroën and put his head on it.

Nott can make nothing of the rest of the story.

Gurdjieff pauses, lights another cigarette, and continues.

"You know, Orage, when you give something to a man, or do something for him, the first time he will kneel and kiss your hand; second time, he takes his hat off; third time, he bows; fourth time, he fawns; fifth time, he nods; sixth time, he insults you; and the seventh time, he sues you for not giving him enough."[39]

39. Interestingly, Gurdjieff repeats this in its entirely—"Such is the nature of man that for your first gift..."— in the *Third Series,* p. 56. The deep meaning of this Orage apparently never fathomed.

Gurdjieff then glances at Nott but says—"You know, Orage, we must pay for everything."

After Gurdjieff leaves, Nott asks Orage what he had meant.

"He is probably getting at us for not knowing how to give," answers Orage. "Neither of us, it seems, has yet learnt. Perhaps Gurdjieff himself has had to learn how to give."[40]

After luncheon one day, Fritz Peters delivers a tray of coffee and brandy to Gurdjieff's room on the second floor. Opening the door, Peters finds Orage standing by one of the windows, impassive and very pale. Gurdjieff stands by his bed raging. In order to put the tray on the table Peters must walk between them. Doing so, he feels "flayed by the fury in Gurdjieff's voice."

Says Peters: "Orage, a tall man, seemed withered and crumpled as he sagged in the window, and Gurdjieff, actually not very tall, looked immense—a complete embodiment of rage.... Suddenly in the space of an instant, Gurdjieff's voice stopped, his whole personality changed, he gave me a broad smile—looking incredibly peaceful and inwardly quiet—motioned me to leave, and then resumed his tirade with undiminished force."

Peters feels great pity and compassion for Orage. Yet upon leaving the room, he says, "my feelings were completely reversed. I was still appalled by the fury I had seen in Gurdjieff; terrified by it. In a sense, I was even more terrified when I left the room because I realized that it was not only *not* 'uncontrollable' but actually under great control and completely conscious on his part."

Peters does not say, if he indeed knew, the subject of Gurdjieff's anger, but it likely had to do with Jesse Dwight.

Gurdjieff has many talks with Orage on love. Though love is of seven kinds, Gurdjieff says, he will only speak of three: instinctive love, emotional love, and conscious love.

> Instinctive love obeys the laws of chemistry or biology and proceeds by affinities.
>
> Emotional love is an aberration. It is not rooted in biology but is often opposed to biology in its direction and character. Often it is a mutual attraction of biological incongruities.
>
> Conscious love, rarely attained, is the only true form of loving.
>
> A conscious lover works on oneself in order to help the loved one perfect themselves, its aim being to bring about rebirth.

40. For an analysis of possible meanings behind this, see p. 236–237.

The summer passes and, given Gurdjieff's accident and Orage's skill at attracting and teaching students, Orage is given a de facto mandate to teach the Work in America.[41]

JULY 29, 1925. PRIEURÉ. Gurdjieff begins a period of intensive work and collaboration with Thomas de Hartmann on music for the movements and ballet.

July, 1925. Prieuré. One morning Gurdjieff, rather sardonically, asks Fritz Peters if he still wanted "to learn everything," or had he changed his mind?

Peters says he hasn't changed his mind.

"Freets, why you not ask about this then, if not change mind?"

He didn't mention it, he says, because he assumed Gurdjieff had not forgotten his request and that he didn't think Gurdjieff would have time since he was so busy.

"If you want something, must ask. You must work. You expect me to remember for you; I already work hard, much harder than you can even imagine, you wrong if also expect me always remember what you want." He then added: "If I busy, this is my business, not your affair. If I say I teach, you must remind me, help me by asking again. This show you want to learn."

With this begins weekly lessons at ten o'clock Tuesday mornings.

Fall 1925. Prieuré. Gurdjieff leaves the Prieuré for a time. Miss Merston, as the Prieuré's director, is to be in complete charge. Jane Heap arranges that Fritz and his brother, beginning with Thanksgiving, visit with Gertrude Stein and Alice B. Tolkas every Thursday in Paris. In time Fritz and Tom come to meet James Joyce, Ernest Hemingway, Constantin Brancusi, Jacques Lipschitz, Man Ray, and Paul Tchelitchev. Soon, Gertrude and Alice are taking the boys on guided tours of Paris in Gertrude's Model-T Ford.

WINTER 1925. PRIEURÉ. Madame Ostrowska's cancer becomes more acute.

DECEMBER 28, 1925. NEW YORK. Orage opens the meeting saying that readings of Gurdjieff's *All and Everything* will begin on January 1st. He speaks of the chapter on Purgatory and says he has read thousands of books and nothing in philosophy, not Plato or Plotinus, compare in lucidity, concentration, and subtlety to this chapter. "It leaves all philosophy behind," he says.

41. While at the Prieuré, based on what Gurdjieff has told him, Orage writes his essay, *On Love*. He appears not to make the connection between what Gurdjieff is telling him and his affair. Like Uspenskii and Bennett, Orage's identification is too strong, even for Gurdjieff.

JANUARY 5, 1926. NEW YORK. Letter from Orage to Jean Toomer: "I haven't plumbed the depths of G.'s thought and probably never shall; but at least certain meanings and interpretations of the colossal parable I now begin to understand."

APRIL 6, 1926. NEW YORK. Orage tells Toomer: "What we say aloud is personality. What we say to ourselves is essence. The aim is to speak what we now withhold, and withhold what we now speak."

APRIL 1926. NEW YORK. Jean Toomer, while awaiting a subway at the 66th Street subway platform, has an out-of-body experience. "I was born above the body into a world of psychological reality....In my private language I shall call this experience the Second Conception." Later in one of his autobiographies, *From Exile into Being*, he describes it:

> I was startled by an uncommon inward event. It was as though I had been touched from within in an extraordinary quiet way that stilled my functioning and momentarily suspended me between what had been and what was to come. My very life had been stopped, so it seemed, and yet I was about to live again, live anew, and strangely. Somehow I understood I was going to be moved, regardless of my wish or will, into a nameless experience.

Of his sensations, Toomer wrote that they "could not have been more strange had my body left the ground and soared into the air." Not only his body but the totality of his presence changed. "My body and my life were in the power of a Power....I was losing my life. It was being taken away by a noble creation...There was Being, Consciousness, and Existence so large and deeply powered—that it would surely absorb me as a particle." He has the feeling of having "a second body, a body in addition to the physical, composed of subtler matters, having its own forces and appropriate functions." And when he looked at his body "It seemed removed from me, placed 'out there,' and below me, as though there were space between myself and it. Though I knew I was still attached to it, or it to me, I felt no relation to it whatsoever. It could have walked off and gone about its business, vanished, and I would not have missed it. I had been torn above the body. To me the body was an object."

SPRING 1926. PRIEURÉ. Gurdjieff returns. A general meeting is called. Miss Merston, who he has left in charge of the Prieuré, reads all of the 'offences' that have occurred during his absence. Fritz Peters, who had rebelled against Miss Merston's authority, has a long list of black marks. Gurdjieff calls him forward and asks if he admits to everything. Peters does so. Gurdjieff then renumerates the offenses, peels off an equal number of 10 franc notes and hands them, a big roll, to Peters. Then the next offender is called forward. At the end of the 'punishments,' Gurdjieff turns to Miss Merston and gives her one 10 franc note for her "conscientious fulfillment of her obligations as director of the Prieuré."

Miss Merston shows no obvious reaction and even thanks Gurdjieff for her reward.

Says Peters: "We were all aghast; we had been taken completely by surprise, of course. But the main thing we all felt was a tremendous compassion for Miss Merston. It seemed to me a senselessly cruel, heartless act against her."

A few days later Peters tells Gurdjieff that he didn't understand why he was rewarded for not doing his tasks and causing Miss Merston so much trouble.

"What you not understand," says Gurdjieff, "is that not everyone can be troublemaker, like you. This important in life—is ingredient, like yeast for making bread. Without trouble, conflict, life become dead. People live in status-quo, live only by habit, automatically, and without conscience. You good for Miss Merston. You irritate Miss Merston all time—more than anyone else, which is why you get most reward. Without you, possibility for Miss Merston's conscience fall asleep. This money should really be reward from Miss Merston, not from me. You help keep Miss Merston alive."

June 26, 1926. Prieuré. Madame Ostrowska dies of cancer. Uspenskii attends the funeral. The two men do not speak. Gurdjieff goes to his room where he stays for two days. Within two years of his car crash, he has lost his wife and mother, and 'closed' his Institute.

Summer 1926. New York. The affair between Jean Toomer and Margaret Naumberg ends. She had financed his spiritual quest. He would find others. As Gorham Munson says, all his life he was "successful in getting people to support him." Toomer again visits the Prieuré.

Summer 1926. Prieuré. Orage arrives from America and continues his translation of *All and Everything* into English. Orage generally comes for only a few months of the year, and Gurdjieff tries to spend as much time as possible with him.

Gurdjieff interacts with Orage in a way quite different from how he usually acts with pupils. The two often can be seen joking with one another and having a great deal of fun. Often, Gurdjieff uses this as a means of teaching. "Few knew better how to joke and have fun with him," says Nott, "without exceeding the bounds between master and pupil."

Every day Gurdjieff works as usual on his book, rewriting and revising. He works in cafés and at the Prieuré, and, when traveling, dictates in Russian to Madame de Hartmann who sits in the back seat of the Citroën furiously writing. In the evening after dinner chapters are read aloud in the salon. Gurdjieff watches the expressions on people's faces and other physiological signs.

He has begun to draft the chapter on "America." Says Nott: "If an American visitor turned up, he would have parts of the chapter read, and always he would begin to laugh during certain passages. We also would join in the laughter, although most us are never sure what he is laughing at. I suspect that it is at ourselves."

C. Daly King is in Europe vacationing with his family and one day arrives at the Prieuré. At the gate he rings the bell marked "Sonnez fort." He is not admitted.

Of this King says, the words sounding rather laconic, "I found nobody of much authority about when I sought entrance and, not insisting, was turned away."

Doubtless he was of many minds about putting himself under Gurdjieff's eye. While he holds Orage in high regard, Gurdjieff remains a bewilderment. King is put off by what he takes to be Gurdjieff's bullying, his manner, the irrationality of his method of teaching. As he will later say:

> No doubt for many years to come there will be discussion regarding the character and personality of Mr. Gurdjieff.... I do not hesitate to say that in my opinion he is not a teacher, and I have seen him both privately and at the meetings conducted by him many times. He is evasive, and I have never yet heard him give a direct answer to any inquiry.... When not evasive, he blusters; in these bullying moods there is more of contempt for his followers than of animosity, but in any case it is scarcely an attitude conducive either to loyalty or to successful instruction. It may well be that he does not wish to instruct—others besides myself have received the idea that he knows much but isn't telling—and my own view is that, insofar as he desires to assist anyone, his principle is that this cannot be done through intellectual information.

Unlike King, both Jean Toomer and Gorham Munson from the Orage group, arrive at the Prieuré and are admitted. Gurdjieff calls Toomer "Mr. Half-Hour-Late," presumably referring to his habit of speaking slowly.

Margaret Anderson and Jane Heap arrive and converse with Orage.

> Orage spoke of Eliot's *Waste Land* and Joyce's *Ulysses* as the two high points of contemporary expression—the artist's statement of the present human bankruptcy.... As he talked Orage seemed to be simultaneously performing several other feats—taking a complete inventory of our mental and emotional equipment, forcing us to lay our cards on the table, realizing that we might not enjoy this, courte-

ously turning his back that we might recover our bearings, but directing every phrase of the conversation as toward a preconceived intention and result. I tried to discover the intention and became baffled. I felt such admiration for Orage's expertness, such sudden panic as I reflected it was a faculty I might never possess, that I became slightly hysterical. I wanted to shake Orage and shout Tell me what it is you know that I don't! Next I wanted to weep, as a token of admiration. Then I decided it would be better to discuss my reactions than to scream or weep. So we did. Orage told of what he had been seeking for all his life, what he had found, what he was working at, what its object was. He made careful distinctions between subjective and objective states of being, the former receiving his taboo. He asked me about my life.

"What is your object in playing the piano?"

"As nearly as I can define it, playing the piano is the logical way to recapture continuously that state of ecstasy without which life is not worth living."

"That is not an object," corrected Orage. "If you say you are playing the piano to make money or to give concert tours you have named objects."

And then he added five words that have changed my outlook upon life:

"Act," said Orage, "don't be acted upon."

FALL 1926. CHICAGO. Jean Toomer arrives and sets up a Gurdjieff study group. He again begins to imitate Gurdjieff, passing himself off as an Eastern mystic or mystery man. Of this Gorham Munson will later say:

> ...a good deal of Jean's life after he went to Chicago was the leading of a life of lying, lying, lying....Jean pretended to be more than he was. He assumed the development and psychology beyond the point that he had ever reached; he ascribed to himself powers and knowledge which he had not really attained. Some would say he had a fantasy which he truly believed about himself as a master of psychological teaching, psychological knowledge. It doesn't seem to me that he could have deceived himself to that extent. He play acts as a spiritual leader.

LATE DECEMBER 1926. PRIEURÉ. Orage leaves for America. "The Prieuré was in debt, Gurdjieff had not a penny and nothing had arrived," he says. Before leaving he gives Gurdjieff $500 of his own money.

CHRISTMAS 1926. PRIEURÉ. Gurdjieff, in reflecting on his productivity in regard to writing, realizes that "in reality at all times [his writing productivity] strictly corresponded in its duration with the length and quality of the, so to say, 'degree of contact,' between my consciousness and the suffering proceeding in me on behalf of my mother and wife." He had written before with Olga de Hartmann, Dr. Stjoernval, and C. S. Nott sitting beside him, they acting as sort of a negative pole in the 'battery' set up. But with his wife and mother Gurdjieff had suffered unconsciously. And so he elicits the use of unconscious suffering as well as conscious. While "watching the children around the Christmas tree and their unrestrained joy," Gurdjieff says he comes to the recognition "of the full possibility of attaining his aims "through the forces of the inner-world struggle."

1927. PRIEURÉ. Hearing from her friends, Margaret Anderson and Jane Heap, that in Gurdjieff she "will see not one man, but a million men in one," Solita Solano arrives. She is a writer and literary critic, and companion of the writer Janet Flanner, who writes for *The New Yorker.* She rejects Gurdjieff on all counts.

"I hoped for a demigod, a superman of saintly countenance, not this 'strange' écru man about whom I could see nothing extraordinary except the size and power of his eyes."

She listened to the reading from his "vaunted book," she says and declares, "It bored me." And so she rejects him intellectually, "although with good humor." Later she hears the "famous music" played. "Almost from the first measures," that she also rejects.

A week or so later, she goes with Margaret and Jane to a restaurant to dine with Gurdjieff and twenty or so others. She is seated next to him. "For two hours [he] muttered in broken English. I rejected his language, the suit he was wearing and his table manners; I decided that I rather disliked him."

SPRING 1927. PRIEURÉ. Gurdjieff is now receiving $1,000 a month from the American groups. He keeps up the demand for money on Orage, who writes: "Gurdjieff is really quite extraordinary about money—but not, unfortunately, unique; we've known many people at college and in life equally extraordinary. However, I'm giving him still the benefit of the doubt, and I'm only sorry I cannot give him a million if only to see if he could be impecunious within a month or so of receiving it."

MAY 1, 1927. PRIEURÉ. Having composed some 300 pieces of music, Gurdjieff ends his collaboration with Thomas de Hartmann.

EARLY SUMMER 1927. CANADA. Jesse Dwight, fighting to hold Orage, has found an ally in C. Daly King, who believes his mentor is too much under Gurdjieff's thumb. The two men have now become quite close, frequently lunching and dining together during the week, with Orage often visiting as King's house guest on weekends. King has just published a book, *Beyond Behaviorism,* which seeks to show the relationship between scientific psychology and Gurdjieff's teaching. Like Uspenskii,

King is enamored of the teaching but regards Gurdjieff as a "dubious messiah, even if an extremely sophisticated one."

Customarily, Orage spends his summers at the Prieuré but this summer, no doubt at the behest of King and Jesse, he asserts his independence. Orage does not go the Prieuré. Instead he vacations in Canada with Jesse and Daly King and his wife, the conversation of the three young people likely turning on the need for fifty-four-year-old Alfred Richard Orage to establish his independence.

SUMMER 1927. PRIEURÉ. Jean Toomer arrives at the Prieuré to spend the summer. As he will be the senior American pupil present, Orage has asked him to oversee the others.

Soon, Gorham Munson and his wife, Elizabeth, arrive and are given a simple room on the third floor, the 'Monks' Corridor. The writer Waldo Frank and his new wife, Alma, had arrived earlier, as had Lincoln Kirstein, Payson Loomis, Carl Zigrosser, Schuyler Jackson, and Edwin Wolfe. Frank is Munson's and Toomer's former literary mentor. Munson finds Toomer showing Frank around the property. The two men seem to be getting on. The group runs into Gurdjieff coming down the walk. He invites them to "the Russian bath" that evening. Munson notes that a few times he hears Gurdjieff speak perfect English and is of the opinion that he speaks broken English because, in making himself hard to understand, his listeners had to give their full attention.

The group has coffee on the terrace. Then Gurdjieff drives them in his Citroën to the Café Henri IV where he at once orders a round of Armagnac and proposes a toast: "Health—ordinary idiots." Then Gurdjieff took another table and began writing a chapter of *All and Everything* in Armenian in a cheap notebook. Frank, a self-important doyen of American letters who had expected red carpet treatment, is put off and says that Gurdjieff acts like a jovial headmaster.

"Health—candidates for idiots," Gurdjieff calls out, raising a glass to a second round of Armagnac.

Munson remembers that Thomas Carlyle had once criticized Jesus for his incompleteness, saying, "He had no Falstaff in him."

"On the biggest scale," thinks Munson, observing Gurdjieff write amid the café noises and passings to-and-fro of waiters and clientele, "he is all that a writer should be: indefatigable, living life to the fullest, inspired with the highest aim in literature—the writing of modern scripture."

Munson sees, too, that despite Gurdjieff's disclaimer that he no longer was teaching, he was teaching all the time. In the late afternoon the men went to the bathhouse but Gurdjieff demanded no anecdotes, as these were for special occasions only. Then Gurdjieff rushed the group back to the château for the evening meal.

Later that week on Saturday evening about sixty people assembled in the English dining room, Gurdjieff sitting in the center of a long table, everyone eating and toasting to the twenty-one different types of idiots.

"Health—squirming idiots," Gurdjieff calls out and everyone drains their glass.

"Health—compassionate idiots."

"Health—squared idiots."

The toasts go as high as eight or nine idiots. Sometimes Gurdjieff toasts with a glass of water: "Health—wise man."

Gurdjieff had seated Frank and his wife on his left and he plays the charming host with important personages.

After dinner Gurdjieff invites everyone into the drawing room to hear a chapter of *All and Everything* read. It becomes clear to Munson that Gurdjieff "is writing to produce intended effects upon an intended audience, and he is checking on the production of designed effects."

Munson says that Gurdjieff had once remarked, "To write my book for conscious men would be easy but to write it for donkeys—very hard."

At the close of the evening, around four o'clock in the morning, Gurdjieff invited Frank and his wife to have a crayfish dinner with him the following evening in Montmartre.

The Franks go but only to tell him—Gurdjieff has left early in the morning for Paris—that they could not join him. As they peered into the restaurant window from the street, Gurdjieff suddenly looked up and waved them inside.

During dinner, Gurdjieff steps on Frank's corns to the point where the author finally stands up and declares—"I think you are a Devil."

Before meeting Gurdjieff, Jean Toomer had already recognized in himself that there is an "I" and a "not-I." He had believed that writing was a means to unify himself. He had found that not to be true. Years later in writing one of his unpublished autobiographies he wrote: "Writing, real writing, it now seemed to me, presupposed the possession of the very thing I knew I lacked, namely, self-purity, self-unification, self-development. I wasn't fit to write. I felt and felt strongly that one ought to be something before one essayed to say something. I felt and felt deeply that a man ought to be a Man before he elected to write." Even so, after *Cane*, he wrote three novels, *Caromb, Gallonwerps,* and *Transatlantic.*

He had published *Cane* in 1923 and did not complete *Caromb* until 1927. Perhaps part of the difficulty was that, though Waldo Frank had written a highly complimentary introduction, he had also spoken of Toomer as being an "African-American." Toomer was white in appearance and manner, but was racially mixed. He took himself to be neither black or white but what he called "American." He took this stand as early as 1914 and never wavered throughout his life, though it was a source of continuing tension and criticism for him with both blacks and whites.

At the Prieuré there is no talk of race and color and, filled with energy and with ideas pouring through him, Toomer writes what he will consider his best novel, *Transatlantic*, or, as he later retitled it, *Eight Day World.* The first draft he writes in seventeen days.

AUGUST 1927. PRIEURÉ. Now Orage arrives, notably alone, to continue work on *All and Everything.* He informs Gurdjieff he must return on September 1st, he has "promised Jesse."

Gurdjieff—who set great importance on completing the translation—"naturally" suddenly can never find the time to work on the translation.

Ten days pass. No work.

Then, the very evening of Orage's departure, Gurdjieff announces translation work will begin the next day. Orage says he has given Jesse his essence-promise to return to New York.

Gurdjieff storms at Orage for leaving his work at the Prieuré "to return to nonentities in New York."

Orage leaves Gurdjieff and returns to Jesse Dwight. His explanation—"I ran out of my first marriage. I will never do so again."

This commitment, so innocent looking and noble sounding, would cost Orage dearly, as it would Gurdjieff.

SEPTEMBER 24, 1927. NEW YORK. Despite his teacher's disapproval, Orage marries Jesse Dwight. She had never had a real feeling for the Work or Gurdjieff, and flaunted her 'independence' in hundreds of little ways.

But Orage is 'in love.'

He describes the situation this way:

"He [Gurdjieff] regarded me as someone who had, so to speak, come with him from another planet with a task to carry out. But I fell in love with a native, and this interfered with his aim."[42]

Before the marriage Orage had been in England. He had promised Gurdjieff to come to the Prieuré before he left for America but instead sailed without seeing him.[43] This would—in light of the aim he had when he first came to the Prieuré in November 1923—have disastrous consequences for Orage.

42. Gurdjieff taught that one person can never give another his understanding. And as it is with Uspenskii and Bennett, so it is with Orage. Gurdjieff had a planetary aim. They had a particular aim.

43. Jean Toomer was at the Prieuré at this time. Gurdjieff's idea, it is thought, was to convince Orage to stay at the Prieuré. This would safely remove him from Jesse Dwight's and C. Daly King's influence, and allow his editorial talents to be applied to the manuscript of the *First Series.* In the interim, Toomer was to have taken over the groups in America.

NOVEMBER 6, 1927. PRIEURÉ. *The sole means now for the saving of the beings of the planet Earth would be to implant again into their presences a new organ...of such properties that every one of these unfortunates during the process of existence should constantly sense and be cognizant of the inevitability of his own death as well as of the death of everyone upon whom his eyes or attention rests....*

After three years of writing, Gurdjieff completes the first draft of *All and Everything,* only to then realize that for anyone not personally associated with him, the book will be unintelligible. *All and Everything* is his *legominism* to be understood and actualized in a future time. It is his last means of completing his mission—and it is unreadable!

The shock of all the intentional effort he has made since his auto accident—the thought of now having to rewrite the whole book—suddenly strips him of the one thing that has never failed him—*self-remembering.*

Gurdjieff no longer has the full sensing of the whole of himself.

There is nothing to do but to begin again. But his health is bad. He has this foreboding that time is running out. He wrestles with the idea of suicide. Gurdjieff finds himself at what is conceivably the lowest point in his life.

Finally, freeing himself from these dark thoughts, he decides to begin the rewriting of *All and Everything.*

This is an important day in other respects. Orage and Jesse Dwight are in England for his divorce proceedings from his wife Jean Walker. On this day his divorce becomes final. Orage has promised Gurdjieff that once the divorce is final he will come to the Prieuré. Instead Orage sends Gurdjieff a wire saying that he and Jesse are sailing back to New York.

It's a crucial moment in Orage's life, a definite fork in the road, for he has allowed Jesse to influence him to break his word to his teacher. Gurdjieff, furious, knowing full well what this portends both for Orage and the establishing of the teaching, writes Orage a letter.[44]

The subject is suffering, and he explains the difference between "voluntary" and "intentional" suffering; a distinction that Orage is unclear about. He also speaks about "noticeable coincidences."

Some years later C. S. Nott gives Uspenskii a copy of *All and Everything.* Uspenskii says that he has not read it.

"You haven't read it?" asks Nott. "Why?"

Answers Uspenskii—"It sticks in my throat."

CHRISTMAS 1927. PRIEURÉ. A tree is cut from the surrounding forest and erected in the main salon and decorated with hundreds of candles. Presents are also hung from the tree. Just as it is beginning to get dark,

44. Given what is going on between the two men—*the struggle between magicians*—it is likely he mentions or alludes to Orage's new wife.

Gurdjieff sends for Fritz Peters and tells him that he is to act as the concierge that evening, that he is expecting a long distance phone call and that it must be answered. Gurdjieff tells him he has chosen him because he trusts him and that he speaks English, French, and enough Russian to be able to cope with any call that might come. Peters is crestfallen, as this is the first Christmas at the Prieuré when Gurdjieff is present. So Peters must watch from the small unheated concierge house outside as the Christmas festivities take place, including the giving of gifts. At this, unable to control himself, Peters goes up to the window of the château and peers in. Gurdjieff sees him and sends for him. "Why not at concierge? Why you here?" he angrily demands. Peters gives some lame answer and he is directed to return. At the end of his shift, he says, "I went back to my room, hating Gurdjieff, hating the Prieuré, and by this time I was almost feeling proud of my 'sacrifice' for him. I vowed that I would never mention that evening to him or to anyone else; also, that Christmas would never mean anything to me again."

Gurdjieff never mentions what happened but Peters says, "He no longer spoke to me as if I were a child, and my private 'lessons' came to an end."

SUNDAY AFTER CHRISTMAS, 1927. PRIEURÉ. Since mid-morning Peters has been drinking with some Americans. They are all angry with Gurdjieff about a recent incident and fourteen-year-old Peters, for the second time in his life, is drunk. By late afternoon Gurdjieff, who is preparing to leave for Paris, sends for him. He and Madame de Hartmann are in his car by the front gate. He asks Peters to go to his room and get a bottle of Nujol, a medicine, explaining that he had locked his door and now could not find the key and Peters, his "caretaker," had the only existing key. Though Peters has the key in his hand, he lies to Gurdjieff declaring that he has also lost his key.

"Gurdjieff became very angry," says Peters, "began to shout at me, talking about my responsibilities and saying that losing the key was practically a crime, all of which only served to make me more determined."

Gurdjieff ordered Peters to go to his own room and search it.

Still gripping the key, Peters tells him that he "would gladly search my room but that I knew I would not find the key because I remembered losing it earlier in the day."

He does go to his room, makes a search, and returns to the car to report that the key is still missing.

"Gurdjieff went into another tantrum," Peters says, "saying that the Nujol was very important—that Madame de Hartmann had to have it while she was in Paris."

She could buy some more at a drugstore, Peters tells him.

Gurdjieff, furious, says that as there was some in his room he was not going to buy any more and, further, that the drugstores were closed on Sunday.

Peters says that "even if there was some in his room, we could not get it without his key or my key, which were both lost, and that since even Fontainebleau had a 'pharmacie de garde' open on Sundays, there must be a similar one in Paris."

With that Gurdjieff, accompanied by Madame de Hartmann, drives off in a rage.

Peters staggers back to his room.

The next evening Gurdjieff returns and Peters, fearing he would lose his job as Gurdjieff's "caretaker," goes to his car.

"I went," he says, "like a lamb to slaughter."

Gurdjieff says nothing to him. Peters carries his luggage to his room, opening the door with his key. When they are alone, Gurdjieff holds up the key, shakes it at Peters, and says: "So, you find key."

"Yes," says Peters who then, unable to contain himself, admits that he never lost his key.

Gurdjieff asks where the key had been when he had asked for it.

It had been in his pocket all the time, Peters says.

Gurdjieff shakes his head and looks at the young boy incredulously... and then laughs. He tells him he will tell him later what he is going to do with him. Peters leaves with the key.

At dusk Gurdjieff sends for him. They meet on the terrace of the Prieuré. Gurdjieff says nothing. Finally, he holds out his hand.

"Give key," he says flatly.

Peters, holding the key in his hand, does not hand it over. His eyes plead with Gurdjieff.

With his hand Gurdjieff makes a firm gesture. The young boy gives up the key.

Gurdjieff puts the key in his pocket and starts to walk down the path.

Peters watches until Gurdjieff is almost out of sight. Then he jumps on a bicycle and races down the path after him. When he is within a few yards of him, Gurdjieff turns and looks back. Peters gets off the bike and rushes up to him. The two stare at each other for a very long time. Finally, Gurdjieff asks, very quietly and seriously—"What you want?"

Peters, his eyes full of tears, holds out his hand. "Please give me the key," he pleads.

Gurdjieff shakes his head. Very slowly but firmly he answers—"No."

"I'll never do anything like that again," Peters cries. "Please."

Gurdjieff puts his hand on Peters head, a very faint smile on his face.

"Not important," he says. "I give you other work. But you now finished with key."

Gurdjieff then takes the two keys out of his pocket and holds them up.

"Have two keys now," he says. "You see, I also not lose key."

With that, he turns away and continues down the path.

MID-JANUARY 1928. PRIEURÉ. Orage and his new wife arrive. Gurdjieff kisses Orage's wife saying—"You are now half mine, whether you like it or not." At dinner one evening Gurdjieff makes sure the Armagnac is poured more liberally than usual. In time, Gurdjieff appears very drunk. But, at one moment, he snatches a small object, a watch or locket, from Orage's wife.

Gurdjieff plays with the object.

Orage, sitting next to him, waits, a tiger-like look on his face.

Suddenly Orage lunges.

But Gurdjieff yanks the object just beyond Orage's grasp.

Before the newlyweds leave the Prieuré, Gurdjieff transfixes Orage's wife with his gaze. He warns her—"If you keep my super-idiot from coming back to me, you burn in boiling oil."

SPRING 1928. PRIEURÉ. At a talk in the salon Gurdjieff is asked about the lack of understanding between Oriental and Occidental mentalities. He answers that this is caused in part by the lack of energy in the East and lack of wisdom in the West. He went on to predict that the importance of the Eastern world would grow to where it would "become a threat to the momentarily all-powerful, all-influential new culture of the Western world." Among the purposes of all messengers from the gods, messiahs and leaders, there is one that is fundamental: "to find some means by which the two sides of man, and, therefore, the two sides of the earth, could live together in peace and harmony....Time is short—it is necessary to achieve this harmony as soon as possible to avoid complete disaster." The only way this can be accomplished is through the individual development of man into a genuine, natural man. One even partially developed individual can influence many others. History, Gurdjieff said, had proven that politics, religion, and any other organized movement which treated man in the mass—and not as individual beings—were failures. The separate, distinct growth of each individual in the world was the only possible solution.

SPRING 1928. ATHENS. Bennett is incarcerated in Athens' central jail, accused of bribing an official to fabricate title deeds relating to an Imperial Ottoman property in which he has a concessionary interest. Bennett receives a telegram:

> Sympathy to Bennett under ninety-six laws.
> —P. D. Uspenskii

To get released, Bennett drinks iodine to fake appendicitis. He is removed to a municipal nursing home. Later, defending himself in Greek, he is acquitted with costs awarded against the government. However, that autumn when Bennett returns to London, Uspenskii refuses all communication.

Later, Bennett learns why. Apparently when the Greek police searched his Athens flat they found several letters from Uspenskii. As his name was Russian, they thought he might be a Communist. This information was forwarded to the Home Office in London which questioned Uspenskii about his political leanings.

Cut off from his teacher, Bennett, with less than five years as a pupil of Uspenskii, forms his own study group. He has reservations, not feeling it is "right for me to set myself up as an expositor of Gurdjieff's System without permission either from him or Uspenskii." He resolves the question by sending Uspenskii a full transcript of each meeting. Bennett says, "I wrote to say that if he disapproved he had only to tell me and I would stop."

MAY 6, 1928. PRIEURÉ. To stimulate his writing, Gurdjieff decides "to remove from my eyesight all those who by this or that make my life too comfortable" and imposes on himself three "will-tasks." One, was to rewrite all his books in a new form which he now understood after the first draft of the *First Series.* Two, to make clear to himself "the very deep questions concerning the common psyche of man." And three, to renew his physical body and spirit so that upon the completion of his writings he "can direct the spreading of them myself, with the energy and persistence which was peculiar to me in my youth." Madame Uspenskii he sends to England and the de Salzmanns to Germany.

LATE SUMMER 1928. PRIEURÉ. Gurdjieff works on the first of what will be three revisions of *All and Everything.* In writing the book, he says he came to hate pencil and paper and the very idea of writing—that he has to force himself every day to begin. Nevertheless, he perseveres.

Of the book Orage says, "It is to be read from the real heart, that is, with emotional understanding." About the book's unusual use of language, he says, "Gurdjieff will not use the language of the intelligentsia—ideas in the book will not be presented in our habitual thought patterns. Our intellectual life is based on chance associations which have become more or less fixed. Only when these are broken up can we begin to think freely." Of values, he says, "The book destroys existing values; it compels the serious reader to re-value all values, and, to a sincere person, it is devastating.... For myself, I realize now that for two years I tried to use these ideas, tried to assimilate them into my own set of values, hoping to enrich the values without giving them up. I thought that the new ideas would widen the scope and extend the perspective of the old and give variety to the content. There comes a time to almost everyone in this work when he asks himself, 'Shall I lose the old values that gave incentive, and shall I then be able to go on to new ones, ones of a different order?'"

"There is," declares Orage, "in the book as a whole, a parallel with the Bible, in that it opens with a cosmology and a cosmogony, an account of how and why the world was created, and of the fall of man.... The anomalies that seem to us incongruous and absurd may be a text within a text, which, when rooted out, may comprise an alphabet of the doctrine."

LATE SUMMER 1928. PRIEURÉ. *Only such a sensation* [the constant sensing of one's death and that of the death of all whom one sees] *and such a cognizance can now destroy the egoism completely crystallized in them* [human beings], *that has swallowed up the whole of their Essence and also that tendency to hate others which flows from it—the tendency, namely, which engenders all those mutual relationships existing there, which serve as the chief cause of all their abnormalities unbecoming to three-brained beings and maleficent for them themselves and for the whole of the Universe....*

With this Gurdjieff finishes his revision of *All and Everything.* He now begins to write the *Second Series* of *All and Everything,* or *Meetings With Remarkable Men.* Having written one book he has profited by the experience and says that now, "I had become more adroit in the art of concealing serious thoughts in an enticing, easily grasped outer form, and in making all those thoughts which I term 'discernible only with the lapse of time' ensue from others usual to the thinking of most contemporary people, I changed the principle I had been following and, instead of seeking to achieve the aim I had set myself in writing by quantity, I adopted the principle of attaining this by quality alone."

FALL 1928. NEW YORK. Orage gives C. Daly King permission to teach two groups, one in New York City, another in New Jersey.

DECEMBER 1928. PRIEURÉ. Fritz Peters receives two letters. One is from his mother in Chicago telling him it is time to return home. In it there is also a note from his stepfather saying that he would be welcome and sent to college. The second is from Jane Heap inviting him and his brother to spend Christmas with her in Paris. In the past his relationship with Jane had been explosive, he said two months before he arrived at the Prieuré she had hit him with a board with nails in it because he refused to do as she asked. As Margaret did, Fritz saw Jane as someone who needed to dominate, have power over others, and who created a continual and compulsive melodrama. Lately, they had reconciled. When told about his desire to leave the Prieuré, she was strongly against it. As Jane Heap and Margaret Anderson had adopted Fritz and his brother, he could only return to America if the adoption was legally broken. Knowing what a rare opportunity it was to be with Gurdjieff at so early an age, Jane vehemently argued against his leaving. Her arguments brought many others onto her side. But to no avail.

JANUARY 23, 1929. NEW YORK. Earlier, Gurdjieff had asked Orage for a donation of $10,000 from his groups. Not receiving it, he now arrives in person. He tells Orage he wants the money within three weeks. "Gurdjieff is more himself than ever," says Orage, "that is to say, he is more impossible than ever. But certainly New York needed a shaking up; and I too must have needed it. . . ."

Orage's wife is now pregnant.

Around this time, and perhaps before, Orage felt he needed a new initiation from Gurdjieff.

"I told Gurdjieff that I'd come to the end of my patience," he says, "and that, without a new initiation, I was as good as dead about the Prieuré. . . ."[45]

Orage would probably beg off responsibility for his action by siding with Uspenskii's Ivan Osokin who says to the magician: "The whole trouble is that we never know for certain what is coming. If we know definitely what would be the result of our actions, do you suppose we should do all that we do?"

"You always know," says the magician, looking at Osokin. "A man may not know what will happen as a result of other people's actions or as the result of unknown causes, but he always knows all possible results of his own actions."

Orage thinks he can have his wife and initiation, too. Submitting to his young wife's self-will and thereby accepting her values, perspective, and all that goes with it, Orage has entered a descending octave. He is now only a shadow of the man who spoke just a few years before at Sunwise Turn, as can be seen in a conversation Orage and Gurdjieff and a few others have about what Gurdjieff calls "a man's whim"[46]—his true desire in life.

Asked what his whim is, Gurdjieff answers—it is to live and teach so that there should be a new conception of God in the world, a change in the very meaning of the word.

Orage, when asked the same question, answers that his whim is to produce and edit the best weekly journal in England.

If Orage was joking, Gurdjieff didn't laugh.

45. Orage does not seem to understand that in disobeying his teacher and in marrying Jesse Dwight he has, in effect, divorced himself from Gurdjieff. Initiation can only take place when there is rapport, not a rupture, between student and teacher. Orage is standing under Ivan Osokin's clock and he does not know it.

46. Gurdjieff's use of the word "whim" is indicative of the care with which he uses words. Follow the line of the dictionary definition of the word as "a capricious or eccentric and often sudden idea or turn of mind," and we come to a deeper insight into the terms "I" and real I; and why, too, Gurdjieff's whim is to make a change in the very meaning of the word.

There is a conversation that goes very close to the heart of the matter between the two men.

"Gurdjieff once told me," recounts Orage, "that he knew my ambition. He said I wanted to be one of the 'elder brothers' of the human race, but that I had not the ability it required."

Then Gurdjieff adds: "You not know how to give. You only let others take. Let them take, you do no good: you lose and they get dependent. Not easy to give. Learn how to give, then you make other people free."[47]

APRIL 5, 1929. NEW YORK. Gurdjieff departs for France. Orage dances on the quay, crying, "Thank God I'm free again!"

Within a fortnight his wife delivers their child, Richard.

JUNE 1929. PRIEURÉ. Louise Goepfert arrives from New York. German-born, this twenty-nine-year-old professor of art comes to put Orage's English translation of *All and Everything* into German. Gurdjieff introduces her to "Jeanna," his name for Madame Jeanne de Salzmann, who is translating the book into French. Then he tells Miss Goepfert, the woman he will come to call "Sausage," to take a bath.

"Take time," says Gurdjieff, "wash off American dirt, then see."

She chooses a room on the third floor of the château, the austere "Monks' Corridor." It is painted in ocher and oxblood red. There is a skull and crossbones painted above the door to her room, which is simply furnished with bed, table, and chair.

Later she meets Gurdjieff's pupils, and his family: his brother Dimitri Ivanovitch, his wife Astrig Gregorevna, and their three daughters, Luba, Jenia, and Lyda. There is also his sister Sophie Ivanovna, and her husband Gyorgi Kapanadze, as well as Gurdjieff's orphaned teenaged nephew Valia.

Within a week of her arrival, Gurdjieff drives Louise Goepfert to Chailly. There, at the scene of his near-fatal auto accident, he reveals himself to her, as he had done to Dr. Stjoernval in Finland, in the image of the suffering Christ. Gurdjieff begs her "to help him, to translate for him." She speaks of her state as: "I am overwhelmed—on my knees before Him who reveals his suffering to me."

She finds that Gurdjieff drives every morning to Paris to the Café de la Paix where he drinks Armagnac or coffee with lemon and revises *All and Everything*. One day she asks him why he doesn't stay at the Prieuré with its fresh air and beautiful surroundings.

47. Orage insisted on being loved by people. He 'gave,' so that by giving, letting people take, he would gain their love. Gurdjieff understood that there are circumstances in which only by *not giving* does one give. Those who are able to take do so, and, in so doing, know and become strong and independent. Wanting to know without nurturing the will and courage can only lead to impotence.

Says Gurdjieff: "I always work in cafés, dance halls, places where I see people, how they are; where I see those most drunk, most abnormal. Seeing them I can produce impulse of love in me. From that I write my books."

EARLY SUMMER 1929. FRANCE. Madame Uspenskii, living in Asnières since 1924, only three miles from Paris, had visited her husband the year before but had no taste for the English and returned. Now she crosses the Channel again. But again returns.

Gurdjieff convinces the de Hartmanns to leave the Prieuré and settle in Courbevoie.

SUMMER 1929. PRIEURÉ. As the months went on and Fritz and Jane remained at loggerheads over the issue of his leaving, Gurdjieff was brought into it. He asked Peters if he "had considered and evaluated my relationships to my mother, to Jane, and to himself and the school conscientiously and if, having done so, I still wanted to go back to America. I said that I thought I had...I felt that I belonged in America."

With that Gurdjieff agreed that he should leave.

AUGUST 3–4, 1929. NUREMBERG. Nazis mount an impressive Party Congress. Thirty trains bring two hundred thousand members and sympathizers. There is a grand parade in which sixty thousand S. A. men in uniform (the Brownshirts) parade before Hitler, their Führer (leader), for three and a half hours.

OCTOBER 1929. PRIEURÉ. Fifteen-year-old Fritz Peters leaves Gurdjieff and the Prieuré for America. Having met Gurdjieff at the age of eleven, he spent four-and-one-half years at the Prieuré as a resident student.

At the gate Gurdjieff shook his hand and with a smile on his face said rather sadly, "So you decide to go?"

Says Peters: "I was only able to nod my head at him. Then he put his arm around me, leaned over and kissed my cheek, and said: "Freets, must not be sad. Sometime maybe you will come back; remember that in life anything can happen."

Says Peters: "At that moment, for the only time in many months, I regretted my decision. Whatever had taken place at the Prieuré, whatever I had or had not experienced or learned, my affection for Gurdjieff had remained essentially undiminished. I realized, although not immediately, that if he had at any time put the question of my departure on a personal, emotional level—the end of my personal association with him—I probably would not have left. He did not; as I have said, he always seemed to me to play fair."

At Cherbourg Jane Heap, gives him a copy of a document dissolving the adoption and says, "You may be shocked when you read this but try to realize my position and remember that it was very difficult to break the adoption without some reason that would be legally valid."

Peters is shocked when he reads it. "The essence of the document," he says, "was that I was being 'expelled' from the Gurdjieff school because I was 'morally unfit.'"

Boarding the *Leviathan*, the world's largest ocean liner, at Cherbourg, he sets off for Chicago to see his mother, stepfather, and seven-year-old half sister. During the voyage Peters hears of the Wall Street Crash.

In Chicago he finds his mother has been hospitalized for nervous collapse. His stepfather, a lawyer, confronts him with the disadoption document and a letter from Jane Heap amplifying the meaning of the words *morally unfit.* "According to the letter," Peters says, "I was some sort of sexually depraved delinquent given, principally, to the practice of corrupting other, smaller, children."

His stepfather wants to hear his side of the story.

Peters says that it seems to him, in general, that people believe what they want to believe. Therefore, if he admitted to the letter's allegations, he would be believed. But if he denied them, inasmuch as the charges had been voiced, the stepfather would always wonder if he was telling the truth or not. "I said further," says Peters, "that since I had no way of proving my 'innocence' the only course left to me was to say nothing. That I would leave it up to him—not to decide which one of us, Jane or myself, had been telling the truth—but simply to decide whether or not Jane had been honest." For the next three hours, despite persistent pressure from his lawyer-stepfather, the young boy resolutely refuses to speak about the subject.[48]

Instead of college, Peters is enrolled in high school as a senior.

1930. GERMANY. Hitler travels the country courting German businessmen. He meets with many of them at the mansion of a piano manufacturer, Carl Bechstein, whose wife is enamored of Hitler. Between now and his election to Chancellor in 1933, industrialists from companies like I. G. Farben, the giant chemical cartel, will contribute 2 million marks a year to the Nazi Party.

JANUARY 1930. CAFÉ DE LA PAIX. In answer to a question about sin, Gurdjieff answers: "If you acknowledge your sin and feel remorse of conscience

48. The maturity and keenness of Fritz Peters' mind and his resolute will are amply demonstrated by this event. Whatever his faults, he was always known to be honest. In his book *Gurdjieff Remembered*, p. 18, in speaking of Chicago's Gurdjieff group which he meets two years after his confrontation with his stepfather, he will say, "Having had, up to that point in my life, no sexual experience..." In an interesting and unconscious way, perhaps, he is practicing the Way of Blame which Gurdjieff spoke about many times.

for having done wrong, your sin is already forgiven. If you continue to do wrong, knowing it to be so, you commit a sin that is difficult to forgive."

FEBRUARY 1930. PARIS. It is the evening before Gurdjieff is to sail for America. He invites Olga de Hartmann to come to the new flat in the rue Marchand. He asks her to give him the key to his little chest of drawers that she keeps for him. Gurdjieff opens it and proceeds to burn all his personal papers, correspondence, certificates, passports—anything which might throw light on his past.

The next morning she returns to his flat and they have what she describes as a "wonderful talk...a talk that could occur only in exceptional moments." Then they go to the railway station and sit in a café where Gurdjieff tells her she is "the only person who never had done what he demanded without wishing it" [for themselves].[49] Gurdjieff then tells her he needs her and her husband, Thomas, in New York in a week's time. Her husband is much too sick and she refuses. The train whistle blows. Gurdjieff mounts the steps to the dining car. He stops on the car's platform. Olga looks up at him from the station's platform.

"Come in a week's time," Gurdjieff says, "or you will never see me again."

"Then...I will never see you again," says Olga Arkadievna.

She had served him loyally for twenty-four years. She, who as he would later say was "the first friend of his inner life," watches as the train disappears from sight.

"In my thoughts," she says, "I saw before me Prince Lubovedsky going away and leaving Mr. Gurdjieff alone. When he was dictating this chapter of *Meetings with Remarkable Men* to me I always wondered about this tragic moment in his life and dreaded that it might happen to me."

The 'death' that Gurdjieff experienced with the Prince, she now experiences. She goes home and goes to bed. Four days pass before she is able to get up and resume her life. Mr. Gurdjieff has set her free in his own inimitable way.

FEBRUARY 1930. NEW YORK. Orage receives a telegram:

> If love not dissipated arrange bath and party.
> — Grandson and Unique phenomenal Grandmother

A second telegram follows:

> Bremen brings thousand kilos disillusion, hundred kilos
> momentary happiness and ten pounds retribution.
> — Ambassador From Hell

FEBRUARY 15, 1930. NEW YORK. "Confess, Orage, that your heart sinks when you hear that I am coming!" Gurdjieff had once told him. There was always a good-natured banter between the two—only Orage and

49. Given what will happen, Gurdjieff may be thinking about Orage here.

Alexander de Salzmann were capable of making Gurdjieff really laugh—and Orage likely riposted. But there was more than a kernel of truth in Gurdjieff's remark.

And so when the *Bremen* docks, Orage is not there to greet his teacher. Nor is he at Gurdjieff's hotel. His absence appears to be making a "statement." The issues: money, initiation, and independence. The first, Gurdjieff demands; the second, he withholds; and the third is premature.

In a letter to C. S. Nott, Orage writes that Gurdjieff is again in search of funds, saying that "... though I doubt whether this time he will get much. His coming has, of course, bust up my group meetings and left me desperately placed for income, but I must be 'clever,' I suppose and find a substitute."[50]

As Gurdjieff will tell Fritz Peters at the end of the Second World War:

> You remember Prieuré and how many times I have struggle with money. I not make money like others make money, and when I have too much money, I spend. But I never need money for self, and I not *make* or earn money, I *ask* for money and people always give, and for this I give opportunity study my teachings, but even when they give money still almost always impossible for them learn anything. Already, they think of reward...now I owe them something because they give me money. When think of reward in this way, impossible learn anything from me.

Orage has interested Alfred Knopf, the publisher of Uspenskii's *Tertium Organum,* in publishing *All and Everything.* Orage has managed to squirrel away enough money in a special bank fund subscribed to by American pupils to pay for the publication of Gurdjieff's book. However when Knopf approaches Gurdjieff about the matter, Gurdjieff tells him certain things are necessary.

"And what are your conditions, Mr. Gurdjieff? I'm sure we can meet your requirements. What would you wish us to do?"

"Not conditions," Gurdjieff replies. "One condition. One small thing."

"And that is?"

"First clean house, your house, then perhaps can have my book!"[51]

50. The Work works by pressure and Gurdjieff knew how to press the "corns" of people. If it wasn't hard manual labor, it was eccentric, even outrageous behavior, or the massive quantities of alcohol consumed during his "toasts to the idiots." And always there was the "material question"—the demand for money. Nothing stops the formatory mind in its tracks, creates projection and doubt like a ceaseless demand for money. America, Gurdjieff said, was a "dollar growing country." And he came often to shear the sheep. Certainly he had need of money to keep the Prieuré afloat. But he never worshipped money. When he spent, he spent lavishly; perhaps, from an ordinary perspective, foolishly. But it also—and this is missed by most of his critics—was a very direct way of teaching.

MARCH 20, 1930. NEW YORK. Orage writes to Toomer saying that Gurdjieff has given him a selection of chapters "to get published or to publish." Knopf, he says, has the typescript.

MARCH 28, 1930. NEW YORK. Writing to Toomer, Orage reports that Knopf has turned the book down. He next tries Doubleday but, again, the same result. "I share your opinion," Orage finally tells Toomer, "that no publisher will accept it."

Speaking of the general condition, Orage says, "The situation is anything but bright and I confess to a little fatigue with Gurdjieff and his ways. Perhaps that is because I've just had to find over two hundred dollars with which to discharge the debts he failed to remember!"

APRIL 1930. NEW YORK. Leaving for France, Gurdjieff returns a gift of an expensive harmonium to its original donor. After he is gone, he says, the world would take note of this event and the harmonium would by then have become...

He searches for the right English word.

Finally he asks a pupil who suggests, "Souvenir."

Not satisfied, Gurdjieff turns to Orage, asking what he would say.

"Sacred relic," answers Orage with a "sacred" intonation.

Gurdjieff breaks into a laughter that sounds like "a giant child's delight."

Says C. S. Nott, "Orage's mind is more nimble than Gurdjieff's and to be with these two is better than a play."

Gurdjieff made many voyages to America. Certainly without American dollars he would not have had the time to write *All and Everything* or been able to maintain the Prieuré. The English had given initially and enabled Gurdjieff to purchase the Prieuré. But that was long ago. The Institute had been established on French soil only because Germany and England proved untenable. As he sometimes gave animal names to people to indicate their chief feature, he did this as well with national character. The Russians he called "turkeys," the Germans "jackals," the English "sheep," and the French "donkeys." Too Cartesian and self-adoring, the French did not begin to take an interest in the teaching until the 1930s and were never a financial factor until long after the war.

Besides their generosity, Gurdjieff was interested in America because, as he told Fritz Peters, "Americans more receptive because not closed up inside yet; they naive, stupid, perhaps, but still real. Americans, particularly, have more chance grow properly as men because have not yet become—like you say—'phony' men." Gurdjieff will also tell him:

51. Perhaps Gurdjieff is alluding to Knopf having published Uspenskii's book. Otherwise, it is difficult to make sense out of his remark.

"Impossible to do my work with all energy if also concerned with money. But all these things very difficult for your contemporaries. Not only cannot do. Cannot even understand why this question of money important. Such people will never understand real teaching or real possibility of learning anything."

What is to happen between Orage and Gurdjieff is foreshadowed in a cab ride Orage takes with C. Daly King. Orage suddenly tells him:

"It is necessary to make these things your own, so that you may never need to rely upon others for them. You must be prepared, for example, to hear Gurdjieff himself deny the validity of the Method."

SPRING 1930. CHICAGO. Though as a high school senior Fritz Peters had made straight A's in all but Zoology, which he detested and flunked, it is decided that he should work in his stepfather's law office rather than go to college.

May 13, 1930. New York. Orage calls the groups together and, as he has so often done in the past, says that the most fortunate event in his life was his meeting with Gurdjieff. He says he is leaving with his wife Jesse and one-year-old son Richard to spend the summer in Rye in Sussex, England. He plans to write essays and articles for a number of American magazines. If he returns, as he hopes, there would be a new kind of Work. He then speaks about the difference between a group and a circle. "The latter meet for themselves individually, to help each other and to help a common cause, 'to make the world safe for consciousness.'" He says that even after six years of attending groups very few of them have a sense of three conscious responsibilities. These three form a triangle which, when functioning, distinguish a circle from a group. The first part of the triangle is individual responsibility toward consciousness and development in one's own everyday life. The second is consciousness "toward our neighbors, the members of our tribe also striving for consciousness." The third center of gravity is consciousness toward some in the group as "'elders.'" He speaks of returning in January and says, "I shall have to be independent of the group financially—no one will have to pay anything again to attend a group of mine." He continues speaking about what he envisions when he returns, saying that to be a member of this new group [whose sole aim is to transform itself into a circle] people must work so hard that one comes to momentary experience of feeling "you are losing your body and your life.... You will have known the fact of death. This is the kind of evidence I shall require for membership in a group." He goes on to say that "I am too tender-hearted to force the pace as Gurdjieff and Uspenskii can so ruthlessly do. But unless you are serious, I cannot be serious—you can hold me back." He then speaks about the five points of objective morality [five being-*obligolnian*-strivings] and ends with "Now having perhaps unfortunately listened to this, you are capable of sin—of refusal to convert verbal form into formal understanding."[52]

MAY 14, 1930. NEW YORK. Orage writes to his friend, C. S. Nott, saying: "We had a farewell group meeting last evening and it would have done your heart good to witness the scene. I *love* the group; and I couldn't bear the thought of being long out of touch with them."

JUNE 11, 1930. SUSSEX, ENGLAND. Orage writes to an American student:

> I told Gurdjieff in New York that I'd come to the end of my patience and that, without a new initiation, I was as good as dead about the Prieuré; furthermore, that I proposed to try the effect of 'growing chungaree' by myself—his reply was so unsatisfying that I shall carry out my plan. In other words, I shall stay here in England doing my best to get a new understanding of the Book on my own resources—in despair, frankly, of Gurdjieff doing anything more for me than he has done for Stjoernval, de Hartmann, etc., however faithfully they have given up all to follow him.... One thing remains unshakably true—the ideas are all the world to me, and I shall always be ready to cooperate in their spread provided I myself continue to increase in their understanding. What I cannot do any longer is to continue teaching without also learning—and Gurdjieff has ceased to teach *me*.

52. At the Prieuré, Orage had experienced the 'death' of which he speaks. During his time at the Prieuré, the physical exhaustion and the elimination of all his spiritual dreams and expectations had brought him to the depths of despair. In fact, he was being tested. He might have easily turned tail and run then, as so many did, but he persisted and had his first initiation. Such 'death,' however, is not undergone once, but many times. Now, though he does not appear to realize it, he is entering a time of a new testing. Having become prematurely independent of Gurdjieff through his marriage to Jesse Dwight, Orage now finds himself being drawn more and more into 'family' life. Marriage and raising a family, of course, seems natural enough. But it is merely biological and, given the mission Gurdjieff has entrusted him with, as a "messenger of my new ideas," as well as his own stated aim of "finding God," it is a 'temptation' to which Orage, given his chief weakness, has blithely and blindly succumbed. Now he comes to another crossroads in which, one, he finds himself psychologically worn down with Gurdjieff's incessant (and what look more and more to him as irrational) demands for money; and, two, having come to the end of what he is able to teach. He needs a new initiation—that recognition is pulling him one way. Pulling him another way is 'familism.' Once again, though he appears to have no presentiment of it, Orage is going to experience the octave of 'death.' Die he must. His choice is: *will he choose to die on an ascending or descending octave?* Will he die for being or die for 'love'? Orage is now capable of sinning; that is, he has sufficient knowledge and will to act as he wishes. Using his own words to his group, will he or will he not refuse "to convert verbal form into formal understanding"? Orage's choice will be difficult for he still looks at the world, as Gurdjieff says, "topsy-turvey." A careful reading of Philip Mairet's otherwise splendid biography, *A. R. Orage: A Memoir*, shows such a viewpoint. What he says seems so sensible, rational, understanding—*until* one realizes what is at issue.

FALL 1930. Fritz Peters' mother and stepfather separate and sue for divorce. When his mother and half-sister go to Europe, his stepfather asks him to leave the law office.

OCTOBER 1930. WARWICK GARDENS, LONDON. Uspenskii decides to expand his work. It is now seven years since he left Gurdjieff. He has been working in strict secrecy with forty or fifty pupils. He will begin a new lecture series, "The Search for Objective Consciousness," at Warwick Hall. Bennett, who Uspenskii has refused to see since Bennett's jailing in Athens two years before, is invited back into the fold. Very soon, he is given the responsibility of reading the lectures aloud in Uspenskii's presence. Later, the two men talk and when the conversation comes to what has become for Uspenskii the perennial question and thorn in his side—Gurdjieff!—he tells Bennett:

> I waited for all these years [to expand the work] because I wanted to see what Mr. Gurdjieff would do. His work has not given the results he hoped for. I am still as certain as ever that there is a Great Source from which our System has come. Mr. Gurdjieff must have had a contact with that Source, but I do not believe that it was a complete contact. Something is missing, and he has not been able to find it. If we cannot find it through him, then our only hope is to have a direct contact with the Source....Our only hope is that the Source will seek us out. That is why I am giving these lectures in London.

NOVEMBER 13, 1930. NEW YORK. For the fourth time, Gurdjieff arrives in America. Significantly, once again, Orage is not at dockside to greet him—he is still in England on holiday with his family. The absence is not lost on Gurdjieff. Neither is the telltale look on the faces of those from Orage's group who are there to greet him. This particular look is what Gurdjieff calls that of a "candidate for the madhouse."[53]

"The charge against Mr. Orage's activities," says C. Daly King, "is that they were intellectually lopsided, placed undue stress upon mental activities at the expense of emotional and practical activities; and that thus, far from being of objective benefit to the pupils who sat under Mr. Orage, it could be guaranteed to render them even more abnormal, objectively, than they had been in the first instance."

King, who prides himself on his rationality, finds himself outraged. "It is difficult to speak of this charge in moderate and serious terms," he says, then declares it to be "brash and blatant nonsense."

53. It can be the result of only one thing: a distorted understanding of the practice of self-observation. That distortion is the responsibility of one man, the man who is absent—A. R. Orage.

Always striving to be fair, he does concede, however, there are a few in the group who think Gurdjieff's assessment correct.

NOVEMBER 28, 1930. STUDIO 61, CARNEGIE HALL, NEW YORK. Between now and December 19th, Gurdjieff gives five talks to the Orage groups. In his first talk he speaks of *initiation*—Orage's question—and makes the distinction between three groups, or levels of understanding. The first group is exoteric, or outer; the second, mesoteric, or middle; and the third, esoteric, or inner. The exoteric group is for those who have newly entered the Work and do not yet merit belonging to the other two groups. The mesoteric group is for those initiated into a theoretical understanding of "all the questions not accessible to the average man." The esoteric group is to be initiated not only theoretically and practically into all relevant questions, but will be introduced to all means for a real possibility of self-perfecting.

Gurdjieff speaks about the exercise of self-observation which enables a person to cognize the "exaggerated importance given to his individuality" and the individual's "almost complete 'nullity.'" He speaks of his so-called "motor car accident," which he regards as the action of *Tzvarnoharno,* and notes that though some of his students "decided to 'prophesize'" his ideas, they all belonged only to the exoteric group. He ends by noting that each nation has its own *idée fixe* regarding the teaching. For Americans, it is *self-observation.*

Having set the foundation with his first talk, Gurdjieff in his second talk launches a full-scale attack on the students' beloved teacher, Mr. Orage. He speaks of Orage as being the consequence of "that abnormality at the basis of family life, crystallized in the life of contemporary people...which consists in the fact that the leading role in the household belongs to the woman." He says that at first Orage was "not yet completely under the influence of his 'left-shoulder Angel,'" a not too subtle reference to Jesse Dwight, but that his marriage to the "saleswoman of 'Sunwise Turn,' a young American pampered out of all proportion to her position," had resulted in the need to meet excessive expenditures. Once the knowledge which he had received at the Institute was used up, Orage had to "manipulate in every way" his very limited knowledge. This led to the practice of self-observation becoming "the center of gravity for the mentation of man," and so a dangerous distortion.

Gurdjieff then asks his secretary, Louise Goepfert, to read aloud a letter addressed to the absent Orage. Then he demands that the "Orage people" sign what he calls an "obligation," or oath, vowing not to have any further contact with Orage unless Gurdjieff so instructs.

A number of Orage's pupils balk, one telling Gurdjieff that Orage was not only his teacher and mentor but his "own loving father."

Blurts out Louise Welch: "If Orage made a mistake or did not know how to go on, it was your fault. He taught us what he learned from you, and you did not give him the additional material he needed."

To which Gurdjieff, pleased at the open expression of resistance, replies: "Bravo!"

The most adamant of the Oragean diehards is C. Daly King. Still, years later King had to admit:

> While I have received no impression that Mr. Gurdjieff is by any means as outstanding intellectually, emotionally or practically as his faithful disciples suppose him to be, I am convinced by my personal experience of him that he possesses another quality that may be more important than any of the foregoing. This quality he possesses to a degree not merely superior to that of any other man whom I have ever encountered but to a degree greater than it would have ever occurred to me to exist, had I not met Mr. Gurdjieff. It is the quality, not of mind or feeling or of successful accomplishment, but simply of *being*. I have never failed to experience this in his presence; one (or I) cannot 'put one's finger on it' but it is most certainly there. It has always prevented the slightest show of impertinence toward him upon my part but, more than that, it has always prevented my (otherwise frequently demonstrated) ability to challenge him even upon those grounds to which he constantly lays himself open to the most obvious challenge. I cannot account to myself for this, in other ways, inexplicable respect in which I hold him than by my admiration of the remarkable degree of being with which I am always impressed when in personal contact with him.

Gurdjieff's third talk[54] is a masterpiece. It reveals the rare level of understanding which he possesses. He speaks of the difficulty of liberation and the need for "the entire sensing of the whole of oneself" and speaks about the use of attention.

DECEMBER 1930. ENGLAND. Learning of the storm Gurdjieff has created, Orage writes to a student:

> It is obvious that my unwillingness to go to all lengths for G., with the group and with myself, indicates an insufficiency of what shall I say?—faith in him? trust? radical conviction that he can do no wrong? Well, to be explicit, that is the fact. I have not that absolute faith. If I were Nahom and G. commanded me to slay my first born, I wouldn't do it. I realize that this degree of faith is perhaps essential to full participation in G.'s teachings. I realize that any degree of belief, short of this makes all services to him ultimately conditional

54. Gurdjieff's *Life is Real only then when "I Am,"* in which the talk appears, works on so many different levels with such comprehensive understanding that summarization is impossible. This is generally true of most of Gurdjieff's writings.

> and therefore, except within limits, not to be counted upon...."Lord," I can say, "I believe"; but I have to add, "Help thou my unbelief." Because, in truth, my belief is not absolute....I can see clearly that from his point of view, believing in himself so absolutely, my half or three-quarters belief in him is titillation, and results only in the titillation of others. He *cannot* but wish either that I shall be absolutely faithful, or cease to be regarded or to regard myself as his chief "minister" in America. I accept this without reproach. But what I pray for is that my own friends, the best I have on earth, the New York group, may not only not suffer on my account, but that, through me, like another Moses, they may find themselves led to the Jordan and transported across by Joshua Gurdjieff!

DECEMBER 10, 1930. NEW YORK. Orage and family return from England. He at once asks to see Gurdjieff, who directs Miss Goepfert to ask Orage to sign the obligation proposed to Orage's groups. Orage, always deft intellectually, comes at once to Gurdjieff's apartment and signs the letter.[55] His apology, from Gurdjieff's description, is ornate and what Gurdjieff terms "philosophizing." This gives Gurdjieff what he calls a "'touchy emotion'... right in the center between the two hemispheres of the brain."[56]

DECEMBFR 12, 1930. NEW YORK. Orage attends the fourth general meeting. Gurdjieff describes Orage and several of his "'first-rank' defenders" as those who sit with their "'tails between their legs' and facial expressions of unchangeable 'plasto-oleaginous' traits."

As with Uspenskii eight years before—and in front of an audience which included Orage—Gurdjieff now attempts to wake Orage up to his situation by a shock technique. He openly humiliates him in front of his students, speaking of the group's "'loving father,' that is to say, Mr. Orage" and his "philosophizing." This tactic did not work with Uspenskii; neither does it work with Orage.[57] And as with Uspenskii, all the years of work with Orage appear to result in nothing. Unable to assimilate and learn from the shock, Uspenskii left to teach his own groups. Orage leaves to edit a magazine which will propagandize for the economic theory of Social Credit.

55. How should Orage have acted? He had defied his teacher in marrying Jesse Dwight. He had broken his promise to Gurdjieff to come to the Prieuré. He had "invented" parts of the teaching and so led his students astray. Wanting to be loved, he had given his students too much of himself, despite Gurdjieff's many warnings against it. If he allowed himself to take the full weight of the shock, it would have opened him and his relationship with Gurdjieff could have begun again on fresh ground with a new understanding. Instead, Orage deflected it with his always facile intellectual center.

When Uspenskii left, Gurdjieff still had a number of promising students. With Orage's leaving, there is nobody. Orage wore many hats for Gurdjieff. He was editor, fund raiser, teacher and, yes, "John, the Baptist." Now all the weight will fall on the shoulders of Jean Toomer.

1931. NEW YORK. Jean Toomer privately publishes *Essentials*, a collection of nearly three hundred aphorisms and definitions largely influenced by Gurdjieff's teaching.[58]

MARCH 1, 1931. NEW YORK. Orage writes Nott: "G.'s going may or may not change things for the better, his effect here having been to kill

56. According to Professor Paul Taylor of the University of Geneva, who is Jean Toomer's adopted son, Orage and his family sailed from England on December 29, 1930, and arrived in New York on January 8, 1931. He and Jesse were invited to Gurdjieff's birthday party on the 13th. They both attended and it was at this time that Gurdjieff humiliated Orage. On the 15th, Orage met with his oldest New York group and first heard about the written pledge Gurdjieff required of Orage's pupils. On the 17th, he wrote to Gurdjieff resigning from all his functions as both group leader and pupil. Thereafter, Gurdjieff and he held a number of meetings but apparently did not reconcile. If these dates are correct, the question remains as to why Gurdjieff shifted the dates in the *Third Series* from January 1931 backwards to December 1930. The shift places the shock Gurdjieff delivers to the New York groups and Orage closer to the November 6th date of 1927 and 1934 which Gurdjieff makes much of in the *Third Series.* If we take the date of November 6, 1927, as the doh of a new octave for Gurdjieff, with each year signifying one note, then on November 6, 1930, we are close to the interval, the shock point. According to Professor Taylor, Gurdjieff saw November 6, 1927, as "the axial moment" in his relationship with Orage. Against Gurdjieff's expressed wishes, Orage had married Jesse Dwight in September. He had promised Gurdjieff that afterward he would come to the Prieuré but did not. Gurdjieff hoped to convince Orage to stay at the Prieuré to help with the rewriting of the *First Series.* While Orage was gone, Jean Toomer was to take his place as the head of the American groups. But Orage broke his promise to Gurdjieff and sent him a wire instead saying he was not coming. Seven years later on November 6, 1934, Gurdjieff began his Introduction to the *Third Series,* the conclusion of his *legominism, All and Everything.*

57. It would seem that Gurdjieff expected Orage to absorb the shock to his chief feature, and continue. But the shock for Orage, as it was for Uspenskii, was too great. It was the moment of truth for each pupil. But neither could totally surrender. They did not wholly trust Gurdjieff and, therefore, reserved the right to judge him. In so doing, they judged themselves. Gurdjieff's action seems a desperate attempt to save both students, not for themselves, not for him—but for his mission. Given their breaking with Gurdjieff, it seems fair to conclude that neither *really* understood his mission. Despite Gurdjieff's knowledge and being, despite the many experiences Uspenskii and Orage had through Gurdjieff and his teaching, in the end they could only follow their teacher part of the way. They could not do as Jesus' apostles did. They could not step out of the web of their lives and follow, as Orage once called him, "Joshua Gurdjieff."

58. The aphorisms are linked together, such as in aphorism XL: • Each of us has in himself a fool who says I'm wise. • Most novices picture themselves as masters—and are content with the picture. This is why there are so few masters. • When I speak I am persuaded. • People mistake their limitations for high standards. • Ordinarily, each person is a cartoon of himself.

the interest of at least three out of four of the old members. I don't know whether they will ever return, *even* if I should be disposed to try to reassemble them. G. talks as if he expects me to carry on as before; but in spite of my constant association with him, I'm not feeling even warm about group work." In fact, Orage will leave Gurdjieff, his decision, no doubt, not protested by his wife.

Gurdjieff, then, at fifty-nine years of age, finds himself utterly alone.

March 14, 1931. New York. Orage to Nott: "Gurdjieff sailed last night, leaving behind him an almost hopelessly scattered and hostile group. He has given the impression, as never before, that he cares for money only and thinks of the N. Y. people in that light alone.... Of course it is not so; but I despair of pointing to any evidence in support, except evidence that he has alienated the rich members as well as the poor."[59]

SPRING 1931. CHICAGO. Jean Toomer meets Margery Latimer, a fellow writer and a student of Orage's. Initially, she is put off by Toomer. In a letter to a friend, she writes: "Toomer I couldn't bear to look at. He sat at the head of the table and I was next to him. I felt he was so tainted with his master, Gurdjieff. I felt he was consciously being G. and also unconsciously being him." But few women could withstand the magnetic personality of Jean Toomer and Latimer is soon captivated.

APRIL 1931. NEW YORK. Orage makes one hundred copies of *All and Everything* from his typescript (the only one besides Gurdjieff's). These are sold for ten dollars apiece. Fifty copies are quickly sold, the remainder taking nearly ten years to dispose of, the last going in 1940 for one hundred dollars.

MAY 1931. NEW YORK. Years later J. G. Bennett, who was not present for Gurdjieff's talks to Orage's groups but who had plenty of contacts, said that during this time Gurdjieff introduced "new methods of work, of which most of his groups had previously no idea. Indeed, the new exercises that were being introduced in 1930 and in the early part of 1931 seem to have been different from the exercises which he had shown people individually at the Prieuré between 1924 and 1929."

59. As Gurdjieff worked with Uspenskii, pressing his corns over "the St. Petersburg conditions," he works in like manner with Orage about money. He will also use money with Jean Toomer. And through Orage and Toomer, he of course works on his American students who form their groups. His continual pressing for more and more money evokes anger and doubt. He seems venal, but it really is Gurdjieff applying what he calls the "Divine principle," see *Third Series*. It is for the student, not the teacher, to resolve and reconcile the contradiction Gurdjieff's behavior creates; to impartially absorb 'the heat.' Many of Gurdjieff's imitators point to this in defending the heavy money demands they make on students.

SUMMER 1931. PRIEURÉ. *A New Model of the Universe* is published in New York. Gurdjieff is shown the book—he turns his back, making a scornful remark.

Declares Dr. Stjoernval: "Mr. Gurdjieff has a very big plan, Uspenskii does not understand this. He does not know what Mr. Gurdjieff's aim is. We who are working with Mr. Gurdjieff have got beyond such books. It only adds to the sum of ordinary knowledge, of which there is already too much. Uspenskii ought to have got beyond it."

Orage, having read a copy, brands it "A New Muddle of the Universe."

Some weeks later at the Café de la Paix, Nott finds Gurdjieff, who, he reports, is in a "worked-up state." Nott tells him that Orage had spoken of Gurdjieff bringing his pupils just so far and then seemingly leaving them up in the air.

With a sardonic grin, Gurdjieff tells him: "I needed rats for my experiments."

"What?" cries Nott.

"I needed rats for my experiments," repeats Gurdjieff.

Nott, who suffered from inferiority feelings, is crestfallen.

Easing the shock, Gurdjieff invites him to lunch at his apartment where they speak of many things. At the end, with a look of compassion, he tells Nott—"You're a good man."

"What is good?" Nott asks, still despondent. "It seems to me that goodness is often a name for weakness. Sometimes I see myself as what I really am—*merde de la merde.*"

A slow smile spreads over Gurdjieff's face.

Meanwhile, in London, everything appears to be going well for Uspenskii. With every passing year, it appears that he made the right decision in leaving Gurdjieff.

Gurdjieff sits on the terrace of the Café Henri IV drinking coffee and cognac and working on a translation of *All and Everything* when the writer Thornton Wilder is introduced to him. Gurdjieff grunts and motions him to sit down and have a coffee and cognac. Asking Wilder a number of questions, he laughs inordinately at every reply.

Wilder is not put off. He sees in Gurdjieff's face someone who is "at once sly and jovial, arrogant and clownish." He looked, says Wilder, "like a very intelligent Armenian rug-dealer."

Gurdjieff orders more coffee and cognac and tells Wilder, "In the world, everybody idiot. Twenty-one kinds of idiot: simple idiot, ambitious idiot, compassionate idiot, objective idiot, subjective idiot—everybody one kind of idiot."

Wilder tells him he thinks he is a subjective idiot.

"Non," answers Gurdjieff, laughing uproariously. "Il ne faut pas aller trop vite. Il faut chercher.—Mais vous êtes idiot type vingt: vous êtes idiot sans espoir!" (No. One mustn't go too fast. One must search.—But you are idiot type twenty: you are idiot without hope.).

Wilder is not offended and Gurdjieff asks him to come to dinner at the Prieuré. Says Wilder: "I had begun to like him, and his eyes rested on me affectionately."

Gurdjieff holds his glass toward Wilder and says—barely able to speak for laughter: "I idiot, too. Everybody idiot. I idiot vingt-et-un (twenty-one). I"—Gurdjieff holds his forefinger emphatically pointed skyward—"I the *unique* idiot." And he breaks into convulsions of laughter.

At the Prieuré Gurdjieff greets him with what Wilder describes as "buffoon joviality" and introduces him to an American lady.

"Smell him and see if he have money," Gurdjieff tells her, sniffing at Wilder. "Yes, I smell him. I think he have money."

Wilder sees this as "brilliant," for he suspects Gurdjieff of pressing people for money.

There are some twenty-five people at dinner, all served at one vast table. Before each place is a bottle of cognac. The principal dish is a sheep brought in on a large platter, its head still on, and lying in a bed of cooked fruits.

Gurdjieff is noisy, jovial and clowning, and constantly toasting Wilder with cognac. The other guests are muted, meditative, and withdrawn.

"Gurdjieff and I," says Wilder, "were the only happy people at the table."

After dinner Gurdjieff offers to let him read *All and Everything,* telling him that when it is published it will cost five thousand dollars.

"I give you five thousand dollars," Gurdjieff says.

After a question from Wilder, Gurdjieff tells him: "You no square idiot, you round idiot." He is given the English typescript of the first chapter of *All and Everything,* which fails to impress Wilder.

Before he leaves Gurdjieff tells him, "You come here and stay. You come three days, three months, or three years."

"I'd like to," replies Wilder, somewhat hesitantly. "But I can't come now. I can come in November."

Gurdjieff suddenly flies into a rage, lashing his arms and stamping his foot—"Not November, now! I no live November. I live *now.*"

Wilder, a keen if conventional observer, says of the rage that "It was terrific and it passed as suddenly as it came. It was not a loss of control; it was a pedagogic emphasis."

MIDSUMMER 1931. FONTAINEBLEAU. Uspenskii unexpectedly arrives at the Prieuré. It has been some eleven years since he last rang the bell at the château's wrought iron gates. He does not gain admittance. The venue of the magicians' last meeting is to be at the Café Henri IV in Fontainebleau. They meet on the terrace with its charming view of the historical Jardin de Prieuré with its roses, goldfish pond, and carefully trimmed plane trees.

Sixteen years have passed since the two first met in a noisy Moscow merchants' café. To any but the most knowledgeable eye, their situations have totally reversed. For here on the quiet terrace of the café stands the former student, fifty-three years of age, fit and in excellent health, now an accepted teacher and magician in his own right, having a large number of pupils, many quite wealthy, and one who enjoys a stainless and growing worldwide reputation as a teacher, serious author, and investigator of the Fourth Dimension.

And here facing him is his former teacher, fifty-nine years old, growing fat and in failing health, the once great teacher and magician, accused of being a charlatan, attacked as having contributed to the death of Katherine Mansfield, his reputation in ruins, heavily in debt, having now only a few pupils, and the author of what is commonly taken as a windy, exasperating, unpublished tome of spaceship fable and myth that strikes all but the initiated as virtually unreadable.

What passed between the two men is not known....

Whatever, it was their great octave's end, the final meeting of the magicians.[60]

Soon after, Sophia Grigorievna Uspenskii, perhaps sent by Gurdjieff, makes her peace with her husband and joins him.

LATE SUMMER 1931. PORTAGE, WISCONSIN. Toomer, Margery Latimer, and six other unmarried people from his Chicago groups experiment with communal living in a small cottage. On weekends, the number may rise into the thirties. Toomer tries to apply, in his own way, some of the principles practiced at the Prieuré. Toomer's aim is to see if artificial societal barriers can be transcended through living in close quarters and the sharing of work and play. Through a combination of work assignments, exercises, games, and discussion, Toomer brings to life what he regarded as the essentials of the Gurdjieff teaching. By summer's end, Toomer feels the experiment is a success. "I am satisfied that it is entirely possible," he says, "to eradicate the false veneer of civilization, with its unnatural inhibitions, its selfishness, petty meanness and unnatural behavior, under proper conditions. Adults can be re-educated to become as natural as little children, before civilization stamps out their true or subconscious

60. Whatever contact they might have hereafter could only occur telepathically. It is likely Uspenskii shut himself down to what in Finland so many years before he regarded as a "miracle." Otherwise, how else might he have any peace of mind? Or as Gurdjieff would say, "self-calm" himself.

instincts." Toomer's experiment causes a scandal with the Portage citizenry. Rumors of Communism, nudity, and sexual license abound.

AUGUST 20, 1931. LONDON. Shortly after his last meeting with his former teacher, Uspenskii finds himself having to deal again with what must seem like a dog that will never die. In a group meeting, a student asks:

> As I understand it, one of the principles of esotericism is that the teaching must be passed from one conscious being to another ...after the general principles of the work are received it is necessary to keep the line unbroken. I ask this because it seems to us as if the line was broken when you left Gurdjieff.

Uspenskii:

> What has all this to do with Gurdjieff and me? I was working with Gurdjieff until I saw a difference in him. This has nothing to do with esotericism. When I found that I could not work with him any longer I left him. That is all....The idea is that one can have only such a teacher as one deserves. But only so long as he is teacher. If he ceases to be teacher—well—then why talk about it? I went to Gurdjieff in 1916, but in 1918 I found that I could not continue to work with him. In 1922 again I started to work with him, and again I came to the conclusion that it was impossible to continue, and in 1924 you remember that I spoke to you about this and said: "I may be wrong but I had to part with him."

Later, in the same meeting, Uspenskii says, "How can I say what number man Gurdjieff is? I know only one thing; that he knows more than I of certain principles. He changed all these principles and I parted from him."

Still later he is asked:

Mr. M: "Was it because of the system that you left Gurdjieff?"

Uspenskii: "What do you mean by this? In a sense, yes."

Mr. M: "Then you must have believed something."

Uspenskii: "There is no question of belief; it is a question of fact. I saw. I saw that things had changed...."

At this point, an argument occurs which results in Uspenskii demanding that Mr. M. write down on a sheet of paper what he said. The two questions are: "Was it because of the system that you left Gurdjieff?" and "Was it in the system that you left Gurdjieff?" Uspenskii reads these aloud and says they are exactly the same question. Mr. M. does not agree. And the conversation goes nowhere.

SEPTEMBER 9, 1931. LONDON. Uspenskii tells Maurice Nicoll, his closest pupil and friend, "Nicoll, you had better go away..." He paused and completed his sentence with "...go away and teach the System." About this time he began to make use of his senior students, such as Dr. Francis

Roles and J. G. Bennett. He deputized them to answer basic questions and to do readings. He also began to speak more about his personal ideas, such as the role of the devil in preventing human evolution.

AUTUMN 1931. LONDON. Orage and his family take a house on Hampstead Heath. He lays plans to return to journalism either as a co-editor of the *New Age* or of a new paper. His days with Gurdjieff, he feels, are over, but he says he still practices the teaching and says he still holds it in high regard.

FALL 1931. CHICAGO. Alone in the world, Fritz Peters has been working as a file clerk and French translator. He comes into contact with Chicago's Gurdjieff group led by Jean Toomer. Peters joins the group. Meetings consist of readings from the *First Series* of *All and Everything* followed by a discussion in which the ideas are related to one's personal life. He has many reservations about the approach.

"Since the writings," he says, "were obviously critical of ordinary values, standards and social morality, the group members usually interpreted these criticisms as meaning that any values which ran counter to the prevailing morality were worthwhile. With this view of life, such things as free love, adultery, or any radical social behavior became almost automatically justified." Most irritating of all is Toomer's affectation of using a Russian accent in answering questions.

OCTOBER 30, 1931. PORTAGE, WISCONSIN. Jean Toomer marries Margery Latimer, whose ancestry can be traced back to the Puritan, Cotton Mather. A few days before their marriage Toomer writes: "There is a new race in America. I am a member of this new race. It is neither white nor black nor in-between. It is the American race, differing as much from white and black as black and white differ from each other.... The old divisions into white, black, brown, red, are outworn in this country. They have had their day. Now is the time of the birth of a new order, a new vision, a new idea of man. I proclaim this new order. My marriage to Margery Latimer is the marriage of two Americans." Understanding perhaps that few are ready to accept such a new order, Toomer lists himself as white on the marriage certificate. Racially, Toomer was more white than negro. But he was going against the social conviction that a drop of negro blood makes a person a negro.

After the initial success of his 1923 novel *Cane*, Toomer has continued to write novel after novel but is unable to get any published. He now commences to write at breakneck speed *Portage Potential* about the experiment in living he conducted with group members at Portage, Wisconsin. His writing has become a 'teaching' and his once fluid and poetic style is now didactic. Gorham Munson, his friend, literary critic, and fellow Gurdjieffian, will point this out but Toomer does not see it.

WINTER 1931. AMERICA. Gurdjieff arrives from France. Following last year's ouster of Orage, Gurdjieff now seems open and approachable. He collects money as usual, and then leaves on the *Bremen* on January 16th.

1932. PARIS. Alexander de Salzmann, who left the Prieuré as things ran down and earned his living in Paris, first as an interior designer and then an antique dealer sits, as has become his custom, in a café on the Boulevard St. Germain, drinking a concoction of beer and Calvados and smoking from a long cigarette holder. All the while his hands are occupied with a pencil which formed what looked like Oriental calligraphy. René Daumal, the poet and writer,[61] who at that time was, as he said, "close to madness and death," is introduced to de Salzmann. A group springs up around de Salzmann which he and his wife, Jeanne, teach.[62]

1932. CARMEL, CALIFORNIA. Toomer completes the manuscript for *Portage Potential.* Marjorie, his wife, says of the book, "It is really a remarkable thing, not involved with people's pains and frustrations but with their growth. I hope there are enough people in America interested in growth rather than the opposite to make its publication and success outstanding."

JANUARY 23, 1932. LONDON. Orage writes to an American student:

> I'm disappointed that you and others found G.'s deprecation of self-observation discouraging, since his reason for his statement was familiar to you all. I never at any time said that there is, ready-made, an actual 'I' that can observe; but I always said—following Gurdjieff—that by feeding this conception I on self-observations (or, rather by its own feeding) it develops as an embryo develops. The whole point of the method lay in its being a means to self-development; not, of course, to self-conception, this latter having been done for us, so to speak, and evidenced by the fact that our planetary body becomes fully formed. The *method* was to be practiced by the conceived but not yet developed I; and it had to start from 'nothing,' since only self-developed individuals rank as individuals....

FEBRUARY 1932. CAFÉ DE LA PAIX. Kathryn Hulme spots Gurdjieff at his table. "With one leg pulled up beneath him Oriental-fashion on the banquette, he looked from a distance like a broad-shouldered Buddha radiating such power that all the people between him and me seemed dead."

61. Daumal will later write an unfinished novel, *Mount Analogue* (Penguin, 1974) which gives his understanding of the Work. He dedicates the book to de Salzmann, who is believed to be the prototype for Pierre Sogol, the book's wisdom figure.

62. Whether Gurdjieff knew of the group at the time is a question.

FEBRUARY 1, 1932. A letter from Clifton Fadiman, a highly regarded literary critic and editor, to Jean Toomer regarding the submission of *Portage Potential* says:

> There are very definite reasons for the rejection; but I hardly know how to list them in a letter. I believe very deeply that since *Cane* [Toomer's first novel published in 1923], which had genius in it, you have traversed the wrong road. Perhaps this post-Gurdjieff period is necessary for your development. In that case, I prefer to look upon books like *Portage* as mere entries in your personal journal rather than as works of art destined for an audience. Unless I speak with you at length, it is difficult to explain. Be assured that I read—and with close attention—every word of *Portage*. I am sorry it is no go with us.

FEBRUARY 29, 1932. NEW YORK. Gorham Munson, a literary critic and a Gurdjieffian, has been a friend of Jean Toomer's for many years. He writes Toomer a letter saying, "I could not resist a rapid reading of the manuscript [*Portage Potential*], and though my opinion is unsolicited, I feel I must give it. Gurdjieffian writings fall into two classes, writings for students and writings for the world.…It is very interesting material for the followers of Gurdjieff, but for the world it won't do."

MARCH 4, 1932. Letter from Gorham Munson to Jean Toomer:

> I wish I could work up an enthusiasm for the book and allay some of my fears about it, but I can't. One thing I will mention are the occasional traces in it of the influence of Mr. G.'s style on you. These I think unfortunate, and I have been hoping in the past that you would see for yourself that G.'s "sublime egoism" at moments is unapproachable by us when we write, and that you would see the difference between his vernacular raciness and what I must call your lapses into a wooden colloquialism. But the main consideration is that the book is not crafty enough to disarm the hostile readers who abound while winning the innocent readers whom we don't know about. Many people are waiting to pounce on the first avowed Gurdjieff exposition that comes along, so we must beware, lest we ourselves work harm to the system of ideas we love.

APRIL 10, 1932. GERMANY. The runoff election for president: Hindenburg receives 19.5 million, or 53%, of the votes. Hitler places second with 13.5 million, or 37%, of the votes.

APRIL 21, 1932. LONDON. Backed by American friends, with one thousand pounds Orage publishes the first issue of the *New English Weekly*, the brainchild of Major C. H. Douglas. Its purpose is to champion Social Credit, a monetary system designed to replace money with a kind of barter and distribute taxes to the poor. That Orage now invests his energy and time in such an endeavor shows how far he has deviated from the octave he began ten years before in 1922, when he first arrived at the Prieuré.[63]

AUGUST 16, 1932. CHICAGO. During childbirth, complications ensue and Margery Toomer dies. The child is saved. She is given her mother's name. Toomer nicknames the baby, Argie.

WINTER 1932. NEW YORK. Fritz Peters, now nineteen years old, visits Gurdjieff at his request. It is the first time the two have seen each other since Peters left the Prieuré in 1929. Gurdjieff tells him that because of his childhood association with him he had certain problems and struggles others would never experience. Says Gurdjieff:

> Freets, you not wish to come to see me tonight, so necessary for me—very busy man—to take time to send for you. This because you now have struggle between real self and personality. You not learn my work from talk and book—you learn in skin, and you cannot escape. These people must make effort, go to meetings, read book. If you never go to meeting, never read book, you still cannot forget what I put inside you when you child. These others, if not go to meeting, will forget even existence of Mr. Gurdjieff. But not you. I already in your blood—make your life miserable forever—but such misery can be good thing for your soul, so even when miserable you must thank your God for suffering I give you.

Gurdjieff tells him that he had been studying the American language and instead of the word "fertilizer," he would now use "shit" as it was a real word. He tells Peters that he, like most young people, look at the world upside down. For example, Gurdjieff tells him that he assumed that anyone he met was good, honest, upright, and so forth. So, when he learned the truth about people, he became disillusioned. This attitude was a long, slow and improper process.

Gurdjieff says:

> You must learn to look right side up. Every person you see, including yourself, is shit. You learn this and then when you find something good in such shit people—some possibility not to be shit—you will have two things: you will feel good inside when you learn this person better than you think, and you will also have made proper observation. Just so, when you can observe self, if you already think self is all shit then when see something good in self will be able to recognize at once and will also feel joy. Important that you think about this.

At a later meeting Peters tells Gurdjieff of his experience with the Chicago group. Ordinarily Gurdjieff had no taste for opinions or gossip

63. It is interesting to recall in this connection Orage saying, "There comes a time to almost everyone in this work when he asks himself, 'Shall I lose the old values that gave incentive, and shall I then be able to go on to new ones, ones of a different order?'"

about others, says Peters, but this time he listened. Peters is concerned with the group's "phony reverence" and its "tendency to use his work as an excuse for sexual promiscuity or at least a good deal of talk about sexual promiscuity."

"America is still very young, strong country," Gurdjieff says. "Like young people everywhere, all Americans very interested, very preoccupied with sex things. So very natural for them talk and act this way. And not bad thing they do. I tell many times that all work must start with body; like I tell many times that if wish observe self must start from outside, by observing movements of body. Only much later can learn how observe emotional and mental centers."

Gurdjieff goes on to say:

> Freets, when you come Prieuré first time you not yet spoiled, have not learn to lie to self. Already even then you can maybe lie to mother or father, but not to self. So you fortunate. But these people very unfortunate. Like you, when child, they learn lie to parents, but as they grow up also learn lie to self and once learn this is very difficult to change. Lying, like all other things, become habit for them. So when I say even ordinary thing, because they wish have reverence for their teacher—this reverence can be very bad thing, but is necessary for their good feeling—and because also wish not disturb their inside sleep, they find other meaning for what I say.

"In that case," Peters asks, "how can they ever learn anything from you—or from anyone else?"

"Maybe they not learn anything new."

"Then why bother to try to teach them?"

Gurdjieff smiled, indulgently. "Because is possibility, even if very small, may learn."

1932. ENGLAND. John Buchan's novel, *The Gap in the Curtain,* is published. Its main character is Professor August Moe, a powerful and brooding man of Central European or perhaps Scandinavian extraction, whose *idée fixe* is time and who casts an intellectual spell over five people at a weekend house party. Professor Moe is the first of three fictionalized depictions of Uspenskii.

1932. LONDON. Orage, perhaps putting his best English face on his rift with Gurdjieff, speaks to Nott in glowing terms about Gurdjieff, saying: "We can never understand the being of man who is on a higher level than our own. Gurdjieff is a kind of walking god—a planetary or even solar god."

EARLY 1930S. LONDON. Uspenskii begins to speak about evil and the devil. One cannot do evil consciously, he says. Some actions require people to be conscious, but evil requires a man to be mechanical, asleep. To discover evil, one must aim to be conscious. Then whatever is an obstacle for that aim is evil. "You can only understand evil in relation to yourself."

Uspenskii says the devil, for him, is "real, quite real. It is not the system; it is my opinion." The devil works through imagination, negative emotions, inner considering and the like. What he wants is man's soul. The devil cannot exist on the level of the sun but "maybe [speaking of the lateral octave] the devil can have his roots in *si*. *Si* is bigger than *la*, *sol*, *fa*. Not all *si*. But maybe when man was invented, the devil was invented also," he says. The devil of which he speaks is not the conception of medieval demonology, that of a concrete image or figure. His idea is that the devil is abstract and general so that the name "devil" can be applied to any who slander, tempt, and so forth. Given what has happened with Gurdjieff, it is to be wondered whether he is speaking about his former teacher.

PART III

THE GREAT BEQUEATHING

1932. PARIS. SINCE 1927 JANE HEAP HAS BEEN PROPOUNDING THE PRINCIPLES OF THE WORK. NOW A GROUP BEGINS TO MEET REGULARLY AT her apartment in Montparnasse. Among its members: Solita Solano, possibly Janet Flanner, and, when in Paris, Margaret Anderson, and Georgette Leblanc.

MAY 1, 1932. CAFÉ DE LA PAIX. Unable to meet mortgage and coal payments, Gurdjieff orders the Prieuré's kitchen closed and the château boarded up within a week. On Tuesday Louise Goepfert goes to the Café de la Paix to say good-bye to Gurdjieff. When they see one another she says "a sharp electric spark passes between us."

She tells him why she is there.

"You are very kind," says Gurdjieff. "I know now there in the Prieuré some hate me. Make worst man of me, I do so and so. They not know how much they cost me, even their shit. To take away their shit, 5000 francs a year…"

Later she will ask him: "Can I do anything for you?"

"Now only money, money. One hundred thousand francs I need at once," is the reply.

MAY 11, 1932. PRIEURÉ. Short of funds, Gurdjieff closes the Prieuré and moves to Paris. The upkeep has been too much and the château has fallen into disrepair, its gardens neglected, the orangery in ruins, the Study House deserted, and some of the precious carpets damaged by rats and mice. According to C. S. Nott, Gurdjieff is able to keep going because of the support of Orage's old New York group of about thirty, the small group of Americans in Paris, and several English students. Only one or two French show any interest.

AUGUST 1932. LONDON. Orage receives a letter from Gurdjieff asking him to come to Paris for a day. Replies Orage:

"There was a time when I would have crossed oceans at your bidding. Now I would not even cross the Channel."

SEPTEMBER 13, 1932. CAFÉ DE LA PAIX, PARIS. Gurdjieff begins writing his appeal to contemporary humanity.

WINTER 1932. AMERICA. Gurdjieff arrives. He demands money and his followers react. Jean Toomer reports several are driven away "with disgust and anger and the conviction that he was using his power merely in order to obtain money, money and more money without cease." But Gurdjieff knows what they cannot know—the bank threatens to foreclose on the Prieuré.

1933. AMERICA. Jean Toomer completes the final draft of his novel, *Transatlantic.* He no longer writes in the rich lyrical style of *Cane* with which he sought answers to human problems. Instead, using Gurdjieff's teaching, Toomer becomes a social critic and spiritual reformer. He cannot find a publisher for the book or any of the books that follow. Still, he doggedly continues to write, here and there publishing an essay or poem. He writes a number of plays, as well, but none are staged with the exception of one produced by a university.

Many years hence, Charles R. Larson, a literary critic, will cut to the heart of Toomer's problem with writing:

> Toomer's own writing became a problem of distance. In *Cane* he wrote as if by possession about a way of life that fascinated yet threatened him. He had touched the forbidden subject yet managed to wriggle away. Thereafter, his subject was not culture in all its song and movement but an individual turned in on himself. The gobbledygook characters and situations in the post-*Cane* works, which were intended to be satirical, more often collapse under their ideological weight. As he pushed Gurdjieffian thought—forced it, one might say—into his fiction, his characters became one-dimensional and bloodless. Thus, race and Gurdjieff both ruined and propelled his work—race, because he couldn't accept his blackness after *Cane* was

completed, and Gurdjieff, because the master's philosophy helped Jean [1] to deny his former self.

SPRING 1933. NEW YORK. Gurdjieff telegrams his followers declaring he is "absolutely destitute" and the Prieuré is about to be sold.

1933. GADDESDEN, KENT. The Uspenskiis are now situated in a Victorian mansion standing on seven acres near Sevenoaks, some twenty-five miles from southeast London. Uspenskii has come to the habit of sitting up half the night drinking claret and reminiscing about his early days in Russia. To Bennett he appears as if he is "obsessed with the need to put himself back into the life he was living before he first met Gurdjieff in 1915." At one such drinking bout, Bennett suddenly finds himself "quite outside myself." He finds himself hearing his own voice and even watching his own thoughts, as if they were going on in someone else. "I saw myself as completely artificial," he relates, "neither my thoughts nor my words were my own. 'I'—whoever at that moment 'I' might be—was a completely indifferent spectator of the performance."

Bennett tells Uspenskii that he now knows what self-observation is.

Replies Uspenskii: "If only you can remember what you have just seen you will be able to work. But you must understand that no one can help you in this. If you do not see for yourself, it is impossible for anyone else to show you."

The conversation turns to Uspenskii's theory of Eternal Recurrence. Bennett is of two minds about it. He believes it contains an important element of truth but does not think it literally true.

Uspenskii tells him: "You are like Madame [Uspenskii]. Both of you have young souls. You have not the experience of living many times on this earth."

1933. PARIS. Alexander de Salzmann dies of tuberculosis. His wife, Jeanne, continues to lead the group.

1. An authentic teaching of transformation like the Fourth Way is like handling a poisonous snake. This esoteric "snake," as such, can give great power, knowledge, and perhaps wisdom; but it must be handled carefully, with great respect, being vigilant to any personal element entering, such as using the teaching to mask, rather than reveal, one's personal problems...for transformation can proceed in either direction. The practices seem simple enough but ignorance of the complexity and interlocking principles that lie behind them make a descent inevitable. Not only did Toomer mix his premature understanding of the teaching with his literary career but the starting of his own groups upon his return from the Prieuré in 1924, with no mandate from either Gurdjieff or Orage, shows a desire for power. Toomer once acknowledged to Orage his need for power but apparently—given his persistent aim of setting up his own institute—it was only an intellectual observation. Still, Toomer was a man of exceptional talent and vision, one who searched all his life, and who made a definite contribution to establishing the Work.

MARCH 7, 1933. PARIS. The previous year Gurdjieff began to write the controversial *Herald of Coming Good* (which was originally titled *Herald of Glad Tidings).* Now he writes a bizarre "Supplementary Announcement" to the book. Though written, the *First* and *Second Series* of Gurdjieff's *All and Everything* are yet to be published. But he does publish *Herald.* With the exception of C. S. Nott and some others, it strikes many as a very strange book. Some, like Uspenskii, think it shows he has lost his mind.

MAY 1933. PRIEURÉ. Unable to meet mortgage payments, the Prieuré, Gurdjieff's home of ten years, is lost and its contents auctioned.

MIDSUMMER 1933. NEW YORK. Gurdjieff spends most of his time in America staying with Fred Leighton, a wealthy student who first learned about Gurdjieff through the Orage groups of the mid-1920s.

AUTUMN 1933. BERLIN. Hitler chooses Albert Speer as his architect. Speer, having heard Hitler speak, joined the Nazi Party in 1931. He says of that time: "After years of frustrated efforts I was wild to accomplish things—and twenty-eight years old. For the commission to do a great building, I would have sold my soul like Faust. Now I had found my Mephistopheles. He seemed no less engaging than Goethe's." Speer went on to design many buildings, as well as create the dramatic lighting effect—deemed "a cathedral of ice"—at the Nazi Party rally in Nuremberg. Speer would later rise to the position of Minister of Armaments and War Production, where his technical ability and organizational mastery excelled.

FALL 1933. HENRY HUDSON HOTEL, NEW YORK. Gurdjieff gives a dinner party for fifteen people he says he considers important for his work. He invites Fritz Peters to help him prepare. He tells Peters that he wants to learn American words for the various parts and functions of the body "that were not in dictionary." For the next two hours, he has Peters repeat every four-letter word and obscene phrase he can think of.

Peters wonders what kind of dinner guests he is having but when they arrive, he finds them well-dressed and well-mannered New Yorkers and serves them drinks. About a half hour after their arrival, Gurdjieff appears. He is very apologetic and crudely flatters the women about how beautiful they are and how everyone does him so much honor in agreeing to be "the guests of a poor, humble man like himself." Peters can't believe that everyone accepts this flattery.

At the dinner table the mood is mellow. The usual round of questions begin as to Gurdjieff's Work and reasons for coming to America. After replying for awhile, Gurdjieff's tone of voice suddenly changes and he gives Peters a sudden sly wink. He says that humanity is in a very bad condition because people—"especially Americans—are never motivated by intelligence or good feelings, but only the needs —usually dirty—of their genital organs." He uses, of course, all the four-letter words and phrases Peters had earlier taught him. Turning to one well-dressed and handsome woman, Gurdjieff copiously compliments her on every aspect of her appearance and then, saying they could be honest with each other, tells her she dressed so because she "wish to fuck" a certain person. Tormented by this sexual urge, Gurdjieff tells her she is very imaginative and can already picture herself performing various sexual acts with this man—"such as, how you say in English? Sixty-nine?" He then launches into a description of his own sexual abilities following it by a detailed description of the sexual habits of various races and nations. After some two hours of such talk, with everyone's behavior becoming completely uninhibited, Gurdjieff eggs them on into having an orgy. When it was in full swing, according to Peters, Gurdjieff suddenly tells them all "in loud, stentorian tones" that they had already confirmed his observations of the decadence of the Americans and that they need no longer demonstrate for him. He points at various individuals, mocks their behavior and then tells them that if they are, thanks to him, now partly conscious of what sort of people they really are, it was an important lesson for them. He says that he deserved to be paid for this lesson and that he would gladly accept checks and cash from them as they left the apartment. To Peters' surprise, Gurdjieff collects several thousand dollars.

WINTER 1933. AMERICA. The problems with Orage and the Prieuré appear to have taken their toll. Gurdjieff looks horrible and has put on a great deal of weight. His *Herald of Coming Good* is misunderstood.

EARLY 1934. NEW YORK. Gurdjieff normally arises at 6–7 A.M. and goes to Child's Restaurant in the Hecksher Building, what he called his "New York office." According to one witness, "He had grown fat. He looked untidy; time had turned his long, black ringmaster's moustache to grey; but he was unmistakably a personage, and the old, arrogant, undaunted look shone forth from his eyes."

APRIL 2, 1934. PARIS. Gurdjieff fulfills his three will-tasks. "First," he says, "'puffed' three small booklets into ten substantial volumes. Second, not only understood from all sides different deep-rooted minutiae of the common psyche of man, suspected by me and intriguing me all my life... Third, my health is now in such condition that I not only, as you may see, live and write such an already ultra-fantastic book, but intend to outlive all my past, present and future enemies."

SPRING 1934. NEW YORK. Fred Leighton introduces Jean Toomer to his friend Marjorie Content. A friend of the painter Georgia O'Keefe, Content was a former partner with Jesse Dwight in the Sunwise Turn bookshop. A photographer and actress, her father is a wealthy Wall Street speculator. Married three times, Content's second husband was Harold A. Loeb, whom Ernest Hemingway portrayed as the infamous character Robert Cohn in *The Sun Also Rises.* Content is familiar with Toomer's writing but has no use for Gurdjieff or his teaching. Toomer, to win her, apparently acts as though he is no longer interested in Gurdjieff.

Jean Toomer sees Gurdjieff about his impending marriage to Marjorie Content. Gurdjieff tells him he is leaving the next day. Knowing he was in need of money, Toomer gives him $200, a large sum in those days.

Gurdjieff tries to get more.[2] Toomer says:

> What could be in the man's mind? Who and what was he? What were his purposes? What aims did he have for me, if any? What aims for the people of the world? Was I a mere tool? Was I not even that, so nothing from his point of view that he need not even consider the way he used or misused me? Was he the supreme egotist? Was he, as some claimed, insane?...This is what is so awful about the situation with Gurdjieff. The situations themselves are always taxing—and you can arrive at no sure reconciliation or fixed understanding because for every fact there is a counter fact, for every reason a counter reason, for every bit of "bad" behavior another bit of "good" behavior, for every son-of-a-bitching thing a counter saintly thing....Insane? He was in full possession of every one of his extraordinary faculties. Debauched and slovenly? Nothing of the sort. Afraid of the dark and being alone? It was ridiculous. Whatever he had gone through, the thing that showed plainly was a decided improvement in every respect.

Toomer asks Gurdjieff about his promise many years before that he would make him "ruler of Africa."[3]

"Something went wrong," replies Gurdjieff, smiling.

Toomer presses him to elaborate.

"You not as I counted," Gurdjieff says.

"How do you mean?"

"In the beginning I counted you. You not as I counted."

2. Both of Gurdjieff's two principal biographers, Webb and Moore, judge Gurdjieff's actions as if he were an ordinary human being. Therefore, to them he is simply being venal. Gurdjieff's actions should be first seen from the highest possible level. Otherwise we diminish his unique being and understanding to that of our own. In so doing, we "psychologize" him and so dismiss him.

3. From this comment, it is clear that Gurdjieff takes Toomer to be black.

"How do you mean?"

"You manifest differently at different times, different from what I expected. You not as I counted and I get angry."

"Angry? Why?"

"You not as I counted."

Gurdjieff tells C. S. Nott:

> The sign of a perfected man and his particularity in ordinary life must be that in regard to everything happening outside him, he is able to, and can in every action, perform to perfection externally the part corresponding to the given situation; but at the same time never blend or agree with it. In my youth, I too...worked on myself for the purpose of attaining such a blessing...and...I finally reached a state when nothing from outside could really touch me internally; and so far as acting was concerned, I brought myself to such perfection as was never dreamed of by the learned people of ancient Babylon for the actors on stage.

Says Fritz Peters, who observed from the Prieuré days onward: "Gurdjieff had an unbelievable (unless you've seen it) *awareness* of other people. It was nothing so limited as mind-reading or thought-transference. He seemed to know so much about the human processes, about the underlying logic in man, that he was conscious of everything that took place within any human being he happened to observe. It is the same kind of faculty that an occasional highly trained psychiatrist seems to have to a limited degree. Gurdjieff had it to an enormous degree."

1934. LYNE PLACE. The Uspenskiis move to a lightly wooded country estate some twenty miles west of central London at Virginia Water, not far from Windsor Castle. The estate includes a large eighteenth-century mansion with the customary English garden, rhododendron walks, ancient trees, a small ornamental lake and boathouse. A short walk from the mansion is the farm with barns, outbuildings, greenhouses, stables, pigsties, chicken houses, and a walled vegetable garden. Beyond this lay the fields all enclosed by hedges.

And of course everywhere Uspenskii is, there are his cats as well. Cats fascinate him. He believes the cat knows and inhabits its body completely; it is aware of itself except when, say, a salmon appears. "Everything *outside itself* it takes for granted, as something given," Uspenskii says. "To *correct* the outside world, to accommodate it to its own comfort, would never occur to a cat. Maybe this is so because a cat lives more in another world, the world of dreams and fantasies, than in this one."

For exercise, Uspenskii rides his favorite horse, Jingles, around the property. A student had given him an expensive Cossack saddle of which he is quite proud. The horse being a symbol of the emotional center, a wag might suggest Uspenskii had things well in hand.

From time to time targets are set up and he practices shooting. He is a crack shot but never shoots anything living. He is fond of Russian prints, and a connoisseur of tea and, of course, vodka.

At this time Uspenskii writes a series of introductory lectures on the teaching which are later published as *The Psychology of Man's Possible Evolution.*

Gurdjieff has copies of *Herald* sent to all of Uspenskii's pupils. Uspenskii has it read to a group of his closest pupils. The general opinion is that it is "almost paranoiac." Uspenskii suggests that perhaps Gurdjieff had syphilis. He instructs his pupils to hand in their copies and has them destroyed.

Later, Gurdjieff repudiates *Herald*, calling in all copies.

Looking for a new home for his Institute, Gurdjieff makes another trip to America and asks the wealthy Mabel Dodge Luhan for the New Mexico ranch she had volunteered eight years before. She refuses.

1934. PARIS. Madame de Salzmann moves her group to Sèvres. In 1935 Philippe Lavastine, the Orientalist, joins the group.

JUNE 30, 1934. BERLIN. Consolidating his power, Hitler orders his chief rival, Ernst Roehm, head of the S. A. (the Brownshirts), and 150 of its leaders shot.

SUMMER 1934. TRAIN FROM NEW YORK TO CHICAGO. Learning that Fritz Peters planned to go to Chicago for a vacation, Gurdjieff decides to go with him and visit the Chicago group. Gurdjieff suggests they take the midnight train. Arriving at Gurdjieff's apartment early that evening, Peters finds Gurdjieff has yet to pack. Leaving the apartment well after eleven they arrive at Penn station with only ten minutes to spare. Gurdjieff has Peters hold up the train's departure while he bids his New York followers good-bye. "Gurdjieff did not manage to complete his urgent farewells," Peters says sarcastically "until the train was actually moving and I had to push him through the door of the last car with his six or seven pieces of luggage." Their sleeping berths thirteen cars ahead, it takes them forty-five minutes to make their way, luggage and all, through the cars. All the while, Gurdjieff's noisy lamentations about Peters' rude treatment angers the sleeping passengers.

Finally in their seats, the exhausted Peters becomes furious when Gurdjieff refuses to go to bed. Instead he eats, drinks, and smokes, all of which he does in very loud tones, still complaining about the shoddy treatment that he, a very important man, is receiving. Peters, in a fit, says he wants to get off the train and away from him. Gurdjieff, with wide-eyed innocence, says he doesn't understand his anger—he "had never imagined that Peters, his only friend, would talk to him in this way, and quite literally, desert him." Enroute many like episodes follow that annoy, irritate, and offend both passengers and Peters. Each time Gurdjieff apologizes profusely then creates new ways to agitate.

At dinner the next evening with his Chicago followers, Gurdjieff publicly praises each follower but berates Peters for how horribly he had treated him. After about an hour of public humiliation Peters bursts into some four-letter words and leaves in disgust.

As Peters later realizes, what he called "the nightmare journey" with Gurdjieff had served to "force me out of the pattern of hero-worship which had unconsciously formed in me in relation to him."

AUGUST 2, 1934. BERLIN. President von Hindenburg dies. Hitler, moving swiftly, abolishes the office of President and combines its power with his own as Chancellor.

SEPTEMBER 1, 1934. TAOS, NEW MEXICO. Jean Toomer and Marjorie Content marry. The painter Georgia O'Keefe, a lover of Toomer's from the year before and a friend of Marjorie's, attends the marriage. The newlyweds return to New York City and the Toomers convene a salon to which the Munsons were frequent guests, as was Georgia O'Keefe and many of Toomer's Gurdjieff friends. Late in the year they buy a large farm outside Doylestown, in Bucks County, Pennsylvania, a center of Quaker-Amish activity. Toomer believes it is the ideal site for the institute he envisions creating.

LATE 1934. DOYLESTOWN, PENNSYLVANIA. At first Toomer and his new wife visit only for weekends. But by spring of 1935 they will move permanently.

With their house guests and the flow of weekend guests, Toomer soon takes the role of the teacher. Often there are a dozen or so people sitting around the dinner table or in a circle around him. Remembers Gorham Munson, who was from time to time a houseguest, "Jean as the host at Doylestown was often embarrassing to me....He would actually go into broken English, too, you know, and he would tear loaves of bread apart. He would use bad, vulgar language at times. He would try to shock people by going into these seemingly rambling discourses. He was all imitative of Gurdjieff and bad, bad, bad imitation." Though Toomer attracts a small number of devotees, he never manages to establish an institute or permanent commune.

Always searching, Toomer, at some point, begins to attend meetings of the Religious Society of Friends, a Quaker group. He and his wife become very involved and in time he begins giving lectures and writing pamphlets. His stomach ailments, which he has suffered now and then throughout his life, increase. He has vision problems which at times necessitates his wearing a patch over one eye. He begins drinking. Toward the end of the decade, Toomer becomes interested in Eastern mysticism.

OCTOBER 1934. Nott has a strong feeling that something serious is about to happen to Orage. A week or so later the two are sauntering up Chancery Lane, as they often did, and are speaking of life at the Prieuré when Orage stops and declares in a tone of complete conviction—"You know, I thank God every day of my life that I met Gurdjieff."

NOVEMBER 5, 1934. LONDON. Orage gives a speech over the radio on Social Credit. At one point, he pauses for a very long time. Later he says that he had not known before how clearly the mind can work with severe pain under the breastbone. The next morning his wife, Jesse, finds him in his study. Orage is dead. He is buried in the churchyard of Old Hampstead Church. On the stone slab covering his grave is carved the enneagram and Krishna's words to Arjuna in the *Gita*, "You grieve for those for whom you should not grieve..."

NOVEMBER 6, 1934. CHILD'S RESTAURANT, NEW YORK. Gurdjieff is with a person who is helping to translate *All and Everything* into English. The word "voluntary" has been substituted for "intentional" in the translated text. Gurdjieff is explaining the difference in meaning between the two words. In an action of synchronicity or what Gurdjieff calls a "noticeable coincidence," he is called to the telephone. The operator has a telegram from C. S. Nott in London—*Orage has died.*

Gurdjieff recalls that this very night exactly seven years before he had dictated a letter to Orage that spoke about suffering and the difference between voluntary and intentional suffering, as well as about "noticeable coincidences."[4]

Orage at that time, says Gurdjieff, "was considered to be, and indeed was, the most important leader in the dissemination of my ideas in the whole northern part of North America." Gurdjieff advised him to regulate his health by means of intentional suffering "in a form corresponding to his individuality and the condition of his ordinary life." But this he would not do.

Gurdjieff must be remembering that great thirst for the truth that was Orage's in the early days, that indomitable desire that was direly tested, as a fifty-year-old man with a largely overweight body forced it all those long days to dig ditch after ditch at the Prieuré. He must have remembered, too, his bright and electric mind, his great warmth and ease with

4. Perhaps Gurdjieff had spoken to Orage then of that fateful evening in January 1924 when Orage first spoke of the teaching at the Sunwise Turn and in the audience sat the manifestation of his chief feature—Jesse Dwight.

people, and, yes, that sense of humor, that wonderful dry English sense of humor full of *metis.*

"How you say it in your country?" asks Gurdjieff, "May his soul reach the Kingdom of Heaven."

Then Gurdjieff wiping the tears from his eyes with his fists says:

"This man...my brother."

On the morning of Orage's death and seven years after Orage's marriage and the blackest moment of Gurdjieff's life—November 6, 1927—he begins to write the *Third Series.* But such was the effect of Orage's death upon him that for two months as he says, "in spite of my constant wish, and constant efforts, I was not able to add a single word to what I had written up to half-past eleven that morning."[5]

JANUARY 6, 1935. NEW YORK. Gurdjieff again resumes the writing of the *Third Series.*

1935. ENGLAND. Uspenskii now has over one thousand pupils. Maurice Nicoll has a group of over a hundred. The Gurdjieff group in London has perhaps twelve people. With Gurdjieff in Paris there are only a few Americans, English, and Russians. In New York, no more than twenty.

1935. SÈVRES, FRANCE. Jeanne de Salzmann's embryonic group consists of René Daumal and his wife, Vera, and Philippe Lavastine and his wife "Boussique," Madame de Salzmann's daughter.

Spring 1935. New York. Toomer goes to Child's Restaurant to see Gurdjieff, who had been shamelessly pressuring everyone for money. "He was in a bad way," Toomer says. "His health was poor. He looked it, liverish, looked as if he had been drawn through a mill, laboring under a heavy strain, physically, and mentally, and in every way." Gurdjieff again pressures him for money,[6] saying he really needs it this time. Toomer says: "My mind flashed over subsequent happenings, the sure result of which was

5. Gurdjieff's reaction shows the extent to which he was counting on Orage to help him in establishing the teaching. Had Orage not died, and had he recognized his chief feature (chief wound, it might be said) and the need to intentionally work with it, he might have returned to Gurdjieff. The result would undoubtedly have been that establishing the teaching in the West would begin on a much higher octave. On another point, it is interesting to recall that Uspenskii, as well, lost the power to write, that is, to formulate, after acceding to Gurdjieff's demand that he give up all his knowledge, see p. 30.

6. Every student thinks themselves and their relationship with the teacher—special. The demand for money, therefore, is usually painful and difficult not to identify with, as money is so associated with power, status, self-esteem and, hence, the false personality. Though Toomer's wife is quite wealthy, Gurdjieff's apparent 'venality' (See Footnote 2, p. 168) is, at the very least, distasteful and creates friction and doubts.

that I felt a great relief when I left New York [he moved to Doylestown, Pennsylvania] and thus left him. To me he seemed like a changed man, changed for the worse. I felt his work was dead. Whether dead or not, there was no place or function for me in it. It was a travesty and hollow mockery of the work I had entered in 1924 with all my heart. I would have nothing to do with what was going on at present. I would have something to do with future work—on the critical basis as if I were meeting him and his work for the first time, taking nothing for granted."

MARCH 1935. NEW YORK. Gurdjieff has been staying with Fred Leighton. Jean Toomer visits and gives him $200. Gurdjieff invites him to lunch the following day. After lunch he invites Toomer into his office, which turns out to be the bathroom, to discuss business. He says he needs an additional $350. He is depending on Toomer, he says. He could get the money elsewhere but due to his policies about different people and aims he doesn't want to. He gives Toomer his essence-word to pay him back in four months and to give him a place in his "future creations." Toomer is incredulous that Gurdjieff is trying to put the bite on him for money again.

"We left the bathroom," Toomer says, "and took chairs in the main room, the typewriters pounding and clacking [typing *All and Everything*]. We smoked and joked. I asked Gurdjieff certain questions about myself. He said I did not deserve to know. I asked, 'If I do not deserve, then who does?' His reply was that nobody deserved. I asked, 'Then for whom are you doing all this work?' [He replied] 'I will live for coming generations. It is for them.'"

"Gurdjieff said some things which threw light on his apparently shameful conduct the past months. The gist of what he said was this. That in order to restore himself, particularly his body, it was necessary that he suffer. In order to suffer he had deliberately done things to people and created situations which would enter into his automatic processes and of themselves cause suffering and make him suffer whenever he remembered them.[7]

"This did somewhat explain the circumstances related by Leighton that throughout the 'worst of it' Gurdjieff had treated him in much the same way as he had always treated him, never mistreating him."

7. Of course Gurdjieff's explanation could be taken as yet another ruse, an arch-clever way of justifying his mendacious and outrageous behavior. What mitigates against it is Gurdjieff's discovery of the special use of suffering—the intentional evoking of blame in others—so that, by working to not identify with the anger-charged energy that blame engenders, new energy can be created and refined. As he wrote: "Although it is possible to attain any self-imposed aim, it can only be done exclusively through conscious suffering." See *Third Series.*

APRIL 2, 1935. NEW YORK. Gurdjieff believes he has successfully completed the three "will-tasks" he imposed on himself on May 6, 1928.

APRIL 9, 1935. NEW YORK. Gurdjieff finishes the prologue to the *Third Series* and begins the chapter "The Inner and Outer World of Man."

APRIL 10, 1935. NEW YORK. Gurdjieff works and reworks the beginning of "The Inner and Outer World of Man." He becomes stuck when he comes to the expression "problem of the prolongation of human life," which he says among all the questions raised in the *Third Series* is "the basic question, or as one might say, the 'clue.'"

APRIL 14, 1935. NEW YORK. Gurdjieff buys the Russian newspaper *Rusky Golos.* He reads P. Mann's article, "The Problem of Old Age," and decides to use it in his chapter on "The Inner and Outer world of Man."

EARLY SPRING 1935. LYNE PLACE. C. S. Nott visits. He finds Uspenskii not the forbidding philosopher he expected, but a sympathetic person "warm, friendly and easy to talk to." Madame Uspenskii, he describes as being small in stature but acting the "Grand Duchess," always maintaining a distance. She does most of the talking. The subject of Orage comes up and Madame Uspenskii, with characteristic directness, says—"There were many things that Mr. Orage did not understand or understood wrongly. Mr. Orage was too formatory for one thing."

Rejoins Nott: "I'm sure Orage would have agreed with you but you had not seen him for ten years, and he had changed very much in that time. And you know, Gurdjieff himself once said that Mr. Uspenskii himself was too formatory."

Nott and Uspenskii would have many talks. Uspenskii would invite Nott into his study and open up a bottle of wine. Gradually, Nott developed a real affection for him, though they were at polar extremes about a never-failing subject of discussion—Gurdjieff.

Of whom Uspenskii would say:

> You know when Gurdjieff started his Institute in Paris I did everything I could for him. I raised money for him and sent him pupils, many of them influential people. When he bought the Prieuré I went there myself and Madame stayed for some time. But I found that he had changed from when I knew him in Russia. He was difficult in Essentuki and Constantinople but more so in Fontainebleau. His behaviour had changed. He did many things I did not like, but it wasn't what he did that upset me, it was the stupid way he did them. He came to London to my group and made things very unpleasant for me. After this I saw that I must break with him, and I told my pupils that they would have to choose between going to Fontainebleau or working with me.

"Gurdjieff's mind never recovered from his accident," maintains Uspenskii.

"I can't accept that," answers Nott. "We cannot judge Gurdjieff from our level. He lives from essence and, in a great measure, according to objective reason, and a person who lives thus can sometimes appear to our minds spoilt by wrong education and conditioning, as not normal. For me Gurdjieff represents objective sanity.... He *lives* the Teaching, while we talk about it."

"No," replies Uspenskii, "he lost contact with the source after Essentuki. His behaviour goes contrary to his teaching. Then the accident. He drives a car as if he were riding a horse."

"I can't agree that he's lost contact with the source," declares Nott. "For me he *is* the source."[8]

Sometime after his first meeting Uspenskii, Nott is in Paris having lunch with Gurdjieff, who makes an unflattering remark about Uspenskii.

"Mr. Gurdjieff," says Nott, always loyal to his friends, "I like Uspenskii and I enjoy talking to him."

"Oh yes, Uspenskii very nice man to talk to and drink vodka with, but he is weak man,"[9] replies Gurdjieff.

Nott reflects on this and concludes that Uspenskii's weakness, as with most people, was his emotional center. It was undeveloped and therefore partial and subjective. "Emotionally," says Nott, "I never felt inferior to Uspenskii."

But he wonders whether his emotional center is too strong. He speaks about it to Gurdjieff who tells him— "A strong feeling center is a gift of God."[10]

MAY 1935. Some, such as J. G. Bennett, believe that Gurdjieff returned to Central Asia between May and July of 1935. There is little evidence to support this. In the late summer of 1935 Gurdjieff is seen again in Paris, taking flats in the rue Marchand and then in the rue Labie.

SEPTEMBER 15, 1935. GERMANY. Nuremberg Laws deprive Jews of German citizenship.

8. Nott sees in Uspenskii's viewpoint about Gurdjieff an inflexibility that is characteristic of the Russian mentality, and "once they have adopted a mental attitude to a given situation they will stick to it, whatever the cost."

9. Gurdjieff here is likely referring to Uspenskii's refusal to allow Gurdjieff to work on his emotional center. Uspenskii's life shows he was a man of great integrity, character, and strength.

10. The formulation of the teaching of the Fourth Way, as given by Uspenskii, is in terms of the intellectual center. But it is just this center which Gurdjieff challenges in *All and Everything*. It cannot begin to be understood unless the emotional center of the reader is evoked. Is this why Gurdjieff's *legominism* is so little read and studied, even by many who practice the Work?

1935. NEW YORK. Gurdjieff again returns. Having finished the Prologue to his *Third Series, Life is real only then, when "I am,"* Gurdjieff travels to Washington, D.C., to meet with Senator Bronson Cutting. The senator is expected to give the financial support needed to repurchase the Prieuré. Cutting, however, dies in a plane crash. Gurdjieff had once told Bennett, "What started in Russia, finish in Russia."[11] Perhaps it isn't entirely surprising then that he now applies for a Russian visa. The Soviets tell him he will be allowed to return, but he cannot teach. With this, all the doors appear to be closing on Gurdjieff.

OCTOBER 19, 1935. PARIS. "I now am old idiot," Gurdjieff says. "Both feet in galosh, moreover old Jewish. I need some church mouse again."[12]

OCTOBER 21, 1935. PARIS. Gurdjieff forms "The Rope," initially a group of four lesbians among whom are Solita Solano,[13] Elizabeth Gordon, Kathryn Hulme and her companion Alice Rohrer. Gurdjieff tells them each person has an "inner animal." One not only had to contend with it, but make friends with it, so it would help them in their work. Gurdjieff gives many of the women animal names. Solita Solano, because she quivers with animation, Gurdjieff calls "Kanari." Kathryn Hulme, because of her overflowing sentimentality, is "Krokodeel." Alice is "Thin One." Elizabeth Gordon apparently does not get a name. Margaret Anderson and Georgette Leblanc become part of the group. Anderson he calls "Yakina," saying her outer animal is a Tibetan yak, a cousin of the European cow. Later, he tells her that her inner animal is a "tapeworm," a lazy animal that seeks a comfortable place and feeds on the labor and effort of others.[14] Georgette Leblanc is not given a name. Jane Heap sometimes attends meetings. He names her "Mees Keep."[15]

11. In none of the historical records does Gurdjieff ever make reference to this again. He did not have a high opinion of theosophy or Rudolph Steiner, but perhaps he believed, as Steiner said, "the importance of the Slavic folk soul as a spiritual bridge between the passive Orient and the active Occident. The religious thought of the Orient belongs to the past; the philosophical-scientific thought of the Occident belongs to the present; the Slavic soul will bridge the two and create a pathway to a spiritual future (in the sixth post-Atlantean age)." From Maria Carlson's *No Religion Higher than Truth*, p. 102.

12. This apparently is Gurdjieff's way of saying that he needs to become more humble.

13. She will later become Gurdjieff's secretary. Why he formed this group is not known, but it is clear that Gurdjieff always experimented with human types. These women were of a very high quality and proved to be among his most loyal students.

14. On the face of it, Gurdjieff's words may seem harsh. If it were words only, it might be. But Gurdjieff's emanation, that of pure impersonal love, provides the necessary background. That is, while the personality is shocked by the words, the essence is experiencing a sense of well-being. Thus, the student finds herself between a 'yes' and a 'no.'

1935. LONDON. Though Uspenskii has managed to attract upwards of one thousand people to the teaching, for him, too, life in the mid-1930s now appears to be contracting.

In the early days his lectures were full of inspiration. He became a sort of underground spiritual figure, "a mystery man," according to one follower, "who kept in the background and conducted very secret meetings somewhere in London."

With the passage of time, the energy that Uspenskii had built up from his contact with Gurdjieff began to run down. Says J. H. Reyner, a student of Uspenskii's and a biographer: "The fact was that Uspenskii had lost his way and was living on stale manna." Says Nott: "The work was too theoretical, too one-centered, intellectual-centered; and often I would leave with a feeling of emptiness, of emotional hunger… I get more from inner work with one lunch with Mr. Gurdjieff than from a year of Mr. Uspenskii's groups."

1936. LONDON. Bennett says that between now and the outbreak of the Second World War in 1939 his relations with Uspenskii changed. Though he went regularly to Lyne, he says "I was no longer in his confidence." No reasons are given as to why.

1936. MILL HOUSE, DOYLESTOWN, PENNSYLVANIA. Despite his wife's concerns, Jean Toomer again tries an experiment in communal living. Working individually and in groups, Toomer's students restore an abandoned grist mill and also farm large tracts of land. Toomer continues to womanize. His wife, determined to make this marriage work, overlooks it.

1936. PARIS. Nott is having lunch with Gurdjieff at his apartment, speaking of idiots. Gurdjieff has told Nott he is a hopeless idiot.

"Which you wish to be, objective or subjective [hopeless idiot]?"

"Subjective, of course," Nott says. "I don't wish to perish like a dog."

"Every man thinks he is God but a subjective hopeless idiot sometimes knows that he is not God. Objective hopeless idiot is shit. Never can be anything, never can do anything. Subjective hopeless idiot has possibility not to be shit. He has come to the place where he knows he is hopeless. He has realized his nothingness, that he is nonentity."

With that Gurdjieff hands Nott a red pepper and says, "Eat, then will remember."

Nott, like the Kurd in *All and Everything*, eats the pepper which sets his whole body on fire.

Says Gurdjieff, "Can be a reminding factor."

15. Kathryn Hulme said Gurdjieff pronounced "h's" gutturally and so "Heap" became "Keep." This seems too literal and ignores Gurdjieff's great sense of humor and understanding of language.

The conversation turns to *All and Everything* and Nott says: "What about people who have never met you, or will never meet you. How will they be able to understand *All and Everything*."

Answers Gurdjieff, "Perhaps will understand better than many always around me. You, by the way, you see much of me and become identified with me. I not wish people identified with me. I wish them identified with my ideas. Many who never will meet me, simple people, will understand my book. Time come perhaps when they read *All and Everything* in churches."

Nott is concerned that so few people know about *All and Everything*. He speaks about this to his friend, Denis Saurat, a professor of French Literature at Kings College, Cambridge and noted author. Saurat has met Gurdjieff and read the typescript of *All and Everything* which Nott has sent him. Saurat assures him that it is "a great book...there is a very great amount of wisdom and knowledge it."

Nott, of course, agrees but if only very few people have the interest, will, and attention to read and understand it—what will become of it?

"Nothing much may happen in our time," says Saurat. "We are in too much of a hurry. We have no sense of real time in the West. Perhaps in fifty, or a hundred years a group of key men will read it. They will say, 'This is what we've been looking for,' and on an understanding of it may start a movement which could raise the level of civilization."

As to Gurdjieff's real identity, Saurat says, "Gurdjieff is a Lohan...a man who has gone to schools and by incredible exertions and study has perfected himself. He then comes back into ordinary life, sits in cafés, drinks, has women, and lives the life of a man, but more intensely. It was accepted [in the East] that the rules of ordinary man did not apply to him. He teaches, and people come to him to learn objective truths...the West does not understand. A teacher in the West must appear to behave like an English gentleman."

Kanari finds Yakina—who the day before had said, "I see I irritate you, Mr. Gurdjieff, so I will go"—sitting with Gurdjieff at a café. Her face is so distressed that Kanari waits until she leaves. Says Gurdjieff: "I nervous and your friend come talk empty to empty.…She too light for this work, too American. In life she perhaps have something good. But not for our work. I thought when she first came that after she had contact with me, something would collect in her empty place, but now I see is not so. Such empty life leave empty place. In fact I could tell is piece of meat with emanations. Good formulation, eh?"

"I think the reason is the result of philosophizing for years with Orage's New York group," says Kanari.

"Yes," answers Gurdjieff, "she is a victim of self-observation."

"Perhaps it is not too late, Mr. Gurdjieff," says Kanari. "She has such a wish to work. She truly knows there is nothing else in life but your work. Don't send her away."

"Well, I will see what I can combinate for her. She must all stop make, wait, begin another way. She has only automatic mind, she not understand that of mind is two kinds and she quite not have real mind mentation. You explain to her, but use my words."

JUNE 18, 1936. PARIS. Says Gurdjieff to Solita Solano and other members of the Rope: "The highest aim of man is to be cunning.[16] I speak of real cunning, not the dirty means of the world. The magus is cunning. The magus is the highest that man can approach to God, because only he can be impartial and fulfill obligation to God. In old times the magus was always made chief because he had cunning. Other magus could do either white or black magic but the magus who had cunning and canning[17] could do both white and black and was chief of the initiates."

During the meetings with the Rope, Gurdjieff drops many pearls. Asked whether man is the result of evolution from animals, he says, "No—man is a different formula." Did man once have a tail which was a continuation of his denying brain? "Yes," he said. About making force, "When you make the body do what it not wish to do, makes force. For making it do just one small thing which it hates doing, makes more force than a day of walking." About intermarriage, "Mixed blood gives less chance of individuality." Of himself, "I am sometimes God and sometimes I have 10,000 devils." At another time, "I am a small man compared to those who sent me." Gurdjieff recalls an old saying, "You can understand and love me only when you love—have passion for—my thorns. Then only I am your slave."

JULY 7, 1936. PARIS. At the Park Café, what he calls his "summer office," Gurdjieff speaks to Solita Solano and other members of the Rope about his auto accident at Chailly.

16. For a discussion of the Greek meaning of cunning, or *metis*, taken from the goddess Metis, see *Cunning Intelligence in Greek Culture and Society* by Marcel Detienne and Jean-Paul Vernant (University of Chicago Press, 1991). From the introduction: "There is no doubt that *metis* is a type of intelligence and of thought, a way of knowing; it implies a complex but very coherent body of mental attitudes and intellectual behavior which combine flair, wisdom, forethought, subtlety of mind, deception, resourcefulness, vigilance, opportunism, various skills, and experience acquired over the years. It is applied to situations which are transient, shifting, disconcerting and ambiguous, situations which do not lend themselves to precise measurement, exact calculation or rigorous logic."

17. See *Third Series* for how Gurdjieff uses the word "canning."

"Yes, all is different since accident," Gurdjieff declares. "Then I die, in truth all die. Everything began then from new. I was born that year, 1924. I am now twelve-year-old boy, not yet responsible age. I can remember how I was then—all thought, feeling. I was heavy, too heavy. Now everything is mixed with light."

Of Madame de Hartmann he says: "She is first friend of my inner life, such thought she had for me."

JULY 1936. PARIS. René Daumal is introduced to Gurdjieff by Madame de Salzmann.

SEPTEMBER 28, 1936. Uspenskii visits Count Keyserling, author and world traveller. About their meeting, the count says: "Mr. Uspenskii controls himself until he is completely suffocated. Oh yes, I do believe in control, but not in complete canalization. I have never seen so rich a character so controlled and stifled....Mr. Uspenskii is one of the greatest men alive; but I have never seen a man subject so much of himself to one part of himself. But he cannot succeed entirely, he is too great."

OCTOBER 1936. PARIS. Gurdjieff sends Jane Heap to London to teach.

1936. WARWICK GARDENS. The biologist Robert de Ropp meets Uspenskii and is much impressed. He believes Uspenskii "was probably at the height of his power....In appearance he was massive and moved with a ponderous intentionality that at times reminded me of an elephant.... The massive body was surmounted by a no less massive head crowned with short-cropped grey hair. The face had considerable strength—an emperor's face, an emperor who was also a scholar and who could very easily become a tyrant."

Uspenskii strikes de Ropp and others as being Russian to his very core. He so typifies that race's strengths and weaknesses that the saying among his older followers is: "One must distinguish between what is the teaching and what is just Russian." The Russian temperament is to be either a total slave or a complete tyrant. "Uspenskii," says de Ropp, "was authoritarian." At the same time, he finds Uspenskii completely free of sentimentality and pretentiousness. He does not pontificate. "Believe nothing, test everything" are his watchwords.

At Warwick Gardens and in London there is lecture upon lecture, the material first being presented by an older student, often by Lord John Pentland, a Cambridge graduate and journalist, or J. G. Bennett. Then the questions are answered by Uspenskii. On the drive back to Lyne Place, Uspenskii never speaks but, once home, he sits in the kitchen, sometimes all night, with male students (Madame Uspenskii will allow no female students[18]) drinking *zoubrovka*, a fiery Polish vodka, and eating lavish spreads of hors d'œuvres. He would often talk about his days in Russia and quote his favorite poet, Lermontov, the author of *A Hero of Our Time.* At such times his manner of cold intellectualism falls away and students see Uspenskii's genuine warmth, kindness, his sense of humor, his innate honesty and extreme modesty.

"Nearly always," says de Ropp, "we were regaled with tales of Moscow and Petersburg. For this was one of Uspenskii's weaknesses. He could not leave Russia. Nostalgia chained him to that land to which he could never return."

Neither could he ever forget Gurdjieff. At one kitchen drinking party Uspenskii speaks of "the week of miracles," referring to the telepathic experience he had with Gurdjieff in August 1916.

"I was in another room," Uspenskii says. "I heard Gurdjieff's voice speaking inside me. He told me something, something very important."

Uspenskii's eyes glaze behind the thick-lensed pince-nez. His concentration in reliving that moment is so great that he seems to those with him to go into a trance.

De Ropp says that Gurdjieff must have been a very strange man.

"Strange! He was extraordinary!" Uspenskii declares. "You cannot possibly imagine how extraordinary Gurdjieff was."

As to why he broke with Gurdjieff, Uspenskii contends that the "real Gurdjieff" had vanished during the flight from Russia. The Gurdjieff of the Prieuré was no longer the real thing; he had either gone mad or switched to the left-hand path and become a black magician. He tells de Ropp and the others: "This new Gurdjieff broke the rules of the Work, took advantage of the weaknesses and credulity of his pupils, and claimed to be personally responsible for the system of knowledge he taught."

Remembering this night many years later, de Ropp still cannot forget the tone in Uspenskii's voice when he spoke of Gurdjieff as being "extraordinary!"

De Ropp trenchantly comments, "So many emotional elements entered into that simple statement: wonder, admiration, regret, bewilderment. I had the feeling that in his relationship with Gurdjieff, Uspen-

18. Adoration is a stage in the student-teacher relationship when it might be said that the student is most open to the teacher, though unconsciously so. When the student works on himself, attention is being freed from identifications and energy is transformed; what is not absorbed is often projected onto the teacher and, in a male-female context, easily becomes sexual. This is likely the reason behind Madame Uspenskii's decree. What exactly her relationship was with Uspenskii is difficult to factually determine. All reports are secondhand. It seems clear that their relationship underwent a major shift when Uspenskii left Constantinople alone in 1921, while his wife left with Gurdjieff and his pupils. The two did not live under one roof again until 1931 when she rejoined him. Perhaps one remark goes to the quick of their relationship. Once the two sat in a Parisian café with a group of students and Uspenskii was particularly withdrawn. "Very hard to make a friend of Mr. Uspenskii," remarked Madame Uspenskii.

skii had confronted a problem that was absolutely beyond his power to solve. He had played the great game with a master and had been checkmated, but he still could not figure out quite how it had happened."

Even so, in an attempt to increase the spread of the teaching, Uspenskii founds the Historico-Psychological Society. Membership is restricted to 300 people. Through it, he also hopes, according to Reyner "to organize expeditions to the East in search of the truths with which he felt that Gurdjieff had made only a partial contact."

The prospectus declares the society's aims to be:

1. The study of man's true evolution, and the necessity for new systems of thought.
2. The study of esoteric schools in different historical periods and countries and their influences on the development of humanity.
3. The practical attainment of conscious living through the techniques of psycho-transformism.

At tea time, Uspenskii is seated at one end of a long table; his wife at the other end, with students on either side. As her husband adjusts his ever-present pince-nez and begins to read the prospectus aloud, Madame Uspenskii—well trained in Gurdjieff's provocative method of teaching which works on a person's emotional center—breaks into gales of laughter, so much so that she begins weeping and dabbing her eyes with a tiny lace handkerchief. But if Gurdjieff could not wake Uspenskii up to his folly, how could his wife?

Talking with Uspenskii about the theory of eternal recurrence presented in his *New Model of the Universe*, De Ropp complained that it was not a very encouraging idea.

Uspenskii smiled enigmatically and insisted that "there was a way of escaping from the treadmill." De Ropp must realize, he said, that time is three dimensional as well as space and that the space-time continuum had not four dimensions but six. In four-dimensional time-space, at every moment only one possibility is realized. In five dimensions, time curves back on itself so the pattern of events is repeated. But in six dimensions all the possibilities inherent in a moment could be realized. So by moving into this other dimension one could, in fact, change one's fate.[19]

The essence of Uspenskii's teaching, de Ropp says, is to remember one's life.[20] "He himself seemed to go over his life again and again as if to impress on his memory all that had happened."

19. Uspenskii's understanding of time's period of dimensions likely accounts for his actions in the last month's of his life.

20. The idea of linking self-remembering with the remembering, or recapitulating, of one's life, is a powerful practice.

De Ropp convinces his friends, the writers Aldous Huxley and Gerald Heard, to attend Uspenskii's lectures. Later Uspenskii invites them to Lyne Place. He enjoys meeting them, saying, "For the first time I meet what we in Russia called intelligentsia." For their part, the two writers speak to Uspenskii about the coming Dark Age and advise him to go to America. Neither is interested in joining the group.

De Ropp does not find this surprising. Huxley and Heard, he says, "were quite unpractical, could never have managed the physical work, and were too fond of their own opinions to work under the direction of someone else."[21]

Later, Huxley and Heard, as well as fellow writers W. H. Auden and Christopher Isherwood, emigrate to America.

De Ropp introduces Rodney Collin to Uspenskii. Collin, now twenty-seven years old, first read *New Model of the Universe* in 1930, the same year he met his future wife, Janet Buckley. He felt then that he was not ready for the Work, but that later it would be important for him. He and Janet, independently wealthy and eight years his senior, married in 1934. In 1935 they attended some lectures of Maurice Nicoll. Immediately, Collin recognized that he had found in Uspenskii and the Fourth Way the teaching he had been searching for. Meeting Uspenskii, he found him to be vigorous, whimsical, and brilliant. He and his wife buy a house close to Lyne Place so as to be near Uspenskii.

EASTER 1937. PARIS. At a café during lunch someone asks, "But before the fishermen, what happened to knowledge?"

"Nothing happened," says Gurdjieff.

"But where was it?"

"Was with initiate people, as always," Gurdjieff replies. "They always go in one stream, it still flows today. You ask question from one stream, I answer from other, then you back your stream with answer. Before there is nothing for man in ordinary stream, but fishermen who knew nothing, so nothing could tell but their wiseacrings. You remember the two streams I write about [in *All and Everything*]. Difference between two steams is the difference between interpretation of events on earth. One make elephant from fly, the other make fly from elephant. Events have two explanations—one for mankind, one for me. My stream is initiate-ism."

"But there have been messengers like you."

Answers Gurdjieff: "Many such there are, even you have in America. For English and Americans they are something, but for me they are shit

21. The description fits Uspenskii as well, though de Ropp gives no indication that he sees this in his teacher. In the objective language Gurdjieff presents, the word *man* has seven definitions. What de Ropp says of Huxley and Heard seems to be a common obstacle for man number three, those in whom ordinary thinking predominates. See *Search*, p. 71.

[in the] objective sense.... You wish believe in your Bible. Your Bible is one thing but mine is quite another. Nobody now believe in Christian thing—not with inner world, especially young ones."

MAY 1937. LYNE PLACE. Boris Mouravieff pays a visit to Uspenskii. He has helped edit the book Uspenskii has been working on since 1920, *Fragments of an Unknown Teaching* (later to be renamed *In Search of the Miraculous*). Mouravieff opposes its publication. "It seemed to me," he says, "that esoteric doctrine, by its very nature, eludes an account described in detail by writing. It must be said that Uspenskii was aware of it. And he ended up agreeing with my way of seeing."[22]

AUGUST 1937. PARIS. A trip Gurdjieff takes to Vichy with Kanari, his brother Dimitri, and others gives a graphic illustration of what Uspenskii, Orage, Bennett, and other pupils must work with. Kanari works the windshield wipers, finds the roads, and lights Gurdjieff's cigarettes. Four times Gurdjieff stops on the road but they make Vichy in less than five hours, arriving before ten o'clock on Friday evening. They can find no rooms, so they park by a curb. Gloomily, Dimitri goes to look for rooms. After visiting 18 of Vichy's many hotels, he finds lodging and at eleven o'clock they have dinner. Gurdjieff says he's caught cold in his left arm and at lunch says he is poisoned by the food. Saturday, Gurdjieff tells them where to meet him but they cannot find him. It turns out he has given the wrong place, the wrong hour, or his watch stopped—whatever. Sunday, he tells Kanari to meet him in the café by the river. For two hours she waits. Finally, someone comes for her and leads her to a café in the middle of the park where Gurdjieff is. Monday, they drive 70 kilometers to picnic. Dimitri is in the back seat with indigestion, muttering "Jamais un peu de repos" (Never a bit of rest). They have with them only watermelon and Armagnac, so they stop many times for provisions. At Clermont-Ferrand Gurdjieff stops to pick up a Russian nurse and her little boy. They sit on the laps of Dimitri and the other two men in the back seat. The heat is intense but Gurdjieff, because of his arm and his cough, insists all the windows be kept closed. For an hour they search for the ideal picnic spot. Passing many wonderful places, Gurdjieff finds the perfect spot—a steep hill—so steep that no one can keep their balance. They sit on sharp rocks, holding onto all the food to keep it from rolling downhill. There is only one glass for everyone. The men tear the chicken apart with their bare hands, wiping their hands on their trousers. Ten minutes later Gurdjieff declares the picnic is over and they leave. Says

22. This will not deter Mouravieff however from later publishing his own massive 759-page, three-volume study, *Gnosis*, which puts forth his idea of esoteric doctrine. Interestingly, the material is a compilation of the Gurdjieff teaching from his Russian period—as interpreted by Uspenskii—and mixed with Mouravieff's idea of a tantric "esoteric Christianity." See Notes.

Dimitri—"Just think, to eat a piece of bread we must come 70 kilometers and spend a thousand francs."

Later this same month Dimitri dies of cancer. Gurdjieff tells his children: "Now my children, you have one hour to cry, then it's finished. I don't want anybody to cry after that. I don't want any black. He's gone; he's happy; everybody else be happy."

SEPTEMBER 5, 1937. PARIS. Gurdjieff leaves his apartment at rue Labie and moves into his brother's apartment at 6 rue des Colonels Rénard, in the Russian quarter.

SEPTEMBER 22, 1937. LONDON. J. B. Priestly's play *I Have Been Here Before* opens, marking the first time Uspenskii's ideas on time and recurrence are popularly portrayed on the stage. The main character is the mysterious Dr. Gortler, who intervenes to halt a series of fated misfortunes (if the other characters behave as they have in the past). Priestly acknowledges his debt to Uspenskii's *A New Model of the Universe.*

OCTOBER 4, 1937. LONDON. Uspenskii is asked at a meeting about whether or not the passage of the ideas into general life would be beneficial to humanity and also might help the school, as well. He answers:

"It will happen by itself. There is no need for us to worry about it. Ideas will spread, maybe in our lifetime and maybe after us. Most of these ideas will enter into scientific or philosophic language, but they will enter in the wrong form. There will be no right distinction between doing and happening, and many thoughts of ordinary thinking will be mixed with these ideas; so they will not be ideas we know, only words will be similar. If you don't understand this, you will lose in this way."

AUTUMN 1937. PARIS. Gurdjieff's lesbian group, the Rope, breaks up. Solita Solano becomes Gurdjieff's secretary.

1938. MILL HOUSE, DOYLESTOWN, PENNSYLVANIA. Faced with deteriorating kidneys impairing his health, along with his wife's rising ire at the cost of upkeep of a farm that can't pay for itself, Jean Toomer is forced to give up the communal experiment. It will mark his last attempt to replicate life at the Prieuré. He is forty-four years old.

MARCH 11–12, 1938. AUSTRIA. Austrians "welcome" German troops into their country.

DECEMBER 18, 1938. GERMANY. Only the Army has the power to depose Hitler. An insight into why it does not is given in the diary of General Freiherr von Fritsch, commander-in-chief of the Army, who on this day writes: "This man—Hitler—is Germany's destiny for good and for evil.

If he now goes over the abyss, he will drag us all down with him. There is nothing we can do."

1939. LONDON. Aldous Huxley's novel *After Many a Summer Dies the Swan* appears. Uspenskii's followers are upset that a main character, Mr. Propter, is thought to be modeled on Uspenskii. Certainly Huxley's Mr. Propter speaks of many Work ideas in the book, such as the liberation from personality, the successive levels of mechanical laws, as well as man's three levels of existence: sub-human, human, and spirit. The first two levels are completely determined and void of God:

> It is in their power to pass from the level of the absence of God to that of God's presence. Each member of the psychological swarm is determined; and so is the conduct of the total swarm. But beyond the swarm, and yet containing and interpenetrating it, lies eternity, ready and waiting to experience itself...let eternity experience itself, let God be sufficiently often present in the absence of human desires and feelings and preoccupations; the result will be a transformation of that life which must be lived, in the intervals, upon the human level.

Most interesting, perhaps, is Huxley's agreement with Gurdjieff that there is no "soul" as such. He writes:

> Madness consists, for example, of thinking of oneself as a soul, a coherent and enduring human entity. But, between the animal below and the spirit above, there is nothing on the human level except a swarm of constellated impulses and sentiments and notions; a swarm brought together by the accidents of heredity and language; a swarm of incongruous and often contradictory thoughts and desires. Memory and the slowly changing body constitute a kind of spatio-temporal cage, within which the swarm is enclosed. To talk of it as though it were a coherent and enduring 'soul' is madness. On the strictly human level there is no such thing as a soul.

1939. 54 RUE DU FOUR, PARIS. Madame de Salzmann's group is now meeting at the apartment of Philippe Lavastine. Among the members are the Daumals, Luc Dietrich, Pauline de Dampier, Henri Tracol and his wife Henriette, Martha de Gaigneron, and Bernard Lemaitre.

SPRING 1939. AMERICA. Gurdjieff visits New York with Solita Solano.

JUNE 1939. DOYLESTOWN, PENNSYLVANIA. Jean Toomer, long suffering from abdominal pains[23] and an unarticulated sense of personal and professional failure, leaves for India with his wife Marjorie and daughter Argie. "He thought," his wife recounts, "that maybe through the mystics he could find

23. As a child of ten, Toomer experienced stomach ailments so intense he was confined to bed. In one of his autobiographies he says the ailments were "largely psychosomatic."

the answers." The journey will take nine months, much of that time spent in travel to and from India, and will cost five thousand dollars.

SUMMER 1939. Madame Uspenskii is stricken with Parkinson's disease.[24] Gurdjieff contemplates a trip to England to help. "If possible I will come," he says. "But she must also make effort." Uspenskii procrastinates. As much as he might reminisce about Gurdjieff during his late night drinking parties, he does not want Gurdjieff in his life.

AUTUMN 1939. COLET GARDENS. In an effort to reach more people, Uspenskii sets up a new London headquarters at 46 Colet Gardens. It has a large lecture hall seating five hundred people, and the lecture program of the fledgling Historico-Psychological Society attracts audiences as large as one thousand people. But war soon intervenes.

AUGUST 23, 1939. MOSCOW AND BERLIN. Hitler and Stalin sign a nonaggression pact.

SEPTEMBER 1, 1939. The Second World War begins. German troops pour across the Polish frontier.

NOVEMBER 9, 1939. BERLIN. The anniversary of Hitler's failed putsch of 1923. Soon 200 synagogues are burned, Jewish stores looted and Jews beaten and killed. Henceforth, this night will be known as *Kristallnacht.*

1940. 6 RUE DES COLONELS RÉNARD. PARIS. American followers try to persuade Gurdjieff to go to America but he insists on staying in Paris. And so he does, closing the blinds and shuttering the windows of his apartment, only a few blocks from the Arc de Triumphe where Hitler's Wermacht will soon parade.

MARCH 1940. MILL HOUSE, DOYLESTOWN, PENNSYLVANIA. The Toomers and his daughter return from India. Describing their journey, his wife says: "We went here, we went there. Usually I stayed in our lodgings with Argie, but sometimes, if I went, Jean would start talking with somebody inside while we were left sitting out in that God-awful heat. And he would stay as long as it pleased him. It became a very unhappy experience."

Says Toomer: "It took India to bring me to my senses.... What hopes I went there with! India did not destroy them; she simply did not fulfill them."

24. Reyner, in his *Ouspensky the Unsung Genius,* p.101, says that Madame Uspenskii had multiple sclerosis.

JUNE 1940. MILL HOUSE, DOYLESTOWN, PENNSYLVANIA. Jean Toomer has a blocked kidney removed. The operation is not successful. He can no longer sit in a chair. He must either stand or lie down. Then arthritis sets in.

JUNE 14, 1940. PARIS. Germans capture the city. A large swastika is hoisted onto the Eiffel Tower. Later Hitler will arrive in a Mercedes to dictate terms of an unconditional surrender.

AUGUST 1940. MILL HOUSE, DOYLESTOWN, PENNSYLVANIA. Toomer, who had studied Quakerism for years, formally becomes a member of the Society of Friends and becomes a much sought after lecturer.

SEPTEMBER 6, 1940. LYNE PLACE. Hitler's night bombing of England has begun. Uspenskii stands on the roof of the house looking toward London some twenty miles distant. The vast night sky is entirely crimson. Searchlights sweep in long arcs through the night skies while streams of tracer bullets rise heavenward and huge explosions rumble and shake the earth. Over four million pounds of bombs fall onto the docks of London, starting fires that only time will put out.Uspenskii, obsessed with the idea that he must have lived this before, shakes his head, saying, "This I cannot remember, this I cannot remember."

It soon becomes clear that the demands of the war effort make large scale implementation of the Work impossible. Uspenskii also fears the success of Fascism and Communism, both of which he considers to be "criminal" parties dominated by Sudras.[25]

AUTUMN 1940. LYNE PLACE. Rodney Collin, his wife, Janet, and their three-year-old daughter, Chloe, move in. Uspenskii speaks of his decision to leave for America in January. Shortly after the Collins' arrival, Janet leaves for America with her daughter to prepare for Uspenskii's arrival.

OCTOBER 19, 1940. 6 RUE DES COLONELS RÉNARD. Madame de Salzmann formally presents her French group to Gurdjieff. With the Germans patrolling the streets, readings of *All and Everything* and movements begin.

1941. NEW YORK. Jean Toomer's father-in-law, Harry Content, dies. He had remarried shortly before his death and the expected estate largely went to the new wife. Says Gorham Munson: "I don't mean to say that they [Jean and Marjorie] were cut off, because they had this place in Doylestown, and had a very comfortable income. In general, he did cut

25. In the Hindu caste system derived from the ancient Laws of Manu, Uspenskii says the Sudras, laborers, "are people without initiative or with wrong initiative, who must obey the will of others." The three other castes are: Brahmans, priests; Kshatriyas, warriors; and Vaisyas, merchants. See *New Model of the Universe*, p. 506. A further analysis of the caste system is given in Frithjof Schuon's *Castes and Races* (Perennial Books, Ltd., 1959).

them off, cut them down, and so it was now clear that Jean would never have the resources, the considerable resources, needed to set up an institute [like the Prieuré]. That was a gone dream."

JANUARY 4, 1941. LYNE PLACE. Madame Uspenskii embarks for America. Uspenskii is soon to follow. He believes it will soon be impossible to continue his teaching in England, as he believes Germany will win the war and this will be a prelude to Communism sweeping over Europe.

Learning of Uspenskii's plan to follow his wife, Bennett sees Uspenskii and asks three questions:

"Is my lack of progress due to lack of effort, or wrong effort, or is it due in part to there being some method or technique we do not know, and have yet to find?"

Replies Uspenskii: "It has nothing to do with methods. Your trouble is that you always make false starts.[26] All your work consists of false starts. And if you keep returning to the starting point, how can you hope to make progress?"

Bennett then asks: "How do I stand in relation to your group here?"

"I can only consider the work at Lyne. The rest, so far as I am concerned, is dissolved. I have given my instructions for continuing the work at Lyne as long as possible. You and your wife can, of course, remain in contact with the work there."

"Have you any objection," inquires Bennett, "to my trying to write out the System as far as I can remember it?"

Answers Uspenskii: "In my opinion, writing is not useful. Mental recapitulation is better. In any case, the System cannot be written in ordinary form. If you do write, it can only be to convince yourself that it is impossible."

JANUARY 29, 1941. LIVERPOOL. Uspenskii leaves Dr. Francis Roles, a noted authority on tuberculosis, in charge of his groups and embarks for America aboard the SS *Georgic*, the same ship that Madame had taken. Even in leaving Europe, symbolically, he cannot get away from the reminder of Georgi Gurdjieff.

Also aboard the ship is Rodney Collin.

For Bennett, Uspenskii's leaving was more than a physical separation.

"It is not a sharp break, or any diminution in my respect and deep gratitude towards him," he says. "He has taught me everything, and the contact with his work has had the supreme advantage for me of teaching me my own weakness and foolishness."

26. Bennett does not explain what is meant by *always make false starts*. It would seem to indicate that Bennett begins from his ego, his self-will, and so no matter the results, the magic circle of the ego is only expanded, not stepped beyond.

Nevertheless, Bennett resolves that he must in the future work independently and sets himself the task of writing all that he can remember of Gurdjieff's system.

SPRING 1941. MENDHAM, NEW JERSEY. Nott arrives and finds Madame Uspenskii quite different from what he had experienced in England. "Here, by herself, away from Lyne Place, a refugee like ourselves," he says, "she has no need to surround herself with a protective facade. She is warm, sympathetic and understanding; a highly developed woman with inner power."

JUNE 21–22, 1941. Operation Barbarossa. German forces invade Russia. Within ten weeks they are at the outskirts of Leningrad.

JULY 1941. NEW YORK. Rodney Collin, who has joined British Security, and who had earlier been posted to Bermuda and then Mexico, arrives.

AUGUST 30, 1941. LENINGRAD. Germans begin a siege of the city that will last 900 days.

SEPTEMBER 29, 1941. BERLIN. The Führer directs his generals "to wipe St. Petersburg off the face of the earth."

DECEMBER 7, 1941. HAWAII. The Japanese attack Pearl Harbor.

DECEMBER 11, 1941. GERMANY. Adolf Hitler formally declares war on the United States.

1941. NEW YORK. Though Orage is seven years dead, the group still functions. Nott, who has come from England, arranges for Uspenskii to speak to the group at Muriel Draper's house on Madison Avenue. Uspenskii must have found Orage's students somewhat led off track, for as he will say years later—"I don't like to say this, but he [Orage] forgot many things and had to invent."

Among those attending is Fritz Peters. Peters had met Uspenskii at the Prieuré and considered him Gurdjieff's most objective critic.

Peters asks:

"Why did you break with Gurdjieff and publicly disassociate yourself from the Gurdjieff work?"

Uspenskii smiles. "The answer is very simple," he says, "When I had found out that Gurdjieff was wrong I had to leave him."

Recounts Peters, "I replied, with much greater feeling than I would have expected of myself, that I did not need to hear any more. It was a revelation to me to find that I was so fiercely loyal to Gurdjieff and to find that I was so positive that he could not have been 'wrong' about anything."

Like Peters, most of those attending find Uspenskii too coldly intellectual and lacking the emotional authority which they had come to expect from Gurdjieff and Orage.

Later, Nott assembles a smaller group, including some from the Orage group, to hear Uspenskii. A group is formed and is reinforced by a number of Uspenskii's English pupils, such as Lord John Pentland, his wife Lucy, and Christopher Fremantle.

C. Daly King, from the original Orage group and one of Orage's most loyal advocates, learns of Uspenskii's meetings. Still interested in the teaching as a modern method for the development of man, King attends several meetings. A rigorous intellectual and scientist, holding a doctorate in psychology from Yale, where he conducts research, King finds Uspenskii to be a "genuine gentleman in the exact sense." However, he also sees Uspenskii as an "incorrigible mystic, no matter how much or how successfully he may or may not have striven against that tendency after his meeting with and his instruction by Mr. Gurdjieff." Of their discussion King says: "I found nothing of serious interest to me in his formulations and had no further contact with these groups."

Later, unable to agree with what he terms "The Ouspenskyan Version" of the teaching and fearing Orage's presentation will be lost, King begins writing the teaching as taught by his mentor, which he titles *The Oragean Version.* Uspenskii's opinion of King is not recorded. As Uspenskii believes Orage "forgot many things and had to invent," he likely puts King in the same boat.

MAY 1942. LONDON. Bennett receives a message reminding him that no one is permitted to write anything about the System without Uspenskii's permission. It could not have come as a surprise. After Uspenskii's departure, Bennett decided to organize the teaching around the triads. He drafts a new chapter of his forthcoming book every week. He reads it to his group of thirty to forty people, then revises it in light of their questions and remarks. Bennett later publishes this as the second in his four-volume *The Dramatic Universe.*[27]

LATE 1942. MENDHAM, NEW JERSEY. Franklin Farms is purchased as a center for Uspenskii's activities. There are rolling vistas of land with a large house of grey granite, once the residence of the governor of the state. Along the driveway leading to the farm's barns are empty silos and outbuildings, and decaying aviaries that had once caged ornamental birds.

27. In his massive 1335-page study, begun in 1940 and continually revised till his death Friday, December 13, 1974, Bennett focuses on value, will, hazard (uncertainty), and triads. While Bennett contends that much of his work is derived "from sources quite unconnected with Gurdjieff's teaching," the roots, in fact, derive from Gurdjieff.

Rodney Collin and his family move in and he commutes to and from his job with the British government in New York City. Collin finds himself exhausted from the commute to New York City and does not attend Uspenskii's meetings. One night he realizes that fatigue is not the problem. He jumps out of bed and goes to the kitchen where he finds Uspenskii alone drinking a glass of wine.

"Why am I afraid of you?" Collin shouts.

Uspenskii looks at him calmly and answers, "Why do you say I?"

The answer has a profound effect on Collin. Thereafter he spends all his free time with Uspenskii.

Slowly, the pattern of life at Lyne Place is now reproduced at Mendham. Groups are formed and students given farmwork and housework. Madame Uspenskii, now crippled and walking with a cane, spends more and more of her time in bed but still manages to direct work activities. For de Ropp and many others, including Lord John Pentland, Madame Uspenskii became the teacher, working drastically, often painfully, on a student's emotional center. As Lord Pentland relates, "She was regarded by all as an independent source of the teaching.…For many of us, she was the senior teacher. Her instruction, tempered in the hard school of revolutionary Russia, at the kitchen of Gurdjieff's Institute [at the Prieuré] was direct, quite free from moralization."

Another of her pupils, who had also met Gurdjieff, says:

> I can still feel the sensation that crept along my spine when I heard Madame approaching, her cane announcing her as she came closer and closer to the terrace of the dining room. Although small in stature, she looked and towered above us all through the sheer strength and poise that radiated from her presence. When she reached the long narrow tables at which we sat, everyone remained motionless, eyes glued to one spot, simultaneously wishing to draw her attention and yet to become invisible to her.

Uspenskii, for his part, only visits Mendham occasionally, spending most of his time in New York. It is de Ropp's opinion that by this time "Uspenskii was no longer a teacher. He had lost his power and wrecked his health by indulgence in two poisons, alcohol and nostalgia." He withdrew more and more into himself, becoming hypersensitive, and perhaps paranoid. "He was apt," says de Ropp, "at the slightest provocation to throw people out of the Work."

Uspenskii revises six introductory lectures which he had published in England shortly before he left. These were later published in 1950 as *The Psychology of Man's Possible Evolution.*

1943. MENDHAM. At sixty-five, Uspenskii's health begins to decline. He had begun to drink heavily which aggravated a kidney problem and sapped his strength. He understands that he shouldn't drink but says it is the only thing he can do to relieve his boredom.

To the end, he never gives any indication that the years without Gurdjieff have brought him to reevaluate his former teacher and their relationship. Frank Pinder felt "Uspenskii knew the theory, better than anyone possibly—he had the knowledge, but he did not understand." Denis Saurat, a professor of French literature at Kings College, believes that "Uspenskii could not submit to the pressure Gurdjieff brought to bear on him to break down his particular kind of vanity."

APRIL 19, 1943. Jean Toomer writes to the psychic Edgar Cayce about the failure of his kidney operation, his lack of stamina, and his continued insomnia.

JUNE 22, 1943. Toomer visits Cayce who recommends a purification of his alimentary canal, X-ray treatments on the sides of the spinal column, and a diet. This helped for a while but the following year the pain returned.

SEPTEMBER 9, 1943. PARIS. During a meeting at Gurdjieff's apartment, someone says: "You said once that even a cow can work alone."

"Excuse me," interrupts Gurdjieff, "I did not say cow. I said donkey. A cow is a parasite—it only gives milk. The donkey works."

1944. MENDHAM. Uspenskii speaks about the devil, saying that while he is not conscious, he is intelligent. "In no period can he have more power than in this," he says. "Now he is in full bloom. Only through man's help can the devil act. Because man has the possibility of evolution [becoming conscious] the devil can stop him by creating conditions and obstacles against man's evolution."

JANUARY 27, 1944. LENINGRAD. The German blockade of St. Petersburg—what was once Uspenskii's beloved city—ends. The city has no pigeons or rats. Without food, people have eaten whatever is available in order to live. There are reports, too, of cannibalism. Of its three million inhabitants, it is estimated that a million to a million-and-a-half people have died, most of starvation.

JUNE 6, 1944. NORMANDY, FRANCE. D-Day landing by Allies.

JULY 20, 1944. WOLFSSCHANZE, EAST PRUSSIA. Colonel Klaus von Stauffenberg plants a bomb in a briefcase at Hitler's headquarters. The bomb explodes but Hitler escapes serious injury.

SPRING 1945. LONDON. Bennett, taking things into his own hands now that Uspenskii is in America, has been giving public lectures on Gurdjieff's system. Some Americans had joined his group and, upon returning home, they went to see Uspenskii (Bennett had given them letters of introduction to Uspenskii). The Americans believe Bennett's lectures are copied from Uspenskii's pre-war lectures.

Soon Bennett receives a letter from Uspenskii's solicitor which demands he return all of Uspenskii's material, including his lectures. In a second letter sent to Lyne Place Uspenskii instructs his pupils to break all relations with Bennett and not to communicate with him on any subject. Then through a letter from a third party Bennett learns he is being called "a charlatan and a thief."

Thinks Bennett: "They [referring to the Americans] must have given him very garbled accounts of what I was doing."[28]

Much like Uspenskii when he broke with Gurdjieff in 1924, Bennett convenes a group meeting and reads the letter in which he is referred to as "a charlatan and a thief." He then tells the group they can decide either to stay with him, or join Uspenskii's group and "never see me again."

APRIL 30, 1945. HITLER'S BUNKER. BERLIN. With Russian troops only a block away, Adolf Hitler marries his mistress, Eva Braun, then he issues a last testament blaming international Jewry and the German General Staff for Germany's defeat. Then Hitler shoots himself in the mouth. Eva Braun takes poison.

MAY 7, 1945. REIMS, FRANCE. Germany unconditionally surrenders.

MAY 1945. MENDHAM. With World War II concluded, Rodney Collin leaves government service to devote all his time to Uspenskii, driving him to and from meetings in New York and spending long evenings with him in his study. Says Collin: "It struck me very much how Uspenskii, in speaking about his parents, relations or old friends, always recalled their possibilities, their best sides, what they might become, and never recalled anything negative or unpleasant."

Besides people, a frequent subject of discussion is the period of dimensions in time and the idea of different times. "For me," says Collin, "the key to the understanding of this idea up to a certain point lies in Uspenskii's theory of six dimensions—the first, second and third [dimensions] are clearly the length, breadth and thickness of space; the fourth is the line of time that we recognize, the line of individual life; the fifth is infinite repetition of this life and all it contains—the 'eternal now'; the sixth must be the dimension in which all exists everywhere, all

28. Bennett never gives any indication that he doubts his own actions and motives. It is always others who do not understand.

possibilities are realized, and all is one. The fourth dimension is 'time,' the fifth 'eternity,' but what shall we call the sixth? For us it is Divinity itself."

AUGUST 6, 1945. JAPAN. The United States drops the world's first atomic bomb on Hiroshima.

LATE SUMMER 1945. 6 RUE DES COLONELS RÉNARD. PARIS. Fritz Peters, now thirty-two-years-old, visits Gurdjieff. Peters had been drafted into the American army and, though behind the lines in a secretarial job, the horror of the war had thrown him into a deep depression. Many narrow escapes—such as, when a group he was with at Torquay on the southern English coast was suddenly strafed by six German fighters and many were killed—had put him in a highly nervous state. Faced with hospitalization, Peters convinces a general to give him a pass to go to Paris. When he left for Paris he had not slept in several days, had no appetite and had lost a great deal of weight. He was, he says, "very close to what I would have to call a form of madness." He has no idea of how to find Gurdjieff but somehow manages to track him down. Gurdjieff is not home when Peters arrives at his apartment and so he waits inside the entrance. After about an hour he hears the sound of a cane tapping on the sidewalk. Presently, Gurdjieff appears and walks up to him. There is no sign of recognition. Peters says his name. Gurdjieff stares at him for a second, then drops his cane and cries out in a loud voice:

"My son!" and embraces him. "Don't talk, you are sick," Gurdjieff tells him and leads him up the stairs to his second floor apartment.

Gurdjieff leads Peters down the hall to a dark bedroom, tells him to lie down and says, "This is your room, for as long as you need it."

Peters lies down but begins to cry uncontrollably, then his head pounds. He gets up and goes to the kitchen where he finds Gurdjieff, who looks alarmed when he sees him. Peters says he wants some aspirin.

Gurdjieff shakes his head, "No medicine. I give you coffee. Drink as hot as you can."

Drinking the coffee Gurdjieff has made and served him, Peters looks at Gurdjieff standing in front of the refrigerator, observing him. Peters suddenly realizes that Gurdjieff looks "incredibly weary—I have never seen anyone look so tired."

Suddenly Peters, slumped over the table, sipping the coffee, becomes aware of an energy rising up within him and he straightens up, staring at Gurdjieff.

"It was as if a violent, electric blue light emanated from him and entered me," says Peters.

All Peters' fatigue drains from his body. He has never felt better in his life. But as his body is renewed, Gurdjieff's body slumps and his massive face turns grey. It is as if Gurdjieff himself, says Peters, "was being drained of life."

"You all right now—watch food on stove—I must go," says Gurdjieff urgently.

In fifteen minutes or so Gurdjieff returns, looking, says Peters, "like a young man again, alert, smiling, sly and full of good spirits."

Gurdjieff and Peters have lunch together. He tells him that he is to come to his apartment for lunch and dinner every day but for the rest of the time he is to go out and "play."

"One thing you never learn, Freets," he said quietly and affectionately, "is how to play, even though I try to teach you this when you child. Now, you go out and do *anything* that will amuse you, any kind of play, then come back here at ten o'clock."

10:00 P.M. THAT EVENING. A large group of students is assembled at Gurdjieff's apartment. He introduces Peters as his "*real* son" who had been at his "real school." During the question and answer a rich woman speaks of the disadvantages of having money in terms of understanding his work and that her so-called friends wouldn't like her if she was poor. Gurdjieff says the answer is simple enough. She could give her money to him, that he would make good use of it, and she would soon learn if she had any real friends. Peters and others laugh. The rich woman objects. Gurdjieff says she should learn that laughter was, in *truth*, a very good medicine. After supper everyone leaves except Peters, who Gurdjieff has asked to help him do the dishes. Then the two drink coffee and Gurdjieff plays on the harmonium much of the music that had been played at the Prieuré. They laugh together and Gurdjieff says that it was a great pleasure to enjoy laughter with someone again—that one of the saddest aspects of his life was that his students were so impressed with him that they could never condescend to anything as low as laughter. The conversation turns to the rich woman. Says Gurdjieff:

> This woman not take me seriously and so will not discover anything. What I tell her is truth. If she could give up money and have to live like poor person she would create possibility for two things. First, would find out what other people like, how they live, and also find out much about herself, that she stupid, shit-person, only have value of her money. Cannot be understanding between rich and poor, because rich and poor, both, only understand money. One understand life with money and despise people without money. Other understand life without money and hate people who have money. This woman now hate self because guilty about being rich. Poor man hate self—or sometimes just life—because feel guilty about not having money or feel cheated by world. With such unreal, false attitude, impossible understand any serious thing like my work. For instance, this woman tell that I most important influ-

> ence in her life—but would be impossible for her to give me her money—so, very simple, she not tell truth. I not important for her life, but only her money important. With poor man can be same thing. Can believe in me and what I teach only if I first teach how to make money—this what poor man think. Not so. If I teach him how make money, then he will have only other problem—he will not be able to live without this money. But such people can learn important thing if can make effort in self to give up money—or, if poor, to give up desire for money. Impossible to do my work with all energy if also concerned with money. But all these things very difficult for your contemporaries. Not only cannot do. Cannot even understand why this question of money important. Such people will never understand real teaching or real possibility of learning anything....You remember Prieuré and how many times I have struggle with money. I not make money like others make money, and when I have too much money, I spend. But I never need money for self, and I not make or earn money. I ask for money and people always give, and for this I give opportunity study my teaching, but even when they give money still almost always impossible for them learn anything. Already, they think of reward...now I owe them something because they give me money. When think of reward in this way, impossible learn anything from me.[29]

Staying at Gurdjieff's apartment, Peters notices that many old and destitute people visit Gurdjieff, who feeds them and gives them gifts or money. One day as he and Gurdjieff drink coffee, Gurdjieff looks at him reflectively and says: "I play many roles in life...this part of my destiny. You think of me as teacher, but in reality, *I also your father...father in many ways you not understand.* I also 'teacher of dancing,' and have many businesses: you not know that I own company which make false eyelashes and also have very good business selling rugs. This way I make money for self and for family. Money I 'shear' from disciples is for work. But other money I make for my family. My family very big, as you see—because this kind old people who come every day to my house, are, also, family. They my family because have no other family." [Author's italics]

"I give you good example why I *must* be family for such people. You not know, even though you hear about this, what life is like in Paris during war, while Germans here. For such people—people who come to see me every day now—was impossible. But for me, not so. I not interested in who win war. Not have patriotism or big ideals about peace. Americans, with ideals, kill millions of Germans, Germans kill—with own ideals—English, French, Russian, Belgian...all have ideals, all have peaceful purpose, all kill. I have only one purpose: existence for self, for students,

29. It is interesting to review Gurdjieff's actions with Orage, Toomer, and others regarding money in the context of what he tells Peters.

and for family, even this big family. So, I do what they cannot do, I make deal with Germans, with policemen, with all kinds idealistic people who make 'black market.' Result: I eat well and continue have tobacco, liquor, and what is necessary for me and for many others. While I do this—very difficult thing for most people—I also can help people."

"But *why* did you do it? Why for *them*?" asks Peters.

Gurdjieff smiles. "Freets, you stupid still. If can do for self and students, can also do for others who *cannot* do such thing." He pauses and then adds, smiling enigmatically now: "Ask self why old lady, with very little money, every day feed birds in park. These people—this family—my birds. But I honest: I say I do this *for* people, and also for self. This give me good feeling. Lady who feed birds in park not tell truth. She tell only do for birds, because love birds. She not tell what pleasure she get."

Peters' question now seems to him somewhat silly and he apologizes for having asked about the "old" people.

Gurdjieff shakes his head. "Not necessary be sorry. Is not bad question you ask me. But one more thing about this question. You notice all such people who come here are already old. Without me not have possibility die properly. Except me, such people not have family, and for future can only look towards death. If I help such people die in right way, this can be very important and very good thing. Someday you understand this better, but you still young."

At Peters' last dinner before leaving Paris, Gurdjieff, as he frequently does, asks that someone tell an anecdote about one of his encounters with a potential student. A man tells the story of a wealthy and well-known Englishwoman who presented herself at Gurdjieff's table at the Café de la Paix, saying that she had been told that he knew "the secret to life." She offers him 1,000 pounds if he would reveal it to her.

Gurdjieff leaves the table. He approaches a well-dressed prostitute who generally worked the sidewalk in front of the café and requests the honor of buying her a drink. She returns with him to the table and, after buying her an expensive drink, he wagers with her that she cannot guess his identity or where he was from. The prostitute says, "Some part of Russia." Gurdjieff tells her his Russian accent was merely part of his disguise and that he is not only not from Russia, he is not even from the planet Earth. He comes, he tells her, from a planet that is unknown to her and all other human beings. The planet, he says, is "Karatas."

The prostitute says nothing. Gurdjieff goes into a long and verbose explanation of how the biggest problem for someone like himself was that he could not sustain himself on the food produced by the Earth and so had to have special food flown in daily from Karatas. Bored and thinking she is with a group of nuts, the prostitute gets up to leave but

Gurdjieff buys her another drink. Asking if she would like to see some of his special food, Gurdjieff takes a few cherries from a paper bag. He says that while this food looks like it was grown on Earth, it is not so.

"Would you be so gracious and so kind," Gurdjieff says, "as to do me the great honor of tasting this superb fruit and telling me how it seems to you? What it resembles?"

The prostitute, saying nothing, takes the two cherries from Gurdjieff's hand. She slowly eats them, putting the pits in a saucer.

"It seems to me that they are cherries," she says sarcastically, holding out her hand.

Gurdjieff gives her some money and escorts her back to the sidewalk, thanking her for doing him such a great service.

Returning to the table, Gurdjieff smiles at the Englishwoman and says simply: "What you have seen is the secret of life."

Giving him a look of disgust and calling him a charlatan, the Englishwoman leaves the table.

Gurdjieff roars and returns to his writing.

The next day the Englishwoman returns to the café and gives him a check for the agreed amount, thanking him for what he had done for her. She later becomes an ardent follower of his teaching.

AUTUMN 1945. 6 RUE DES COLONELS RÉNARD. PARIS. Peters wangles another pass from the army, returning to Paris to see Gurdjieff. The two discuss many things and laugh a lot together. The day Peters is to leave, Gurdjieff, seventy-three years old now, tells him he is very tired and that when he finishes the *Third Series*, "my work will be done. So now I can die, because my task in life is coming to an end." He then looks at Peters gravely, saying this also means that he can do nothing more for him.

"So when you get out of army," Gurdjieff says, "do not come back here but go home where you belong and where you will find much work for self, and many experiences."

Gurdjieff says Peters was "necessary" to him for two reasons. One, he came to the Prieuré "as a wounded animal" and suggests he research the meaning of the word in French (which is *blesser* which comes from the word *blessed).* And two, Gurdjieff says that because of his particular heredity and conditioning and the fact that he somehow managed to remain "open" despite his early physical traumas that he, Peters, had been an appropriate receptacle or "garbage can" in which he could "dump" some of the accumulation of his life's work.

They have lunch that day at Gurdjieff's apartment with some twenty other students. Many stories are told and there is much laughter. But at the end of lunch Gurdjieff's mood changes suddenly and he looks very ill. He rises and supports himself by leaning on a chair. He then raises one arm and makes a large sweeping gesture around the room. The act galvanizes everyone's attention.

"Must make announcement," he says dramatically in English. "My last book is now finished, except for work with editor."

He pauses...taking in every person individually, as if he is weighing them.

"This mean," he continues, "my work is through—finished. Mean at last I can die..." Again a pause, the silence in the room deafening. "...but not just because book is finished. In life is only necessary for man to find one person to whom can give accumulation of learning in life. When find such receptacle then is possible die."

He gives a kind smile and continues: "So now two good things happen for me. I finish work and I also find one person to whom can give results my life's work."

Once more he raises his arm, this time with the index finger extended. Slowly the arm arcs about the room, the outstretched finger pointing at one person then another.

When the finger points at Fritz Peters, the arm stops.

The silence, the tension, in the room is immense.

Gurdjieff and Peters look at one another fixedly....

Finally, Gurdjieff drops his arm and leaves the room.

Momentarily, everyone seems transfixed. Peters finally breaks the silence by walking across the room. At the doorway he is stopped by one of the women instructors. She grabs his arm tightly and looks at him with a malevolent sneering smile.

"You will never learn, will you?" she says.

Peters pulls his arm away. "What does that mean?"

She laughs.

"How does it feel to be chosen?" she demands. "From the look on your face, I can tell you exactly what you are feeling. He pointed at you, didn't he? And now—with your colossal ego—you march out of the room...the triumphant successor."

Peters returns her smile.

"Your guess is as good as mine," he replies and leaves the apartment.

Peters, swamped with questions and doubts about what Gurdjieff had said, goes to see him one last time. The war in Europe is now over. Shortly after his previous visit America dropped another atomic bomb on Japan.

Peters knocks at the door of Gurdjieff's apartment. He answers, looking sleepy and giving Peters a cold look.

"Already," Gurdjieff says, "I tell you good-bye, and already I think you in America. Why you come?"

Peters says he is on his way to America and has just come to say good-bye.

Gurdjieff, without hostility, says: "Cannot say good-bye again—this already done."

He gives Peters a final, impersonal handshake.

Peters turns to leave but Gurdjieff stops him with a gesture, saying sharply, with a smile on his face—"Americans drop bomb on Japan, yes?"

Peters nods.

"What you think of your America now?"

Peters goes to reply but Gurdjieff closes the door, gently, in his face.

1945. MENDHAM. Nott sees Uspenskii often. The two sit alone as they had in England, talking and drinking. Though Uspenskii has become what Nott describes as "a sick man, suffering from the weaknesses and lawful infirmities of old age, as well as from some specific disease [kidneys]," he finds Uspenskii mixing and drinking concoctions that were too powerful for him.

"You must have a stomach of iron!" exclaims Nott, taking a sip. "It's too strong for me."

"It's the only thing," says Uspenskii, "that relieves the boredom and depression that comes over me at times."

Long ago in *Tertium Organum*, Uspenskii had written about what he called the secret of the power of alcohol over human souls. "Alcohol," he wrote, "produces the illusion of communion of souls and stimulates fantasy simultaneously in two or more people."

MENDHAM. The effects of Uspenskii's long years of self-willed isolation from Gurdjieff, the failure to contact a school, nostalgia for the Russia of his youth, and the increasing amounts of alcohol have all taken their toll.

His secretary and pupil, Marie Seton, gives an alarming picture of Uspenskii in his final days in America. After lectures, she says, Uspenskii would ask a few of the group to go out with him to supper. But the party began to break up later and later, Uspenskii beginning to show a greater disinclination to leave the restaurant. Says Seton:

> The others would go and he would ask me to stay on. With the others gone he would have another drink and another and yet another, though he never became drunk; or at least, did not show it. One, two, three, four in the morning and still he would urge me to stay longer, and hour after hour he would talk—extremely interesting—about his homeland.
>
> He instructed me to cancel the lecture. Uspenskii then asked me to go out to dinner. I felt the time had come when I must ask him for an explanation as to how he could consider that dinner justified the sudden cancellation of a lecture. Where did such action fit into the System, and also where did his violent temper towards some people fit in?

> "They are such fools," Uspenskii said. "I've lost control of my temper."
>
> "But surely, if we are to try to control our negative emotions, we cannot learn from you, if you can't control yours," I said.
>
> Uspenskii answered bluntly: "I took over the leadership to save the System. But I took it over before I had gained enough control over myself. I was not ready. I have lost control over myself. It is a long time since I could control my state of mind."
>
> "Why don't you give up the lectures and try to gain control over yourself again?" I asked.
>
> "The System has become a profession with me," Uspenskii answered.
>
> One day he said something that was somehow more revealing than anything else as to the way a man becomes entangled in a role, or a vocation.
>
> "In Russia," he said, "there used to be a thousand or two thousand people at my lectures. Here there are a hundred—too few."
>
> One day he said: "I have become dependent on the comfort, the luxury. I can't give it up."
>
> Here was a man who was at heart honest; a man who was not by any means devoid of compassion for people. But adulation and comfort and the dearth of friends and the terror of a period of war had sapped his will to keep theory and practice united.
>
> If a man of the undeniable qualities of Uspenskii can go off the track and become absorbed in egotism and dependent on easy living, and become callous as to the effects on himself and on others, what of the gurus who are less basically honest?
>
> When I went to the country house for practical work, I began to notice what I had not noticed in England: that the people who were the 'old members' and had been living under Madame's direction were drab in clothes, joyless, and strangely closed-up people with one another. All were fearful of her displeasure....I began to see the pursuit of self-knowledge had to, as it seemed, eliminate an atmosphere of warmth between people and something that might be described as a lack of lovingness.

SUMMER 1946. Uspenskii, ill with a kidney disease[30] but refusing to submit to treatment, gives his last New York lectures. At the end of the final lecture he announces to his sixty-some followers that he is returning to England.

1947. SPANDAU PRISON. BERLIN. Albert Speer, sentenced to ten years in prison, writes in his diary: "The catastrophe of this war has proved the sensitivity of the system of modern civilization evolved in the course of

30. Aristotle held that the kidneys were seat of the soul.

centuries. Now we know that we do not live in an earthquake-proof structure. The build-up of negative impulses, each reinforcing the other, can inexorably shake to pieces the complicated apparatus of the modern world. There is no halting this process by will alone. The danger is that the automatism of progress will depersonalize man further and withdraw more and more of his self-responsibility."[31]

JANUARY 18, 1947. MENDHAM. Against doctor's orders and pleas of his wife, Uspenskii returns to England aboard the SS *Queen Elizabeth.* His skin is pale, his face flabby, from lack of exercise and a chronic kidney condition; Uspenskii is, physically, much older than his sixty-eight years. De Ropp, Collin, and others at Mendham watch as Uspenskii slowly walks towards a waiting car. The England that Uspenskii will return to will be for weeks under heavy snow and cold. Electricity will be restricted and food rationed.

Within days of his arrival Madame de Salzmann, at Gurdjieff's behest, invites Uspenskii to see him. Uspenskii refuses.[32]

FEBRUARY 24, 1947. COLET GARDENS. Uspenskii holds the first of what will be six meetings at Colet Gardens. During the long years of his absence, Dr. Francis Roles and his followers faithfully continued to meet and study the System as Uspenskii had constituted it. The atmosphere is tense with expectation. Presently, Uspenskii appears. He is noticeably older looking. Using a cane, every movement obviously a painful effort, he mounts the two steps to the platform. He takes his seat as he has done since his first lecture in England twenty-six years before. With an impassive glance he looks out over the audience. The questions begin....

He is asked: "Do you wish us to continue with the program you gave us in 1940?"

"Program?" Uspenskii replies. "I don't know program. Which program?"

"Program which you gave in 1940."

"No, I don't remember," says Uspenskii.

31. As early as 1916 Gurdjieff warned against a growth of automatism and personality. "Contemporary culture," he declared, "requires automatons....Man is becoming a willing slave. He no longer needs chains. He begins to grow fond of his slavery, to be proud of it. And this is the most terrible thing that can happen to a man." *Search,* p. 309.

32. Had they met, their meeting would have been the complete reversal of their last at the Café Henry IV sixteen years before in midsummer 1931. Then, Gurdjieff's outer life was nearing the lowest point of its descending octave, while Uspenskii's was reaching its highest. Gurdjieff has now completed the *Third Series* of his *legominism, All and Everything;* he has a strong Paris group; his older students are returning to him, and the teaching is ready to go forward. Whereas with Uspenskii there are no more books to be written; he will no longer teach; has failed to find the school for which he searched; and is suffering from illness and disillusionment.

Later in the meeting the subject is re-explored.

"We have been trying to follow out the teaching you gave us years ago," someone says.

Declares Uspenskii, "I gave no teaching."

"You told us certain things to help us."

"You misunderstand."

"Where can we begin to work now?"

"I will see what you want to know and where you want to begin," Uspenskii says, "and then we will see first step, and perhaps we will find second step. We don't know first step, that is the question. That you must remember."

MARCH 12, 1947. COLET GARDENS. At this meeting someone asks Uspenskii if he has abandoned the system.

"I never taught system," Uspenskii says.

"What are you going to try to teach us now?"

"That we may see."

Time and again, Uspenskii returns the question to the questioner, saying either he does not know or does not understand. His answers are short, simple. He urges people to make attempts for themselves. But some questions he does answer.

"Is there anything one can do at any given moment now to make sure that one will remember that moment later?" he is asked.

Replies Uspenskii, "No, we have nothing of that kind—no help in that way. Each one must find chief thing for himself—why one cannot remember."

"I believe that when I want something I only want it because I am selfish and possessive," someone says. "I need an aim which is outside myself."

"Right. Very good."

"How can I make my will come into action as quickly as my desire?"

"Very good—we may see something from that."

Uspenskii is asked, "You said that many of our questions do not refer to you."

"Yes," answers Uspenskii, "quite right."

"Is it because there is no understanding of a purpose other than one's own small purpose?"

"I don't even see small purpose."

"I mean that the questions are based on the inevitable point of view—the personal one—and is it that they lack any idea of a larger purpose? Your purpose, or possible purpose for everyone here?"

Uspenskii: "Well? Further."

Finally, comes this exchange:

"Can we learn to be more humble?"

Says Uspenskii, "I never was humble myself, and I don't know how I can."

APRIL 1947. MENDHAM. Rodney Collin leaves for England just before Easter to be with Uspenskii. He will spend all summer and autumn with his teacher.

MAY 21, 1947. COLET GARDENS. At this meeting the question of memory is introduced by Dr. Roles.

"People who have been trying to do things," Dr. Roles says, "tell me that they simply don't remember to go on with it. They forget every minute. They do it once a day. Is it possible to start by trying to improve memory in some way?"

"Yes, if it is what I call memory," answers Uspenskii. He adds, "There are many misunderstandings about this."

What Uspenskii is most likely referring to in regard to memory can be found in Rodney Collin's book *The Theory of Eternal Life*. Collin writes that what we commonly understand can only refer to the denser worlds in which "perception travels through time slowly enough to yield a sense of past, present and future." But in the higher worlds there can be no memory. This is "because everything is *now* and everything known."

Later Collin writes: "For familiar levels of consciousness and for the impulses of memory arising from them death is an *absolute insulator*. To pass through death in the next life memory would have to be of a far greater force, that is, it would have to arise from an immensely higher intensity of consciousness than any we ordinarily know."

JUNE 18, 1947. COLET GARDENS. This is the last time Uspenskii appears in public. At this meeting he is asked:

"I think that what I have learned from these meetings is that I know even less than I thought I did. Is that a desirable result?"

Uspenskii, giving no ground, replies—"Sometimes it may be."

Many were baffled and bewildered by Uspenskii, among them the Harley Street surgeon, Kenneth Walker. He sees Uspenskii as a "very deeply disappointed man.…Something had gone wrong and somebody had failed, but who it was that had failed was never very clear to me."

Others see it differently. Says Rodney Collin, "At Uspenskii's last meetings at Colet Gardens, he reached the deepest level [of sincerity] I ever met in a living man."

Said another:

> Uspenskii seemed very tired at first but I have noticed before how he seems to gain energy as the evening goes on. There were many questions and many answers, but it was from the emotional feeling that I

> gained the answers and not from the words. He seemed to be indicating that each must find for himself the particular personal difficulty that prevents remembering. I also felt that he conveyed that remembering was the whole thing and that with that everything else was added in the degree in which one could remember. I also felt that it was a very simple thing and that we could not be simple.

Of Uspenskii's return to England, Collin says: "He was a different man. So much of the vigorous, whimsical, brilliant personality, which his friends had known and enjoyed for so many years, had been left behind, that many meeting him again were shocked, baffled, or else were given a quite new understanding of what was possible in the way of development.... He spoke to them in a new way. He said that he abandoned the system. He asked them what they wanted, and said that only from that could they begin on the way of self-remembering and consciousness." Those who understood the way that Uspenskii was now showing, he says, "realized that in the way of development true knowledge must first be acquired and then abandoned. That exactly what makes possible the opening of one door may make impossible the opening of the next."

SUMMER 1947. LYNE PLACE. After the meetings at Colet Gardens, Uspenskii retired to his country home. Concluding that a new start could not be made in England, he instructs Collin and others to prepare for his return to America that autumn. He withdraws from life, sees very few people, and rarely speaks. But his silence is alive.[33]

Says Collin: "He would have two or three people sit with him, not doing anything, just sitting, smoking, occasionally making a remark, drinking a glass of wine, for hours on end. At first it was very difficult—one racked one's brains for what to say, how to start a conversation, thoughts of all kinds of imaginary duties elsewhere. Many people could not bear it. But after a while, these became the most interesting times of all. One began to feel—everything is possible in *this* moment." When Uspenskii does speak, the topic is often eternal recurrence.

Uspenskii is emphatic in his declaration that *Fragments of an Unknown Teaching* (later retitled by its publisher, *In Search of the Miraculous)* is not to be published. He does, however, retitle his 1915 novel *Kinemadrama* as *The Strange Life of Ivan Osokin.* The book is published in English before he dies.

SEPTEMBER 4, 1947. SOUTHAMPTON. Collin drives to the dock and puts Uspenskii's luggage on board a ship bound for America. A few hours

33. Perhaps this reminded Uspenskii of the time when he visited Gurdjieff's small Moscow apartment on the Bolshaia Dmitrovka and noted that Gurdjieff's pupils *"were not afraid to keep silent."*

before its departure, Uspenskii arrives. However, he has realized perhaps, that to return to America is futile and too passive, for he tells Collin to unload his luggage. "I am not going to America *this time,*" he says.[34] [Author's italics]

To Collin, the experience "was like the 'stop' exercise on the scale of the whole Work. A stop was made in many lives, everyone's personal plans were turned upside down, and a space made in the momentum of time where something quite new could be done. Then a most extraordinary and indescribable time began...."

SEPTEMBER 1947. LYNE PLACE. In what will be the final month of his life, though weak and sick of body, Uspenskii wills himself to make the super efforts needed to increase his vibration. Watching Uspenskii staying up day and night, demanding more and more impossible tasks of his body, it seems to Collin that his teacher is rising "in a crescendo of effort to meet the moment of death."

To impress familiar locations on his memory, Uspenskii has Collin drive him all over the south of England to places he had known, such as his former flat at Gwendwr Road, the house at Gaddesden, and to Alley Cottage, Maurice Nicoll's old seaside cottage in Sussex. These excursions often last throughout the night, Uspenskii sitting silently in the back seat, always in the company of his beloved cats.

Says Collin: "When almost unable to set one foot before the other he would make his dying body walk step by step for an hour at a time through the rough lanes; force it to rise in the small hours, dress, descend and climb long flights of stairs; turn night into day; and require of his companions in order to remain with him, such feats of endurance as they in full possession of health and strength were scarcely able to accomplish."

One night not long before his death Uspenskii, having spent the whole night forcing his body to stay awake, says to Collin—"Now do you understand that things come right by themselves?"

"At that moment," says Collin, "I saw clearly that if we really understood that everything is done by effort, all our life would be on another basis. We would not be able to hope....We, ourselves, have to develop our own will up to the highest possible point; that is, the power of putting into practice what we know."

In these last months Uspenskii communicates his ideas telepathically.[35] Finally, one of his attendants, fearing that her imagination might overrun her, asks that he speak audibly. He did as she asked. Increasingly,

34. Uspenskii's wording suggests that he perhaps has remembered that in another lifetime he did return to America and it came to nothing.

35. Where once with Gurdjieff in 1916 Uspenskii was receiving telepathic messages, he now is generating them.

many people at Lyne Place begin to have a sense of the miraculous taking place. (Later, Rodney Collin will write about this in an account he entitles *Last Remembrances of a Magician.*)

The coming of death creates an intensity that gives to the so-called ordinary occurrences of life a dimension and significance not usually seen. Sitting with Uspenskii at the dinner table, Rodney Collin watches him crumbling a bread roll on the cloth while under the table a cat ate the crumbs. As Uspenskii's love of cats was well known, Collin realizes the animal could have jumped on the table and Uspenskii would have given him the whole roll. He watches the cat eat in the peculiar way well-fed cats have who will eat things they find for themselves but to which, if offered in a dish, they would pay no notice.

Francis Roles speaks with Uspenskii who tells him, "You must go and find a method by which to remember yourSelf. If you find the method you may find the source. What you find will help me; somehow it is arranged like that."[36]

OCTOBER 2, 1947. LYNE PLACE. At dawn Uspenskii dies in Rodney Collin's arms.

After his teacher's body is taken away for burial, Collin returns to the bedroom where Uspenskii had died and locks himself in. There he remains for six days heeding no knocks or calls. Then a bell is heard in the kitchen, the same one that Uspenskii was accustomed to ringing. Collin's wife Janet enters the bedroom and finds her husband on Uspenskii's bed, emaciated, dirty, unshaven, his legs in a half-lotus position, looking as though he had been through a tremendous traumatic experience. During this vigil he had taken neither food nor drink. He believes he has been in telepathic communication with his teacher who has given him the knowledge which he will write about in *The Theory of Eternal Life.*

For Robert de Ropp, "Uspenskii, during the last phase of his life in America, had not lived like a Warrior [but] he certainly died like one."

Just a fortnight before his death, Uspenskii had said to a few friends who were with him: "You must start again. You must make a new beginning. You must reconstruct everything for yourselves—from the very beginning." This, Collin feels is "the true meaning of 'abandoning the

36. Many years later Roles is in India and speaks to the Shankaracharya of the North (there are two) about his teacher. He is told: "You should not worry about the liberation of such a man, because he seems to have finished his work in this world—in this revolution of the Cosmos. He finds a Divine Body and will be in peace until the creation dissolves in Brahma. Do not worry about him."

system.'" As Uspenskii's use of English was imperfect, Collin believes what Uspenskii meant to say was "reconstructing everything *in* oneself (instead of *for* oneself)." Thus, each student had to both create in themselves anew the understanding which the system had made possible and achieve its aim of permanently overcoming the false personality and acquiring a new level of consciousness.

Over the years, Rodney Collin has grown quite close to Uspenskii, who seemed to regard the young man like a son. There appears to be what might be a "heart connection" between the student and teacher. "Uspenskii," he says, "never worked for the moment. It might even be said that he did not work for time—he worked only for recurrence."

Says Bennett upon hearing of Uspenskii's death: "Throughout the day I felt a great love towards him, such as I had never known while he was alive. Nevertheless, I was strongly aware of the difference between death after a long life on the earth and a premature departure. Uspenskii's potentialities had been brought into time, and they had undergone an irreversible transformation. There was something that I could not understand and should not try to understand. A great cycle of my own life which had lasted twenty-seven years had closed. I felt love and gratitude towards Uspenskii, but I felt no nearer to him than I had before."

Years before his death, Uspenskii had told Bennett—who was concerned that business ventures would keep him away from meetings for months, if not years—of a Russian fairy tale:

> A knight sets out on a great adventure. He arrives at a place where the road divides into three. Unable to decide which to choose, the knight sees an old man, who tells him that if he goes to the right he will lose his horse, to the left he will lose himself; while if he takes the road in the center, he will lose both himself and his horse. The knight reasons with himself that a knight without a horse is helpless, and a horse without a knight is useless, so he might as well risk losing both. He chooses the middle path, and after desperate adventures, in which the old man's prophecy is fulfilled, he finally reaches his goal.

Uspenskii told Bennett, "You are now in that position. But I may as well tell you that if the knight had chosen either of the other two paths, it would have been the same in the end. Only it was necessary that he should persist and never give up. That is the only condition."

Like the Russian knight, Pyotr Demianovich Uspenskii had chosen his solitary path and, however low he went, he never gave up and, in the eyes of many of his students, he reached his goal.

At Uspenskii's death, Gurdjieff's students in Paris, New York, and London number about 200. Uspenskii's students in London alone number some 1,000. Madame Uspenskii tells her husband's students that Gurdjieff is alive in Paris and to go see him. More than half, believing what Uspenskii had told them—that Gurdjieff had forsaken the system after Essentuki—do not go. Dr. Francis Roles becomes the leader of the Uspenskii people in England.[37] Others follow Rodney Collin.

Says Rodney Collin: "I believe that Gurdjieff and Uspenskii were the two chosen agents of at least one stage of a new revelation. They were partners and complements, chosen because they represented and could transmit opposite aspects of the same truth. Two poles have to be separated for electric current to jump between them and make light. This was the reason for the separation of Gurdjieff and Uspenskii—it was by mutual agreement, to create a field of tension in which important preparations could be made."[38]

A requiem service is held for Pyotr Demianovich Uspenskii in the Russian Church at Pimlico. His body is buried in the courtyard of Lyne Church.

1948. Tlalpam. Following Uspenskii's death, Rodney Collin appeared, to a number of people, to have come to a new level of being and authority. Now he and his family and followers arrive in Mexico and buy an old hacienda on the outskirts of Mexico City. He also buys land in the hills and begins to build a planetarium. Thus the Uspenskii version of the Work is planted in the ancient world of the Aztecs and Teotihuacans.

January 1948. England. Cecil Lewis, an airman, author, and cofounder of the British Broadcasting Company, had become a student of John Bennett's. Lewis describes his initial impressions of Bennett:

37. Later, Dr. Roles will link up his people with the English barrister Leon McLaren's London-based School of Economic Science, which will come to stress an Indian Advaita Vedanta approach. In the 1960s McLaren and Roles consider turning the school over to the Maharishi Mahesh Yogi and his Transcendental Meditation movement. For an informative look at these days, see Joyce Collin-Smith's *Call No Man Master* (Gateway, 1988). She also recounts her visit in Mexico City with her brother-in-law, Rodney Collin.

38. Rodney Collin, of course, never met Gurdjieff. Collin's only knowledge of the teaching came through Uspenskii. To compare Uspenskii's *Search* with Gurdjieff's *All and Everything* offers the possibility of seeing, as Orage did when the two men were on the same platform, who clearly is the teacher and who the student, see p. 77. Collin, like many still, puts them both on the same level and so seals himself off from Gurdjieff's far richer and more profound exposition. The distortion is fundamental and continues to be perpetuated today not only by students of Uspenskii but students of Nicoll and Bennett as well.

> In stature he was a tall, good-looking man [who] had the air of being used to command. He spoke several languages, was widely read and seemed as much at home in philosophy or psychology as he was in higher mathematics. But all this variety was, so to speak, hidden beneath genial conversation and an evident open-hearted generosity of nature. He met all problems with assurance and authority, was never at a loss for an answer and, though, in fact, he had only received a limited part of the Teaching he brought to us, it was quite enough to draw us to it and later, when the source of it all appeared, for him to seem to know it already.

With the death of Uspenskii, and Gurdjieff believed to be dead, Lewis says that "He, Bennett, alone remained as the custodian of these tremendous possibilities, which were Gurdjieff's legacy to the world. How could we preserve them for posterity?"

Believing the international situation to be unstable enough that a third world war might break out and the teaching be lost, Bennett's solution was to establish the teaching in a safe haven. Says Lewis: "With practically no further investigation...Bennett swept us all off our feet by deciding that something must be done at once. He suggested that South Africa was our best choice."

Presently, Bennett, Cecil Lewis and his wife Olga, and a few others fly in a converted Lancaster bomber 6,000 miles to South Africa. The purpose of the trip: to scout feasible sites to set up the teaching.

Eastern Transvaal is finally chosen. The site, says Lewis, "is in a magnificent lonely valley, unspoiled by any 'civilization' and complete with river and hundred-foot waterfall." The idea is to prepare a commune for some two hundred people.

Bennett, however, begins to have second thoughts. He prays for guidance. Deep into the night he says he becomes aware of a Presence that tells him: "You are not meant to stay in Africa. Your place is in London. Trouble will come; not as you imagine, but differently, and you have to be in the midst of it. There is no need for Noah's Ark, for this time there will be no flood. The task before you is quite different from what you suppose."

Later, Bennett sees South Africa's Prime Minister, Field Marshall Jan Smuts, who tells him:

> You think that if European civilization is destroyed, something can still be preserved. I do not believe this. Europe is still, and for at least a century will continue to be, the bearer of the hopes of the human race....There is nothing like it in the rest of the world....The crisis in human affairs, as I see it, consists in the premature acquisition by mankind of powers which it cannot use wisely. But this crisis cannot be solved by running away from it. If you have understood the situa-

tion a little better than others, then your place is at home. Go back and preach the supreme importance of our European heritage.

Bennett returns to London, and the Lewises, and a handful of others stay to build the commune. Bennett apparently never tells Lewis of his experience with the Presence.

1948. MENDHAM. Bennett visits Madame Uspenskii. He had tried to find Gurdjieff in Paris, but without success. He thinks Gurdjieff had either died or gone mad. "Gurdjieff is not mad. He has never been mad," Madame Uspenskii tells Bennett. "He is living in Paris now," Madame declares. "Why don't you go to him?"

Earlier she had also told her more mature students, like Lord John Pentland and Christopher Fremantle,[39] that Gurdjieff is alive—"Hurry, don't waste a moment. Go to him."

1948. ENGLAND. Maurice Nicoll is told that Gurdjieff is living in Paris, but he shows no interest in seeing his former teacher. Perhaps he has heard that Gurdjieff, in speaking to those who have gone to see him, has accused Uspenskii and him of "stealing his teaching."

1948. 6 RUE DES COLONELS RÉNARD. Sometime after the war Gurdjieff receives another visitor, Jesse Orage. Everyone is already eating lunch. After a short conversation, Gurdjieff says to her:

"Jesse, you have my plate, my dinner."

"No, I've had it," she replies.[40]

Gurdjieff then begins to speak about a certain man who knew everything but lacked "the simple understanding.... He tried for such and was too intelligent to grasp it."

Jesse begins to cry.

Gurdjieff never takes his eyes off her.

1948. NEW YORK. Jean Toomer meets Gurdjieff. After the meeting Toomer writes: "I do not really know myself, who I am, my selfhood, my spiritual identity, or what I am. I have some information about it, but also some misinformation, some understanding, but much illusion. Real knowledge, real recognition, realization? No. What are my complex motivations? What is my aim, assuming that I have but one aim? I do not really know my wife, my child, my closest friends. I do not really know anyone or anything."[41]

39. Christopher Fremantle would later play a significant role in helping to establish the Work in Mexico and later America. See his book *On Attention* (Indications Press, 1993).

40. An interesting reply, given what has happened between her, Gurdjieff, and Orage.

AUGUST 14, 1948. COOMBE SPRINGS. ENGLAND. Bennett writes to Cecil Lewis in South Africa: "I am writing this on the eve of our journey into the unknown. At this time tomorrow Polly and I will be in Paris and we shall see G on Friday.... Today, I feel like a new boy creeping timidly into the Great Hall of some ancient school—where even the other boys seem to be supermen and all about is a mystery. Somehow I cannot bring myself to realize that, at last, I have come to the possibility of real guidance and help.... I will write you from Paris.

"We think of you battling with Nature in the distant South and we here struggling to keep our minds clear...."

AUGUST 15, 1948. 6 RUE DES COLONELS RÉNARD. It is twenty-five years to the month when fifty-one-year-old John Godolphin Bennett, a powerful business executive and leader of his own groups, rings the bell. With him is his seventy-five-year-old wife, Winifred, known as "Polly."

Madame de Salzmann answers and motions them inside.

They walk down the dark, dingy hallway, every inch of the walls covered with paintings, either ugly, bizarre, or decidedly amateurish.

The two are motioned into a small sitting room on the right. Its walls are also covered with paintings of the same dubious quality. Though it is early afternoon, the windows are shuttered and the only illumination is provided by electric lights. Bennett notices the furniture is shabby and the carpets threadbare. On either side of the fireplace hang representations of the enneagram, made from mother-of-pearl and sewn to fabric-covered black disks. In the corners of the room, abutting the street, sit two odd, glittering artifacts. One is a sort of stylized Christmas tree, made out of some gold-colored metal or gilded wood. It gleams from light reflected from countless prisms of glass. The other is a cabinet containing a large collection of dolls dressed in different national costumes, as well as an assortment of keepsakes, pipes, musical instruments, Orientalia. When the room is properly lit, the cheap materials scintillate and sparkle, giving the feeling of being in Aladdin's cave.

Presently, in the doorway, Gurdjieff appears.

Quite heavy now, he holds himself as erect as ever. He moves into the room with the same grace and economy of gesture as Bennett remembers from the Prieuré.

The moustaches are white now and the face has lost its firm outline, but the skin is still smooth. He wears a tasselled magenta fez, open shirt and rumpled trousers.

41. What a heartbreaking recognition this must be for Toomer after twenty-five years in the Work. But the courage of such sincerity signals a new start. However, Toomer's physical condition steadily grows worse. After 1955 he is unable to take care of himself and his wife must put him in a nursing home, where he will die on March 30, 1967.

Madame de Salzmann introduces the Bennetts.

Gurdjieff does not remember them.

For a few moments he takes Bennett in and then says:

"You are Number Eighteen. Not a big Number Eighteen but small Number Eighteen."

Soon, it is past two o'clock. There are only a few people in the flat. Gurdjieff suddenly says, "Chain. Chain."

People form a line from the kitchen to the dining room and pass plates of food. Bennett is seated on Gurdjieff's right, Bennett's wife on the left. Lunch is eaten. With his fingers, Gurdjieff slowly eats morsels of lamb and hard bits of goat cheese and fresh tarragon leaves. At one point the toasts to the idiots begin.

After the meal, which does not end until nearly five o'clock, Gurdjieff invites Bennett into the pantry for coffee. Though food is still rationed, the shelves of the pantry are stocked thick with tins and jars of food while dried fish and sausages of camel's meat, bunches of dried scarlet peppers, and sprays of rosemary hang from the ceiling.

"You know what is the first Commandment of God to man?" Gurdjieff asks, as he pours some coffee out of a battered old thermos bottle, takes a piece of sugar, puts it into his mouth, and sips coffee through it.

Bennett fumbles for an answer.

"Hand wash hand!"

Gurdjieff pauses to let Bennett absorb that. Then he says:

"You need help and I need help. If I help you, you have to help me."

Bennett says he is ready to do whatever Gurdjieff wants.

Gurdjieff speaks about his money difficulties, then asks Bennett what he wants from him.

"Will you show me how to work for my Being?"

"It is right," Gurdjieff declares. "Now you have much Knowledge, but in Being you are a nullity. If you wish, I will show you how to work, but you must do it as I say."

They speak quite seriously. Bennett is amazed. It is an exact continuation of the conversation they had had in Constantinople twenty-seven years before.

"I know my situation is hopeless," says Bennett at one point. "That is why I have come back to you."

Gurdjieff repeats: "If you will do as I say, I will show you how to change. Only you must stop thinking. You think too much. You must begin to sense." He then asks if Bennett understands the distinction between sensing and feeling.

Bennett's answer is an intellectual definition.

"More or less. But you only know this with your mind. You do not understand with your whole being. This you must learn."

SEVERAL DAYS LATER. Gurdjieff has gone on a trip to Cannes with a large sum of money that Bennett has given him. There is an accident as he drives through the town of Montargis: a small truck with a drunken driver comes out of a side road and ploughs into Gurdjieff's car; the impact is so great that the drunken driver and his passenger are instantly killed. Bennett had not gone on the trip but he is there when Gurdjieff arrives back at his apartment. It is dusk when the door of the car opens and Gurdjieff slowly gets out. "His clothes were covered with blood," reports Bennett. "His face was black with bruises....It was a dead man, a corpse, that came out of the car; and yet it walked."

Somehow, Gurdjieff gets to his room and sits down.

"Now all organs are destroyed. Must make new," he says.

Seeing Bennett, he says: "Tonight you come dinner. I must make body work."

With that the pain gives his body a great spasm and blood flows from his ear. Bennett thinks that he has a cerebral hemorrhage and, if he continues to force his body to move, that he will kill himself.

Gurdjieff asks Madame de Salzmann about some man. Told that he is in the American Hospital, he tells her to go see him. Then he adds:

"I wish watermelon. Buy watermelon when you come back."

Now Bennett realizes that Gurdjieff has to do this, for "if he allows his body to stop moving, he will die. He has power over his body."

AUGUST 1948. 6 RUE DES COLONELS RÉNARD. Bennett has brought about sixty students to Gurdjieff's flat. C. S. Nott, having coffee with Gurdjieff at the Café des Acacias, says to him that Mr. Bennett's return will be a very good thing for the Work, as he has a large organization and many of his students seem to have money. He says Gurdjieff replied laconically:

"Bennett is small thing. Useful for money, yes. He will bring me a thousand pupils and out of these I shall choose perhaps ten."

Reports one English person about lunches at Gurdjieff's apartment:

> We all eat jammed around the table with our elbows in each other's tummies almost. The meal always starts with so-called "salade" too disgusting, floating about in a little bowl. "Not such salade never was"—and indeed I hope so. Then there is usually meat or bird with rice and a big dish of radishes, onions, etc. passed round to eat with it. Then a sweet—always very sweet and syrupy—and fruit, melon, grapes, etc. Sometimes coffee, sometimes not. Throughout the meal he [Gurdjieff] passes round oddments of food—apparently quite indiscriminately, so that one may easily find oneself eating sprats or bear meat with one's sweet, sheeps' meat from Bokhara, camel sausage from Kayseri—one never knows what to expect. Once he broke up fish in his fingers and then held out a fistful across the table, say-

> ing benevolently "Who not squeamish?" The last evening we were there one of Brynn's goat cheeses was handed round which G. described as "special Scotch cheese from Scotland" and enveloped us all with a baleful stare, defying us to deny it. All this is washed down with, mainly, bread or white vodka for the toasts, but there is also Mare, Calvados, Armagnac—most things…

Another comments on the music:

> After the meal is over we go into the salon and settle ourselves on the chairs, the divan, the stools and the floor. G. sits in his chair and Lise [Tracol] brings him his little portable organ which he rests on his knee playing with one hand while he works the bellows with the other.
>
> He then makes the strangest music—the most wonderful music. He says it is "objective"—that is, the vibrations he produces have a definite effect on people, both organically and psychologically. It affects people in different ways, tough business men and scientists sit with the tears streaming down their faces, others are merely bored or puzzled, others again are moved but do not know why.
>
> He is asked about this music. A woman says she found she did not listen to it with her ears. He said: "Ears are no good for this music, the whole presence must be open to it. It is a matter of vibrations." Then he added, "But tears must come first." He also said he had to put the whole of himself into these vibrations, it was very difficult for him. He is always exhausted after playing. Often he does not play. Then we play the records of the music.

This is the end of the session. The lunch session lasts from 1:30 to 4:30 or later; the evening session from 10:30 to 2 or 3 in the morning.

LATE AUGUST 1948. LASCAUX. Gurdjieff visits the caves. He tells Bennett that the enneagram, like the Sphinx, is not a symbol but an emblem of an esoteric society. Something happens and Gurdjieff makes it clear he does not want Bennett to travel with him.

"I go right," Gurdjieff says, "you go left."

"Then we must say good-bye to you?" asks Bennett, hoping to keep an opening.

"Yes, good-bye!"

Back in Paris, Bennett experiences again being out of the body and separate from the mind.

When he meets Gurdjieff again, he is treated "as if I were an outcast." Gurdjieff complains that he had not been able to eat on the drive back from Lascaux for lack of company.

"But you sent me away," says Bennett.

"But you tell me you have to go fetch wife—" says Gurdjieff, "but she here all the time. You are not honest. Your manifestations are disgusting."

SEPTEMBER 4, 1948. PARIS. Bennett goes to Gurdjieff's café in the rue des Acacias. Gurdjieff is there but he ignores him. He responds only after much time and much prodding and only after Bennett tells him, "I cannot thank you for what you have done for me. That I can never repay."

Gurdjieff says nothing for a long time. People come and go. Finally he turns towards Bennett and says slowly:

"What you say about never repay—this is stupidity. *Only* you can repay. Only *you* can repay for all my labours. What you think is money? I can buy all your England. Only *you* can repay me by work. But what you do? Before trip I give you task. Do you fulfil? No; you do just the opposite. Never once I see you struggle with *yourself.* All the time you are occupied with your cheap animal."

Later, at lunch Gurdjieff speaks of conscience, saying that "When conscience and consciousness are together, then you will not make such mistakes."

Bennett drives Madame de Salzmann home after lunch and tells her of his sense of having failed Gurdjieff.

"The work changes," she says. "Up to one point, one gets fairly clear guidance. Then comes a time when it is made so confusing that you can easily do exactly the wrong thing in the conviction that it is right."

1948. 6 RUE DES COLONELS RÉNARD. Lord Pentland[42] had been Uspenskii's chief deputy in the 1930s. During the 1940s he worked under Uspenskii's and Madame Uspenskii's guidance at Franklin Farms in Mendham, New Jersey. Learning that Gurdjieff was in Paris he and his wife, Lucy, and young daughter, Mary, come to lunch. Mary sits by her mother's side and just in front of Gurdjieff. She becomes bored. Gurdjieff suddenly speaks to her, saying—"In life it is never possible to do everything."

The child is puzzled. Having her attention, Gurdjieff points to the mess Mary has made at the table. "On my table you cannot make this mess," he says. "Perhaps at home Mother permits. Then if you want to do this thing, you must stay at home. But if you stay at home, you will not be able to come here and see me. So you see, you can never do everything."

In the evening at the end of the dinner, Gurdjieff asks Mary, "Who do you respect most?"

She doesn't understand the question.

"Who do you think is the most important person here?" her mother asks.

Without hesitating, Mary declares—"My Daddy."

Gurdjieff beams.

42. He is later appointed by Gurdjieff to lead the Work in America. He will be a leading force in creating and establishing both the Gurdjieff Foundation in New York in 1953 and similar foundations and groups throughout America. He will act as the president of the New York and California Foundations until his death February 14, 1984.

"I am not offended," he says. "God is not offended either."

Gurdjieff explains that a person who loves his parents loves God, and he says, "If people love their parents all the time that their parents are alive, then, when their parents die, there is a space left in them for Him to fill."

As the Pentlands prepare to leave, Gurdjieff pats Mary on the shoulder, saying to everyone present: "For my aim, I want twenty such. If I had twenty like her, I get my aim. Not because she special, but because she not spoilt."

OCTOBER 30, 1948. FRANCE. Gurdjieff sails for America with Madame de Salzmann. On the boat train there is a large luncheon. Bennett is the director of the toasts. He breaks the ritual by proposing a toast to Mr. Gurdjieff's health.

"No," says Gurdjieff, "I will propose myself health of English. Thanks to the English I sail to New York free from all debts. Pure comme bébé."

His parting message to everyone is: "Before I return I hope with all my being that everyone here will have learned the difference between sensation and feeling."

NOVEMBER 18, 1948. SOUTH AFRICA. Cecil Lewis receives another letter from Bennett:

> The truth is that everything is so exciting here [London] at the moment that hardly anyone can bear the thought of being separated from it. At the same time if and when disaster strikes, the very people who are reluctant to do anything to share in building up a home for us to go to, will be only too ready and anxious to take advantage of what has been done....I am equally certain that within two or three years we shall enter that period of acute nervous tension which Gurdjieff called *solioonensius.* Such periods induce intense incentive to work in those who are capable of it, but they engender madness in those who have lost touch with the real aim of life. Whenever the process of *solioonensius* occurs on earth, a state of tension is created in which it is impossible for people to exist quietly like cows. They have either to work on themselves or they begin "to destroy everything within sight." As I understand it, the next *solioonensius* will be the most intense of all. As an outcome, either mankind will change to a different mode of existence or there will occur the most terrible process of mutual destruction....So our decision to seek a place in SA remains just as valid as it was three years ago.

WINTER 1948–1949. NEW YORK. Gurdjieff stays at the Wellington Hotel in Manhattan. He visits Madame Uspenskii at Franklin Farms. He wants to begin to consolidate the groups, putting the "Uspenskii people" in contact with the dozen or so "Gurdjieff people," most of whom, like Peggy Flinsch and Dr. William Welch and his wife Louise, come from the original Orage groups. As a result, some of the Uspenskii group begin to visit Gurdjieff regularly at his hotel. Among them are Lord and Lady Pentland, Christopher Freemantle and his wife Anne, and Tom Forman. After every luncheon there are the toasts. Bennett has arrived from England.

Says Louise Goepfert: "Bennett returned to Gurdjieff's table and pronounced himself Mr. Gurdjieff's oldest pupil. When Bennett was put into the Round Idiot category, the same as me, it sat badly with me." Gurdjieff said of the Round Idiots—"those that never stop, but day-night-year-round continue."

Madame Uspenskii has sent Gurdjieff a chapter from her husband's *Fragments of an Unknown Teaching*, asking if it should be published. After the toasts, the chapter is read aloud to the group. About one passage, Gurdjieff says, "Is too liquid. Lost something." Overall, though, Gurdjieff praises it. "Very exact is. Good memory. Truth was so."

EARLY 1949. NEW YORK. During a dinner conversation, Gurdjieff says that when Hitler came to power a critical phase of history had begun. In terms of the teaching, he had been obliged to wait until it became clear how mankind would react.

JANUARY 13, 1949. NEW YORK. *It was in the year 223 after the creation of the World by objective time-calculation, or, as it would be said here on the "Earth," in the year 1921 after the birth of Christ.*

Twenty-five years after having first dictated these lines, Gurdjieff decides to publish the first series of *All and Everything—Beelzebub's Tales to his Grandson.*

In the morning at Child's Cafe on Fifth Avenue, Gurdjieff's "New York Office," he tells Bennett to write a circular letter to all his students telling of his decision to publish the first series of *All and Everything.*

Says Bennett: "I asked for a sheet of paper, and wrote without knowing how or what I should write.... The manner of writing was completely foreign to me. I had used the word 'adept' instead of pupil. This both surprised and annoyed me, as the word 'adept' grated harshly on my ear as savouring too much of occultism."

At lunch that day, Gurdjieff's rooms at the Hotel Wellington are jammed wall to wall with his students, overcoats piled four feet deep the length of the foyer. Early arrivals are seated cross-legged on the floor around the sofa, everyone else standing, Gurdjieff sits on the sofa with one leg characteristically tucked under him, parting his moustaches with the thumb and index finger of his hand. Finally, he takes a letter from his pocket and hands it to Bennett, sitting near him.

"Read, read—is for everybody," Gurdjieff says in a low voice. He listens as if weighing each word.

Bennett, who says Gurdjieff handed him the letter as if he had never seen it before, reads: "This circular is addressed to all my present and former adepts and to all who have been directly or indirectly influenced by my ideas and have sensed and understood that they contain something which is necessary for the food of humanity. After fifty years of preparation and having overcome the greatest difficulties and obstacles, I have decided to publish..."

Following the reading, Gurdjieff says three representatives are needed, for France, England and America. For America he appoints Lord John Pentland;[43] for France, René Zuber; and for England, J. G. Bennett.

In the afternoon there is a children's party at Gurdjieff's hotel room. At the party's end everyone leaves, Bennett finds himself alone with Gurdjieff. Gurdjieff is at the end of a long drawing room seated on a low couch. Bennett goes up and kneels beside him, thanking Gurdjieff for all that he has done for him. Says Gurdjieff:

"What I have done up to now for you is nothing. Soon I return to Europe. You come to me, and I will show you how to work. If you do what I tell, I will show you how to become immortal. Now you have nothing, but if you will work you can soon have soul."

EARLY 1949. C. S. Nott says:

> One day, I read in the paper that he [Uspenskii] had died, and a deep feeling of compassion came over me and wished that I had been able to have kept in contact with him. He was a good man and helped hundreds of people. His attitude towards the ideas was one of absolute integrity and the evidence is *Fragments of an Unknown Teaching*, a masterpiece of objective reporting but some kink in him had caused him to reject Gurdjieff as a teacher. Ouspensky always had wanted to found a religious philosophical school; and he had founded a very successful one, with a large organization in England and America. Yet it had not given him real "being satisfaction." At the end of his life he had, it seems, come to realize that a philosophical school was not the basically important thing for him. It may be that he, like others, had had to work out something from the pattern of his life: his philosophical school and all his theories in connection with it, and "next time" he may be better equipped to understand the real work of the inner Teaching.

MAY 26, 1949. NEW JERSEY. C. Daly King completes *The Oragean Version.*[44] He does so because he feels Orage's understanding was different

43. For an account of his unique capacity to teach and his understanding of leadership, refer to the author's book, *Eating the "I"* (Arete Communications, 1992).

than both Gurdjieff's and Uspenskii's and was on "the verge of being irrecoverably lost." In a later book, *The States of Human Consciousness,* King will say of Gurdjieff:

> With one exception the writer has never encountered anyone of whom he felt assured that the latter was living permanently in a state of Awakeness. The exception was Gurdjieff himself....In these respects [the mode of living and the manner of contact with other persons, friendly, hostile or neutral] and many more, Gurdjieff manifested himself in ways never encountered by the writer, in ways so different from those of others that they constituted a plain and perceptible difference in level of existence upon his part. His famous reputation as an enigmatic rested largely upon this circumstance. He is the only person ever met by the writer who gave the indubitable impression that all his responses, mental, emotional and practical, were mutually *in balance* and thus the further impression that everyone else was out of step, but not this man himself.
>
> The writer has no hesitation in calling him [Gurdjieff] one of the hundred, perhaps one of the fifty, most remarkable men known to us in our history. Although he did not claim personally to have discovered all of it, the mere range of his knowledge was so far beyond that of others as to make comparisons not merely invidious but impossible. His methods of instructing his pupils were highly individual and highly unusual and one of his principles seems to be to guard against their acquirement of too much knowledge prematurely; a corresponding degree of understanding was to be demanded and, until it had been attained, additional knowledge was inadvisable.

AUGUST 1949. 6 RUE DES COLONELS RÉNARD. While reading aloud at the evening meal, Bennett suddenly has the experience of leaving his body. "I found myself several feet away from my body," he says. "My voice was still speaking, but it was not 'my' voice any more, but a stranger's....The sense of separation from the body persisted for several hours, although I remained inside it."

One mealtime Gurdjieff speaks to Bennett in a low voice on the Last Supper and the role of Judas. He tells Bennett that Judas was Jesus' best and closest friend and that he alone understood why Jesus was on the planet. By his selfless action Judas had saved the work of Jesus from being destroyed. Then Gurdjieff asks him:

44. In the book (privately published), King faithfully records the teaching, such as he received it from Orage. He makes some interesting points concerning self-observation and his book is worth studying. But, just as Gurdjieff pointed out eighteen years before to Orage and his groups, he overvalues the practice and appears to misunderstand its intent. Sure in his confidence in his intellection, C. Daly King will die in 1962 at the age of sixty-seven, not once in his published work questioning his viewpoint about Gurdjieff or the teaching.

"You know what I say of Judas and how differently the church teaches. Which do you believe is true?"

To Bennett it seems that somehow the crowded dining room and time disappears and he finds himself back in the Jerusalem of A.D. 33. He becomes aware of the good and evil forces at war and sees that Judas was unmistakably on the good side.

"You are right," Bennett answers. "Judas was the friend of Jesus, and he was on the side of good."

In a voice so low as to be almost inaudible Gurdjieff says: "I am pleased what you understand."

Several other times during the coming days Gurdjieff tells Bennett that his relationship with him is the same as that between Judas and Jesus.

Bennett says that once he and Lord Pentland were sitting next to one another and Gurdjieff says:

"Mr. Bennett is like Judas; he is responsible that my work is not destroyed. You," he says to Lord Pentland, "are like Paul; you must spread my ideas."

During these last days, Bennett says, Gurdjieff "never spoke of death, but of going far away."

OCTOBER 1949. LONDON. Bennett gives a series of lectures in London called, "Gurdjieff: The Making of a New World."

OCTOBER 14, 1949. SALLE PLEYEL 32, PARIS. Gurdjieff collapses during a movements class and is taken back to his apartment where he is nursed by Lise Tracol. His condition fluctuates throughout the coming days.

OCTOBER 19, 1949. MILL HOUSE, DOYLESTOWN, PENNSYLVANIA. Letter to Paul Anderson, who is helping Lord Pentland with the publication of *All and Everything*. It is from Jean Toomer, who has fallen away from his involvement with the Quakers, after having given the prestigious William Penn Lecture and who is now seeing a Jungian therapist:

> I said yes to the idea of having lunch with you and Lord Pentland because I had interest in such a meeting and also because I wanted to convince you that I have no interest in doing anything about either Uspenskii's or Gurdjieff's books at this time. My life and needs run in other directions....Gurdjieff and his projects are, for me, nothing to touch unless you want to get deeply involved in them....For some reasons known to me, and some unknown, I am, for better or worse, out of it—and I want to remain out, quite out—until such time, if and when that time comes, that I again move towards it by impulses arising within myself. As you know, some drinks mix; some don't. I must not mix what I am doing now with the world and works of Mr. G....You are in the work. I know the feeling. You want to leave no

> stone unturned in your efforts to fulfill your function in the work. Splendid. It is a grand active sense of purpose. When I was an active agent I liked it too. It was meat and bread and life. So I, from my side, say more power to you. And do you then, from your side, understand that I do not like being on the passive end.[45]

OCTOBER 21, 1949. PARIS. Gurdjieff sees the first proofs of the American edition of *All and Everything*. As Gurdjieff had said in 1945, "I now very tired and I know that when I finish this last book my work will be done. So now I can die, because my task in life is coming to an end."

OCTOBER 22, 1949. PARIS. Bennett finds Gurdjieff at his café in the rue des Acacias. He is dressed in his coat with the astrakhan collar, sheepskin boots, a brown and red woolen scarf folded over his chest and his black astrakhan cap. His appearance—that of a sick old man—is shocking. He looks ill, his face very dark, the eyes sunken with black rings around them. Gurdjieff speaks of the future.

"The next five years," he says, "will decide. It is the beginning of a new world. Either the old world will make me 'Tchik' [squash me like a louse], or I will make the old world 'Tchik.' Then the new world can begin."

OCTOBER 24, 1949. 6 RUE DES COLONEL RÉNARD. Still seriously ill, Gurdjieff oversees the toast to the idiots.

OCTOBER 26, 1949. 6 RUE DES COLONEL RÉNARD. The decision is made to take Gurdjieff to the American Hospital. A stretcher is brought to his bedroom but he refuses to use it. Instead, he gets out of bed and appears in the hallway wearing his pajamas and a red fez. On seeing the stretcher he says, "Oy!" He sits on it upright, his fez at a rakish angle and lights a cigarette. Outside, as the stretcher is carried to the ambulance, the cigarette between his lips, he makes a sort of wave and says, *"Au revoir, tout le monde!"*

OCTOBER 27, 1949. AMERICAN HOSPITAL AT NEUILLY. Early this morning the American doctor, William Welch, who has flown in from New York, prepares to perform an abdominal puncture to tap and drain the bloated abdomen. Gurdjieff rests in bed wearing his red fez and cloaked by his camel hair coat, holding a cup of coffee and wooden cigarette holder. Asked if he is ready, Gurdjieff, the old fox, replies—"Only if you not tired, Doctor."

Gurdjieff gives his last instructions to Madame de Salzmann.

45. After Gurdjieff's death Toomer, always searching, became involved with Scientology. His interest in the Work was reignited after hearing a lecture by J. G. Bennett in 1954 and he began attending meetings with Madame de Salzmann at Uspenskii's former residence in Mendham, New Jersey.

"Publish as and when you are sure that the time has come. Publish the *First* and *Second Series* [of *All and Everything*]. The essential thing, the first thing, is to prepare a nucleus of people capable of responding to the demand which will arise.

"So long as there is no responsible nucleus, the action of the ideas will not go beyond a certain threshold. That will take time... a lot of time, even.

"To publish the *Third Series* is not necessary.

"It was written for another purpose.

"Nevertheless, if you believe you ought to do so one day, publish it."

OCTOBER 28, 1949. AMERICAN HOSPITAL AT NEUILLY. Gurdjieff falls unconscious.

OCTOBER 29, 1949. AMERICAN HOSPITAL AT NEUILLY. Mr. Gurdjieff dies about 10:30 A.M. He died of cancer.[46] Dr. William Welch sits in the kitchen of Mr. Gurdjieff's flat drinking a big bowl of coffee. He says that Mr. Gurdjieff died peacefully, the sickness disappearing from his face. "I have seen many men die. He died like a king."

OCTOBER 30, 1949. PARIS. The funeral service takes place in the Russian Orthodox Church in the rue Daru. Mr. Gurdjieff's body is too large for the coffin; a larger one must be found. In absolute silence, the congregation stands for an hour waiting for the coffin to arrive. The priest is dressed in the old tradition with robe, silver cross and a chain, long black hair and beard. In a honeyed voice he asks:

"What did this man Gurdjieff teach? For my whole life I've wanted a congregation like this."

The chapel is lit with candles. Mr. Gurdjieff's body is dressed in his best suit, bought for the forthcoming American trip. It is covered with a pale cloth piled high with red roses, pink orchids, and white flowers. On either side of his head are two enormous bouquets of violets.

Says one pupil: "The face is like a statue's. Yesterday he looked alive still, a slight smile made him seem so; his skin had a most curious lavender tinge. Today he is darker, the smile has gone, he's already far away, the eyes have begun to sink, the lips are in a grave line, though not quite

46. See the Solita Solano papers at the Library of Congress. His followers did not admit the real cause of Mr. Gurdjieff's death in that he himself had said that cancer and heart disease "were almost always the inevitable results of living in an unharmonious atmosphere under constant strain and pressure." (See Fritz Peters, *Gurdjieff Remembered*, p. 62.) But this was Gurdjieff's great sacrifice: his own life. It must be remembered that he took a vow on September 14, 1911, "to live an *artificial* life " in order to establish the ancient teaching of the Fourth Way in the West. [Author's italics.] Given the abnormal conditions and customs and deviations of our contemporary world, a constant and unflagging colossal super-effort would be demanded that must, of course, be paid for in terms of continual strain and pressure. What was taken as a negative was really quite otherwise, when truly seen.

stern....He looks as if he had just said: 'Now I go away with all my secrets and my mystery. My work is finished here.'"

Says another pupil:

> I was overwhelmed by the force that came from him. One could not be near his body without feeling unmistakably his power. He looked magnificent; composed, content, *intentional*, for want of a better word. Not simply a body placed by someone else. He was undisguised, nothing was concealed from us. Everything belonging to him, his inner and outer life and all the circumstances and results of it, were there to be seen, if one could see. What force there was in him then! I have never seen anything in any way like it. This, I think, was what I had dreaded: I could not bear to see him with the force gone from him. Yet in fact I saw his power for the first time unobscured.

The priest reads the eulogy Thomas de Hartmann had prepared. He wrote it in such a way that the last words pronounced by the priest in front of Mr. Gurdjieff's coffin in the Russian church are the words from Gurdjieff's ballet *The Struggle of the Magicians*:

> *Lord Creator and all you His assistants, help us to be able to remember ourselves at all times in order that we may avoid involuntary actions, as only through them can evil manifest itself.*

Five white-and-gold-robed Russian priests and a cantor perform ceremonies, chanting and praying and singing, all in Russian. One by one all those assembled pass by the coffin, making a genuflection at his head, stepping up to the icon at his feet, kissing it and walking off to the left.

The Russian "Service for the Dead" begins for Mr. Georgi Ivanovitch Gurdjieff. It concludes:

> *Give rest eternal in the blessed falling asleep, O Lord,*
> *to the soul thy servant departed this life,*
> *and make his memory eternal.*
> *Memory eternal!*
> *Memory eternal!*
> *Memory eternal!*

Just as the funeral ends, the electric lights in the church and in that entire quarter of Paris fail.

NOVEMBER 2, 1949. PARIS. It is a cold but sunny day. Crowds stand along the street as Mr. Gurdjieff's coffin, still topped by flowers, is carried out and put into the large black funeral carriage. His family rides with him. Private cars and four large buses carry his students. The streets around the church are closed to traffic for blocks. At Avon Cemetery at Fontainebleau, in an icy wind, hundreds walk through the cemetery gates to the family plot. Mr. Gurdjieff's grave lies between his mother's and his wife's, each of whose tombstones, with time, have bent towards one another, forming a stone triangle with the earth. At sunset the coffin, a golden cross at its head, is slowly lowered into the ground. The long pale coffin in place now, a great sigh involuntarily issues from the people—the only sound they have made. The priest now begins to chant as, one by one, in accordance with the old Russian custom, people begin to pass by the grave of their Teacher, kneeling, making the sign of the cross, throwing a handful of earth on the coffin, and passing on. Thrown with a handful of dark earth are a few red and white roses....

Lord John Pentland says that when Mr. Gurdjieff died the feeling was that "it was impossible to go on. Because up till a few days before he died, he was seeing everybody and appearing at meals...and refusing to allow various feelings to start [that he was going to die]. Fortunately, there were people who understood enough to help us all once he did die. Of course there were very few people....Fortunately, somebody was able to show the way to go on without at once trying to manifest everything that they understood. In other words, to go on learning from each other, and in a way not too obvious."

That evening, following Mr. Gurdjieff's burial, Madame de Salzmann speaks with her French students and a few English people.

"When a Teacher like Mr. Gurdjieff goes, he cannot be replaced. Those who remain cannot create the same conditions. We have only one hope: to make something together. What no one of us could do, perhaps a group can. Let us make this our chief aim in the future."

Bennett, having witnessed the friction between Mr. Gurdjieff's close pupils and marveling at Madame de Salzmann's optimism, says: "I was bound to agree that in unity lay our only hope."[47]

Says Mr. Gurdjieff's secretary, Solita Solano:

"Madame de Salzmann will carry on his work as best she can, and I suppose we will all help her."

"We have so pledged...."

47. Later, a group of eight of Gurdjieff's students was formed to carry on Gurdjieff's work. Among them were Madame de Salzmann, Lord John Pentland, Henri Tracol, and John Bennett. Within a year Bennett said "I believed that unity was all-important...but I was also quite sure that unity does not mean uniformity." By the summer of 1954 Bennett left the group. He felt in particular that *All and Everything* "was being treated as a disreputable elderly relative, best kept in the background. This alienated me from those who did not share my feelings." Of his own actions, he said, "I could make real sacrifices for the sake of unity and then destroy all the goodwill I had gained by following a course of action I had agreed to forswear." See *Witness*, pp. 284, 306.

Declares Frank Pinder:

> Gurdjieff came to strike a big Doh, to help the upflow of the Law of Seven against the current of mechanical life....Gurdjieff came to give us a New World, a new idea of God, of the purpose of life, of sex, of war. But who are "Us"? "Us" are those who accept him and his teaching and help to carry out this work. This world of ours cannot be saved in our measure of time. Had it been possible it would have been "saved" long ago by prophets and teachers who have been sent. Those who look for the world to be saved by a single teacher in a given time are shirking their own responsibility. They wait in hope of a "second coming" with no effort on their part—indulging in the disease of tomorrow.

By the end of 1949, Mr. Gurdjieff's *All and Everything* and Uspenskii's *In Search of the Miraculous* simultaneously appear in print. Mr. Gurdjieff's Prieuré becomes a convalescent home for physical invalids. Uspenskii's Lyne Place becomes a sanatorium for mental invalids.

So ends the extraordinary struggle of—how do we see it?—a teacher and his pupils, a magician and his adepts, an avatar and his disciples, a Messenger from Above and his would-be helper-instructors.

GURDJIEFF,
USPENSKII, ORAGE, & BENNETT

USPENSKII, ORAGE, AND BENNETT WERE NOT ORDINARY MEN, NOT ORDINARY SEEKERS. EACH WAS BLESSED WITH A RARE AND STRONG intellect, a deep occult understanding, great will, and an enduring thirst for self-knowledge. Each could hold and direct the attention of a great many people, many quite powerful in ordinary life. Each in his own right, was a magician. Though none could take that final step beyond themselves, each took many steps, passed many tests, made many sacrifices. Each *developed*—in Gurdjieff's sense of the term. Yet none to a point where he could totally sacrifice himself to Gurdjieff's mission. Uspenskii could not sacrifice his independence of mind; nor Orage, his feelings; nor Bennett, his thirst for adventure, his ability to create.

Despite their time and training with Gurdjieff, none of the three seemed to really understand the idea, monumental in its implications, that Gurdjieff had brought an ancient teaching, reformulated for our time, which was as he himself said "completely self-supporting and independent of other lines and completely unknown up to the present time"—a teaching, he said that could save the world from destroying itself. Like all seekers, understandably, what they searched for was a teaching for themselves, not for mankind. In this way only were these men ordinary. What Gurdjieff searched for was a man or men, who would help to step-down the teaching. Gurdjieff's aim in founding the Institute for the Harmonious Development of Man, as he states quite clearly in *All and Everything,* was to prepare helper-instructors who would help him disseminate and establish the teaching in the major capitals of the world. His Institute, which he once described as a "hatching place for eggs," had a very short life. Within twenty-three months of its purchase, Gurdjieff closed its doors. What precipitated this was his near-fatal car crash. But well before, he likely realized that no 'eggs' would hatch—that none of his pupils could make the necessary transformation in so short a time. Despite Gurdjieff's awesome powers, the immensity of his will and understanding, and the quality of his students—their egoism, the deep identification with themselves, was too hardened. The car crash was the shock he needed to admit the hard truth to himself—in terms of his mission, the Institute was a dead end.

Looking back, it seems that what Gurdjieff had to do was what he never could do: convince Uspenskii, Orage, and Bennett of the full authenticity of his message and his authenticity as its messenger.[1]

It was not difficult back then to miss the mark...to miss the amazing fact and grace that a teaching so practical and powerful, and a man as unique as Gurdjieff, could appear at all.

So it was then, so it is now.

Of the three pupils, Uspenskii seems the oldest soul. Certainly, of the three, he was the first to meet Gurdjieff—and the depth of his understanding appears much deeper then either Orage's or Bennett's, both of whom had been Uspenskii's pupils. If Gurdjieff's *idée fixe* was the purpose of man's existence on earth, Uspenskii's was time in its fullest dimension.

Early on, Uspenskii had felt the gnawing emptiness of death. In his bones he realized that life was about dying. Growing up, he saw through the sham of ordinary life, its deceits and absurdities. He knew that all the carrots life offered were only dream carrots. He was the black sheep that could not be tempted with being a lion or eagle—or even a man. He had left the herd long before he met Gurdjieff, searching for a way to break out of life's magic circle. He realized that to break out took time and that each

1. It is not surprising, for how many—even these many years later—would agree that Gurdjieff brought an ancient teaching that would save the world from destroying itself and that he, yes, this *kaphir,* was a Messenger from Above? If true, such an understanding could be likened to having a *revelation.* Uspenskii, Orage, and Bennett may have had such a revelation but their actions show they could not sustain it. There were many, of course, who did have the revelation, most notably Dr. Stjoernval, Thomas and Olga de Hartmann, Jeanne de Salzmann, and Louise March. But Stjoernval, the de Hartmanns, and March were not equipped for the role Gurdjieff needed to be played and Madame de Salzmann would come into maturity only in his life's final phase.

human being had only so much time. "I formulated my own aim quite clearly several years ago," he told Gurdjieff, "I want to know the future." He had come to the conclusion, he said, that "the future can be known." And, further, that a man "has the right to know the day and hour of his death...for what is the good of beginning any kind of work when one doesn't know whether one will have time to finish it or not."

Uspenskii's great and singular achievement was his objective reporting of the ancient teaching Gurdjieff brought. His ability to absorb and so cleanly communicate the teaching shines with intelligence and integrity. The pity was, knowing the teaching, he could not fully live it. Two factors stood in his way. One was what he called his "extreme individualism." This, Uspenskii himself admitted, was the fundamental feature of his attitude toward life. The other was the emotional scarring caused by the death of his father when Uspenskii was not yet four years old, followed the next year by the death of his grandfather. "I didn't play with toys as a child," he said. "From an early age I knew what life was about."

It wasn't until he was twelve or thirteen years old, he says, speaking of his wonderment upon reading a book on levers, that "For the first time in my life, my world emerges from chaos." However, death continued to dog his footsteps. At sixteen his mother died and at twenty-nine his sister. That he fathered no children of his own seems significant. Protecting him against feeling the grief of these losses was the isolation, the alienation that must have been the background of his "extreme individualism." These two factors—individualism and death—entwined within him like two snakes, the one feeding the other.

"Wraps Up The Thought." That was Gurdjieff's early nickname for Uspenskii. (Nicknames, Gurdjieff said, often point towards a pupil's chief feature or chief fault.) What Gurdjieff saw was that when Uspenskii was asked a question, he would answer so completely that nothing would be left of the question. In effect, he demolished it. Answering in this way not only demonstrated, one could say showed off, his great intellectual capacity, but also pointed to a need to control; a word he used quite often. What Uspenskii was likely controlling was his emotional center. Later, Gurdjieff said that some people's chief feature was so buried beneath its formal manifestations that it was incapable of discovery. "Then," wrote Uspenskii, "a man can consider *himself* as his chief feature just as I could call my chief feature 'Uspenskii,' or, as Gurdjieff always called it, 'Pyotr Demianovich.'"[2]

One wonders, in this regard, if Uspenskii actually felt Gurdjieff's presence. Virtually everyone, friend or foe, who encountered Gurdjieff remarked on the rare quality of *hanbledzoin* he emanated. As detailed as Uspenskii's account of his first meeting with Gurdjieff is, he does not speak of it. Nor does he mention it later. Unlikely though it seems, could it be that *Pyotr Demianovich* was so armored and so identified with knowledge that he did not experience it? Why did he never mention it? How was it he could withstand Gurdjieff's many direct attacks to break through his chief feature and to set him right? Did Uspenskii register it but in some way discount it? These can only remain questions.

We do know that his *Pyotr Demianovich* began to weaken as a result of Uspenskii's work on himself and the telepathic experiences Gurdjieff induced in him in Finland. As a result, he began to feel his community more with other people. Uspenskii did not see, however, that—because of his insincerity[3] with Gurdjieff—his rapport with his teacher was also weakened. Within a year-and-a-half of first meeting Gurdjieff, Uspenskii was already distancing himself psychologically. Though he would relive his days with Gurdjieff until the end of his life, the fact is he remained blind to the real significance of the events in Finland, thus giving testimony to the incredible power of buffers, regardless of the quality of the pupil.

The seed of premature separation which Uspenskii planted in himself in Finland grew and festered, until in Essentuki he began to divide Gurdjieff from the teaching. Once sufficiently divided, Uspenskii, of course, was in a position (another of his favorite words) to judge Gurdjieff, who, he convinced himself, was a "tainted channel." This was not surprising. Next to "time," the subject of "good and evil" seemed to be Uspenskii's major interest, likely stemming from his feelings about having his loved ones taken away from him. "Good and evil" was one of the chief contexts

2. A possible deduction might be that Gurdjieff could *not* discover Uspenskii's chief feature. It was too hidden. Which would mean that Gurdjieff, at root, didn't understand Uspenskii. This would account perhaps for Gurdjieff's failure, or inability, to change roles, or at least refrain from playing a role with Uspenskii to a point of no return. More likely, Gurdjieff understood that for Uspenskii to be of any real use to him, he had to work directly on Uspenskii's emotional center. Though the odds against a breakthrough were great, Gurdjieff's mission and the urgency of the time meant that he had no time to coddle Uspenskii. It was *all or nothing.* Moreover, if the personality, that is, *Pyotr Demianovich,* was the chief feature it meant that it was thick enough to resist any penetration, any discovery. In psychological terms the "armor" of personality was the chief feature—that which was always protecting, controlling, interpreting. *Pyotr Demianovich* did weaken, become penetrable. Uspenskii did achieve a new level of being with Gurdjieff but then *Pyotr Demianovich* reappeared. It wasn't until his chief feature played its last card and Uspenskii faced death that he finally came to the clarity and will to make the super-effort necessary to free himself.

3. Speaking of his telepathic experience, Uspenskii wrote: "I knew that he [Gurdjieff] would not believe me and that he would laugh at me if I showed him this other thing. But for myself it was indubitable and what happened later showed that I was right." *Search,* p. 263. What happened later is most likely his break with Gurdjieff in Essentuki. In that case, "this other thing" would relate to why he broke with him, i.e., "Gurdjieff was leading us in fact towards the way of religion." *Search,* p. 375.

through which he saw life. It was the subtle interpretation coloring all his impressions. For Uspenskii to have kept the good end of the stick for himself, transferring the bad end to Gurdjieff (whose seemingly erratic behavior, it may be said, gave ample room for doing so) was in the cards from the start. From what Uspenskii reports, Gurdjieff invited, even fostered, such negative attitudes, intentionally creating division in his pupils. It was up to his pupils to see and work with it. A powerful and dangerous way to teach, but time, Gurdjieff knew, was short.

In breaking with Gurdjieff, Uspenskii made his premature understanding of the teaching the basis of a new line. "I took over the leadership to save the System," Uspenskii said. There is no reason to doubt that this is what he believed. But to save it from what? To save it from Gurdjieff! From the very first, Gurdjieff's 'play' had upset Uspenskii, made him wary. Gurdjieff's 'play' was like that of no holy man, no teacher or guru known to Uspenskii. That Gurdjieff seemed to go out of his way to create negative and false impressions, that he cultivated people's worst fears about himself, Uspenskii could not fathom. It was the doubt—that Gurdjieff was irrational—that would continue to grow in Uspenskii. In Essentuki, Gurdjieff's stern and seemingly pitiless handling of Uspenskii's friend Zacharov, together with Uspenskii's concern over where he believed Gurdjieff was leading them, ultimately led Uspenskii to admit: "I gradually began to see that there were many things I could not understand and that I had to go." Uspenskii does not mention what he termed the "St. Petersburg Conditions"[4] with which Gurdjieff worked on his emotional center. Opening this center would do what Uspenskii most feared—plunge him into the feelings of death and chaos he once felt as a child. This was the 'wound' he carried, his burden, and, it was dressed in irrationality. Ironically, he used his power of rationality to protect his irrationality.

Though he was quite successful in establishing his version of the teaching in England, and later America, Uspenskii's divorce from Gurdjieff would dog him for the rest of his life. It was a wound upon a wound. When asked in a meeting "if the line [of teacher to student; the passage, or octave, of the teaching] was broken when you left Gurdjieff?" Uspenskii answered huffily: "What has all this to do with Gurdjieff and me? I was working with Gurdjieff until I saw a difference in him. This has nothing to do with esotericism." But, of course, it does. It was a lie that this very honest man had to live with.

If he refused to suffer emotionally with Gurdjieff, one German bombing of London was all it took to convince Uspenskii to sail for America. The reasons he left England are rational enough, but the fact is Uspenskii did what Gurdjieff never did: *he left his pupils*. Gurdjieff brought his pupils

4. See pp. 25 and 91.

through a raging civil war, took responsibility for them in Constantinople, Berlin, at the Prieuré, and stayed on in Paris during the Nazi occupation.

At Franklin Farms in Mendham, the estate-farm in New Jersey that his followers had provided for him, Uspenskii gave his lectures as always, but grew increasingly reclusive. He began to see, in part, what had happened. "I took it [the leadership of the Work] over," he admitted, "before I had gained enough control over myself. I was not ready. I have lost control over myself. It is a long time since I could control my state of mind." And later: "The System has become a profession with me."

Not only did the teaching, or "the System" as Uspenskii called it, become a profession for him, but his interpretation of it became—and still is to this day—the most widespread and influential representation of it. Gurdjieff is spoken about, of course, but it is largely the "Gurdjieff" and the "teaching" as Uspenskii saw them. Not only do his books dwarf Gurdjieff's in terms of readership, but many more people study them than they do Gurdjieff's *All and Everything.* They thereby base their practice entirely upon Uspenskii's version of the teaching, which is comprised of his understanding of Gurdjieff's Russian and early French periods (1915–1924) and his later interpolations. In terms of students, whereas Uspenskii was teaching upwards of a thousand people at Lyne Place, perhaps not more than a hundred or so passed through the Prieuré before it was disbanded in 1924. Afterwards, Gurdjieff worked only with small groups of people. It was not until 1948 that people came to him in any numbers.

So what has largely been taught is Uspenskii's version of the Work, a version which stresses intellect, work with negative emotions, pessimism, 'good' and 'evil,' perfectionism and, most of all, psychology. When once asked if he had altered the teaching much, Uspenskii said he had not altered it at all [as he understood it]. "But I prefer," he said, "to start with the psychological side." It might be recalled that during their first meeting Gurdjieff reminds Uspenskii that "in his work, which was chiefly psychological in character, *chemistry* played a big part." Uspenskii spoke at length about psychology in his *New Model of the Universe.* He took a dim view of psychoanalysis, as did Gurdjieff. But many people do not carefully distinguish between it and what Uspenskii means by psychology as he explains it in *Psychology of Man's Possible Evolution.* Uspenskii's emphasis on psychology from Gurdjieff's Russian period has come to dominate many of the forms of the teaching and has led perhaps to some of these being unduly psychologized.

In his *First Series* Gurdjieff speaks of psychoanalysis as being a maleficent means of distorting the psyche, calling it as one of the "pseudo teachings." This is especially true of New Age psychologists who fold the teaching into their professional practice and who even, with little to no Work experience, start their own groups. In any case, such has been

Uspenskii's imprint on the Work that it might be said that the full development of the teaching as given by Gurdjieff has yet to be fully appreciated and practiced. The sense of the sacred, of community, in particular, often seems to be missing.

Plagued with depression and kidney problems, and against the advice of his wife and doctors, Uspenskii left America after the war to return to England. Though nearly sixty-nine years old, he hoped to make a new start with the pupils who had stayed behind. So in his lectures upon his return, time and again, he turned questions back on the questioners, trying to break them free of their doctrinal reliance on the teaching. He had taken the teaching, that is, his version or understanding of the teaching, as far as he could and had reached a dead end. He needed to begin anew. For his pupils, he saw, that was not possible. In one of his last public meetings, he was asked: "Can we learn to be more humble?" Uspenskii answered: "I never was humble myself, and I don't know how I can." But, in fact, he was becoming humble through the means by which, unfortunately, most of us become humble—*humiliation.* His life, his search, had come to nothing. Yet he had the self-sincerity, no small thing, to admit this to himself. And so, at the last minute, his bags already aboard a ship that would return him to America, he ordered them to be unloaded. "I am not going to America this time," he said.

What did he mean—*this time*? It must mean that he remembered...remembered having gone to America before in his previous life in the great wheel of eternal recurrence. It was now, having reached the nadir of his life, that he began his valiant climb to the zenith and his ultimate triumph of stepping through time, of dying a conscious death. His last days, his great struggle with his body and emotions, and his breakthrough, are all recorded by his pupil and spiritual friend, Rodney Collin. So, at the very end, Uspenskii was able to return to where he began, to find the miraculous, to penetrate "beyond the thin film of false reality." In his thirst for the truth, his self-sacrifice, his faults, confusion, and rebellion, we can all perhaps see aspects of ourselves and know, too, through the testament of his life, that there is always the grace of redemption, no matter how far we stray, if we are open to it.

It is not recorded what idiot Gurdjieff ascribed to Uspenskii, but one that must be considered is 'enlightened' idiot. Nor did Alexander de Salzmann paint Uspenskii's animal on the wall of the Study House of the Prieuré. Had he done so, the animal would have been highly intelligent, visionary, mystical, stubborn, fiercely independent to a fault. Perhaps a 'white,' or even a 'black' swan.

Orage was altogether a different type of animal. De Salzmann painted him as an elephant. But Orage was also part fox—clever, possessed of breadth of intellect, charm, and benevolence. He wanted to be loved and so he was. He was the classic 'white knight,' a 'St. George' in a tweed jacket.

Of Uspenskii, Orage, and Bennett, the dynamic of relationship with Gurdjieff was deepest with Orage. Orage, could as only Alexander de Salzmann and Fritz Peters could, make Gurdjieff laugh. It is no small thing that upon hearing of Orage's death, Gurdjieff, wiping the tears from his eyes with his fists, declared: "How you say it in your country? May his soul reach the Kingdom of Heaven! This man...my brother."

With an impartial self-honesty—not often found in Uspenskii or Bennett—Orage, brother of Gurdjieff, pinpointed the problem. He said he lacked (like Uspenskii and Bennett) the *absolute* faith. The difference was—and this is considerable—Orage recognized it. He did not foist his problem off on his teacher. As Orage wrote to a friend:

> I cannot go more than half a hog, let us say. I can regret it and wish that I had been different; but the fact remains that I cannot "sell all"—and everybody—to follow G. in person. His method I continue to regard as the Word of God; I practice it to the best of my powers. His system I regard also as probably the very latest word of truth; but, as I cannot verify it myself, and have lost hope that I ever shall be able; and as, furthermore, I cannot merely believe and, still less, try to persuade others of just my beliefs—I see no probability of my resumption of G. groups or teaching for the rest of my life.

It is significant that the figure of Orage, the 'compassionate idiot,' dominates Gurdjieff's *Third Series.*[5] Orage, in a sense, symbolizes the teacher-student problem even more than Uspenskii and Bennett. He was closer to Gurdjieff than either of the others and so, perhaps, well knew Gurdjieff's human side and his weaknesses. Orage's remark to Gurdjieff, for example, about the harmonium being a "sacred relic" was a pulling of the Messenger from Above's tail. Both Uspenskii and Bennett wanted to set up their own teaching. Orage simply wanted to remain a 'human being.' He was blind to the reason why he could not have his Jesse and his Gurdjieff, too.[6]

Gurdjieff tried to warn him but Orage was not listening. How deaf he had become is shown in the scene between Gurdjieff, Orage, and C. S. Nott in which Gurdjieff speaks to the two men about his auto accident.[7]

5. It is said that in the original version Gurdjieff was much harder on Orage.

6. Gurdjieff's great generosity and compassion are seen in the *Third Series* where, along with the skewering of Orage and the reason for his failure, Gurdjieff revealed a great deal about himself and his own failures. Of the four books Gurdjieff wrote, it is the author's opinion, contrary to present opinion, that it is his greatest testament and that the text is *complete*, not incomplete, but it is for us to complete it.

Gurdjieff told them that he habitually picked an apple from a tree when driving from Paris to Fontainebleau. To do this, he drove with only one hand. On this particular day, he said, the wheel of his car must have bumped into something for afterward he could remember nothing. He was found with his head lying on a car cushion.

Having told this story, Gurdjieff continued, "You know, Orage," addressing him directly. Then he related to Orage how a man reacts when you do something for him. A man's attitude, he declared, would go from "kneeling and kissing your hand" to "suing you for not giving him enough." Gurdjieff ended by again repeating, "You know, Orage…we must pay for everything." After Gurdjieff leaves, Orage comments: "He was probably getting at us for not knowing how to give…."[8]

To understand the true import of what has transpired we must know the issue between Orage and Gurdjieff. Like all students, Orage wanted knowledge but he had fallen in love with Jesse Dwight, a strong willed woman who seemed to have had little sense of or feeling for the Work, much less Gurdjieff's mission. She saw everything in the ordinary, formatory way. She posed a great danger, therefore, to both Orage and Gurdjieff. In this sense, it could be said that the 'apple' represented Jesse Dwight. Orage, given his many episodes with women over the years, thought, if with regard to this subject he was thinking at all, that he could have his 'native'[9] and Gurdjieff, too. He did not take this woman and the force she unconsciously represented seriously. Just as in Gurdjieff's story when his vehicle hit an unexpected bump when he was not in full control of the car, Gurdjieff was warning Orage that his body would receive so great a shock from her that he would lose control over himself, i.e., lose his head. The result would be that Orage will remember nothing of his intention to awaken and the mission Gurdjieff has given him. Orage would self-calm himself from the spiritual catastrophe he has brought upon himself by resting his head on a cushion; that is, no longer thinking but enjoying creature comforts. It might be worthwhile, too, to consider the apple as the symbol representing knowledge in the Garden of Eden. (And for this, the serpent must be included as well.)

Gurdjieff had given Orage a great deal and demanded the same in return. But with the giving, Orage's attitude changed. His self-love convinced him that he deserved and had assimilated what he had been given, and so he had no qualms about asking for more. As for Orage's

7. See p. 121.

8. The importance of this, not only for Orage but for every seeker, is indicated by Gurdjieff having repeated it as a saying of popular wisdom in the prologue to his *Life is real only then when "I am,"* p. 56.

9. A 'native' is a person totally identified with materialism.

remark that he and Nott don't know "how to give" (interesting how Orage includes Nott in this when Gurdjieff was clearly speaking to him), the real issue was not giving but that Orage was taking without paying. In effect, he was spiritually stealing. That he might have been "paying" in other ways was of no import. Only the teacher, the giver, can say how what he gives must be paid for.

Bennett's animal, had de Salzmann painted it, would likely have been a chameleon, or perhaps an elephant, "lord of the beasts," as Bennett himself said. Certainly, of the three men, Bennett was the most elusive. With time, the lives of Uspenskii and Orage took definite shape and proceeded along established lines, but Bennett's seemed to carom erratically from cushion to cushion, like a cue ball stroked with too much English. Where Uspenskii was focused on finding "the new or forgotten road," the teaching that would release him from the circle of eternal recurrence...where the aim for Orage was becoming an elder brother of the human race—for Bennett the two constants throughout his life were the fifth dimension and making his own "contribution" to the teaching. Of the three Bennett left behind the largest body of writing. Certainly in terms of sheer volume he published more books on the teaching, and his version of it, than Gurdjieff, Uspenskii, and Orage combined. His books *Gurdjieff: Making a New World, Gurdjieff: A Very Great Enigma,* and *Talks on Beelzebub's Tales* offer many important insights into Gurdjieff, his mission and his teaching. Others, such as *The Dramatic Universe,* give Bennett's own interpretation and interpolation of the teaching. He introduced his work with the enneagram and systematics to the corporate business world, where these once esoteric concepts are now being applied to organization, design, and manufacturing.

Gurdjieff recognized Bennett's capabilities, his brilliance, but thought his students, and therefore Bennett as well, "lunatics", that is, having unreliable values. Bennett appeared quite candid about his shortcomings. For example, he confessed he had the "particularly irritating habit of telling lies, either from the desire to please people or from the impulse to avoid awkward situations." "I was well aware that I had no stable attitude," he wrote. "I had often compared myself to a chameleon that takes the colour of every background." He admitted: "My exasperating habit of agreeing upon a course of action and then doing something quite different is tolerable only for those who can value a little gold even when mixed with much dross. I could make real sacrifices for the sake of unity and then destroy all the good-will I had gained by following a course of action I had agreed to forswear." That, intellectually at least, Bennett saw a great deal about himself cannot be doubted. But did his admissions ever really reach his essence? Did he ever come to realize his own powerlessness, nothingness, in the face of his weaknesses? Or, did he buffer himself by admitting his weaknesses, but not suffering them?

One prevalent weakness he does not admit is his need to be in control This may stem from his problematic relationship with his father. Whereas Uspenskii's and Orage's fathers died early in their lives—each son becoming at that time the 'man of the family'—Bennett was an adult when his father died. However, Bennett gives the impression in his memoir *Witness* that his father was absent from the home. He characterized his father as being "incurably optimistic...constantly making plans for new journeys and new undertakings to make us all rich." Bennett's mother,[10] coming from a puritanical New England family, likely held her husband in contempt for, as Bennett framed it, his father had an "inability to behave properly either in sexual or in financial matters." In effect, although for different reasons, Bennett became, like Uspenskii and Orage, his household's surrogate father. The archetypal role of the father in the family is that of a king, and all three men were 'kings' before they were adults. They became accustomed to being adored and having their own way.

Kings do not lightly become princes. This is aptly demonstrated when the twenty-seven-year-old Bennett first came to the Prieuré in August 1923, and Gurdjieff gave him what he called his "great experience." Gurdjieff infused Bennett with his *hanbledzoin*—"I was filled with the influx of an immense power," said Bennett. Gurdjieff told him: "There are some people in the world, but they are very rare, who are connected to a great reservoir or accumulator of this energy...those who have this quality belong to a special part of the highest caste of humanity...what you have received today is a taste of what is possible for you." Gurdjieff then asked Bennett to stay on at the Prieuré. But Bennett was wary. His life was a long string of 'great experiences.' It was Bennett's blessing and curse. Always in motion, he feasted on experience. A 'young king,' he was wary of coming under another man's will and direction.

Looking for a way to decline Gurdjieff's invitation, Bennett asked Gurdjieff—"If I should stay with you, how much time would be needed?" He said he expected Gurdjieff would tell him twenty years. Instead Gurdjieff answered—"If you will devote all your energies to the task, it may take two years before you can work alone." *You can work alone.* Gurdjieff saw Bennett's chief feature and spoke to it.

To no other pupil is it recorded that Gurdjieff ever gave such a promise. Whether Gurdjieff was serious is another matter. Speaking even more explicit, Gurdjieff said he would take Bennett with him to America to act as his interpreter. Bennett insisted he must leave, he had debts to

10. Their relationship must have been problematic in that he only makes a brief mention of her in his memoir and admits, p. 326, of "the need to hide from myself my deep fear of women."

pay off. Gurdjieff, under heavy financial burdens and cash-strapped himself, said he would pay all Bennett's bills. (From Bennett's description, one gets the sense that Gurdjieff was almost pleading with Bennett to stay on.) But Bennett was having none of it. In *Witness,* Bennett obscures the real reason for his leaving by saying that "It was much rather as if Gurdjieff himself had withdrawn from me, and would not let me follow him."

It would be twenty-five years before Bennett would reunite with Gurdjieff. Though Bennett was now fifty-one years old, Gurdjieff found Bennett immature and ignorant.[11] Even so, Gurdjieff realized his possibilities and, according to Bennett, on several occasions likened their relationship to that between Judas and Jesus. "Mr. Bennett," says Gurdjieff, "is like Judas; he is responsible for that my work is not destroyed...." Bennett's critics, given the eclectic teaching he later put together, wonder if he strayed into the more ordinary meaning of the word.

Of all the ideas Bennett put forward, two in particular need to be noted. One was the idea that Gurdjieff sent students away for their own development, thus taking the onus from those who left Gurdjieff. This idea along with its companion idea of 'graduating'[12] from the Work, has created much confusion. Gurdjieff was preparing "helper-instructors" who would be instrumental in enlarging the Work and who could take part, as he expressed it, "in God's government." Certainly, some people were sent away. But this was because they were either unsuitable, or could be of no further use, or needed to withdraw from the world for a time. Both of Bennett's ideas—being sent away and graduating—appear self-serving. Both support his own leaving of Gurdjieff, his disobeying of Uspenskii, and, later establishing his own 'line' of teaching.

Throughout his life Bennett, a creative, mercurial, and willful man, always posed problems for other people. For Uspenskii, Bennett became a problem as early as the spring of 1928 when he was jailed in Athens. Upon Bennett's return to London later that year, Uspenskii vowed never to speak with him. So Bennett, always the consummate political chess player, formed his own group. Slyly he made what is called in chess a "forking" move; that is, a move that attacks in two directions simultaneously. He sent Uspenskii transcripts of his meetings, implying that if Uspenskii disapproved of what he read, then, as Bennett said, "I would

11. Perhaps what he was really pointing to was that Bennett was a young soul, much younger than Uspenskii or Orage. As Uspenskii once told Bennett: "You are like Madame [Uspenskii]. Both of you have young souls. You have not the experience of living many times on this earth."

12. In no place does Gurdjieff mention graduating, but he does speak of initiation. "A change of being," he says, "cannot be brought about by any rites....There is not nor can there be, any outward initiation. In reality only self-initiation, self-presentation exist." *Search,* pp. 314–15.

stop." As Bennett had been a pupil of Uspenskii less than five years at best, it was indeed presumptuous of him to start, unauthorized, his own group. At the very least it revealed a lack of valuation. Moreover, exactly what he meant by saying "I would stop," Bennett left, quite characteristically, ambiguous. Would he stop speaking about whatever Uspenskii objected to? Or did he mean he would disband his group? In any event, Bennett would have forced Uspenskii to do what Uspenskii had decided not to do—to make a move, that is, to break his vow and communicate with him. No matter what Uspenskii's response, whether he moved or didn't move, communicated or remained silent, Bennett 'won.' For if Uspenskii made no reply (and he didn't reply) Bennett could then interpret this lack of response favorably—as Uspenskii's tacit approval of his activities.

However, only two years later in 1930 Uspenskii, seeking to expand his Work and needing able helpers, made his peace with the 'devil.' He invited Bennett to join him. Towards the end of the decade Uspenskii, concluding that Bennett was too erratic to be trusted, moved him outside his inner circle. All my life I had acted willfully," said Bennett of himself, "with little regard for the opinion of others, but I never trusted myself...my way of acting had always been exasperation to my best friends because of this constant vacillation between self-will and self-effacement."

In January 1941, with Uspenskii leaving for America, Bennett asked him about the reason for his own lack of progress in the Work, wondering if it was because of a lack of a certain method or technique.

Uspenskii told him straight away: "It has nothing to do with methods. Your trouble is that you always make false starts. All your work consists of false starts."

Bennett then shifted the conversation to the subject of group work; that is, Bennett's own groups. Again, Uspenskii was quite direct.

"I can only consider the work [groups] at Lyne. The rest, so far as I am concerned, is dissolved."

The clear implication is that Uspenskii was telling Bennett to dissolve his groups.

Bennett, however, did not follow up on this, but again shifted to another subject. "Have you any objection to my trying to write out the System as far as I can remember?" he asked, making it sound—"trying to write out the System"—as if this would be an outline for his own purposes, and not the four volume study he planned to write.

Uspenskii told him: "In my opinion, writing is not useful."

Bennett makes no mention of how he views what Uspenskii said concerning his "false starts," but a characteristic of Bennett's, if not his chief one, is his willfulness. Even nine years after his conversation with Uspenskii, Bennett is still in its grip, for as his wife, Elizabeth Bennett, says: "So certain that he knew how to work, so blind to the opportunities in front of him, so humorless, *so determined that force*—physical, mental, and moral—would bring him to the gates of heaven! In that month of August 1949 he was obsessed with himself and his own subjective states, to the point of *distorting Gurdjieff's instructions* so that they would fit his own preconceived picture of what was needed to bring about liberation." [Author's italics]

Following Uspenskii's embarkation for America, Bennett began writing his book—contrary to Uspenskii's instructions—drafting one chapter every week. Hearing of this, Uspenskii sent a message to Bennett telling him no one was permitted to write anything about the System without his permission. Bennett neatly sidestepped this by evolving his own philosophy, or teaching, centering it on will, hazard, and the triads. Later, in 1945, Bennett gave public lectures. This caused Uspenskii to break completely with Bennett. Uspenskii demanded Bennett return all his materials and instructed his pupils to have nothing to do with him. Bennett was also charged with being "a charlatan and a thief."

After Gurdjieff's death, Bennett crusaded for the Work, but his ideas and actions met with resistance from Madame de Salzmann in France and Lord Pentland in America. Stymied, he turned to Subud. Having a number of experiences with Subud which he felt opened his heart, he travelled the world proselytizing in its behalf. By 1962, seeing the limitations of Subud, he came under the influence of Idries Shah who professed that he, Shah, was a messenger from the "Guardians of the Tradition." Eventually, Bennett became a believer. In 1965, after much pressure from Shah, he offered Shah his own home and meeting place, Coombe Springs (at that time valued at $300,000). Shah accepted but insisted that "his hands be perfectly free." He told Bennett "the gift must be absolute, irrevocable and completely voluntary." As soon as Shah took possession of Coombe Springs, he made Bennett feel unwelcome and banned all Bennett's students. Shortly thereafter Shah had Coombe Springs bulldozed and sold off for development.[13]

Shah's demolition was a tremendous public humiliation. It shocked Bennett, as he said, into "the idea of self-effacement and withdrawal." For his seventieth birthday in 1967 his friends collected a large sum of money as a gift. Said Bennett: "In a very boorish and unkind way, I refused everything...and said I did not even want a birthday party. This uncivil behavior was attributable to my inner turmoil."

Six years passed. An inner voice—one Bennett said had always spoken to him in moments of crisis told him—"You are to found a school." He said there "then entered my awareness the significance of the 'Fourth Way.'

13. J. G. Bennett, *Witness*, pp. 359–62.

There was a task for me to do and I had to prepare people who could help me in it. The school to be founded was a school of the Fourth Way."[14] And so on October 15, 1971, envisioning a coming crisis for humanity,[15] Bennett opened his own school in England, the International Academy for Continuous Education. Student residency was limited to ten months. Thus, Bennett proposed to do in less than a year what Gurdjieff himself had failed to do at the Prieuré in two years—prepare a core of helper-instructors. His experiment in accelerated development was called by his critics the "Bennettron." Bennett introduced his students to an eclectic sampling of exercises and ideas taken from many different ways. They studied Gurdjieff's books, as well, heard lectures by Bennett that ranged far and wide over esoterica, practiced the movements and *zikr,* fasted, staged theatricals, and did community service. Thus, the Fourth Way—which Gurdjieff had said "is completely self-supporting and independent of all other lines and completely unknown up to the present time"—was mixed with others. From this emerged the Bennett version.

Of Bennett's critics, it is perhaps biologist and author Robert de Ropp who offered the most balanced insight into the complexity of the man.

> The man was a Warrior of the first order, but ambitious. That was his problem. There were two men in Bennett. The first was a very sincere Seeker After Truth, who would spare no expense, no trouble, to learn more about the great game [transformation]. That aspect of Bennett I admired. But there was a second aspect. I called it the Arch-Vainglorious Greek. It was a Gurdjieffian term and referred to Alexander of Macedon, the strutting hero who had spread havoc all the way from Greece to India and then expressed regret that there

14. Here Bennett assumes the role of the Teacher by putting himself, unconsciously or not, on a level with Gurdjieff and his mission. A Fourth Way school emanating directly from Gurdjieff already existed. What was the need for another? Gurdjieff had told Bennett to take the Fourth Way teaching into the world. Instead, Bennett took a teaching of his own formulation into the world and called it the Fourth Way. Had he been able to resist such an impulse, or 'voice,' he would not have contributed to the present day confusion of Fourth Way tongues. It is because of this that Bennett's most militant critics charge him with being a Judas who betrayed Gurdjieff and his mission.

15. It is interesting to consider Uspenskii, Orage, and Bennett in terms of their perception of the future. Uspenskii, given his theory of eternal recurrence, is looking backward in time. Orage gives little indication of what he thinks but seems to believe that Social Credit, a barter system, would help the world. Of the three men, Bennett is the most future-oriented. His insights and assessments are mostly on target and his recognition of what was needed following Gurdjieff's death seems now, in hindsight, to be largely true. Many of his ideas could have been helpful. But he was not as developed as he thought he was and could not subsume himself for long to any group effort which he did not lead. He was a slave to his own brilliance. He left perhaps three hundred or so students who had taken his ten month course, some of whom are still connected with communities that he envisioned would act as "arks" in what he saw as the certain collapse of society; a collapse he believed would come about in the 1980s.

> were no more worlds to conquer....The Seeker After Truth was basically humble and sincere, content with little, modest and retiring. But the Greek was ambitious, full of great schemes, always liable to overextend himself, to attempt too much.

De Ropp, a student of Uspenskii's since 1936, had also started a center to teach the Work. Some of his pupils left to study with Bennett. Upon their return, de Ropp says he "had expected well-trained, obedient, ready-for-service disciples." Instead he received "rebellious, starry-eyed, self-opinionated 'adepts.'...They were, as they put it, 'Messengers of the Higher Powers.'"

However one looks at Bennett, the feeling is that one has no sure footing. What can be said is that Bennett mixed the teaching. Naively 'democratic' in his thinking, Bennett never seemed to understand or value the Work's need to be the hermetic. Others, however, might argue that he only did what Gurdjieff asked him to do and, further, that the rapidly increasing "terror of the situation" confronting humankind demanded all gates be opened. For all the dross, Bennett does have his gold. Many of his ideas are thought-provoking, potent, and visionary.

More important: In terms of the line of the teaching, the octave of the Work, its force, as it had been with Uspenskii, was again halved with Bennett. Today there is still talk of the "Bennett Work," as if it were a teaching in its own right and Bennett were on the same level as Gurdjieff, or, for that matter, Uspenskii and Orage. With the passage of the current generation of Uspenskii's and Bennett's students, these versions of Gurdjieff's teaching are likely to play themselves out. Should they then be reintegrated with the original teaching, the teaching that Gurdjieff paid so dearly to bring to those of mankind for whom it was prepared might regain its original force and play the role in the world for which it was destined.

Of course Gurdjieff more than anyone understood how in *heropass* all things, particularly a teaching as potent as the Fourth Way, are subject to deflection, distortion, and finally deviation. That is why he labored so to bequeath to the world *All and Everything.* Of the significance of Gurdjieff's *legominism,* one can fully agree with Professor Denis Saurat's vision in the 1930s:

> Nothing much may happen in our time. We are in too much of a hurry. We have no sense of real time in the West. Perhaps in fifty, or a hundred years a group of key men will read it. They will say, "This is what we've been looking for," and on an understanding of it may start a movement which could raise the level of civilization.

GURDJIEFF & FRITZ PETERS

MUCH HAS BEEN WRITTEN OF GURDJIEFF'S RELATIONSHIP WITH HIS CHIEF PUPILS, BUT HIS RELATIONSHIP WITH FRITZ PETERS IS RARELY, IF ever, mentioned. And yet, it is unique. Only eleven years old when he first met Gurdjieff in 1924, just a month before Gurdjieff's car crash, Fritz Peters was quickly drawn into the life of the Prieuré. In the months following the accident, the young boy acted as Gurdjieff's "chair-carrier" following him everywhere, watching out for his safety. Later, "Freets," as Gurdjieff called him, was enlisted as Gurdjieff's personal servant, delivering messages, doing errands, cleaning his room. And soon every Tuesday morning the young Fritz—who, when Gurdjieff first asked what he wanted most to know, had answered: "I want to know everything"—was receiving private lessons from Gurdjieff.

At such a young and impressionable age to be taken under the wing of a master like Gurdjieff is a blessing as great as it is unique. But it can be a kind of 'curse,' as well, if not taken rightly. One learns only by consciously living one's errors and Peters' later life shows how harrowing a journey that can be. Leaving the Prieuré in October 1929, Fritz Peters, then fifteen years old, was immediately thrown into a turbulent adult world where he found himself totally alone, blamed and victimized, fighting for his very survival. Developed and shaped by his Prieuré training, Fritz Peters walked his life's path, always the outsider, the rebel, the malcontent. He would become a member of the Chicago and New York groups, but, though the teaching and Gurdjieff were in his blood, he never found his place in the Work. His days with Gurdjieff at the Prieuré were over. Neither the Chicago nor New York groups were serious enough for him. Too much reverence for Gurdjieff. Too many members he saw as "phony." His experience at the Prieuré was undeniably special, but as Gurdjieff warned—"Every stick has two ends" But Peters never saw the other end of the Prieuré stick. Though keenly observant and detesting any sign of falseness, he didn't see that he had allowed it to make him too special, too separate. He became, as it was expressed one day in 1945 at 6 rue des Colonels Rénard—"a colossal egotist."

That thirty-two-year-old Fritz Peters standing amidst a group of wartime French pupils in Gurdjieff's apartment that autumn day could for even a moment have believed it when seventy-three-year-old Gurdjieff pointed to him as his successor....Well, to the assembled pupils, who regularly had to pass Nazi checkpoints to get to meetings at Gurdjieff's apartment, it was yet another vivid proof of Peters' overweening self-love.

That Gurdjieff's act had evoked, as well, a trace of will-to-power and envy in those who had *not* grown up at the Prieuré, or enjoyed as intimate a relationship with Gurdjieff, was perhaps neither recognized nor appreciated. And certainly the later life of Fritz Peters, filled as it was with seizures of anger, jealousy, rejection, vengeance, nervous breakdowns[1] and alcoholism, would do nothing to mitigate the sweeping indictment of him on that autumn day in postwar Paris. It would forever brand Peters as a nullity, a fool, no one to take seriously. The one group of people then that might have understood Fritz Peters all but disowned him. Though he was to later write *Boyhood with Gurdjieff* and *Gurdjieff Remembered,* two books that are without rival in portraying the heart and soul of Gurdjieff in the last period of his life, Fritz Peters remained, and remains, maligned and marginalized, his relationship with Gurdjieff never seriously considered.

Meeting such a monumental father-figure so early in life, it took nearly a lifetime for Peters to digest it. For years Peters struggled with Gurdjieff's identity and his relationship to Gurdjieff and to the teaching. In his last book, *Balanced Man,* Peters recounts how as late as 1960, forty-six years

1. Throughout his life, Peters would have a number of nervous breakdowns. He once told Margaret Anderson that "I had enjoyed my last crisis of 'madness'—it gave me great pleasure, really." It was so serious that she thought he might never have another. "I think his collapses are unconscious, half-conscious and conscious," she said. "And one can see this time that, though he broke with, and cursed, everyone except William Segal [a well-regarded member of the New York Foundation], he was quite conscious of wanting to keep them as friends."

after he first met Gurdjieff, he says "I was still laboring under the impression that I was *special*—the *real* son of a Messiah. In an emotional sense, I was Gurdjieff's son. I loved him more than anyone I had ever known. But times change...I no longer feel like anyone's 'son.'" As Gurdjieff foresaw, he would not lead a happy life. He had a broken marriage, alcoholism, homosexuality, and relationships that inevitably turned contentious.

Troublemaker. That's how Fritz Peters was commonly seen. And not simply a troublemaker but "a born troublemaker," according to Gurdjieff. Like Rachmilevitch, a lawyer and member of the St. Petersburg group and later a Prieuré resident, Peters had the inborn knack of setting people's teeth on edge, bringing up the animal in them. Although Gurdjieff said that we should thank anyone who gives us the opportunity to see ourselves. . .to see a little "I" or two in us, yes—but to see the "animal-I?" Who wants that? Uspenskii didn't want it. Nor Orage. Certainly not Bennett.

The similarity between the young boy and Rachmilevitch was seen at once by Gurdjieff. "You remember, how I tell you that you make trouble?" Gurdjieff said. "This true, but you only child. Rachmilevitch grown man and not mischievous, like you, but have such personality that he constantly cause friction whatever he do, wherever he live. He not make serious trouble, but he make friction on surface of life, all the time. He cannot help this—he too old to change now. . . .I know no one person like him, no person who just by existence, without conscious effort, produce friction in all people around him." Like the caring father that Peters never had—his father having deserted the family when he was only eighteen months of age—Gurdjieff was using the figure of Rachmilevitch to show Peters what he would become if he continued to act as he did. All children are naturally mischievous at times, but if Fritz allowed this characteristic, this "I," to grow and become fixed in personality, if he did not work to control it, in adulthood it would control him.

To be a "troublemaker" is, in itself, nothing bad, Gurdjieff told him. Troublemakers, in fact, play an important role in life. "What you not understand," Gurdjieff said, "is that not everyone can be troublemaker, like you. This important in life—is ingredient, like yeast for making bread. Without trouble, conflict, life become dead. People live in status quo, live only by habit, automatically, and without conscience. . . ."

Gurdjieff confided that he, too, was a "troublemaker." The difference between them is that he plays the role consciously, molding it to circumstances; creating conditions and friction in the service of awakening people to what keeps them asleep. This stepping on toes is a "Divine principle"[2] when consciously directed, when not born of the mechanical reaction to make others suffer; make them pay for trespasses, injustices, psychic

2. G. I. Gurdjieff, *All and Everything, Third Series.*

wounds. To be able to call up a role in oneself and play it, that is one thing; to be controlled by it, quite another.

Of trespasses, injustices and psychic wounds, Fritz Peters' life would be filled to the brim. After his father divorced his mother, Lois, she married an Englishman, a Chicago lawyer, who was far from fatherly. His early life was marred by physical calamities—"disasters" he called them and rightly so. His older brother Tom, for example, stuck a crochet hook in his right eye, which permanently blinded Fritz in that eye. His grandmother put him in the bathtub and then went to answer the telephone. He turned on the hot water and could not turn it off. As his grandmother was deaf,[3] it wasn't until his screams were heard by a neighbor that he, now "partly parboiled," was rescued.

When he was nine years old, Fritz's mother was hospitalized with a nervous breakdown that lasted about a year. It was then that his mother's sister Margaret Anderson and her companion Jane Heap took on the responsibility of caring for Fritz[4] and his older brother Tom. That was in 1923. In June of 1924 Fritz and his brother were brought by Anderson and Heap to the Prieuré. Upon meeting Gurdjieff the eleven-year-old is asked, among other things, what he wants to know.

"I want to know everything," Fritz replied.

"You cannot know everything," Gurdjieff told him. "Everything about what?"

"Everything about man. In English I think it is called psychology or maybe philosophy."

Gurdjieff sighed and after a short silence answered: "You can stay. But your answer makes life difficult for me. I am the only one who teaches what you ask. You make more work for me."

This exchange, like so many others, gives an indication of Peters' quality of mind and mental maturity.

3. He doesn't explain how if she was deaf she heard the phone. Perhaps it was only one ear, the one she held to the receiver.

4. His given name is Arthur D. Peters. He did not know this until as an adult he wanted to learn his exact birth date and time. Writing to the county seat where he was born, they had no record of a "Fritz Peters." He then tried to recall his earliest memory. "I thought and thought and finally remembered when I was a fat little kid crawling up into my chair and banging the table with my spoon, yelling, 'I want my breakfast!' and Jane Heap coming into the room and saying, 'You sound just like a Prussian general, let's call you 'Fritz.' Later I found out that my real name was 'Arthur,' but who wants to be called 'Art.'" Given the strong animus personality of Jane Heap, the naming seems a projection and also a means of belittling, cutting the boy's power. Given the emotional deprivation he was subject to, it was not physical food for which Fritz yearned. For children whose mothers are bonded to them, it is not an issue.

In October of that year Fritz and his brother left the Prieuré to return to New York. There, the boys' mother, their real father and Jane Heap became involved in an emotional struggle for their allegiance. Fritz and his brother were shunted back and forth so much that Fritz began "to feel even more alone than I had before—like a piece of unwanted luggage for which storage space was needed."

It seems Jane won and, as Margaret had stayed on in Europe with her new friend, the actress and singer Georgette Leblanc, the primary care for the boys devolved to her. Of his relationship with Jane, Fritz said that it was "highly volatile and explosive. There was, at times, a great deal of emotion, of love, between us, but the very emotionality of the relationship frightened me. More and more I tended to shut out everything that was outside of myself. People, for me, were something I had to exist with, had to bear. As much as possible, I lived alone, day-dreaming in my own world, longing for a time when I could escape from the complex, and often totally incomprehensible, world around me. I wanted to grow up and be alone—away from all of them." With characteristic insight and frankness, he says of these early years: "Obstinate and independent because of my feeling of aloneness, I was usually in trouble, frequently punished." He said that Jane once went so far as to hit him with a board with nails in it because he refused to do as he was told. Even so, Jane eventually came to the idea that she and Margaret[5] should adopt the boys. And so they did. "I am not at all sure that I understand why Margaret and Jane took on this responsibility. It was a strange form of 'planned parenthood' for two women neither of whom, it seemed to me, would have wished for children of their own, and a mixed blessing from any point of view."[6]

Fritz and his brother returned to the Prieuré in the spring of 1925. When Gurdjieff saw him he put his hand on the boy's head, and Fritz "looked up at his fierce mustaches, the broad, open smile underneath the shining, bald head. Like some large, warm animal, he pulled me to his side, squeezing me affectionately with his arm and hand, and saying… 'So…you come back?'" In the middle of that summer, reminding Fritz of his desire "to know everything," Gurdjieff began giving him private lessons. Every Tuesday morning

5. Jane and Margaret had been together as a couple since 1916. When Margaret met Georgette Leblanc, formerly the mistress of Maeterlinck, she became entranced and the two women went off to Europe together in a relationship that would last until Georgette's death in 1941. It might be that the idea of adoption was Jane's way of getting Margaret back.

6. Fritz and Margaret's relationship, both inordinately strongwilled and hot-tempered, was an emotional roller coaster with long periods of silence, some lasting years, followed by tearful reconciliations and then outbursts such as when Fritz once called Margaret "a bitch of a mother." Of their separations Margaret once said "It is like losing one of my most cherished and interesting friends."

at 10 o'clock sharp Peters was to go the second floor of the château, the "Ritz," as it was called, and report to Gurdjieff's room.

The lessons and all of his ensuing experiences at the Prieuré with its adult population are well-documented in Peters' book *Boyhood With Gurdjieff.* The unusual maturity, clarity, and will of Peters is demonstrated many times in the book but one incident in particular is striking. Gurdjieff was having the lawns of the Prieuré resown and had all the pupils out on the lawns. But Gurdjieff had them working so close together that planting new seed was a useless activity since it immediately got trampled underfoot. Days passed. No one said a thing. Finally Rachmilevitch, thick with rage, confronted Gurdjieff. He told him the work was insane and stalked off. It was the first time Gurdjieff had ever been publicly defied.

An hour passed and Rachmilevitch did not return. Peters was sent to find him and bring him back. Peters protested, saying he didn't know where he had gone. Trust your instincts, Gurdjieff told him. It was then that Peters demonstrated, though he didn't know it, a lesson Gurdjieff had been teaching him. Not knowing where Rachmilevitch had gone, he put himself in the Russian's place, experiencing empathy with him. A hunch came as to where he might be and Peters "set off towards the woods beyond the main, formal gardens." He said, "It seemed to me that he could only have gone to one of the distant vegetable gardens—a walk of at least a mile, and I headed for the furthest one, at the very end of the property." There, he found the sixty-year-old sitting up in an apple tree.

He wouldn't go back to the château, Rachmilevitch insisted. What to do? How could Fritz Peters argue with a man who was not only five times his age, but a lawyer[7] as well? So he did the only thing possible and he did it with all his will. Said Peters: "I did not know of any arguments—I could not think of any good reasons—with which to persuade him to come back, so I said that I would wait there as long as he did; that I could not return without him." Finally, after a long silence, Rachmilevitch dropped out of the apple tree and returned to the château with him.

What did Gurdjieff see in Fritz Peters? Why did he take him so intimately into his life? Why did he give him personal lessons? He spoke about this in part in 1931 when he told Peters: "When you come Prieuré first time *you not yet spoiled, have not learn to lie to self.* Already even then you can maybe lie to mother or father, but not to self. So you fortunate. But these people [Jean Toomer's Chicago group who Peters thinks are

7. It is interesting how much of Peters' life is involved with lawyers. His stepfather, with whom he later will contend, is a lawyer. He later works in his law office as a clerk and as an adult will be employed as a paralegal. When he answers the questions posed in the last issue of Margaret Anderson and Jane Heap's *Little Review,* he will write that what he fears most is that "I might have to lead the business man's life."

phonies] very unfortunate. Like you, when child, they learn lie to parents, but as they grow up also learn lie to self and once learn this is very difficult to change. Lying, like all other things, become habit for them." [Author's italics] It is this quality of self-honesty suffusing Peters' writing that makes his books so immediate and vivid. His evocation of his experiences with Gurdjieff at the Prieuré and later as an adult, along with his portraits of Gurdjieff through the years (1924–1945), are without parallel.[8]

The extraordinary significance of Gurdjieff's work with him at the Prieuré is revealed when Gurdjieff tells Peters that others "must make effort, go to meetings, read book. *If you never go to meeting, never read book, you still cannot forget what I put inside you when you child.* These others, if not go to meeting, will forget even existence of Mr. Gurdjieff. But not you. *I already in your blood—make your life miserable forever*—but such misery can be good thing for your soul, so even when miserable you must thank your God for suffering I give you." [Author's italics]

Five or so years later Peters complains to Gurdjieff about the New York group, saying he disagreed with the reverence Gurdjieff was given and felt uncomfortable and so did not attend meetings. Gurdjieff tells him. "You remember I tell you that *what I teach is in your blood; that you cannot forget, no matter how you try*? What you tell me is proof of just this teaching. Group work is important, when people work together they can help each other, can make work easier; but since you have not right feeling with group you now make, unconsciously, difficulties and suffering for yourself. Just because of what I teach you in past you now make extra struggles for yourself. This can be good for your future, but also very difficult. *You poisoned for life.*" [Author's italics]

As an adult Peters' most telling experience with Gurdjieff came in the late summer of 1945. Peters, having had several near-death experiences in the Army, in a dangerous state of nervous exhaustion, sought Gurdjieff out in his Paris apartment. When Gurdjieff saw him he cried out—"My son!" Later, slumped in a chair in the kitchen, Gurdjieff filled him full of "a violent, electric blue light," his *hanbledzoin*, to recharge Peters' energy and atmosphere. Afterward the two sat and drank coffee. It was then that Gurdjieff spoke to Peters of being his father. "I play many roles in life," Gurdjieff told him "...this part of my destiny. You think of me as teacher, but in reality, *I also your father...father in many ways you not understand.*" [Author's italics]

They continued talking, joking and laughing together. This is significant. Only two pupils had been able to joke with Gurdjieff. Both were extremely close. One is Orage of whom, when he died, Gurdjieff said, "This man...my brother." The other was Alexander de Salzmann, one of

8. The only other books that approximate Peters' are Thomas and Olga de Hartmann's *Our Life with Mr. Gurdjieff* and Margaret Anderson's *The Unknowable Gurdjieff.*

Gurdjieff's oldest pupils. "Among the devout there were a few who fenced with him verbally," said Peters, "but, in the long run, they seemed to be the ones who were the most 'possessed' or 'convinced'; daring to joke with him [Gurdjieff] became proof of a certain intimacy with him—a privilege accorded to them because of their total agreement with his ideas—and in no sense an indication of rebellion."

The author saw Peters only twice. On both occasions it was in a remodeled basement in a Manhattan townhouse a block from the Foundation known as the Gallery. A probationary group of some twelve people met there under Lord Pentland's direction. Lord Pentland had said that at this particular meeting we would discuss sex. To make it easier to speak, the group would be divided into two groups, one male, one female. Males would meet first. Someone special would speak with us he said. At the meeting I had no idea who the man was sitting up front next to Lord Pentland. He looked rather preppy in glasses, a bow tie, and striped shirt with a tweed sports coat, khaki slacks and brown loafers. The line of our questions—all about sex—seemed to surprise him. I don't think Lord Pentland had told him of the topic. He seemed uncomfortable, smoking one cigarette after another. I felt embarrassed, sorry for him. But as the questioning continued, my respect grew. He was answering as honestly as he could. Often when he had no answer he said so, without excuse. Only later did I learn that the man was Fritz Peters.

A few weeks afterward we held a small bazaar in the Gallery, selling handmade Christmas items. During my shift as a salesperson, I noticed Fritz enter the basement. He looked much the same as he had, still wearing a bow tie, sports jacket, slacks. It was like a uniform, a disguise of sorts, I felt. Almost immediately he was pounced upon—I use that word because energetically that's what it felt like—by Anthony, an Italian from Massachusetts whose father, or was it his brother?, was in the Mafia. Anthony, aggressive, intense, and perhaps gay, made a show of displaying the crafts, bullying Fritz to buy one. Suddenly, Fritz flushed, broke away and stalked out. Ten minutes later he returned, gripping an ugly-looking snub-nosed black revolver. He was in Anthony's face in a second, sticking the revolver into his chest and shouting—"Here, shoot yourself!" Then he put the revolver in Anthony's hand, turned, and stormed out. The revolver turned out to be a toy. Although I had yet to read his books or hear anything about him, I sensed that much of Fritz's life was like that—*tormented.*

I had always assumed from those experiences and the stories I heard that Fritz Peters had never developed, was certainly not conscious in any real degree. How could anyone who lived the life he lived have come to anything? I enjoyed his books on Gurdjieff and that was about it. Then, in writing this book, I read and reread his books and saw that among the portraits and scenes there was a lot of valuable information, even teaching. It's interesting when you come upon an unconscious assumption. Suddenly you see what it's been blocking out. I began to take seriously what Gurdjieff said to him about being in his blood, being poisoned for life—and about being his son. Peters' life seemed fated to be disharmonious.[9]

In seeing these things, I realized I had assumed that someone who developed in the Work, say to the fifth level, would lead a conscious and therefore harmonious life. On reflection, that's obviously not true. One's life depends on one's fate. So one could live a tormented life without it being indicative of their level of development. I saw that I had never separated a person's outer life from their inner life. I had unconsciously judged one by the other. That let Fritz Peters live for me again. I saw I didn't know who he was. Then everything I had read, like the turn of a kaleidoscope, instantaneously took on a new shape. Just as it could be said that Orage was Gurdjieff's brother, Bennett his Judas, and Lord Pentland his St. Paul (all of which Gurdjieff said outright), Fritz Peters was Gurdjieff's son.[10]

Now a number of insights flashed. What did Peters have to work through in life? "A colossal ego"—inordinate self-love. And who had the identical chief fault? Wasn't it Beelzebub, hero of Gurdjieff's *First Series*? This very Beelzebub, a being with an "extraordinarily resourceful intelligence" who had "an exceptionally strong, fiery, and splendid youth" but whose "unformed Reason due to his youth" led him to make trouble about something which he found "illogical" in the government of the World and consequently, along with the rest of his tribe,[11] was sent into exile...couldn't this in miniature be the life of Fritz Peters? From start to finish he had lived[12] the life of an outsider, a maverick, a rebel, "a lone wolf," as he called himself and, definitely, like his 'father' before him, that of a born troublemaker. That said, his intelligence, will, honesty, and capacity to suffer stand without question.

After that day in 1945 at 6 rue des Colonels Rénard when Gurdjieff pointed him out as his successor, Peters says that in reflecting on what happened he "was forced to admit to myself that I had, at least momentarily, felt chosen.[13] That, in fact, I still did. I was pleased with my behav-

9. One can isolate oneself from the general laws which govern collective fate. Living in essence, not personality one can escape accident and have the fate that belongs to his type. See *Search,* pp. 161, 164.

10. Blood sons of powerful fathers usually have difficult lives and perhaps it is no different with the spiritual.

11. The sins of the father...

12. To the *Little Review* question "What is your world view?", Peters answered "I am not reasonable and I am not in a reasonable scheme."

ior at that moment—I had learned enough from him to be cagey about it when I had been accused by the lady—but the feeling of triumph was not unadulterated, and I was besieged by questions and doubts." He then begins to objectify his doubts, make a list of them, and to recapitulate his work with Gurdjieff; as he says, "to think back over my entire experience with this man." He sees that "It is at least possible that he [Gurdjieff] was actually referring to me as his 'successor.' It was possible on many counts: a) it was actually true; b) it was intended to 'expose' my ego to myself; c) it was intended to produce various reactions in the other persons present; and d) it was a huge joke on the devout followers." He sees, too, that "I did not honestly know in what his 'work' consisted. How then [given he was the successor] could I carry it on?" Assuming that he could "carry on" Gurdjieff's Work, he reasons that "...if there was some way in which I could 'cull,' as it were, what had seemed valuable to me from what had seemed, if not valueless, at least 'incomprehensible,' *I would like to be able to pass it on in some way.*" [Author's italics]

And that Fritz Peters certainly does in *Boyhood With Gurdjieff* and *Gurdjieff Remembered,* both of which give a unique sense of Gurdjieff and his relationship with the young man and adult he knew as 'Freets.' Without doubt Fritz Peters fulfilled the task he set himself. That was his gift to his 'father,' to himself and to us. From the life of Fritz Peters and his relationship with Gurdjieff we can all learn a good deal. He deserves a re-evaluation, a serious one.

13. In 1951 Fritz Peters published his autobiographical novel, *Finistère,* meaning "the end of the earth." With it he cut the ground away beneath himself, for in it he spoke candidly of his homosexual affair with an older man. It was a fragile time for the Work as Gurdjieff had only been gone two years, so if Peters had any thought of leading the Work in some way, of being the conventional successor to Gurdjieff, *Finistère* surely ended it. One wonders if his subsequent collapses were not in part, or in full, caused by his having bared a truth he found difficult to integrate.

THE TEACHER-STUDENT EXPERIENCE

OF ALL HUMAN RELATIONSHIPS, THAT BETWEEN TEACHER AND STUDENT OFFERS THE GREATEST REWARD, FOR IT ALONE IS FOUNDED IN THE impersonal. However various the paths of spiritual transformation, the form and substance of the teacher-student relationship is archetypal. In its essence—no matter its time—it is forever the same. Truly formed, the relationship develops, evoking by turns remembering, observing, discovery, joy. But also engendered is a collision of worlds—a collision of the objective with the subjective, the time-free with the time-bound, the real with the unreal. As such, friction, confusion, clash, rebellion must result. For no matter its shape or surface appearance, the relationship between teacher and student is born in and of a primordial struggle.

The stronger the student, the stronger this struggle. This is seen most vividly in the relationship G. I. Gurdjieff had with Uspenskii and Orage. Both students were blessed with a great depth of intellect and will and, better, a great thirst for knowledge,[1] truth. Powerful in ordinary life, confident of their abilities, neither was easy to impress or to lead. They demanded a great deal of Gurdjieff. And he of them.

Awakening through the grace of vision, born usually of deep disappointment with ordinary life and himself,[2] the student is magnetized to seek. Influences, conscious in origin, enter his life. A book, a poem, an image, an impression, a person—some representation that transcends the personal, the ordinary, speaks to him. There is a flash of awakening. He responds, resonates, the world suddenly appears greater, more mysterious. Jubilant, inspired, he identifies, imagines himself a spiritual being, and seeks a teacher.[3] His expectations are as great as his 'spiritual' dream of himself, his capabilities. He doesn't see that aligned against his permanent awakening are massive mechanical forces, both personal and collective, societal and natural, all of which contrive to keep him 'in place.' Nor does he see that only a very small part of him, his essence, wishes to awaken; his personality has no desire to awaken. And so it obfuscates, lies, and defends.

In meeting his teacher, he experiences "roses, roses." He absorbs directly a conscious influence, perhaps a dynamic stillness, a wholeness and clarity, an unimagined scale and sweep of perception. Invited to join a group working to awaken, he, in the role now of the student, learns the rudiments of self-observation, of self-remembering. He has lived, so he believes, in a subject-object world, but the truth of his observations show him *his world has been all object and no subject.* That is, he sees objects, what and who is around him, but never in his perceptions includes himself, the subject. And so his perception is 'one-dimensional.' (He may think about himself, his actions later—but this is memory, not the raw vividness of immediate perception/impression.) Now, dividing his attention between himself and the object—not directing it all on the object—he includes himself in his perception. If his attention becomes absorbed in either the subject or the object he, of course, reverts again into one-dimensional perception.

1. Today, it is often energy, rather than knowledge. Energy is attractive perhaps because of the energy-draining pressures of the technologized world and the pervasive use of drugs and stimulants. Energy, the student believes, is the magic elixir—energy will solve all problems. Instead of submitting to the suffering and remorse that self-seeing must bring, instead of working with his lower centers, he thinks he can finesse the process by adopting techniques for refining energy, such as breathing exercises. As he increases vibration without correspondingly increasing discernment and understanding, he unknowingly projects his ignorance and delusion on the higher levels of energy, thus creating imagination in higher emotional center (where, once imprinted, it is difficult to erase). Hence, the prevalent contemporary fascination with a variety of psychic phenomena: channeling, the "higher Self," talking with angels, and what not. All of this is part of the current spiritual materialism masking itself in New Age and Transpersonal rhetoric. For an astute analysis of the phenomenon see René Guénon's *The Reign of Quantity* (Penguin, 1972), particularly the chapters "Neo-Spiritualism" and "Confusion of Psychic and the Spiritual."

2. The use of the masculine here denotes force, not gender.

3. The awakening is only temporary and so those who try to teach themselves lose their possibility in the hubris of what they take to be their 'individuality.' Said Gurdjieff: "A man cannot awaken *by himself.*" *Search,* p. 143.

With his fellow students, he reports to his teacher what he can of his struggle to awaken. Directly, perhaps indirectly, the teacher points out the gaps in the student's perception, his unconscious and automatic identification with one-dimensional seeing—either all object, no subject; or all subject, no object. He does *not* observe himself. Reading that Gurdjieff said "man is asleep," he agreed—others are asleep. Now he sees that *he is asleep.* But likely, self-love and vanity being so ingrained in his perception, in the next breath the personality comforts him with the notion that now *he* is waking up. But he begins to see by *the evidence of his own observed experience* that what he has taken to be himself is simply whatever "I" is last to appear. He is not one permanent indivisible I—he is, in fact, many "I"s. The unity that he has taken himself to be is a false unity, a false self, ruled by the "I"-structure of personality. To become one, he must first become two. He does this by reperceiving himself. That is, by dividing his attention, breaking the hypnotic 'oneness,' and impartially observing his functioning, his states, his motives. By trying to remember himself in this way he will see the most important first fact of his wish to awaken—that *he does not remember himself.*

Galvanized now to remember to observe himself, he eagerly reports on what he observes. He begins to sense himself, if only momentarily. A long and fruitful period follows in which he has glimpses of his mechanicality, his self-absorption, his imaginings. Still, despite his intention to do so, though, whole days may pass without him once seeing himself. He may identify, become depressed. The teacher tells him not to work for results and reminds him of his wish to awaken. The teacher "holds the level," instructs and shocks, creates a magnetic contact that reconnects the student with his essence. Slowly, the student discerns the taste of self-remembering, gives it value, works to prolong it—and more important, sees, if only by reconstruction, the crossroads, the point at which he lost himself. He begins to understand with more than his intellectual center that when his attention is divided, redirected and recirculated, his center of gravity moves from head to body. Now, he is no longer simply an idea, a self-image asleep to itself in time and space, but, when remembering both subject and object, when in two-dimensional perception, he inhabits the body, is aware of its reactions, aware of his thoughts; and, aware, too, of what is around him. Maintaining this perception requires a special energy and so he cannot see in this way for more than a short time before he unconsciously identifies, becomes one "I" or another, or becomes entranced with the object. Eager to attain, he easily misses the interval of a deeper attention and so may mistake his sleep for awakening. What he is awakening to is identification and imagination, but he doesn't want to see this...see how asleep he really is. For to begin to see impartially is suffering, a suffering of a very special quality. Heretofore, his 'suffering' has only been the suffering of personality.

The student must repeatedly wake up in his sleep, not identify with its contents, emerge from his world of fantasy to the world of fact. For at this stage, as says Gurdjieff's Mullah Nassr Eddin, "there is everything in him except himself." By the evidence of his own observed experience the student will see that his actions and inactions are automatic, predetermined. There is nothing free about them at all. He is gripped by the ever-changing shadow hands of his own conditioning, the assemblage of "I"s that purport to be his real I, but are only poseurs. Continuing—making persistent efforts to observe himself in his various life-situations, moods, attitudes—he is certain to see a 'himself' and a 'world' he never imagined. Virtually all of it dung. Unable to remain impartial to these impressions, he will justify, blame, excuse, and finally fall into an inner well of self-pity and hopelessness. The teacher, pointing out his lack of impartiality and the resultant identification, will time and again release him from his vicious circle.

All the student's efforts have alerted the I-structure of personality to the recognition that to be undressed, to allow itself to be seen as it is, is to give up its power of illusion, its position of supremacy. And so, divided now between that which wants to see and that which does not, he must suffer. Trained well by the teacher, the student will recognize that such suffering is necessary. For in no other way can he be freed from his entanglements, his identifications. But as Gurdjieff says, "the last thing he [the student] will give up is his suffering." To intellectually recognize that his suffering is rooted in his "I"-hood doesn't lessen the flames.

Only the truth, his own suffered truth, can free him. But its price is high. For first, the truth kills. It kills the student's lies about himself, that which divides and isolates him, freezes him into his self-image. To put this self-image in question, he is handed the 'tools' of the teaching, its practice, its scale of perception, intuitions, ideas—all of which ultimately may lead him to Objective Reason and Conscience. He is asked to observe himself as he exists in actuality, adding nothing, deleting nothing. Such observing entails a self-inflicted suffering; that is, in the seeing of himself he suffers himself. This is work on oneself in the real sense. And this work must be voluntary, for if it is coerced, freedom is lost...and only freedom can engender freedom. Waking up to deeper and deeper levels of sleep in himself he may observe, for example, that on his best days, when he feels most himself, that is precisely when he is most apt to be asleep. But he is not likely to be keen enough to observe this, given the blindness of his self-love.

He has many ideas about himself and others, few grounded in actual experience. In a group with other students, contrary to his expectations, they may seem ordinary. Ordinary or not, they share with him the aspiration to awaken. If he will strive to work instead of reacting, he will come to understand that each student represents for him a reflection of what he himself is. His covert and overt complaints, accusations, tirades against others—all is fertile material. He must learn to live with his negativity, listen to the "I"s having their day in the court of the mind, sense the mounting pressure to run, hide or "get it off his chest"...and should he do so, lose the very energy he is working to balance. Or, at the right time, prepared and sensing himself, he may express himself with the intention of hearing himself as well as making himself understood.

At the Prieuré, Gurdjieff asked people to observe themselves by "opposing I to it." The "I" was the potential consciousness, the observing; the "it," the body. Observing, they were to try to see themselves as others saw them, that is, to see impartially. Only much later were they to criticize what was seen. First, the effort was simply to see (which, of course, is not so simple). Observing oneself—seeing the outer manifestations, the inner reactions—short circuits the habitual one-dimensional perception pattern and breaks the hypnotic identification pattern one has with oneself. It impedes the driving force of assumptions, the silent tide of dreams that propel and prop up one's life. Observing brings one out of the dream of life, allows a separation, a necessary distance, creating a true subject-object relationship. Previously, perception was all object or all subject: one-dimensional. By including himself in his perception, he became, as said earlier, an object for himself. As he knows others, he now has the potentiality to know himself. And he can know himself to a degree he has never known others, because he can observe both the outer manifestation and the inner reaction. And so, *for the first time,* he is in a position to know himself.

His work to see himself becoming more serious, the teacher may indicate the student's hidden motivations and agendas, his indulgences and avoidances, his deeper identifications and imagining. The fact is that his awareness—and the word is used in the most rudimentary sense—lacks duration and depth. And more: the student is likely to identify with himself as the observer; a special spiritual being. Unknowingly, then his egoism is transferred to a more subtle level. The teacher warns against making the observing into an observer, the making of a verb into a noun. Again and again, he leads the student to see that which he continually refuses to see: his mechanicality, heaviness, self-love, his capacity for self-deceit, for violence.

As the world of remembered attention, inclusive and choiceless, becomes a primary value, the student will realize that his attention, fixed as it habitually is in his head brain, must be redirected again and again into the instinctive center. This brings the body alive, makes it known to itself, creates space in the head brain. When the body comes alive, with the head free and clear, direct observation can take place. Only then, can impressions, outer and inner, be received. The student must be passive on the surface, active beneath. And, so poised and balanced, impressions are elaborated, "eaten," the content digested and eliminated, the essence extracted and absorbed, the vibration refined, all going to create and coat a more sensitive body of awareness. In this way, practiced over a long period, an inner separation, a "distance," not dissociation, may occur whereby one can observe the functioning of the identification without distorting or stopping it. The body's sensation becoming strong enough to form a backdrop for activity so that both are known simultaneously; the one in the other, the other in the one.

The student by definition, of course, is an egoist, albeit an unconscious egoist. In struggling with himself he may, after much observation momentarily see his nothingness—that in a true sense he cannot do. The impression of nullity he must register many times, for the personality always "backfills," quickly explains and obfuscates. By the evidence of his own self-observation, the student gathers material to attack not others but himself—the 'himself' that is his own self-image, conditioned personality. "Personality defends itself," Gurdjieff said. Now the student may encounter a personality he never knew he had. Where once self-observation attracted his interest, his attention, now it may repel him. He doesn't want to see anymore. He's had enough. This is a sign that he's close to the bone of himself—the so-called negative is in actuality a positive. However, the totality of his experience—his sensation, feeling, thought—litigates against this.

Once so eager to observe—now he coasts, pretends, excuses. A new 'search' may begin: the search for a reason to run. The teaching, the teacher, the other students—none are as perfect as imagined. Images, idealizations, clash with actuality. What is the aim, the value, of it all? And, yes, when is he going to graduate? Informed that it is not a matter of "graduating" but working to self-initiate himself into less subjective levels of consciousness, he may bolt. If he stays, the emotional heat doesn't dissipate but increases. He must endure the truth of his observations and report upon them. To see oneself as he actually is, and not as he imagines, engenders a great suffering; a suffering of a type and quality only known to those sincere enough to endure it. In this way sincerity is developed, tested, forged. Only after much work will the student develop the power of sincerity where the background as well as the foreground of his observation—the subject *and* object—is sensed and awared with any duration and depth. It is then that his perception may enlarge beyond the two-dimensional.

At the Prieuré Gurdjieff advised people to become "conscious egotists," to work for themselves, to thank everyone who supplied the material for work, i.e., was unpleasant or exasperating to be around, and to remember why they came. Working in such a way the student will come to the primary impression beyond that of not understanding anything—to the impression of actually being nothing, having no real I. Moment after self-remembered moment, observation poised at the cusp of this perception—this quality of nothingness will not be seen. For who wants to admit the hard fact that all of what we take to be real about ourselves is rooted in imagination, identification, I-images? The truth shall set us free, yes, but first it kills us—kills what is untrue. He who has, not as an impulse or wish but as a requirement, *taken the role* of the teacher[4] must mirror that impersonal truth.

As he moves along the octave of the teacher-student experience, he may become proprietary toward the teacher and teaching. His relationship with the teacher becomes something to guard, to defend. Other students, now projected as rivals, are scrutinized to determine how close they may be to the teacher. On the surface the student exhibits a postured calm while inwardly waging a bitter, relentless, invisible competition. (So, with regard to not expressing negative emotions, a great deal of material is activated for assimilation by the student.)

Seeing the student's preoccupations and desires, his deep identifications, the teacher may choose to "feed" them. He will let the student come close, perhaps let the student lead him. Or, as Gurdjieff did, the teacher may put into question or challenge the student's assumptions, "press on his corns." If the student never moves beyond the "roses, roses" stage, or otherwise escapes the stage of "thorns, thorns," then the teacher-student octave soon retrogresses and devolves into its opposite. Instead of rising toward a life of higher vibration, the student falls to a 'death' in a denser world.

In the pitch of intensified observation, extremes are likely to appear, 'blacks' and 'whites' each demanding resolution—a strong 'yes,' contends with an equally strong 'no.' In the foreground, the urge to do battles with the urge not to do; in the background, in the silent seeing and being, the triad of observation and remembrance transforms and coats. For only in the fire of emotion, of desire, of a 'yes' and a 'no,' can an inner separation occur, an inner space and distance in which intelligence might separate sensation from feeling, and so evoke, if momentarily, the triadic state of true self-remembering.

Round and round it all spirals, moving up and down, out and in...wherever the student's state, the teacher leads him, time and again, to those unexplored, subconscious areas of himself that the student alone must discern. Like a young stallion, the horse of himself is not easily ridden. It bucks and snorts, kicking up dust and a lot of dirt. Ten thousand

4. The teacher is always at risk, given the projections of his students, to slip into identification of himself as *the teacher.* He functions as such but must never identify as such. Otherwise he limits himself, his awareness, to the duality of subject-object.

times the rider will be sent sprawling. This is when the teacher must be a good spiritual friend. For the teacher has, in his own way, taken those very falls. He can speak to the student from his experience—*his own suffered truth, the anguish of essence.* There is a bonding then whose origin lies not in desire but empathy, truth. The rapport between them flows, the non-verbal becoming more audible. The teaching is moving beyond words.

Such spiritual friendship, as we see with Gurdjieff and Orage, wonderful as it is, has its dangers. For, drawing close to the teacher, the student can overstep himself, take liberties, personalize the relationship, think himself 'higher' than he actually is. We see this amply demonstrated when Fritz Peters visits Gurdjieff after the war. The octave of teacher-student is then in danger of deflecting. Mistaking the rapport with the teacher as a right rather than a gift, the student weakens the relationship. As it was with Orage, the appearance of the student's chief feature, or chief weakness, at this moment can drive a deep wedge between him and the teacher. It is for this reason, perhaps, that many ancient spiritual texts begin with a prayer and immediately speak about the moral qualifications of the student. For only a deep and ruthless self-sincerity can ride the horse of emotionality.

At some point in their relationship, the student may realize that despite all he may know, he doesn't know. And so he wants knowledge. The teacher points out the difference between intellectual knowledge and self-knowledge, and so points the student back to the toil of observing himself—impartially. The teacher speaks of self-sacrifice. Self-sacrifice is the last thing the student wants. But the teacher knows what the student does not: *there is no knowledge without sacrifice.* He knows that the student, even a student of the caliber of Uspenskii or Orage, is a half-developed world, asleep to his true self. No matter how great the thirst for spiritual transformation, the student protects with all his power everything which he stakes claim to with the name "I." For the student to develop, this deep identification with his "I" must be self-experienced, observed, explored, questioned. Direct impressions are what is sought, not analysis. He must come alive to himself, to his inner and outer world, through being present to himself, to his body-feelings-thoughts. Stepping out of the dream of "I," he is now in the immediate and can impartially receive-observe the registry of his senses. That for a long time this call to remembering and observing himself will neither be organic nor whole, that it will come through mental reminder only, be discreet, have little depth and even less duration is, in itself, a necessary exoteric stage of the esoteric process.

Working on himself, the student's identification with personality slowly weakens, becomes more porous. Thereby, his knowledge will grow commensurate with his power to absorb, assimilate, and connect that knowledge; that is, commensurate with his degree of being. With growth of self-knowledge and being, understanding deepens. He is growing. But the day will come when what he sees is so far beyond the familiar categories of mind that he will understand, as Uspenskii told Gurdjieff, that he understands *absolutely nothing.*

Declared Uspenskii: "Formerly I used to think that sometimes at any rate there were some things I understood but now I do not understand anything."

Answered Gurdjieff: "It means you have begun to understand. When you understood nothing you thought you understood everything or at any rate that you were able to understand everything. Now, when you have begun to understand, you think you do not understand."

This perhaps is one of the meanings of Gurdjieff's saying that we see the world "topsy-turvey." And it is a significant one, for he then told Uspenskii:

"This comes about [the thinking that he understands absolutely nothing] because the taste of understanding was quite unknown to you before. And now the *taste of understanding* seems to you to be a lack of understanding."

This new taste and its opposite, the old taste of 'head knowing,' is what the teacher will point out as he sifts the student's reports of his observations. But the old taste, like the old Adam, dies hard. One often has a strange bond to it, a kind of perverse 'loyalty.' There may be a sense, too, of 'taboo,' subtle inner warnings that he go no further, look no deeper. In fairytales the entrance to the cave of knowledge is always guarded by dragons—dragons of one's own subconscious design. To name them is to know them, but to name one must first have the power to discern. And dragons can be very subtle creatures. Like chimera, they present themselves in a variety of crafty guises not easily divined, the oft-depicted fire-breathing dragon usually being only an initial manifestation. So diverse are the dragons' poses, description is defied. What can be said is that the student tastes a sense of threat, of danger, of the terrible. And so he may halt, withhold, deflect. The relationship between teacher and student is bound by, and dependent upon, a covenant—the student is to tell the teacher *the whole truth.*[5] He must learn to speak from essence, not personality. In so doing he slowly learns a different taste, that of sincerity. To withhold from the teacher is to weaken the rapport that is being established between them. It was just that which happened with Uspenskii in Finland after Gurdjieff induced in him an intense telepathic experiencing.

5. Said Gurdjieff: "They [members of the group] must tell the *teacher* of the group the whole truth....People do not realize what a big place in their lives is occupied by lying or even if only by *the suppression of truth.* People are unable to be sincere either with themselves or with others." *Search,* p. 224.

Said Uspenskii: "I saw that Gurdjieff was right; that what I had considered to be firm and reliable in myself in reality did not exist." But having realized that he says: "But I had found something else. *I knew that he would not believe me and that he would laugh at me if I showed him this other thing.*" [Author's italics]

In this way Uspenskii began to separate himself from Gurdjieff, engendering what his subsequent actions indicate may have been a "wrong or incomplete crystallization." That is, crystallization occurs—but on a wrong foundation. Gurdjieff gives instances of this such as crystallizing on the foundation of "a fanatical belief in some or other idea, or on the 'fear of sin.'" The fanatical belief can be, of course, the belief in oneself. Uspenskii said his chief feature, or chief fault, is his "excessive individualism." Gurdjieff, however, gave him the nickname "Wraps Up The Thought." Like a spider, Uspenskii spun a web around any thought that entered his mind. He was difficult to get through to, since he was always wrapping up, modeling his own world. Ask a question and he spoke for half an hour, taking the question apart bit by bit, demolishing it with facts—completely oblivious to the person who posed the question or, as was the case with Gurdjieff, the level above his from which the question was asked. Uspenskii's formidable intellectual center was both his blessing and his work.

In his relationship with his teacher, the student will feel himself in a very vulnerable position. He has agreed, in a fashion, to become a student (though he doesn't know really what that means). However harmonious the relationship may appear on the surface, at deeper levels there is unrelenting struggle. Over the table there may be smiles and handshakes. But beneath the table there is the conscious demand of the teacher that the student see himself for what he is, and is not. Opposed to this is the student's need to hide his vulnerability, to not submit, keep his self-will, get the gold and run: survive as his "I." The teacher represents an ascending evolutionary octave; the student, still mixing the unreal with the real, the descending. If the process of evolution, of transformation, does not abort, if the student is able to blend, he will attain the middle. Otherwise, aborting, breaking the ascension, the octave descends, carrying the student even deeper into the imaginary world from which he had been extricating himself. At some point, the student may fear being swallowed up by the teacher, by the teaching. In unconscious reaction, he establishes requirements, boundaries. The teacher, the teaching, the other students are blamed while the student's lack of spine is now trumpeted as a triumph—rather than as the spiritual tragedy it is.

The task of the teacher is therefore to encourage and to challenge the student to investigate his belief system, his notion of "I"-hood; to see by the evidence of his own self-observed experience that he is not the individual he takes himself to be; to see that however strong his wish for self-knowledge and being, it is registered in only a part of him, a very small part. This part he is prone to personalize and aggrandize. For, if he rightly observes, he will see that he is forever telling himself, and all who will listen, the one great story which he is always updating, editing, expurgating, polishing, and forever repeating—*The Great Story of "I."*

The belief in this story, and the assemblage of "I"s that drive it is almost sacrosanct. The underpinnings of 'the story' are his unconscious assumptions—static, unchallenged, and self-fulfilling. Every person is mechanically living and fulfilling his own story's prophecy. Observing at a deeper level, one sees the animating force that comes from his conditioned sense and feeling of "I"-hood. It is like a dark hole into which everything is sucked. Whatever the impression, when one is asleep the raw energy of that impression is immediately interrupted, its content filtered through and interpreted from the viewpoint of the current "I" and whatever chain of "I"s the impression's energy and content may activate.

So a kind of 'transformation' is taking place but it's a tilling of soil that bears only sterile fruit. Every impression is reduced and filtered, then tagged and sorted according to previously established categories of memory. A harmony may be produced but since it is bereft of the vivifying quality that only refined impressions can give, the atmosphere is hollow, dank. Divorced from a direct reception of impressions, the student decorates his Plato's cave of shadows, mistaking the false for the real in the like-dislike world of his supposed individuality, which is simply a product of the consumerist-technologized-psychologized world in which he lives. All of life is filtered through and interpreted by this self-referential world of herd consensus of so-called societal reality. Since all impressions are immediately reduced to the student's world, to his level and type, nothing and no one can enter. Tell him that people are asleep and he might agree. Certainly others are asleep. Point out that there is not one level of knowledge and being but that these are relative to their place on a scale of vibration, and that experience, and therefore knowledge, is specific to the level of being on which it is received—this is simply beyond his comprehension, if he would be sincere enough to admit it.

For example, what knowledge Uspenskii did have was, as Gurdjieff told him, mixed with fabrication—so how could he discriminate fact from falsity? Therefore, Gurdjieff directs him "to put it all in the fire." In an act of rare spiritual courage, Uspenskii gave up his very considerable knowledge. The trauma of the sacrifice was so great that for two years, he said, he lost the power to write. Knowledge and power go together, so in sacrificing one, he sacrificed the other. How difficult that must have been for Uspenskii, a leading theosophist in Russia, a man who lectured before thousands. (If the reader thinks of what he does well, what he prides himself in, what gives him power and respect, what he would have to give up, he might have a taste of what Uspenskii felt.)

Of course there is not just one process but many going on in the relationship between teacher and student. Among the more primary is the reenactment of the relationship the student had or has with his parents. An old drama, formerly played out in sleep, is now recast. The teacher, the spiritual father,[6] is also the surrogate for the physical father and the student now has the opportunity to live the relationship consciously. So often his idea of relationship is to share his life with the teacher, rather than to share in the teacher's. As with his physical parent, the student seeks to know his 'father,' but the motivating factor may be to become his equal or better, rather than fully accept the role of the son. The student's wish for, or better, assumption of, an 'equal' position relative to the teacher is in fact a psychological strategy to prevent his seeing. All his observation and all the teacher's actions and inactions can thus be filtered, interpreted, and judged. Such was the case in Uspenskii's relationship with Gurdjieff when, having with others been given the keys to the teaching in Essentuki, Uspenskii suddenly elevated himself to a position where he believed he knew what his teacher was doing and thereby judged him. In fact, he was only judging himself.

Ideas, like people, age. What is today fresh and life-giving is tomorrow stale and death-dealing. The notion of 'equality' has become one of the sicknesses of our time. Like 'individualism,' 'equality' is one of the presiding, unquestioned self-evident assumptions of our time.[7] It is used to justify and promote deviation and degeneracy as legitimate, progressive. Such is the general inversion of traditional values and aspirations that all is confused, all allowable. The drive, infernal in origin, is to bastardize and animalize all of human life in the service of the basest and most deviate impulses, yet frame it as just the opposite. The flag-word of 'equality' waved, no true thinking can appear; critical faculties are severed. The power of such words lies in their very indefiniteness, their lack of precision. They are the magic-symbol tools by which the unthinking are herded, hammered, and shaped in the societal dream state. As Gurdjieff said of our time—"It is an empty and aborted interval."

In the world of transformation, all words must be experienced and understood as they apply in the scale of creation and to the processes and the laws which govern it. The desire to eliminate inequality on the physical level is only a mentalism. As Gurdjieff said, "To destroy inequality would mean destroying the possibility of evolution." Given the suffering

6. If the teacher is a female, she would be the surrogate mother.

7. As are also 'peace,' 'progress,' and 'freedom' as currently used; that is, distorted with secular desire forms.

and misery of the ordinary world, it is very difficult for the student to acknowledge that there is and must be inequality—especially as he becomes more familiar with the teacher and teaching. Waking up to what heretofore he was asleep to, he may want to "save the world," another cunning way personality may defend itself. Beyond this is the recognition of hierarchy; a hierarchy of being-understanding. Raised and conditioned in a 'democracy,' the notions of inequality and hierarchy are difficult to accept, let alone think about. But to see this he need only look at the relationship between teacher and student. It is not one of equals.

Inhabiting a different world, the student can never really 'see' the teacher, never 'know' the true import of his actions and non-actions. Therefore, he cannot judge the teacher.[8] If he presumes to do so, the octave aborts as it did with Uspenskii's relationship with Gurdjieff in Essentuki, and later in London. The student may think, as Uspenskii did, that he can carry on by himself. And certainly he may for a time, running on the fuel he has stored up and what understanding he has come to. But in time he must arrive at a dead-end, as Uspenskii saw when he admitted that "I took it [leadership of the System] over before I had gained enough control over myself. I was not ready. I have lost control over myself. It is a long time since I could control my state of mind."

"Time is counted," says Gurdjieff. He does not mean someone is counting time, rather that to step beyond psychological time one first must be in time. To have the great blessing of the opportunity to be in time and then to dither and doubt, to not move, makes what is heard and learned in time—old. Truth formulated, not truth as directly experienced, is what Gurdjieff calls a B influence, its origin residing outside of the circle of time, in its esoteric center. A influences are all that which is within time. They are born of time, live on only borrowed life, have no life of their own. All B influences must—because they have been manifested within the circle of time—devolve into A influences.

The truth, in the sense of formulated truth, must decay. One day's truth is another's worm. And so, the student, first hearing the truth, receives a fundamental shock to essence. It is like a whiff of the breath of Life. It will lead him to his teacher. Here, he will receive C influence—a living and direct contact, an influence that is intimate yet impersonal. In that timeless immediacy, the student is awakened to the resonance of his real nature. So inspired, the great octave of evolution, of development and transformation, thus initiates itself. Galvanized, the student is open, eager to learn. *He will become conscious, it's right here, he can do it*—these thoughts keep him eating the new energy which is released. It may take years, many years, for him to realize that his formulation is in error. That

8. He may in time be able to see the person of the teacher but he should not confuse the two.

the 'he' that he speaks of is a phantom. It is just this *he*, this *spiritual he*, that must be seen for what it is: a nothing.

If pressure becomes too great he is likely to run, and the resulting energy, not being assimilated, implodes, then explodes. Projections abound, judgments are justified, and the student, not yet fixed, crystallized, at a higher vibration, falls back into either a one-dimensional perception of an object world only, or he maintains the two-dimensional but now coats it with ego and so further devolves into mere power. The magnetic tie between teacher and student broken, no longer under conscious influence and using up his store of internal substances refined by previous hard work on himself, the student often tries to sustain his level of energy and perception through the 'help' of drugs. In truth, although the student can parrot the language, mimic the circumstances, play judge and jury, he has never passed from misunderstanding to understanding. Icarus-like, he may be able to fly but his wings are wax. Flight into the face of the sun can be sustained only so long. This is what Uspenskii found. He had done a great deal of work in a very short time and had comprehended much. Leaving Gurdjieff, he was quickly surrounded by students, given large estates and an esteemed place in society. It took many years for the energy he had assimilated to diminish and the knowledge he had acquired to become static.

Some think they can bypass the rigors of the teaching like Albrecht in Wagner's *Twilight of the Gods,* who developed himself through sublimation powered by an emotional deformity; in his case, his hatred of the feminine. At their roots such trees are weak and so, in time, must fall. Experience is always filtered through a still intact "I." Acquiring power, they progressively seal themselves off from their humanity, their nascent conscience. It is in the nature of the essential lie they manifest, that they soon, in Christian terms, sin against the Holy Ghost; that they use the real in the service of the unreal, the sacred in the service of the profane. That inevitably they must find themselves alone and forsaken, cast into a *Hasnamussian* world of their own ill-desire, awaits only the conclusion of the course of events which began with trying to get nothing with something. Or, to be more precise, to consciously be their no-thingness while remaining a some-thing, a somebody—the two being mutually exclusive.

As in Ibsen's play *Brand,* the relationship between student and teacher is always "all or nothing." The demand for spiritual inquiry is always such; just this point is always in question for the student. He is willing to go only so far, to open only so much. But the opening is not just once and for all time, but again and again, level after level. It is demanded. Whenever the teacher is active, the student must be receptive. Only then can the higher relate to and blend with the lower to form the reconciling. This action is beyond the psychological realm. It is beyond the corporeal. Yet it includes both. The action is vibrational, dynamic, living. More intimate than intimate and yet impersonal. In this way, the teacher may supply "the gold" that the student needs to make gold. Thus enriched, the student can work to process the material and so raise his level. If the student, rooted as he is in the psychological and corporeal, and so automatically rooting every impression in the personal, the static, the finite...if the student does not discriminate and so makes the impersonal, personal, then that, too, must be observed. If correctly observed, he will learn by his mistakes. If he does, if he can receive the action impersonally, then he may intuit That which lies behind all action, of whatever quality and substance. But this is well down the road.

Only in a time as confused as ours could one think that the teacher-student relationship—an archetypal and sacred form—exists as an option rather than as a necessary requirement, a station on the way. Some seekers attempt to circumvent the suffering inherent in any true student-teacher relationship by becoming their own teachers, studying what they will, when they will. Or they read the books and listen to the tapes of some now dead or far away teacher who they never meet in the body, face to face, but who they proudly declare is their teacher. Others subscribe to mail-order courses of teachings long dead.[9]

By such means these 'seekers' believe they avert the possibility of entering into a relationship with a teacher who is a fraud. But there is risk in whatever one does. Few people give up money-making or love-making because of bad experiences. No, the real issue is the worship of the fatted calf of our time—the 'individual.' The idea of being an individual is so deeply embedded in the contemporary psyche that it has become a societal flashword that short circuits what remains of most people's span of attention. And, of course, always riding shotgun with such 'individuals' is the notion of 'respect.' The person, so construed, is an authority to himself. No other authority is recognized. And what this 'authority' consists of, when seriously investigated, is nothing more than dreams and animal impulses.

While the relationship between teacher and student is archetypal, the time in which it occurs is always unique. Today, we live in a time of great technological transition which is changing the face, customs and mores of society. The old world is dying, the new still being born. Egoism has always ruled the ordinary world but now, through the powers of technology, it has the means to work its will. It thus shows its true colors and so creates conditions for its own eventual demise. In the meantime, it pollutes society with its false gods and animal values. And so, society pro-

9. There are even mail-order courses that purport to teach the Fourth Way. There are also Internet groups who think they can work in cyberspace (developing, perhaps, their cyber-"I").

vides a condition for work, for it no longer supports or is neutral to awakening but— opposes it.

Society is the seedbed of all paths. It is that from which all aspirants come. When society devolves into rank materialism, honoring only the mercantile, the mercenary, and the animal impulses, barbarism seeps into every avenue of life. Values, customs, thinking, and speaking coarsen, the profane becomes commonplace, acceptable. In such an atmosphere, communication—and especially spiritual communication—has little common ground.

In *New Model of the Universe*, Uspenskii points out: "The culture of barbarism grows simultaneously with the culture of civilization. But the important point is the fact that the two cannot develop on parallel lines indefinitely. The moment must inevitably arrive when the culture of barbarism arrests the development of civilization and gradually, or possibly very swiftly, completely destroys it." This is not speculation on his part, for in 1917, on the streets of his beloved St. Petersburg, he looked this moment in its brutish face. And it is interesting that this very moment is the one into which Gurdjieff would come bringing a way of understanding, a way of conscience, a way out which is a way through.

In essence the relationship between teacher and student is as Gurdjieff described in the *First Series:* "The higher blends with the lower...." A connection occurs, is elaborated, a dynamic flows, an atmosphere forms, expands, emerging is the full solid emptiness of being and knowledge in which oral transmission is, itself, silently breathed, and courageously lived. What was once only object has evolved into subject-object, and in that silent crucible, the subconscious becomes conscious, the scale of vibration, of creation, opens...and, in that transcending, the hard lines of duality disappear and what was two-dimensional has become three, and the three leads to four, and one begins to live the burning of desire within non-desire. And so whatever the historical time that one lives, it is a good time...to live.

Note: The relationship between teacher and student is as unique as it is archetypal. And, as such, its scale is too dynamic to ever fully represent in words. This preliminary sketch then is meant simply as an opening of the question, not its closure.

NOTES

ANDERSON, MARGARET (1889–1973). A woman of high energy, great beauty and sensitivity, Margaret Anderson lived a large portion of her life by her feelings and emotions, trying to attain one of three states: liberty, ecstasy, and peace. The way many live out of the intellectual center, Margaret lived out of the emotional. Wrote Hugh Ford, in his *Four Lives in Paris*, "Feeling, emotion, sensation, nuance, fine distinctions, and emanations were the qualities Margaret pursued and celebrated, none of which, in her opinion, intellectuals comprehended or considered useful. She prided herself on knowing what they did not know or did not care about." When Orage advised her, "Remember you're a pianist, not a piano," a recodification of Gurdjieff's "Act, don't be acted upon," she came to learn, as she phrased it, "The quality of every life is determined exclusively by its position in relation to acting or being acted upon." Her longtime companion, Georgette Leblanc, a singer and great beauty herself, never felt comfortable with intellectuals for, as she said, "We live for emotions...they live for events. In our relations with people, we wait on the development of personal atmosphere; they don't wait, they crouch....They become critics." Margaret Anderson appears to be a classic representative of man number two, who refers everything to the emotional center.

BUTKOVSKY, ANNA ILINISHNA. In her book, *With Gurdjieff in St. Petersburg and Paris,* she twice writes that she first met Uspenskii in 1916. Later, she mentions his going to India and then returning. But we know from *In Search of the Miraculous* that he returned to Russia in November 1914. She also writes that she first heard of Uspenskii through his book, *Tertium Organum,* which was published in 1912. She writes her book in 1975 at ninety years of age and is likely to have been confused about dates. With James Moore, we take her first meeting with Uspenskii to be in 1912. However, Moore has Uspenskii first speaking to Anna about Gurdjieff when he returns from Moscow after a week of meetings with Gurdjieff in April 1915. In Anna's book, however, she writes: "You remember I told you [says Uspenskii] the time I went to Moscow...Well, that man is here now, in Petersburg. I've just come from him this moment." On the preceding page she writes: "Now that Uspenskii was back in St. Petersburg we resumed our morning meetings..." Clearly, a good deal of time had elapsed.

THE DEVIL ACCORDING TO USPENSKII. "'The Devil,' that is, the slanderer or tempter," wrote Uspenskii, "was in the original text [of the New Testament] simply a name or description which could be applied to any 'slanderer' or 'tempter.' And it is possible to suppose that these names were often used to designate the visible, deceptive, illusory, phenomenal world, 'Maya.' But we are too much under the influence of mediaeval demonology. And it is difficult for us to understand that in the New Testament there is no *general idea* of the devil. There is the idea of evil, the idea of temptation, the idea of demons, the idea of an unclean spirit, the idea of the prince of the demons; there is Satan who tempted Jesus; but all these ideas are separate and distinct from one another, always allegorical and very far from the mediaeval conception of the Devil." Speaking of the biblical phrase where Christ says, "get thee hence, Satan," Uspenskii says that in this case Satan "represented the visible, phenomenal world, which must not 'get hence' by any means, but must only serve the inner world, follow it, *go behind it.*" *A New Model of the Universe,* "Christianity and The New Testament," pp. 154–55. For a serious study of this area, see *The Old Enemy: Satan & The Combat Myth* by Neil Forsyth (Princeton University Press, 1987).

EVIL. Uspenskii quotes Gurdjieff in *Search* as saying that there can be no conscious evil. But in a deleted passage from the original draft he writes: "I said, 'Do you wish to say that there can be conscious evil, and he [Gurdjieff] certainly said it can be. Anything that produces big phenomena can have mind and intelligence behind it. Then I remember he said—'Why are you upset?' I was upset because it meant changing all I thought before. He said, 'It becomes even more interesting—it is one thing to have against you only mechanical forces and quite another to have intelligence; it is one thing to struggle with intelligence, and another to struggle with mechanical forces.'" Gurdjieff added that, "If in a full sense conscious evil is possible, it is only possible in a very elaborate way and a very rare case." In *All and Everything*, Gurdjieff gives another perspective on the word 'evil,' p. 1139.

FERAPONTOFF, BORIS. The notes of Boris Ferapontoff, which extend from February 1920 through the summer of 1921, give an impression of how the teaching was presented at that time. It was said, for example, that "sol 12 can sometimes pass to la 6, if the shock was sufficiently strong, for instance, with the help of artificial, or sometimes, natural breathing." Ferapontoff stayed with Gurdjieff through the Prieuré period and was appointed along with five others, including Sophia Uspenskii, Jeanne de Salzmann, Olga Hinzenberg, Elizabeta Galumnian, and Dr. Konstantin Kiselev, as an Assistant Instructor of the Institute of Harmonious Development of Man. He taught movements at the Prieuré and, of all the Russian pupils, spoke the most fluent English. Ferapontoff died in 1930.

FOURTH DIMENSION. In 1898, at the age of twenty, Uspenskii published his first book The Fourth Dimension. The two books by the Englishman C. H. Hinton, *A New Era of Thought* (1910) and *The Fourth Dimension* (1912), were a great influence on Uspenskii's later thought on the subject.

GURDJIEFF'S BIRTH. In February 1930 Gurdjieff burned all his private papers, documents, and passports before going to America so, to date, there is no factual authentication of his date of birth. Most authors have taken this date as being 1877. However, biographer James Moore, argues for 1866. He bases this largely on *Meetings with Remarkable Men* (p. 41) where Gurdjieff remarks that he was "about seven years old" when a cattle plague happened. Moore has evidence that in 1872–73 a rinderpest cattle plague developed in the area where Gurdjieff lived, thus Gurdjieff was born in 1866.

I believe that Gurdjieff was born not in 1877 or 1866 but in 1872. This is based on dates Gurdjieff gives in *Meetings*. The year 1888 (pp. 64–65) plays a big part in Gurdjieff's life. It is then that he sees the Yezidi in the circle, learns of the evil spirit in the corpse of the Tartar, drinks for the first time, is accidently shot in the leg, has a "silent romance" with a girl twelve or thirteen years old, and has the artillery range duel with Karpenko. If as Moore suggests, Gurdjieff was born in 1866, Gurdjieff would have been twenty-two years old when he fell in love with a girl nine to ten years his junior. This hardly seems likely. Born in 1877, Gurdjieff would have been eleven in 1888; if in 1872, he would have been sixteen. Both dates are feasible, though logic tends toward the 1872 date. We know from *Meetings* that Bogachevsky, or Father Evlissi, Gurdjieff's teacher, arrived in Kars in 1886, the year Gurdjieff's sister dies and he becomes interested in "abstract questions." Using the 1866 birth date, Gurdjieff would be twenty years old when Bogachevsky arrived; if 1872, fourteen; if 1877, nine years old. Again, the 1872 birth date seems the more reasonable. Further, Gurdjieff would be either twenty-two, sixteen, or ten years of age when he 'dueled' with Karpenko. It's hard to believe that Gurdjieff at twenty-two would do anything so mad.

Olga de Hartmann felt Gurdjieff was considerably older than the birth date of 1877 but was unable to prove it. As her passport gave her birth date as 1896 when she was actually born in 1885, she dismissed the 1877 date given on Gurdjieff's passport. And, as stated in the footnotes, Louise Goepfert (March), Gurdjieff's secretary for many years, gives his birthday as 1872 in an unpublished essay she wrote within a year of his death, "Gurdjieff: An Indication of His Life and Work." Of all his followers J. G. Bennett has perhaps made the most intensive search into Gurdjieff's background. In his *Gurdjieff: A Very Great Enigma*, p. 8, he stated: "So far as I myself can make out from various sources, from what he himself and his family have told us, it does seem probable that he was born in 1872, in Alexandropol." Lastly, the first edition of *All and Everything* gave the year of his birth as 1872 on the dust jacket. In later editions, at his younger sister's insistence, the year was changed to 1877.

GURDJIEFF IN RUSSIA. The general consensus is that Gurdjieff arrived in Moscow in 1912. However, he is remembered to say in "The Material Question," an addition to *Meetings With Remarkable Men*, that he arrived in Moscow the late part of 1913 (p. 270). In the Institute's prospectus circulated in 1922 it says, "Only a small number of them [Seekers After Truth] returned to Russia in 1913, with Mr. Gurdjieff at their head."

A HERO OF OUR TIME. Uspenskii speaks about the author, Mikhail Lermontov, in the chapter "Eternal Recurrence and the Laws of Manu" of his *A New Model of the Universe,* pp. 472–73. "The feeling of the repetition of events was very strong in Lermontov," wrote Uspenskii. "He is full of presentiments, expectations, 'memories.' He constantly alludes to these sensations, especially in his prose. 'The Fatalist' [a chapter in *A Hero of Our Time*] is practically written on the theme of repetition and of remembering that which seems to have happened in some unknown past. Many passages in 'The Princess' and in 'Bela,' especially the philosophical digressions, produce the impression that Lermontov himself is trying to remember something that he has forgotten.... In our time the idea of recurrence and even the possibility of half-conscious remembering becomes more and more pressing and necessary. In *The Life of Napoleon* (1928), D. S. Merejkovsky constantly alludes to Napoleon in the phrases 'he knew' ('remembered'). And later, in dealing with Napoleon's last years in Europe, 'he forgot' ('he ceased to remember').... I wished only to show that the idea of repetition and recollection of the *past* which is not in our time is far from being foreign to Western thought."

Translated by Vladimir and Dmitri Nabokov, the novel is published by Everyman's Library (Alfred A. Knopf, Inc., 1992). For a review of the book see *Telos* #8.

THE IDEAS. Uspenskii's appreciation for the ideas that Gurdjieff brought never wavered. Though he recognized that "some separate fragments of it could be found elsewhere, but not connected and put together" in the form that Gurdjieff presented. He always understood that their origin was beyond ordinary life. In 1926 he wrote in *Fragments*, "The system is waiting for workers. There is no statement and no thought in it which would not require and admit further development and elaboration.... [However] ordinary intellectual study of the system is quite insufficient; and there are very few people who agree to other methods of study who are at the same time capable of working by these methods." He understood that the power of the ideas and the course of involution would have them eventually entering into scientific and philosophic language. "But," he says, "they will enter in the wrong form. There will be no right distinction between doing and happening, and many thoughts of ordinary thinking will be mixed with these ideas; so they will not be ideas we know now, only [the] words will be similar."

INTELLIGENTSIA. The word first entered the English language through Russian émigrés. It had been adopted from French and German, where in the 1830s–1840s the term was used to designate educated citizens with progressive interests. Having a university education was not enough; one had to also have a strong interest in the public good. The word, then, referred to academics, men of letters, journalists, writers, and professional revolutionaries. With the twin emergence of scientific advances and secular societies, European intellectuals appeared in the sixteenth century as a distinct group who considered traditional philosophical questions outside the clerical and theological bulwarks. Dominating thought in the sixteenth and seventeenth centuries was the Socratic idea of innate ideas, which had entered Western thought through St. Augustine. The immutability of human nature posited in such thought meant that people's behavior was also immutable. In 1690

John Locke's *Essay on Human Understanding* rejected the concept of innate ideas, declaring that all ideas had their genesis in sensory experience (thus, the beginnings of Behaviorism). In 1758 Claude Helvétius, the French philosopher, siphoned off the political ramifications of Locke's theory of knowledge and made a great leap of reasoning, arguing that since all of man's knowledge and values were the result of sensory experience, then if that experience can be controlled, it is possible to affect and determine people's thought and behavior. Says Richard Pipes in *The Russian Revolution*, "This is one of the most revolutionary ideas in the history of political thought: by extrapolation from an esoteric theory of knowledge, a new political theory is born with the most momentous practical implications." The control of sensory data, i.e., environment, is to be through reason, through rationality, which is of course the province of the intellectuals, the intelligentsia, or what we today would call the "cognitive elite." Unlike in England, the intelligentsia in Russia (as in France) was not allowed to participate in public life, a fact observed by de Tocqueville, and so they tended to run aground in extreme ideologies based on reason alone.

Only in an open and egalitarian society in which independent opinion can flourish can the intelligentsia have influence. The Russian intelligentsia came into being in the 1860s as the result of the Great Reforms of Tsar Alexander II. "To understand the [Russian] intelligentsia," writes Pipes, "it is imperative to keep in mind at all times its deliberate detachment from reality: for while the revolutionaries can be ruthlessly pragmatic in exploiting, for tactical purposes, the people's grievances, their notion of what the people desire is the product of sheer abstraction." There could be no belief in God or the immortality of the soul or accident in human affairs if one was to be a 'pure' Russian intellectual.

JEAN TOOMER ON GORHAM MUNSON. As many of Munson's perspectives concerning Jean Toomer have been quoted, this is how Jean Toomer (writing about himself in the third person) saw Munson:

> He is always uneasy in his presence. He wishes to be Jean's equal. He can convince himself that he is when Jean is absent. But even Jean's absence does not bring real peace. For he is never absent altogether. Somewhere on the horizon he looms up (what things he might be doing over there!) a dark, unpredictable object which at any moment may sweep near, burst in, and upset the chairs and tables. Even were the things just narrated to be cancelled, still Gorham would be uneasy in Jean's presence. For Gorham feels Jean to posses an essential energy that displaces his own and which he is unable to cope with. If it were not that Gorham is a literary critic, needs literary material, and has stated his belief that Jean is a significant potential, he could be well rid of him. He sincerely likes Jean personally, but

their affection would not have a ghost of a chance against his need of security and peace of mind. Gorham thinks that all of Jean's silences are critical, and that, for the most part, they are destructively critical of those about him, Gorham himself included. But Gorham does not wish therefore that Jean should speak, for his spoken thought might prove to be more disturbing than his silence. Jean's quickness, power, and command of words and thought in discourse is in an unpleasant contrast to his own slowness. Moreover, Gorham can never tell when Jean will break out with an opposition to some pet theory or prejudice which he, Gorham, has been laboriously building and hence does not wish demolished in a moment, particularly by Jean. Nor can Gorham tell when Jean will narrate some strange, unusual effect or experience. Such things are in unfortunate contrast to Gorham's commonplaces. They give evidence too vividly of Jean's greater range in life. And whether Jean is silent or otherwise, Gorham always feels in him an assumption of greater maturity, an attitude which says that he, Jean, is on the one right road, and that he has already achieved a degree of calm mastery. In short, Gorham thinks that Jean always feels himself to be superior. Gorham greatly resents this feeling, he would like to disrupt it, but he fears to attempt it.

KING, C. DALY. King (1895–1962) believes Orage, and not Uspenskii, taught the true Gurdjieff canon. Uspenskii he sees as having introduced into the Work "a sort of overlay of religious enthusiasm and of mystical atmosphere." In particular he finds Uspenskii's characterizations of self-remembering and self-observation as fuzzy, saying they lack "rigorous and conclusive definition" and finding them "far more introspective than genuinely objective." He also disagrees with the concept that man has many "I"s. Wrote King in his last book, *The States of Human Consciousness* (1963) "In the waking state, as elsewhere, there can be only a single 'I'-entity involved." Earlier, wishing to preserve the teaching as he had received it from Orage, King had written *The Oragean Version* (1951) which is privately published. His other books include: *Integrative Psychology* (1931), *The Psychology of Consciousness* (1932), and *Heritage, A Social Interpretation of the History of Ancient Egypt,* unpublished. King appears to be a classic representative of man number three, the man who refers everything to the intellect.

LENIN. Brilliant, compulsive, and secretive, Lenin's chief feature was hatred. Says Peter Struve, who had frequent dealings with Lenin in the 1890s: "His principal *Einstellung*—to use the new popular German psychological term—was *hatred.* Lenin took to Marx's doctrine primarily because it found response in that principal *Einstellung* of his mind. The doctrine of the class war, relentless and thoroughgoing, aiming at the final destruction and extermination of the enemy, proved congenial to Lenin's emotional attitude to surrounding reality. He hated not only the existing autocracy (the Tsar) and the bureaucracy, not only lawlessness and arbitrary rule of the police, but also their antipodes—the 'liberals' and the 'bourgeoisie.' That hatred had something repulsive and terrible in it; for being rooted in the concrete, I should say even animal, emotions and repulsions, it was at the same time abstract and cold like Lenin's whole being." According to Lenin the decisive influence on him as a young man were the writings of Nicholas Chernyshevskii. A leading radical of the 1860s, Chernyshevskii was the author of *What is to be done?*, a novel portraying the existing world as corrupt and doomed. Its hero, Rakhmetov, is the "new man" of iron will who is totally dedicated to radical change. Lenin borrowed the novel's title for his first political tract. Born in April 1870 to a well-off bureaucratic family, Lenin was expelled from the university for revolutionary activity. In 1893 he moved to St. Petersburg where he studied Marx's *Das Kapital* and agitated the workers. He was consequently jailed in 1895 and later given a Siberian exile from 1897 to 1900. After he was deported, he lived in a number of European capitals before finally taking residence in Switzerland. In appearance, Lenin was quite provincial looking and not at all attractive. In his *The Russian Revolution*, Pipes writes: "His strength of will, indomitable discipline, energy, asceticism, and unshakable faith in the [revolutionary] cause had an effect that can only be conveyed by the overused term of 'charisma.'" But he alone, of everyone, whatever side they were on, proved himself the grand master at revolutionary chess. His analysis was far deeper and more realistic. At all times he knew exactly his position on the 'board,' its strengths and weaknesses in terms of material force and time, and that of his opponents. Without illusion, he was an implacable foe. His will to win was absolute. No costs were too large. Tactics he could adapt to the moment, but the overall rightness of his strategy was never in doubt. He had long studied the French Revolution and would not make the mistakes of Robespierre, whose cardinal mistake, according to Lenin was its "excessive generosity—it should have *exterminated its enemies*." He would seem to be a classic prototype for the Gurdjieffian hasnamus. "The question of power is the fundamental question of every revolution," said Lenin. And in his most famous remark, "Kto kogo?" or "Who-whom?" he says, that is, "Who masters whom?"

MERCOUROV, SERGEI DMITRIEVICH. Fifteen years younger than Gurdjieff, Mercourov was born on October 21, 1988, in Alexandropol. A cousin of Gurdjieff's, Mercourov's family were next-door neighbors of Gurdjieff's family. Growing up, he developed somewhat of an interest in the occult and Hindu philosophy, but his passion was sculpting. His first commissions were of the Khan of Nakhichevan's concubines. Well regarded in Moscow circles before and after the Revolution, he took the death mask of Leo Tolstoi in 1910. Later in 1924 he took Lenin's death mask, executed a number of statues of him, and in 1939 was awarded the Order of Lenin. The first mention of Mercourov as the "M" to which Uspenskii alludes appears in James Webb's 1980 biography, *The Harmonious Circle,* p. 93.

MOURAVIEFF, BORIS PETROVITCH (1880–1966). Born in Kronstadt, the naval base at St. Petersburg, his father was Graf Piotr Petrovitch Mouravieff, admiral of the Russian fleet and vice minister of the Russian navy of the last imperial government before Tsar Nicholas II's abdication. An ancestor, Andre Mouravieff, was chamberlain at the Russian Imperial Court and a member of the Holy Synod of the Russian Orthodox Church; he founded the monastery of St. Andrew on Mount Athos. In 1917 when Kerensky took office as the second prime minister of the new Russian Republic, Boris Mouravieff became his principal private secretary. Meeting Uspenskii in Constantinople, he then, through Uspenskii, was introduced to Gurdjieff. Mouravieff later emigrated to Paris where Uspenskii asked that he help in editing his manuscript *Fragments of an Unknown Teaching* (later retitled *In Search of the Miraculous*). Always on the fringe of the Gurdjieff circles, casting doubt, criticizing, he apparently could never get Gurdjieff and the teaching out of his system. In 1944 he and his wife moved to Switzerland where, studying at the University of Geneva, Mouravieff obtained a Ph.D. He then taught Russian history and Eastern philosophy at the Institute of International Studies in Geneva. In 1958 he lectured on "An Introduction to Esoteric Philosophy" which was eventually expanded into his three-volume work *Gnosis.* He then opened a Center for Christian Esoteric Studies. When he died in 1966 the institute closed and his books went out of print. Recently they have been republished.

Mouravieff's intention is to cut the teaching from its Fourth Way and Gurdjieffian mooring and link it to what he calls a "fifth way," a Christianity of his own design (many of his views being heretical). Interestingly, Mouravieff's fifth way is clearly an amalgamation of Uspenskii's Gurdjieff-Eastern Christianity-Cathars. The material he presents in *Gnosis* is a rewriting of Uspenskii's *Search,* which, of course, is from Gurdjieff's Russian period and lacks the fuller development that Gurdjieff gave the teaching in *All and Everything.* Mouravieff's perspective, as well as his writing, is at a level far below that of Uspenskii and, of course, does not even begin to approach Gurdjieff's. For a detailed study of The Mouravieff Phenomenon represents see *Telos* Vol. 3, Issue 4, and Vol. 4, Issue 1.

ORAGE AND KATHERINE MANSFIELD. One of the few letters preserved among Orage's personal papers was a letter Katherine Mansfield had written to him on February 9, 1921

> Dear Orage,
>
> This letter has been on the tip of my pen for many months.
>
> I want to tell you how sensible I am of your wonderful unfailing kindness to me in the "old days." And to thank you for all you let me learn from you. I am still—more shame to me—very low down in the school. But you taught me to write, you taught me to think; you showed me what there was to be done and what not to do.
>
> My dear Orage, I cannot tell you how often I call to mind your conversation or how often, in writing, I remember my master. Does that sound impertinent? Forgive me if it does.
>
> But let me thank you, Orage—thank you for everything. If only one day I might write a book of stories good enough to "offer" you...If I don't succeed in keeping the coffin from the door you will know this was my ambition.
>
> Yours, in admiration and gratitude
> Katherine Mansfield
>
> I haven't said a bit of what I want to say. This letter sounds as if it was written by a screwdriver, and I wanted it to sound like an admiring, respectful, but warm piping beneath your windows. I'd like to send my love too, if I wasn't so frightened.

PAUL DUKES AND 'PRINCE OZAY.' In his book, *Unending Quest* (Cassell & Co. Ltd., 1950), Dukes writes that he and P. D. Uspenskii "used to sit up long nights discussing mysticism, in particular the system of G. I. Gurdjieff, undoubtedly one of the great living teachers, whom Uspenskii acknowledged as master, but from whom he had none the less parted company." It is difficult to believe that a man of Dukes' intelligence and worldliness (he earned a knighthood by the age of thirty as Secret Agent ST 25) would not make the connection that Prince Ozay is Gurdjieff. Simply in terms of ideas it appears that many of Ozay's are similar to, if not identical, with Gurdjieff's. It seems odd that Dukes does not at least mention the similarity in ideas. Moreover, Dukes clearly holds the Prince in high repute—he made a lifelong impression on him. If he believed Ozay was Gurdjieff, he would certainly have sought Gurdjieff out in Paris after the war. But Dukes makes no mention of it. So either the two are of different identities or, for some reason Dukes—could he have believed Uspenskii's depiction of Gurdjieff as having gone mad?!—does not wish to acknowledge it. The only facts Dukes gives that mitigate against Gurdjieff being Ozay is that the Prince speaks better English than

Russian and claims to have been in "many churches in England and America." Some people report hearing Gurdjieff speak perfect English. Perhaps he 'played' with language.

THE QUEST SOCIETY. Formed in 1909 by G. R. S. Mead, Madame Blavatsky's secretary and a leading theosophical writer and gnostic historian, because of the readmittance of C. W. Leadbetter into membership in the Theosophical Society by Annie Besant, its president. Leadbetter had been accused of pedophilia. The Quest Society still followed the theosophical teachings and so the link between Uspenskii and theosophy continued when Uspenskii arrived in London.

THE REVOLUTION. Lenin understood the crucial importance of timing. Writes Trotsky: "If we had not seized power in October we would not have seized it at all. Our strength before October lay in the uninterrupted influx of the masses, who believed that this party would do what the others had not done. If they had seen any vacillation at this moment on our part, any delay, any incongruity between word and deed, then in the course of two or three months they would have drifted away from us....It was just this that made Lenin decide to act."

RUSSIAN THEOSOPHY. Though theosophy had its adherents in Russia, it took root only through the efforts of Anna Alekseevna Kamenskaia (1867–1952), who organized the Russian Theosophical Society in 1908, lectured endlessly, and edited the Society's journal *Vestnik Teosofii.* The Society's headquarters was in St. Petersburg and Uspenskii was considered one of the leading theosophical thinkers and writers. A detailed history of the theosophical movement in Russia is given in Maria Carlson's *No Religion Higher than Truth* (Princeton University Press, 1993).

SEEKERS AFTER TRUTH. Gurdjieff tells the names of thirteen members of the group: Prince Yuri Lubovedsky; Professor Skridlov, anthropologist; Dr. Ekim Bey, hypnotist; Piotr Karpenko, mining engineer; Abram Yelov, linguist; Sarkis Pogossian, priest; Dashtamirov, astronomer; Baron X, ardent occultist; Vitvitskaia; Soloviev; Prince Nijeradze; Dr. Sari-Ogli; and Samsanov. Thomas de Hartmann, in his and his wife's book, *Our Life With Mr. Gurdjieff,* p. 72, reports Gurdjieff saying there were fifteen members of the group, and that "There were also women...." So the last and unnamed member of the group must have been a woman. Three of the fifteen died during their expeditions. In terms of religion they were Orthodox, Catholic, Muslim, Jew, and Buddhist.

In the original manuscript of *Meetings With Remarkable Men,* Gurdjieff devoted a chapter to Prince Nijeradze. Several times Gurdjieff rewrote this chapter but never completed it. Writes Bennett in *Gurdjieff:*

Making a New World, p. 178, "We gather that Prince Nijeradze had been concerned in some embarrassing episode connected with the difficulty Gurdjieff came up against, through having broken some of the rules of one of the Brotherhoods where he had been receiving help and teaching. One who heard the chapter read in 1933, recounts that it produced a profound impression by its account of the state of man who wakes up after dying and realizes that he has lost the chief instrument of his life, his body, and recalls all he could have done with it while he was still alive."

SINCERITY. "I remember Uspenskii speaking very interestingly once in New York about sincerity. We think we have only to decide to be and we can be. But sincerity has to be learnt, slowly and painfully. Takes a long time. And when one finds sincerity on one level, one realizes that there is another completely different level of sincerity hidden beneath."—Rodney Collin, *The Theory of Conscious Harmony,* p. 77. Said Gurdjieff in a meeting:

> Many things are necessary for observing oneself, the first is being sincere with oneself. It is much easier to be sincere with a friend. Man is afraid to see something bad, and if by accident, looking deep down, he sees his own bad, he sees his nothingness. We have the habit of driving away thoughts about ourselves because we fear remorse. Sincerity may be the key which will open the door through which one part can see another part. With sincerity man may look and see something. Sincerity with oneself is very difficult, for a thick crust has grown over essence. Each year man puts on a new dress, new mask, one after another. All must be gradually removed, for until they are removed, man cannot see.

THE STRANGE LIFE OF IVAN OSOKIN. Did Uspenskii self-publish the book before or after his April 1915 meeting with Gurdjieff? The likelihood is afterward, and if so, then he would have rewritten the scenes in which the magician appears. The magician then is Gurdjieff. And Zinaida may be Anna Butkovsky. On p. 131, Zinaida asks Osokin: "Well, are you going to Australia soon?" In Butkovsky's book, p. 30, Uspenskii talks to Anna about going to Australia.

THEOSOPHY. Originated with Helena Blavatsky, a Russian occultist, medium, and author of *Isis Unveiled, Voice of Silence,* and *The Secret Doctrine.* Blavatsky's teaching draws heavily on esoteric Buddhism. In Gurdjieff's view theosophy, and Western occultism, represent "a mixture of fundamental lines. Both lines bear in themselves grains of truth, but neither of them possesses full knowledge and therefore attempts to bring them to practical realization give only negative results." *Search,* p. 286.

TRIADS. Intellectually, one of the most interesting of Bennett's many ideas is that every law has both a pure and impure form. This was why there had been no headway made with the triads. "Uspenskii had failed to recognize the true cosmic character of several of the triads," says Bennett.

USPENSKII'S MOTHER, SISTER, AND WIFE. It is unclear when Uspenskii's mother and sister died. In J. H. Reyner's biography, *Ouspensky: Unsung Genius,* he has the twenty-year-old Uspenskii and his mother visiting Paris in 1898 and her dying "shortly afterwards." Colin Wilson in his *The Strange Life of P. D. Ouspensky* says she died in 1894. Neither cite sources. Reyner states that the sister died "a few years after" her 1905 imprisonment. Wilson has her dying in 1908, the year when Uspenskii writes in his "Autobiographical Fragment" that he traveled to Constantinople, Smyrna, Greece, and Egypt. Reyner, oddly, speaks of Uspenskii meeting Sophia Grigorievna about 1905, well before his 1912 meeting with Anna Butkovsky. Wilson says nothing of when they met. James Webb in his *The Harmonious Circle* ignores Uspenskii's early life, as does James Moore in his *Gurdjieff: An Anatomy of a Myth.*

SELECTED BIBLIOGRAPHY

All and Everything. G. I. Gurdjieff (1st Edition, Harcourt Brace and Company, New York, 1950)

Meetings with Remarkable Men. G. I. Gurdjieff (E. P. Dutton and Co., New York, 1963)

Life is real only then when "I am." G. I. Gurdjieff (Triangle Editions Inc., New York, 1975)

The Struggle of the Magicians. G. I. Gurdjieff (The Stourton Press, Cape Town, South Africa, 1954)

The Herald of Coming Good. G. I. Gurdjieff (Surefire Press, 1988)

Views from the Real World. G. I. Gurdjieff (E. P. Dutton and Co., Inc., New York, 1975)

In Search of the Miraculous. P. D. Ouspensky (Harcourt Brace and Company, New York, 1949)

A New Model of the Universe. P. D. Ouspensky (Alfred A. Knopf, 1934)

Tertium Organum. P. D. Ouspensky (Vintage Books, New York, 1982)

The Psychology of Man's Possible Evolution. P. D. Ouspensky (Alfred A. Knopf, 1954)

The Strange Life of Ivan Osokin. P. D. Ouspensky (Arkana, London, New York, 1987)

Letters from Russia. 1919. P. D. Ouspensky (Routledge & Kegan Paul Ltd., London, Henley, Boston, 1978)

Conscience. P. D. Ouspensky (Routledge & Kegan Paul Ltd., 1979)

Talks with a Devil. P. D. Ouspensky (Turnstone Press Ltd., London, 1972)

The Fourth Way. P. D. Ouspensky (Vintage Books, New York, 1971)

P. D. Uspenskii Collection. (Sterling Library, 1978)

A Record of Meetings. P. D. Ouspensky (Arkana, New York, 1992)

A Further Record. P. D. Ouspensky (Arkana, 1986)

A. R. Orage's Commentaries on All and Everything. (Two Rivers Press, Aurora, OR, 1985)

On Love. A. R. Orage (Samuel Weiser, Inc., New York, 1974)

Gurdjieff: Making a New World. J. G. Bennett (Turnstone Books, Ltd., London, 1973)

Gurdjieff: A Very Great Enigma. J. G. Bennett (Samuel Weiser Inc., New York, 1973)

Idiots in Paris. J. G. and Elizabeth Bennett (Coombe Springs Press, York Beach, Maine, 1980)

Witness. J. G. Bennett (Claymount Communications, Charles Town, WV, 1983)

Exchanges Within. Questions from Gurdjieff Group Meetings with John Pentland in California 1955–1984 (Continuum, 1997)

Gurdjieff: An Annotated Bibliography. J. Walter Driscoll and The Gurdjieff Foundation of California (Garland Publishing, Inc., 1985)

Essentials. Jean Toomer (University of Georgia Press, 1991)

Portage Potential. Jean Toomer (Unpublished)

The Wayward and the Seeking: A Collection of Writings by Jean Toomer. Edited by Darwin T. Turner (Howard University Press, 1982)

The Collected Poems of Jean Toomer. Edited by Robert B. Jones and Margery Toomer Latimer (The University of North Carolina Press, 1988)

Jean Toomer's Years with Gurdjieff. Rudolph P. Byrd (University of Georgia Press, 1990)

Katherine Mansfield: A Biography. Antony Alpers (Alfred A. Knopf, New York, 1953)

Katherine Mansfield, Selected Letters. Edited by Vincent O'Sullivan (Oxford University Press, New York, 1989)

The Fiery Fountains. Margaret Anderson (Horizon Press, New York, 1951)

My Thirty Years War. Margaret Anderson (Horizon Press, New York, 1969)

The Notes of Jane Heap. Jane Heap (Two Rivers Press, Aurora, OR, 1994)

Diary of Madame Egout Pour Sweet. Rina Hands (Two Rivers Press, Aurora, OR, 1991)

Memories of Gurdjieff. A. L. Staveley (Two Rivers Press, Aurora, Oregon, 1978)

Undiscovered Country. Kathryn Hulme (Little, Brown and Co., Boston, 1966)

Extracts from Nine Letters. Rosamund Bland (The Stourton Press, Capetown, South Africa, 1952)

More Lives than One. Claude Bragdon (Alfred A. Knopf, 1938)

With Gurdjieff in St. Petersburg and Paris. Anna Butkovsky-Hewitt (Samuel Weiser Inc., 1978)

On Attention. Christopher Freemantle (Indications Press, 1993)

"No Religion Higher than Truth." Maria Carlson (Princeton University Press, 1993)

The Theory of Conscious Harmony. Rodney Collin (Robinson & Watkins Books, Ltd., London, 1958)

The Theory of Eternal Life. Rodney Collin (Stuart & Watkins, 1954)

"Beloved Icarus." Joyce Collin-Smith. *British Astrological Journal* (1963)

Call No Man Master. Joyce Collin-Smith. (Gateway Books, Bath, England, 1988)

Unforgotten Fragments. Edited by Lewis Creed (Quacks Books, York, England, 1994)

The Unending Quest. Paul Dukes (Cassell & Co. Ltd., London, 1950)

Talks by Madame Ouspensky. Robert de Ropp (Logos Press, 1974)

Warrior's Way. Robert de Ropp (Dell Publishing Co., Inc., New York, 1979)

Four Lives in Paris. Hugh Ford (North Point Press, 1987)

Luba Gurdjieff: A Memoir with Recipes. Luba Gurdjieff Everitt (Ten Speed Press, Berkeley, CA, 1993)

Time Exposures. Waldo Frank (Boni & Liveright, New York, 1926)

Our Life with Mr. Gurdjieff. Thomas and Olga de Hartmann (Arkana, New York, 1983)

After Many a Summer Dies the Swan. Aldous Huxley (Ivan R. Dee, 1993)

The Oragean Version. C. Daly King (Unpublished)

The States of Human Consciousness. C. Daly King (University Books, 1963)

The Psychology of Consciousness. C. Daly King (Kegan Paul, 1932)

Invisible Darkness. Charles Larson (University of Iowa Press, 1993)

All My Yesterdays. Cecil Lewis (Element, 1993)

A. R. Orage. Philip Mairet (University Books, 1966)

The Gurdjieff Years 1929–1949: Recollections of Louise March. Beth McCorkle (The Work Study Association, New York, 1990)

Gurdjieff and Mansfield. James Moore (Routledge & Kegan Paul Ltd., 1980)

Gurdjieff: Anatomy of a Myth. James Moore (Element, Great Britain, 1991)

The Awakening Years. Gorham Munson (Louisiana State University Press, 1985)

Psychological Commentaries on the Teachings of Gurdjieff and Ouspensky. Maurice Nicoll (Shambhala, Boston and London, 1984)

Teachings of Gurdjieff. C. S. Nott (Samuel Weiser Inc., New York, 1961)

Journey through this World. C. S. Nott (Routledge & Kegan Paul Ltd., 1966)

Eating The "I". William Patrick Patterson (Arete Communications, Fairfax, CA, 1992)

Law of the Sun, Law of the Moon. William Patrick Patterson (Arete Communications, Fairfax, CA, 1998)

Conscious Survival. William Patrick Patterson (Arete Communications, Fairfax, CA, 1998)

Ladies of The Rope. William Patrick Patterson (Arete Communications, Fairfax, CA, 1998)

Boyhood with Gurdjieff. Fritz Peters (E. P. Dutton & Co., 1964)

Gurdjieff Remembered. Fritz Peters (Samuel Weiser Inc., New York, 1971)

Balanced Man. Fritz Peters (Wildwood House Ltd., London, 1978)

Maurice Nicoll: A Portrait. Beryl Pogson (Globe Press Books, 1987)

Ouspensky: The Unsung Genius. J. H. Reyner (George Allen & Unwin Ltd., 1981)

A Lasting Freedom. Francis Roles (Society for the Study of Normal Psychology, 1972)

"The Case of P. D. Ouspensky." Marie Seton. *Quest* (Calcutta, #34, July–Sept. 1962)

Remembering Pyotr Demianovich Uspenskii. Edited by Merrily E. Taylor (Yale University Library, 1978)

The Harmonious Circle. James Webb (G. P. Putnam's Sons, New York, 1980)

The Strange Life of P. D. Ouspensky. Colin Wilson (Aquarian Press, London, 1993)

Orage with Gurdjieff in America. Louise Welch (Routledge & Kegan Paul Ltd., 1982)

Who Are You, Monsieur Gurdjieff? René Zuber (Routledge & Kegan Paul Ltd., 1980)

Hitler and Stalin. Alan Bullock (Alfred A. Knopf, 1992)

The Life of Lenin. Louis Fisher (Harper & Row, 1964)

Comrades: 1917—Russia in Revolution. Brian Moynahan (Little, Brown and Company, 1992)

The Russian Revolution. Richard Pipes (Alfred A. Knopf, 1990)

The Rise and Fall of the Third Reich. William L. Shirer (Simon and Schuster, 1960)

Inside the Third Reich. Albert Speer (The Macmillan Company, 1970)

REFERENCES

Guide to References

Each quotation or significant fact is designated by the code for the source material and the page upon which it appears. Thus:

I waited all these years. OLWG 54

means the material will be found in the book *Our Life with Mr. Gurdjieff* on page 54.

Key to Titles

AE .... *All and Everything.* G. I. Gurdjieff
ALF .... *A Lasting Freedom.* Francis Roles
AMDS...... *After Many a Summer Dies the Swan.* Aldous Huxley
AMY .... *All My Yesterdays.* Cecil Lewis
ARO......... *A. R. Orage.* Philip Mairet
BWG........ *Boyhood with Gurdjieff.* Fritz Peters
BI .... "Beloved Icarus." Joyce Collin-Smith
BL .... Beinecke Library
BM........... *Balanced Man.* Fritz Peters
CPDO...... "The Case of P. D. Ouspensky." Marie Seton
E............... *Essentials.* Jean Toomer
FLP .... *Four Lives In Paris.* Hugh Ford
FR .... *A Further Record.* P. D. Ouspensky
GAB .... *Gurdjieff: An Annotated Bibliography.* J. Walter Driscoll
GAM........ *Gurdjieff: Anatomy of a Myth.* James Moore
GGE......... *Gurdjieff: A Very Great Enigma.* John G. Bennett
GKM........ *Gurdjieff and Katherine Mansfield.* James Moore

GMNW... *Gurdjieff: Making a New World.* John G. Bennett
GR........... *Gurdjieff Remembered.* Fritz Peters
GY........... *The Gurdjieff Years: 1929–1949. Recollections of Lousie March.* Beth McCorkle
HCG .... *Herald of Coming Good.* G. I. Gurdjieff
ID .... *Invisible Darkness.* Charles Larson
IP .... *Idiots in Paris.* John G. Bennett
ISM .... *In Search of the Miraculous.* P. D. Ouspensky
JTG.......... *Jean Toomer's Years with Gurdjieff.* Rudolph P. Byrd
JTW......... *Journey through this World.* C. S. Nott
KMB........ *Katherine Mansfield, Biography.* Antony Alpers
KML........ *Katherine Mansfield, Selected Letters.* Vincent O'Sullivan
LG .... *Luba Gurdjieff: A Memoir with Recipes.* Luba Gurdjieff
LFR .... *Letters from Russia. 1919.* P. D. Ouspensky
LRIA........ *Life is real only then when "I am."* G. I. Gurdjieff
MAP .... *Margaret Anderson Papers.* University of Wisconsin
MEPS ...... *Diary of Madame Egout Pour Sweet.* Rina Hands
MLO .... *More Lives than One.* Claude Bragdon
MNP .... *Maurice Nicoll: A Portrait.* Beryl Pogson
MRM....... *Meetings with Remarkable Men.* G. I. Gurdjieff
MTYW .... *My Thirty Years War.* Margaret Anderson
NL .... *Nine Letters.* Rosamund Bland
NMU....... *A New Model of the Universe.* P. D. Ouspensky
NRHT..... *No Religion Higher than Truth.* Maria Carlson
OGA........ *Orage with Gurdjieff in America.* Louise Welch
OL........... *On Love.* A. R. Orage
OLWG...... *Our Life with Mr. Gurdjieff.* Thomas and Olga de Hartmann
OUG .... *Ouspensky the Unsung Genius.* J. H. Reyner
PC .... *Psychological Commentaries.* Maurice Nicoll
RM .... *A Record of Meetings.* P. D. Ouspensky
RPDU.......*Remembering Pyotr Demianovich Uspenskii.* Merrily E. Taylor
SL .... Sterling Library
SLIO........ *The Strange Life of Ivan Osokin.* P. D. Ouspensky
SLPDO.... *The Strange Life of P. D. Ouspensky.* Colin Wilson
SOHC ..... *The States of Human Consciousness.* C. Daly King
SSP .... *Solita Solano Papers.* Library of Congress
TSTM...... *The Struggle of the Magicians.* G. I. Gurdjieff
T.............. *Telos 7*
TAY.......... *The Awakening Years.* Gorham Munson
TCH........ *The Theory of Conscious Harmony.* Rodney Collin
TE .... *Time Exposures.* Waldo Frank
TEL .... *The Theory of Eternal Life.* Rodney Collin
TFF .... *The Fiery Fountains.* Margaret Anderson

TG .... *Teachings of Gurdjieff.* C. S. Nott
THC .... *The Harmonious Circle.* James Webb
TMO .... *Talks by Madame Ouspensky.* Robert de Ropp
TO .... *Tertium Organum.* P. D. Ouspensky
TOV......... *The Oragean Version.* C. Daly King
TWD .... *Talks With a Devil.* P. D. Ouspensky
TWS .... *The Wayward and the Seeking: A Collection of Writings by Jean Toomer.* Edited by Darwin T. Turner
UC .... *Undiscovered Country.* Kathryn Hulme
UF............ *Unforgotten Fragments.* Lewis Creed
UG .... *Unknowable Gurdjieff.* Margaret Anderson
UQ........... *The Unending Quest.* Paul Dukes
VRW .... *Views from the Real World.* G. I. Gurdjieff
W .... *Witness.* John G. Bennett
WGP .... *With Gurdjieff in St. Petersburg and Paris.* Anna Butkovsky-Hewitt
WW .... *Warrior's Way.* Robert de Ropp

∾

EPIGRAPH

iii...........The Magus is the highest. SL
iii...........God give you the strength. THC, 321
iii...........a kind of walking God. JTW, 31

PREFACE

ix ....My work in the future would proceed quite independently. ISM, 389
xii ....Very good is. GY, 74–75
xiv ....on the 15th of October. ISM, 369
xv ....Never poke your stick. AE, 44

INTRODUCTION

xvii ....thin film of false reality. ISM, 3
xix ....by origin a kaphir. MRM, 148
xix ....clear realization. MRM, 205
xix ....specific 'delicacies.' LRIA, 8
xxi ....our Lord Sovereign. AE, 53
xxi ....common welfare. LRIA, 2
xxiii ....Contemporary culture needs automatism. ISM, 309
xxiii ....Unless the 'wisdom.' GR, 122
xxiii ....All leaders. BWG, 160

A NEW OR FORGOTTEN ROAD

1 .... a new or forgotten road. ISM, 3
1 .... a more rational kind. ISM, 5
2 .... the ballet will have. ISM, 6
2 .... born in Moscow. RPDU, 9
2 .... clear mental pictures. RPDU, 9
3 .... I was under less imagination. RPDU, 14
3 .... a dead wall everywhere. RPDU, 10
3 .... Work at school was dull. RPDU, 10
3 .... he sensed the unity of all things. NMU, 1–2
4 .... very anarchistically inclined. RPDU, 10
5 .... unbroken line of thought and knowledge. NMU, 5
5 .... the idea of searching for those schools. NMU, 7
5 .... schools of the distant past. ISM, 4
6 .... Here was a book. WGP, 16
6 .... the most independent and talented. NRHT, 74
6 .... These ordinary members. WGP, 17
7 .... self-consciousness. TO, 277
7 .... must always feel equal. WGP, 19
8 .... across your orbit like a comet. WGP, 24
8 .... almost boyish enthusiasm. WGP, 22
8 .... women have taken. SLIO, 128
9 .... driving force and a will to seek. WGP, 19
10 .... as extraordinarily real. NMU, 309–10
10 .... there was no I. NMU, 321
10 .... Uspenskii Fourth. OUG, 19
10 .... I was watching the play. TO, 258
11 .... why don't you go. WGP, 30
11 .... Speaking sincerely. SL
12 .... Why on earth did I ever go. WGP, 31
12 .... P.D. Uspenskii's lectures attracted a huge audience. NRHT, 73
13 .... a mixture of superstition. ISM, 7
13 .... Indian raja. ISM, 7
14 .... Narcotics. TO, 278
15 .... chemistry. ISM, 8
15 .... great knowledge of the human machine. ISM, 8
16 .... feline grace and assurance. ISM, 10
16 .... at once, without delay. ISM, 11
16 .... Gurdjieff knew more. SL
16 .... seclusion. ISM, 16
18 .... man is responsible. ISM, 20
18 .... an artificial life. HCG, 12
19 .... empty and aborted interval. MRM, 8

19..........Moscow in 1912. LRIA, p. 28
19..........necessary to be independent. MRM, 249
19..........unavoidable friction. MRM, 270
20..........You believe in ventilation! UQ, 100
20..........You are a musical instrument. UQ, 107
20..........God is achieved not through activity. UQ, 108
20..........Are you afraid of risks? UQ, 113
20..........Sergei Dmitrievich Mercourov, Gurdjieff's cousin. THC, 93
21..........Uspenskii received a letter. SL
22..........Everything was beginning to totter. ISM, 29
23..........I have found the miracle! WGP, 35
23..........fine, virile features. WGP, 36
24..........in the presence of a Guru. WGP, 36
24..........Listen, Georgi Ivanovitch. SL
25..........People do not value a thing. ISM, 12
25..........all outward manifestation. WGP, 75
26..........People are machines. ISM, 52
26..........you do not remember yourselves. ISM, 117
26..........I remembered that I had forgotten. ISM, 121
26..........We are undoubtedly moving on to a higher level. NRHT, 77
28..........the matter of knowledge. ISM, 38
28..........Our ordinary European logical method. SL
29..........did not see me. SL
29..........fuller, ancient esoteric teaching. ISM, 205
30..........Time is breath. ISM, 213
30..........after a great struggle. SL
31..........fear of losing myself. RPDU, 8
31..........Whatever is this rubbish. WGP, 79
31..........impossible to deceive Gurdjieff. WGP
31..........Wraps Up The Thought. WGP, 103
31..........The first camp. SL
32..........his eternal and continual playing. SL
33..........spread out before our eyes. MRM, 245
34..........I believe that Georgi Ivanovitch. WGP, 67
35..........People around Gurdjieff. SL
35..........Gurdjieff was a genius in his own domain. SL
36..........Every man's personal work. ISM, 226
36..........a state of unusual tension. ISM, 260
37..........I saw this man in motion. THC, 282
37..........the miracle began. ISM, 262
38..........I knew that he would not believe me. ISM, 263
39..........extreme individualism. ISM, 266
39..........Pyotr Demianovich. ISM, 267

39 .... difficult to climb the hill. ISM, 271
40 .... not afraid to keep silent. ISM, 271
40 .... give up his suffering. ISM, 274
40 .... suffered from ill-health. SL
40 .... I felt myself growing. WGP
40 .... I will try to hammer. WGP, 104
41 .... 'play' is indispensable. SL
41 .... usually more whores here. OLWG, 8
42 .... he knew how to explain. OLWG, 9
42 .... when you live among wolves. OLWG, 12
44 .... oil king. ISM, 325–26
44 .... What a great and all-encompassing mission. NRHT, 171
45 .... we must go abroad. ISM, 328
46 .... If you want to rest. ISM, 340
46 .... irresistible inclination to destroy. AE, 406
47 .... those with guns. LFR, 21
47 .... catastrophe, a shipwreck. LFR, 28
48 .... how can one strengthen the feeling of "I"? ISM, 343
49 .... all responsibility towards myself. ISM, 344
49 .... I am a difficult, pretentious man. WGP, 105
49 .... the plan of the whole. ISM, 346
50 .... School is necessary. ISM, 347
50 .... a very strange feeling. ISM, 346
51 .... began to waver. ISM, 368
51 .... What the matter was. ISM, 368
52 .... their very existence which corrupts. LFR
52 .... a very absurd quarrel. ISM, 370
52 .... I am a svolotch. OLWG, 54
53 .... I have now already spent. ISM, 371
53 .... light of Eternity. NRHT, 80
54 .... Society for Struggle. OLWG, 58
55 .... man of being. OLWG, 68
55 .... Why always a suggestion of charlatanism. OLWG, 74
55 .... drove away many useful. SL
55 .... basis of his Work. OLWG, 69–70
56 .... the way of religion. ISM, 375
56 .... Infuriated beasts. MRM, 274
58 .... The expedition intends. OLWG, 78
58 .... devoted to me. MRM, 273
58 .... we got out safely. MRM, 274–75
59 .... she—is intelligent. OLWG, 122
59 .... Why are you so astonished? OLWG, 147
60 .... prices of all products. LFR, 6

61..........very characteristic. ISM, 381
61..........weakness of the intelligentsia. LFR, 33
61..........the ground had fallen. LFR
61..........Only scoundrels will survive. SLIO, 140
62..........strange confidence. ISM, 380
62..........I saw the same capacity in myself. SL
62..........negative frame of mind. ISM, 381–82
63..........striking appearance. THC, 178
63..........I finally gave up. MRM, 281
65..........He had a circle. THC, 178
65..........sheep's heads. OLWG, 152
66..........would come to Constantinople. SL
66..........one of the very few men. W, 55
67..........being understood better. W, 55
68..........no effort. SL
69..........Lord Creator. TSTM, 47
70..........make one line out of that. ISM, 383
70..........Nothing but dirty jokes. SL
70..........problem of this 'play.' SL
71..........In former Russia. NMU, 388
71..........Deeply impressed. GAM, 152

MAGICIANS AT WAR

74..........conscious of his aura. ARO, 24–25
74..........he was the novice. ARO, xxi
75..........a bird's strong beak. THC, 219
75..........Come if you like. W, 73
75..........I spent two hours with the man. NL, 5
76..........Uspenskii seemed rather depressed. NL, 63
76..........ordinarily we speak of 'I'. VRW, 75
77..........Everything more vivid. MNP, 72
77..........Gurdjieff was the teacher. TG, 27–28
77..........wrong lines. JTW, 98-99
78..........Normal human beings. GAM, 164
78..........I had decided. ISM, 385
78..........a hard outer shell. WGP, 22–23
79..........I don't feel influenced. KMB, 345
79..........This child I conceived. MRM, 292
80..........I want to learn. KML, 275
82..........build more solidly. PC Vol. 1, 14
83..........I cannot change your being. MNP, 83
83..........halfway to death. ISM, 385

83 .... people who have suffered shipwreck. ISM, 386
83 .... My intellectual life was leading me nowhere. TG, 27
84 .... Now what have I? TG, 28
84 .... a hatching place for eggs. MNP, 89
84 .... For the average person. GR, 126–27
84 .... complete submission to a will not his own, ARO, 93
85 .... the very depths of despair. TG, 28
85 .... I think you dig enough. TG, 28
85 .... a house of devotion. ARO, 93
85 .... her face shone. KMB, 356
86 .... an opportunity. KMB, 356–357
86 .... celebrate Christmas in tremendous style. KML, 280
86 .... You see, my love. KML, 282
87 .... a very tame semi-existence. KML, 284
87 .... a being transfigured. KMB, 359
87 .... I have heard enough about that place. GKM, 3
88 .... temptation. ISM, 389
88 .... from the very beginning. SL
89 .... When you return. MNP, 89
90 .... Did you understand. SL
90 .... Gurdjieff and I. THC, 382
90 .... Institute work was not necessary. SL
91 .... Dear Mrs. Page. SL
91 .... If they repeat. SL
91 .... Uspenskii was a brilliant. W
92 .... All that Uspenskii had of value. JTW, 90–91
93 .... People who did not belong. SL
93 .... Now only your mind is awake. W, 108
93 .... the possibility of learning to work. W, 121
94 .... too much knowledge. W, 121
95 .... conscientious egotist. SSP
95 .... a big, brindled beast. MNP, 97
96 .... Uncle George. LG, 28
96 .... enjoy life. LG, 19
96 .... his family had suffered much. TG, 34–35
97 .... a super-unique-tragi-comic situation. MRM, 293
97 .... gone off the rails. CPDO, 34
97 .... break off all relations. SL
98 .... successful religious teacher. JTW, 91
99 .... 'preach' about it. WGP, 84
100 .... The life of our time. TG, 1–3
100 .... the most persuasive man. THC, 281
100 .... enjoy the talk. ARO, 79

101........a feminine element. THC, 214
102........None at all. TG, 6
103........I was a mere youth. TG, 20
103........All I had formerly. GAM
103........his complexion is swarthy. ID, 40
104........Power—something more than strength of body. JTG, 71–72
104........The sensation in New York for the past month. ID, 35–36
105........a messiah? TFF, 111–12
105........claims of humanness. GAM
106........I felt that this man's note was intelligence. TAY, 253–54
106........genuine lover. ID, 24
107........Here were true intellectuals. TE, 151
108........American women. TG, 31–32
108........the attitude to finance. TG, 35
109........the perfect disciple. MLO, 324
109........acted like a small boy. UG, 83–84
109........a planet too limited. UG, 136
110........'Messiah' or not. BWG, 5
110........against my will. GR, 138
110........only admit. THC, 362
111........bit of live meat. AE, 1186
111........law of accident. THC, 294–5
112........their usual superficial understanding. LRIA, 80–81
112........a stubborn belief that I could make my own way. JTG, 72
113........Damnation! TG, 83
113........Things begin to hum. JTG, 75
113........the real value of manual work. JTG, 74–75
113........manual work as chemistry. BL
114........thanking those. BL
114........more effort and more experience. JTG, 75
114........I had been strong. TWS, 74
115........I had to die. OLWG, 233
115........shot straight into the air. JTG, 77
116........the principle of seniority. SL
116........For me he is X. W, 158
116........He certainly was under some special kind of obligation. GGE, 98–99
116........impact which his work and ideas could have on the world. GMNW, 173
117........totally unusual and impressive. TOV, 4
117........Jean had a lot of nerve. ID, 42
117........When desire ends. BL
117........It happened in the 223rd year. AE, 51
117........beneficial truths elucidated. LRIA, 4
118........very rare case. SL

118 .... He wasted his substance. ARO
118 .... Substances in me. THC, 339
118 .... sincerely beloved. LRIA, 31-32
119 .... four animals. LRIA, 36–38
119 .... in the category of scripture. TG, 93
119 .... desire for power. BL
120 .... cancer grows worse. LRIA, 31–32
120 .... very old soul. BWG, 78
122 .... we must pay for everything. TG, 100–101
122 .... flayed by the fury. BWG, 33
123 .... must ask. BWG, 33
123 .... leaves all philosophy behind. BL
124 .... plumbed the depths. THC, 360
124 .... Orage tells Toomer. BL
124 .... I was startled by an uncommon inward event. ID, 46
125 .... troublemaker. BWG, 60–62
125 .... people to support him. ID, 25
126 .... he is not a teacher. TOV, 11
127 .... Act. MTYW, 268–69
127 .... a good deal of Jean's life after he went to Chicago. ID, 45–46
127 .... Prieuré was in debt. THC, 359
127 .... degree of contact. LRIA, 40–42
128 .... million men in one. UG, 28
128 .... I rejected his language. UG, 29
128 .... quite extraordinary about money. THC, 360
129 .... Health—candidates for idiots. TAY, 265–70
130 .... Writing, real writing. JTG, 63–64
131 .... I ran out of my first marriage. OGA, 49
131 .... love with a native. GAM, 215
132 .... The sole means. AE, 1183
132 .... The subject is suffering. LRIA, 151–152
132 .... It sticks in my throat. JTW, 106
133 .... hating Gurdjieff. BWG, 97–100
133 .... Nujol. BWG, 141–43
135 .... you burn in boiling oil. THC, 363
135 .... become a threat. BWG, 172
135 .... Sympathy to Bennett. W, 149
136 .... an expositor of Gurdjieff's System. W, 153
136 .... comfortable. LRIA, 44-45
137 .... parallel with Bible. TG, 193
137 .... nails. BM, 62
137 .... melodrama. BM, 60
138 .... he is more impossible than ever. THC, 364

138........The whole trouble. SLIO, 17
138........a man's whim. ARO, 115
139........one of the 'elder brothers.' ARO, 115
139........American dirt. GY, 17
140........I always work in cafés. GY, 25
140........play fair. BWG, 171–74
141........telling the truth. GR, 7–15
141........acknowledge your sin. SL
142........the only person. OLWG, 256
142........If love not dissipated. GAM, 235
142........Confess, Orage. JTW, 21
143........think of reward. GR, 89–90
144........Americans more receptive. GR, 27
145........real possibility of learning anything. GR, 89
145........necessary to make these things your own. UF, 33
145........'elders.' OGA, 103–07
146........I love the group. OGA, 107
146........the end of my patience. OGA, 108–09
147........all these years. W, 154
147........candidate for the madhouse. LRIA, 70
147........The charge against. TOV, 9
148........Orage's ideé fixe. LRIA
148........very limited knowledge. LRIA, 96
149........Orage made a mistake. OGA, 111
149........simply of being. TOV, 13
149........entire sensing of the whole of oneself. LRIA, 111
150........Joshua Gurdjieff. OGA, 115–17
150........what Gurdjieff terms "philosophizing." LRIA, 123
150........tails between their legs. LRIA, 127
150........'loving father'. LRIA, 119
151........G.'s going may or may not change things. JTW, 14
152........cares for money only. JTW, 14
152........Toomer I couldn't bear to look at. ID, 124
152........ten dollars apiece. JTW, 19
152........new methods of work. MNW, 175
153........Mr. Gurdjieff has a very big plan. JTW, 38
153........A New Muddle. JTW, 37
153........I needed rats. JTW, 38
155........I am satisfied that it is entirely possible. ID, 125
156........why talk about it. RM, 15–17
156........go away and teach. MNP, 109
157........free love. GR, 17
157........There is a new race in America. BL

158 .... whole point of the method. OGA, 124
158 .... With one leg pulled. UC, 64
159 .... it is no go with us. BL
159 .... for the world it won't do. BL
159 .... wooden colloquialism. BL
160 .... thank your God. GR, 25–26
160 .... fertilizer. GR, 24
161 .... not yet spoiled. GR, 28
162 .... real, quite real. RM, 568–69

THE GREAT BEQUEATHING

163 .... 5000 francs a year. GY, 61
164 .... There was a time. THC, 371
164 .... problem of distance. ID, 203
165 .... obsessed with the need. W, 168
167 .... orgy. GR, 30–36
167 .... He had grown fat. THC, 421
167 .... 'puffed' three small booklets. LRIA, 46
168 .... What could be in the man's mind? THC, 422–23
168 .... You not as I counted. THC, 424
171 .... nightmare journey. GR, 37–43
172 .... I thank God. JTW, 52
172 .... the most important leader. LRIA, 153
173 .... I loved Orage as a brother. OGA, 137
173 .... constant wish. LRIA, 153
173 .... He was in a bad way. BL
174 .... I will live for coming generations. BL
175 .... prologue. LRIA, 161
175 .... clue. LRIA, 161
175 .... Old Age. LRIA, 165
175 .... Grand Duchess. TG, 107
175 .... stupid way. JTW, 97
176 .... but he is weak man. JTW, 107
176 .... gift of God. JTW, 108
177 .... What started in Russia. GMW, 108
177 .... I now am old idiot. SL
177 .... inner animal. UC, 80
178 .... living on stale manna. UG, 94
178 .... no longer in his confidence. W, 173
178 .... a hopeless idiot. JTW, 76–77
179 .... I not wish people. JTW, 77
179 .... key men. JTW, 46–47
179 .... too light for this work. FLP, 280

179........victim of self-observation. SL
180........The magus. SL
181........twelve-year-old boy. SL
181........Count Keyserling. SL
181........height of his power. WW, 87
182........He was extraordinary! WW, 99
183........escaping from the treadmill. WW, 104
183........go over his life again. WW, 105
184........intelligentsia. WW, 87
184........initiate people. SL
186........Just think. SL
186........one hour to cry. LG, 25
186........enter in the wrong form. RPDU, 36
187........psychological swarm. AMDS, 304
187........there is no "soul" as such. AMDS, 304
187........maybe through the mystics he could find the answers. ID, 150–51
189........This I cannot remember. WW, 123
190........a gone dream. ID, 157
190........Is my lack of progress. W, 178
190........not a sharp break. W, 179
191........break with Gurdjieff. GR, 72
192........genuine gentleman in the exact sense. TOV, 284
192........Orage "forgot many things..." RM, 492
193........Why am I afraid of you? BI, 5
193........no longer a teacher. WW, 152
194........Uspenskii knew the theory. JTW, 91
194........he is in full bloom. RM, 569
195........key to the understanding. TCH, 92
196........My son. GR, 92
197........money. GR, 86–90
198........I also your father. GR, 92
198........family. GR, 92–93
199........Karatas. GR, 101–04
201........Your guess. GR, 112–13
202........relieves the boredom. JTW, 161
202........Uspenskii began to show a greater disinclination. CPDO
203........lack of lovingness. CPDO, 34
204........I don't know program. RM, 585
205........never taught system. RM, 616
206........never was humble myself. RM, 624
206........what I call memory. RM, 634
206........absolute insulator. TEL, 85
206........Sometimes it may be. RM, 642

206 .... deeply disappointed man. SL
207 .... He was a different man. TCI, xx
208 .... not going to America this time. TCH, 179–80
208 .... everything is done by effort. TCH, 6
209 .... Collin returns to the bedroom where Uspenskii had died. BI, 5–6
209 .... he certainly died like one. WW, 159
209 .... You must start again. TCI, xxi
210 .... he worked only for recurrence. TCI, xix
210 .... I felt no nearer to him. W, 219
210 .... Russian fairy tale. W, 128–29
211 .... two chosen agents. TCH, 133
211 .... he and his family and followers arrive in Mexico. BI, 9
212 .... Gurdjieff's legacy to the world. AMY, 137–38
212 .... he becomes aware of a Presence. W, 223
212 .... if European civilization is destroyed. W, 226–27
213 .... living in Paris now. W, 232
213 .... you have my plate. THC, 372
213 .... I do not really know myself. BL
214 .... the eve of our journey into the unknown. AMY, 142
215 .... You are Number Eighteen. W, 238
216 .... black with bruises. UG, 185
216 .... Bennett is small thing. JTW, 241
216 .... We all eat jammed around the table. AMY, 145–46
217 .... I go right. W, 265
218 .... Only you can repay. W, 267
218 .... you can never do everything. MEPS, 54
219 .... health of English. W, 249
219 .... everything is so exciting here at the moment. AMY, 142–43
220 .... Round Idiot category. GY, 75
220 .... when Hitler came to power. GMNW, 216
220 .... adept. W, 253
221 .... He was a good man. JTW, 238-9
222 .... exception was Gurdjieff himself. SOHC, 100
222 .... The writer has no hesitation. SOHC, 5-6
222 .... not 'my' voice. W, 261
224 .... the passive end. BL
224 .... I can die. GR, 110
224 .... The next five years. W, 270
224 .... Au revoir, tout le monde! IP, 104
224 .... Only if you not tired. GAM, 315
225 .... The essential thing. LRIA, xi–xii
225 .... He died like a king. IP, 104
225 .... What did this man. GY, 89

226........eulogy. OLWG, 259
227........various feelings. T, 7
227........chief aim in the future. W, 274
227........in unity lay our only hope. W, 274
227........We have so pledged. UG, 212

GURDJIEFF, USPENSKII, ORAGE, & BENNETT

230........hatching place for eggs. MNP, 89
231........I want to know the future. ISM, 99
231........extreme individualism. ISM, 266
231........I could call my chief feature 'Uspenskii.' ISM, 267
233........Gurdjieff and me. RM, 15–17
234........the psychological side. THC, 398
234........chemistry. ISM, 8
234........psychoanalysis. AE, 577–78
234........pseudo teaching. AE, 249
236........This man…my brother. OGA, 137
236........I cannot go more than half a hog. OGA, 124–25
238........lunatic. W, 252
239........incurably optimistic…constantly making plans. W, 9
239........connected to a great reservoir. W, 121
240........as if Gurdjieff himself had withdrawn from me. W, 126
240........is like Judas. W, 262
241........you always make false starts. W, 178
242........So certain that he knew. IP, xi
242........turmoil. W, 362
243........a Warrior of the first order, but ambitious. WW, 327–28
244........key men. JTW, 46–47

GURDJIEFF & FRITZ PETERS

246........collapses. MAP
247........special. BM, 9
247........troublemaker. BWG, 62
247........cause friction. BWG, 72
248........disasters. BM, 53–55
249........highly volatile. BWG, 21
249........So…you come back? BWG, 26
250........insane. BWG, 67–69
250........not yet spoiled. GR, 28
251........in your blood. GR, 26
251........poisoned for life. GR, 48
251........My son! GR, 81
251........I also your father. GR, 92
252........daring to joke. BWG, 119

253 .... lone wolf. GR, 115
253 .... felt chosen. GR, 114

THE TEACHER-STUDENT EXPERIENCE

259 .... opposing I to it. BWG, 10
263 .... taste of understanding. ISM, 245–46
264 .... wrong crystallization. ISM, 32

NOTES

276 .... always uneasy. BL

INDEX

Eating The "I":
A Direct Account of The Fourth Way— The Way of Self-Transformation in Ordinary Life

by William Patrick Patterson

"Most books on the Work, while quite valuable, are too dry. *Eating The "I"* is a major step in changing that: here we have a real human being, like you and I, struggling with Gurdjieff's teachings, sharing moments of despair and moments of insight and liberation."

—Charles T. Tart, Ph. D.
Author of *Waking Up*

"Eating The "I" gives as full a picture of the Work as it may be possible to get without joining it. The book comes from a great depth and carries much conviction." — *Gnosis*

"Eating The "I" eloquently describes the author's struggles and realizations as he practices the esoteric techniques of Gurdjieff's Fourth Way. In vivid detail, Patterson interweaves his encounters with the formal teachings with his daily adventures as he tries to apply the teachings. The characters are memorable, the dialogue lively, and the narrative never lapses into sentimentality or grandiosity." — *Yoga Journal*

"Patterson is an excellent writer, with a gifted novelist's ability to capture a character through a few lines of dialogue or seemingly casual notes on expression or dress. As for honesty about himself, Patterson's work is in a class with Christopher Isherwood's devastatingly frank, and brilliant, story of his spiritual quest, *My Guru and his Disciple*. Writers in the Gurdjieff tradition tend to do autobiography. There are the classic accounts of life with Mr. Gurdjieff by Ouspensky, de Hartmann, Peters and others. *Eating The "I"* will find an honored place in that series."

—Robert S. Ellwood, Chairman, Dept. of Religious Studies
University of Southern California

Eating The "I" is available at all serious bookstores.

Or write the publisher: Arete Communications, 773 Center Boulevard #58, Fairfax, CA 94978-0058; Fax: (510) 848-0159. Add $3.50 for postage within continental U.S.A. Outside, add $7.00 for surface; $14 for air mail.

Four-color cover. 6 x 9. 370 pgs. Acid-Free Paper. Bibliography and Index. Softcover. ISBN: 1-879514-77-X. $19.95.

Distributors: *Partners, Bookpeople, New Leaf, Moving Books, Samuel Weiser, Baker & Taylor.* In Australia: *Banyan Tree,* P.O. Box 269, Stirling 5152, South Australia. In Europe: *Eureka Booksellers,* Utrecht, Netherlands; and *Golden Square Books,* 16 The Village Golden Square, London, WIR 3AG, England.

Excerpts from

Eating The "I"
A Direct Account of The Fourth Way—
The Way of Self-Transformation
in Ordinary Life

Prologue

I HAD BEEN IN THE WORK ONLY A SHORT TIME WHEN JOHN PENTLAND, MY teacher, told me, "Perhaps someday you'll write a book about The Fourth Way—the way of transformation in life." His words went in like a sword. Now, some twenty years after receiving this task, that sword is coming out of the stone.

With the recent passing of Madame Jeanne de Salzmann, Gurdjieff's personal secretary and, since his death in 1949, the leader of the worldwide Work, most of Gurdjieff's direct students are gone. A few have left accounts of their experiences with Gurdjieff and their understanding of the teaching he brought at so great a cost. The book you hold now comes from a different place in the octave of the teaching. For my generation, like all succeeding, can commonly encounter Gurdjieff only through his books. Yet his spirit lives on in the powerful ideas and practices of the Work. But, effectively, what matters is not how close or remote one is to Gurdjieff in terms of ordinary time, but how sincere and persistent is the search.

The intent here is to give a direct and unvarnished account of my years in an esoteric school of The Fourth Way. My interest is in the collision that occurs between the teaching and the "I," the conditioned self-identity. This meeting is ancient and archetypal, an evoked alchemy between the impersonal and personal; the objective and subjective. My aim is to portray the wonder and misunderstanding, the discovery and resistance, that marks the seed of this potentiality for a new life.

Eating The "I" is a story of my struggle with ignorance and arrogance, the friction between the desires and the non-desires, that led to many suffered truths and some hard-won understanding, all coming under the masterful teaching and example of the remarkable man who Gurdjieff chose to lead the Work in America, Lord John Pentland.

In writing of my search, I made a compact with myself: I would invent nothing—I would tell the story exactly as I experienced it. The reason is both simple and beautiful. Life needs no invention. So-called ordinary life is extraordinary when I pay attention. Free attention frees the moment. Impressions once static are now dynamic, multidimensional. The moment expands. The physical "becomes" the metaphysical. The symbolic and mythological come into play.

The dance begins. Do I identify? Through hard experience I learn that, though rarified, the symbolic, the mythological, are still content, still things. Beyond them lie emptiness, silence, real I. Awakening to the elegance of this truth, I see the work is not to change myself, but my vibration. In certain places, then, to reflect this change in fluidity and inclusiveness, tenses are changed.

This book is not, nor is it intended to be—a "pure" reflection of the Work. The aim instead is to give an intimate report of how I worked and did not work with the ideas. And how, too, they influenced and inspired me and, yes, how they tore me, the "I," apart. I have not painted any sparrows yellow, nor otherwise gilded my idiocy. It should be noted, however, that there is a "mixing" of ideas here. This is because of my attraction to not only the ideas of Gurdjieff, but also those of Jung, Heidegger and certain others. So read with a critical eye.

There is, of course, concern about publishing an intimate work on the esoteric. Gurdjieff's teaching is not for everyone. Nor should it be. The Esoteric Tradition is just that: esoteric. Without the material necessary to understand in Gurdjieff's sense the relativity of the scale of vibration, recognition of this fact is not commonly possible. Gurdjieff took great pains to "bury the bones," to guard against the teaching falling into unprepared or profane hands. As is well-known: when the esoteric is made exoteric, when real knowledge is bought too cheaply—a lawful deflection and distortion must result. Once again then we witness the spectre, too common to our time, of a once sacred channel giving only ordinary tap water. Let us keep in mind, as well, what Rene´ Guénon wrote in his masterwork *The Reign of Quantity:*

> *Every truth of a transcendent order necessarily partakes of the inexpressible; it is essentially in this fact that the profound significance of the initiatic secret really lies; no kind of exterior secret can ever have any value except as an image or symbol of the initiatic secret... But it must be understood that these are things of which the meaning and the range are completely lost to the modern mentality, and incomprehension of them quite naturally engenders hostility; besides the ordinary man always has an instinctive fear of what he does not understand and fear engenders hatred only too easily.*

Perhaps a warning is also in order. Namely, that to practice any of the ideas mentioned herein, independent of the inner knowledge and objective pressure that only an authentic teacher and school can apply, will only cement the person further into his or her most cherished "I"; and so produce yet another instance of the ego burying the essence alive, the true "living death."

My wish and intent here is to walk the razor's edge between the exoteric and esoteric, casting a little sacrificial human flesh into the public fires as payment. In striving to fulfill the task given to me over twenty years ago, I must of necessity put my "I" on display. It might just as well be anyone's fixed idea of themselves. Idiots are idiots. The heart of the matter lies in the essential collision of worlds, that of the timeless with the temporal, and That which remains ever the same. This account describes, then, what it is like to voluntarily undergo the unorthodox and uncompromising spiritual discipline of the mainstream school, yet ever honors its hidden core and tradition.

Chapter 1
A Son's Search
(Excerpt)

At this time of evening the RCA Building seemed like a massive burial tomb. Inside it was cool, dark and silent, bereft of people, save for a few grizzled guards whiling away the time. I took the elevator to his floor and slowly made my way down the dimly lighted corridor, the only sound was that of my soles squeaking on the marble floor. Finally, I came to a door reading:

John Pentland
The American-British Electric Corporation
The Hunting Group of Companies

I knocked several times. I expected to meet a portly and dour English gentleman wearing a vest and a gold watch chain. He'd have jowls, wear glasses. Perhaps have a crop of white hair. No answer. I waited. The office was dark. Empty. I cursed. Had he forgotten? Was he playing a trick? I was about to leave when, on impulse, I tried the brass door knob. It clicked. The door opened. The light was faint, ghostly, the office painted in shadows and blackness. I felt like a burglar. An ordinary business office. On the walls were large geological and topographical maps. I glanced at some papers on a desk. This "Lord Pentland" was the company's president.

I was about to leave when I heard the sound of a door opening. I took a few furtive steps forward and peered down a long corridor. In the pale light I saw a tall silent figure, very erect, slender, moving through the shadows toward me. He seemed like some prehistoric bird. He was upon me almost before I knew it. The face was totally impassive. The eyes aware. Yet without expression. The neck was very long, reed-like. It seemed too slender for the head. The eyebrows were dark and bushy. The shoulders were broad. He was balding.

"Hello," I said feigning cheeriness.

No greeting, no response. It was as if I hadn't said anything.

Weird. The two of us, strangers, standing in a dark hallway, half our faces in shadow, and him just standing there. He regarded me impersonally and without the slightest embarrassment. I felt as if he was drinking me in, weighing me in some way. What an odd duck! I could see him as perhaps the abbot of some distant, time-forgotten monastery—but hardly a disciple of a man like Gurdjieff. No, he must be just a caretaker. The teaching must have died with Gurdjieff.

Finally, the eyes and face still without expression, his lips formed a smile. In a low voice, just above a whisper, he said:

"Would you follow me?" A long arm motioned me down the corridor.

We walked down the dusky hallway; the only sounds in my ears were the soft pad of his slippers and the squeak of my shoes. His office was large and ordinary, a little sparse. Without ornamentation. No exotic souvenirs of travels with the Seekers of Truth. No secret symbols of knowledge. Only a few framed family photos. The view was impressive. St. Patrick's Cathedral, Saks, the traffic and crowds along Fifth Avenue, the Manhattan skyline, the bridge to New Jersey. I turned from the bank of windows. He had brought a chair to the side of his desk.

"Sit wherever you like," he said, half-motioning me to a chair by his desk.

Deliberately, I took a chair in front of the windows. He noted that, then took a seat opposite me on a small couch against the wall. His look was as impassive as it had been in the hallway. I took him in now as well. I noticed his ears. They were large, without lobes, nearly coming to a point at the top. Rather elfin-like. This "Lord" wasn't much of a dresser, even for a businessman. He wore charcoal trousers, baggy and beltless, an old dull pea green cardigan, white business shirt, a nondescript wool tie. The dress of a professor of archeology, a scientist maybe. Hardly the stuff of a sly, swashbuckling man like Gurdjieff.

We continued looking at one another. We hadn't sat long when the last rays of the day's sun streamed into my eyes forcing me to move my chair. I was glad for the excuse to move. I thought that might break this awful silence but he continued watching me. I felt like a bug under a microscope. There was something unnerving about him. I sensed he wasn't there in some way. At least not the way I was; the way normal people are. Was he playing some game? I vowed not to speak before he did. Just then he spoke:

"Why have you come?" His voice was soft, unhurried, almost indifferent.

The same question as on the telephone. Again, I felt the same doubt, same bewilderment. *Why* was I there? *What* did I want? *What* had brought me here? I had no answers. I began talking, rambling on, telling him of my early life, how my parents had spoiled me, treating me like a rich kid, buying me anything I ever wanted.

"Well, at least," I said, "it made me realize that material things couldn't make you happy and then, too, death took it all away, so what was the meaning of it all?"

He went on listening

I recounted how I'd studied psychology and philosophy and found no answer with either. Just mind games. Religion seemed too ordinary, played out, and you had to accept its answers on faith.

He made no comment.

"I don't know what life is about," I told him, "but something in me just can't accept that it is all meaningless—there has to be some reason for human life."

I thought he might respond, but he didn't. I waited. He motioned that I should continue.

I told him, too, how after college I'd gone to San Francisco to work in advertising, but was drafted into the Army. Afterward, I'd come to New York. Worked as a copywriter for Montgomery Wards. Later for J. Walter Thompson and BBD&O. Finally ended up at IBM. I told him about how I had started *In New York,* its success, then about the fast buck boys.

Like a broken water main, the whole story burst out of me. I must have talked for a good hour. But he listened, however long and convoluted. He had an amazing ability to listening. He gave no sign of how he felt. Perhaps he only appeared to follow. I couldn't tell. When I got to my theories of what life might be about, its purpose and meaning and all, well, I did notice he seemed to tire visibly. He was in his sixties. Probably had a long day.

I ended by telling him of my spiritual experiences, the light and the telepathy, the inner knowing. I was just getting to the good part when—unbelievably:

He yawned!

Right in my face. No attempt to cover his mouth. No, "excuse me." Not the least embarrassment. He acted as if nothing had happened. Perhaps the "Lord" was a bit senile? Was this another Murphy deal? A wild goose chase? Gurdjieff had died in 1949. This old gaffer—was he just a museum piece?

I hurried then to the end of the story. I was about to excuse myself and leave when—the bastard yawned again!

It was the most incredible yawn I had ever seen. The mouth opened wide, showing a huge cave of teeth and tongue. The neck muscles and tendons stretched full out. Then a loud sucking in of air and the mouth clapped shut, the nostrils exhaling a stream of spent air. The whole mechanical movement of the musculature happened in slow motion, like it was all under his control. He kept his eyes on mine the entire time. They showed nothing. Not the least guilt or apology. Was all this deliberate? If so, why?

I wanted to get the hell out of there, fast. But I didn't. I thought of moving, but couldn't. The thought wasn't strong enough. So we just sat, wrapped in all that heavy silence, all that empty space. It was withering.

"Tell me..." he inquired, feigning a curiosity, "can you experience all that now?"

There was a slight undertone of challenge in his voice. I saw immediately what he meant: I'd talked about my "spiritual experiences" as if they were a continuing part of my life. I felt like a fish with a hook in its mouth.

"No," I finally admitted, a bit reluctantly.

He nodded, acknowledging the truth of my admission.

"But I could then," I added tersely.

"Can you do this now?" He wasn't going to let me off the hook.

I looked out the window. The Manhattan skyline stood in sharp black silhouette against the graying twilight. The lights in the buildings, all yellow—they seemed like thousands of impenetrable cat eyes. What was his point? What was he trying to prove? That I was an idiot?

"No," I finally said somewhat sheepishly, "I can't do it now."

"That's true," he shot back quickly.

It was as if we had come to something now, something important. His voice was so direct, sharp, not whispery at all. And the way he pronounced the word "true"—the elongated tail he put on the 'rue'—flashed right through me. Was he suggesting everything I'd said up to that moment wasn't true? Or only half-true? That only my admission—that *I couldn't do it now*—was worth anything?

The chair felt uncomfortable, unforgiving. I shifted in it uneasily, crossing my legs, clasping my hands around my knee, leaning forward. He shifted as well. More hard silence. I had the most unusual feeling then. It was like a "double feeling." It was as if I was lying and telling the truth—and at the same time.

But everything I'd told him was true! It had happened. I wasn't making it up. So why this feeling of lying? Mentally, I kept seeing reruns of my actions, my words rebounding on me. It was as if I was in some kind of instant replay.

Then his original question—*Why have you come?*—bubbled up in me again.

Suddenly I understood. I hadn't answered his question. I hadn't admitted I didn't know why.

That unlocked something. For immediately I remembered what had brought me—what I wanted. Why had I forgotten?

"I want to become conscious," I told him, another tone in my voice.

Something happened in the room then. There was a shift of some type. Same room, same two people, yet it was all different. I felt the space growing, getting larger and larger, like an invisible balloon expanding. The sense of time changed. It was as if time "thinned out." The moment was electric. The whole atmosphere was more subtle, alive.

"Can you help me?" I asked softly.

He sat there, very still, not immediately answering. His hands were folded on his lap, palms up. For a long time he peered into them. It was as though he was reading tea leaves or studying a yantra. He seemed to weigh my question carefully, evaluating my strengths and weaknesses, pitting them against all the obstacles I would encounter. At last he looked up.

"Yes...I think we can."

I felt elated. But inside me the undertone in his voice echoed. I realized that he had said "yes" only by a hair's breath. That I was more a long shot than a calculated gamble.

Lord Pentland's face seemed ancient, timeless.

"Yes, you can be helped," he continued, a small measure of certainty in his voice. Then he added "...if you are *sincere.*"

Sincerity! The word exploded in me. I was telling him the truth. How had I been insincere? I hadn't lied. I was serious.

Again, the whole atmosphere and tempo changed.

Lord Pentland suddenly began speaking in a brisk, matter-of-fact manner. It seemed that he and some others met once a week to discuss some of Mr. Gurdjieff's ideas. "If you would care to attend, why I suppose that might be all right...and if you chose to do so, well, of course, your becoming part of this group would be of some trouble but, then again, not so much as to preclude your at least attending a meeting or two; provided, of course, that you actually want to do so...*do you?*"

This was an entirely different "Lord Pentland."

I nodded, thinking to myself that he pronounced the name "Mr. Gurdjieff" with so much feeling, respect; yes, even reverence. I'd pronounced the name.

Lord Pentland mentioned that since Christmas was so near there would be no meetings until January. He would be going to San Francisco for a time but when he returned he promised to be in touch.

We both got up then and went to the doorway. Instead of motioning me through it, he paused to glance at me. It was as if he was considering taking me into his confidence.

"Would you like to read another of Mr. Gurdjieff's books?" he asked, his voice a near whisper.

For some reason, I couldn't speak. I felt paralyzed. All I could do was nod.

He turned and reached into a bookcase behind his desk, taking from it a thick dark blue book the size of a travel guide. The binding was worn. It had obviously been read and reread many times. He looked at me directly and began to hand me the book. I put my hand out to receive it—but his hand stopped just inches from my outstretched fingers. It was as if we were caught in a freeze frame—him holding the book, me with my hand out. I felt stupid. Why didn't he just give me the book?

"You know," Lord Pentland mused, taking a long breath, "a man like Mr. Gurdjieff comes along only once in a million years."

What did that mean? Whatever, I nodded politely.

"That's *very hard* to appreciate...if you know what I mean?" he said softly, peering at me, as if he were trying to detect my level of understanding.

Was he saying Gurdjieff was a saint? An avatar? A messiah of some kind? What was he talking about?

"Would you like to read my copy of *All and Everything?"* Lord Pentland asked, his eyes pinning mine.

Again, all I could manage was nod.

"Mr. Gurdjieff gave it to me himself," he added, his voice exceedingly low as if he wanted no one else to hear.

"All right," I answered. "Sure."

"Would you like to borrow it?" he asked.

I couldn't speak. I felt like I was cut in two. One part standing there inert, one part watching. But watching what? It took an enormous effort of will, but I got it out—

"I would like to—yes!"

The corners of Lord Pentland's mouth turned up into something of a smile, a kind of small acknowledgment. But of what? That I had wanted to read the book? That I had asked for it?

He still made no motion to give me the book. Did he want me to reach for it? Was I dreaming this? I couldn't tell.

He actually smiled now. A kindly smile, soft and radiant. It was wonderful. I felt all this energy. My body was suddenly alive with all this energy. Then he turned to the bookshelf, carefully replacing the threadbare copy.

I stood there bewildered, with this ridiculous feeling of having been rejected. Like he had given me a test which I'd almost passed. But—but what was the test? And why?

Lord Pentland gestured me silently out into the pitch black hallway. I felt this was a goodbye. I walked slowly, awkwardly, past the empty row of desks, my soles squeaking in my ears, struck with this deep sense of rejection.

The shadowy office, the desks and chairs, business machines—who would ever suspect that such a conversation (if that was what it was) could happen here in ordinary life, in the RCA building? It felt unreal. Like everything was a prop in some movie set. It was as if I had auditioned for a role in some rare movie. I'd almost gotten it, but wasn't right for the part.

At the outer door, trying to put the best face on it, I turned to say goodbye.

Lord Pentland loomed tall in the darkness. He appeared quite fatherly now. I felt a strong feeling for him, like some connection had been made. He smiled. "I'll be getting back to you sometime after the holidays," he said.

I stared at him blankly.

He added, "You might look into what it means to remember oneself."

I nodded. I was accepted after all!

Lord Pentland extended his hand. His gesture released all the swirling energy inside me and I grabbed it. I shook his hand so strongly, that both our hands pumped madly up and down. I smiled from ear to ear but he just stood there impassively, looking on without expression. Weird. I felt embarrassed. Suddenly this sinking recognition washed over me—*only my hand was doing the shaking!*

A dead fish! The bastard had given me a dead fish handshake. Lord Pentland's hand was completely passive, limp. Mine was pumping both our hands up and down like a piston. My mind was thinking one thing, my body doing another. And this weirdo is just standing there. I felt like a fool. What was he doing to me! And *why?*

"Goodbye, Pat," Lord Pentland said warmly, as he ushered me out and gently, but quite deliberately, shut the door right in my face.

Explore Telos

TELOS

INQUIRIES INTO SELF-TRANSFORMATION IN THE CONTEMPORARY WORLD

Why Uspenskii ... Gurdjieff

Part VI

TELOS

Inquiries Into Self-Transformation in the Contemporary World

Gurdjieff in Egypt

Interview: Struggle of the Magicians

VOLUME 2 NUMBER 1

TELOS

Gurdjieff in Egypt

Part II

TELOS

Inquiries into Self-Transformation in the Contemporary World

St. George

Gurdjieff's Special Saint

Contents

If the ideas and perspectives you've found in *Struggle of the Magicians* are of interest, you may be want to explore *Telos.*

The sole focus of *Telos* is inquiry into self-transformation in our contemporary world. An international sixteen-page quarterly, *Telos* publishes interviews, book excerpts, essays and book reviews. It does not, and will not, carry advertising. For its publication, it relies solely on the support of its readership.

If you would like a complimentary copy, please send the postcard, or write:

Telos
Box 58, 773 Center Boulevard
Fairfax, California 94978-0058

E-mail: Telos9@aol.com
WWW: http://members.aol.com/Telos9

Three New Titles
by William Patrick Patterson

Conscious Survivial
in a Decaying World Time

ISBN: 1-879514-99-0
Available April 1998

Law of the Sun, Law of the Moon

ISBN: 1-879514-99-1
Available 1998

Ladies of The Rope

ISBN: 1-879514-41-9
Available 1998

Published by

Arete Communications
773 Center Boulevard Box 58
Fairfax, California 94978-0058

William Patrick Patterson
Biography

A longtime student of John Pentland, the man Gurdjieff chose to lead the Work in America, Mr. Patterson has actively practiced the principles of the teaching for over twenty-five years. He is the founder and editor of *Telos*, the first international quarterly devoted to the Fourth Way. A seasoned public speaker, Mr. Patterson regularly lectures on transformational themes, leads seminars, and conducts applied research.

For many years he worked as an editor in publishing and advertising in New York City, and later in Silicon Valley and San Francisco. His work in journalism won many awards including the Jesse H. Neal Award, considered the Pulitzer Prize of business press journalism. While in New York, he founded and edited his own magazine, *In New York*. He lives in a small town in Northern California with his wife and two sons. An avid traveller, he has visited Egypt, Israel, Greece, Turkey, India, Ireland, England, Mexico and Japan, as well as Europe and Scandinavia. He looks forward to visiting Antarctica.